Classic Southport Cooking

Recipes and Reminiscences of Old Southport, North Carolina

by
Lewis J. Hardee, Jr.

Published by
THE SOUTHPORT HISTORICAL SOCIETY, INC.
Southport, North Carolina.

ISBN 1-892444-14-3

Manufactured by
Cushing-Malloy
Ann Arbor, Michigan

Fourth Printing
2008

For my mother
Dorothy Dosher Hardee
whom everyone calls
Sweetheart

And the memory of her mother
Alta Wescott Dosher
whom everyone called
Ma-Ma

Front cover: A 1951 watercolor painting by Southport artist Arthur Newton depicting the Southport waterfront at the foot of Howe Street at that time. The original is owned by Anne Baker Adams who has graciously permitted us to reproduce it. The old cedar tree which grew at the Whittlers' Bench is seen at the right. Lewis Hardee's Colonial Shrimp Company packing house is at the center; his 1938 Chevrolet pickup truck is in the foreground. The back cover is part of the same painting, and shows Dan Harrelson's, one of the principal grocery stores. Two of Dallas Pigott's boats are seen in the distance.

Contents

Preface

For some time I have looked forward to writing a memoir of growing up in Southport, and in the back of my mind has been a cookbook of the wonderful foods I grew up with. But I had no point of view for either. Then my dear childhood friend, the author and editor Cousin Brooks Newton Preik, invited our friend Jean Evelyn Poole, Cousin Vivian McKeithan Jones, my mother and me for lunch. She asked,

"Is there anything in particular you want me to serve?"

"There most certainly is," I replied. "I want some of Annie Lou's fried chicken and her potato salad. Don't ask me a question like that if you don't want me to answer." Annie Lou Knox Newton, Brookie's mother, was one of the best cooks in town—in a town of many good cooks, I might add.

On a very hot noon soon thereafter we drove up in front of Brookie's exquisite home in Wilmington to find her toiling over a hot stove, dripping perspiration into a skillet of chicken hissing and popping in hot grease. I played bartender, fixed Bloody Marys all around. Vivian, being a good Baptist, stuck to iced tea.

"Aren't you ashamed of yourself, having Brookie go to all this trouble?" asked my mother with a scolding air. To parents, their children are always five years old.

"Not one bit," I replied. "I know how good it's going to be."

And it was. We had a grand time swapping Old Southport stories, and devouring the best fried chicken and potato salad we had tasted for many a moon.

Brookie's luncheon rekindled my cookbook and memoir ambitions. The mind is a wonderful thing. Feed it the information and it will do the work, like putting yeast in wet flour and letting it rise. *You* don't make it rise—*the yeast* does the work. A light bulb went on—a memoir based around Old Southport Cooking would allow me to set down the recipes and at the same time place them within the context of Old Southport stories. Thus, *Classic Southport Cooking.*

MID PLEASURES AND PALACES

Such cooking as I know came about of necessity. I was raised in Southport, but my calling took me to New York, where dining out is expensive. So I learned to cook. By the time I retired as head of a big music theatre department at Wagner College, Staten Island, New York, I had had the good fortune to acquaint myself with some of the world's

vii

great cuisines, for New York has the widest variety of any city on the planet. The broiled lamb chops at Jimmy Neary's Irish restaurant on New York's East Side cannot be surpassed, nor can the sweet, rum-drenched babas down at the century-old Ferrara's Bakery in Little Italy. Foreign travel has been a delightful part of my life. In Hawaii I have tasted mouth-watering pork made with pineapple and spices known only to the Gods of the Volcanoes; in England at the little visitors' cafeteria on Churchill's estate, Chartwell, an absolutely delicious steak and kidney pie with strong, rich, brown gravy; in Vienna, the world famous chocolate Sacher torte, its fame well deserved. But, "Mid pleasures and palaces, wherever I may roam, be it ever so humble, there is no place like home." At the end of the day, I want my Down Home, Southport Cooking.

How lucky was I to have been born in the last generation in America raised on good food gathered and cooked the way it was for a hundred years and many more before I arrived on this earth. For I was raised on seafood plucked straight from unpolluted creeks and the clear, rolling sea, crops homegrown in back yards, in the old Swamp Garden that I tell about in Chapter 10, and in nearby farms; on breads baked in slow ovens or fried in cast iron skillets on wood stoves, on pork barbecue roasted all night over a smoking pit by church volunteers, with loving and caring.

WORDS OF THANKS

My mother, Dorothy Dosher Hardee, has been a virtual collaborator on this book. I am further grateful to the following for their contributions: My great friend, Peter Monteleone; my brothers and their wives, Mikael and Genie, Don and Vickie Hardee; Cash and Irma Caroon, Delores Fortiscue, John Carr Davis, Ronald Hood, Dean Rhodes, Toni Oliver, Jean Gilbert Smith, Vivian McKeithan Jones, Afton and Edyth Smith, Jim M. Harper, Lorraine Cranston, Capt. Jimmy Moore and May White Moore, Don Frink, Pat Marlowe, Mary Johnson, Marc Baron, Ann Baker Adams, Betty McGlamery Cochran. Amelia Parker, Dickie Marlowe, Patrick Connaughton and Carl Gregory. I am especially thankful to these churches and organizations for the use of some of the recipes in their published cookbooks: The Southport Baptist Church, St. Philip's Episcopal Church, Trinity United Methodist Church; and the local chapters of the Daughters of America and the Eastern Star. I am indebted to the Southport Historical Society for publishing this book, and especially to Wolfgang Furstenau, with whom I worked most closely during the process.

Introduction

My aim is to record the essential recipes that define Southport's cooking, as well as I can determine, within the context of historical notes and personal reminiscences. Some of the recipes date from the town's earliest days when it was called Smithville, some are fairly recent, and most are somewhere in between.

I have personally tested many, but not all, of the hundreds of recipes included herein. Some have been revised or adapted to make them more accessible to modern users, and here and there I have suggested how to recreate the classic Southport taste with timesaving modern appliances. Others I have left untouched—particularly those with instructions enclosed in quotation marks, from the very old, 19th Century cookbooks. You may have to experiment yourself.

Most recipes in this book call for made-from-scratch cooking. To represent an authentic, classic Southport cooking, I have tried to stay with those that call for basic foodstuffs, avoiding most that call for ready-made, brand-name package mixes and foods.

A DOLLOP, A PINCH, A SMIDGEON AND A DASH

Many of the recipes, particularly those from the old Southport cookbooks, were written down by cooks who assumed a familiarity with certain cooking methods of their day, are often inexact and do not spell out details of mixing procedures, temperatures or cooking times. You were expected to know these things. Ask your grandma how she made such great biscuits, and she'd answer impatiently as if you were the most stupid person on earth, "All you do is put flour in your bowl, cut in a dollop of shortening, add a pinch of soda, a smidgen of sugar and a dash of salt." Not much help today when trying to stir up a batch of her biscuit dough.

Moreover, the techniques and terminology of cooking have changed. To make corn cakes, an old recipe may read, "Have your spider well heated…" Not everyone today knows that a spider is a skillet with a long handle, and takes its name from very old skillets with legs that fan out like a spider for cooking over coals. Few people today have a peck container handy in their kitchen, or wish to measure flour or sugar in pounds rather than in cup measurements.

The dietary cautious will note that many of the recipes are heavy on lard, butter and cream. Vegetable shortening and margarine may be substituted if you wish, with nearly the same results. In times past, sugar was used without guilt; if you could afford it, you used it joyfully. The old rule of thumb was to add a pinch of salt to every sweet dish, and a pinch of sugar to every salty dish. "It rounds out the flavor."

ABOUT COOKING TECHNIQUES

As the emphasis of this book is on recipes and reminiscences, cooking techniques are included only here and there. For the techniques of home canning and candy making particularly, the user should consult specialty cookbooks, or chapters in comprehensive cookbooks. Canning foods by one of the standard methods such as the open kettle or the pressure cooker can be tricky. Years ago my great-aunt Margarette Dozier was putting up tomatoes in a huge pressure cooker when the petcock blew and a bushel of tomatoes plastered her ceiling bright red.

Similarly, candy making can be a challenge, and often requires special skills.

ABOUT SOUTHERN AND SOUTHPORT COOKING

Southern cooking is essentially English cooking, as is most American cooking, even with the steadily increasing diversity of our population. But from Colonial times, the regions began to develop different cooking styles. The South, with its dependence on African slaves for much of its cooking, developed a distinctive cuisine quite different from the North. Dishes with African foods such as eggplant, banana, and okra (of which "gumbo" is the African name), became a familiar part of the Southern diet. Crops grown only in the South naturally led to their wide use in Southern dishes; rice, for instance, is an essential part of Southern fare, as is molasses, which is made from sugar cane.

The classic diet of Southport is Down Home Cooking, for want of a better term, but with its own distinct coastal flavor and characteristics due to its location and other factors, especially sea traffic. For most of its existence, Southport was a fishing village clustered around a military garrison dating from Colonial times. It was a pilot town also, home to the intrepid men who would compete for the sailing ships that must be met far out at sea off Cape Fear. Ships' captains not infrequently made a gift of some special bottle of wine or spirits or other exotic delicacies to the good pilot who guided them across the treacherous Frying Pan shoals into the safety of the Cape Fear River.[*]

---

[*] In 1663 the adventurer William Hilton entered the river and called it the "Cape-Fair." Both names are apt; the Cape is both fair, and to be feared.

Since its early days Southport has also been a resort. During summers, visitors flocked here from the sweltering inland to enjoy the cool breezes on the piazzas of the boarding homes and hotels on the bluff overlooking the river. So the interaction of sea traffic, the military and tourists influenced Southport's cooking, giving it an edge of greater variety and sophistication over many larger towns locked inland.

Southport sits on a high bluff at the mouth of the Cape Fear River looking out across the bar to the ocean from under a huge grove of live oaks. Some of the streets twist and turn in deference to these trees, many of which are hundreds of years old. The ancient, massive trunk of the "Indian Trail Tree" crooks down into the earth, then hurls back up to the sky; it is believed that when it was a sapling, native Americans staked down its neck to mark their trail, accounting for its humped back trunk.

As Southport is surrounded by creeks and marshes, the diet naturally features seafood in abundance, but also chicken, turkey, game, pork, venison and other meats, and endless vegetables and fruits. Since so much of Southport's cooking is centered around social events, I recount a crab boil, a shrimp boil, a fish fry, an oyster roast, and an all-night pit barbecue. There are recipes for casseroles of many sorts, as these have long been popular, especially for pot-luck dinners at churches, clubs, and family gatherings. Southport was born with a sweet tooth, and there are plenty of recipes for cakes, pies and other desserts.

A BRIEF HISTORICAL PERSPECTIVE ABOUT COOKING AND FOOD PRESERVATION

Until the 19th Century, ways of cooking changed very little from Medieval times. Most cooking was at the hearth or an outdoor fire. Shakespeare's upper-middle-class family of Renaissance England possessed state-of-the art cooking facilities that may be seen today in their homes at Stratford-Upon-Avon. The kitchen of Shakespeare's mother, Mary Arden, features a massive hearth with a cauldron suspended on a small crane for stewing and boiling that could be moved toward or away from the heat to adjust the temperature. There is a spit for roasting, turned by iron weights which were hoisted up, then allowed to descend slowly to turn the spit, much like the driver mechanism of a grandfather clock. This released the cook for other duties, and dispensed with the need for a family member or servant to constantly turn the spit. A deep, arched brick oven adjacent to the hearth, its front door, or gap, closed during baking by a fitted arched plank on a pole called the "stopgap," from which comes the modern day term.

The iron range revolutionized cooking. By mid-19th Century it was becoming commonplace in Northern kitchens; in the South it lagged behind, as slaves could turn the spit before the hearth. But by the end of the 19th Century the iron range, or its economy model, the "tin Lizzie," was universal. The progression of fuel has been from wood to coal, kerosene, gas, and electricity,

Food preservation by salting or drying was of course known in ancient times. The Romans used the sealing method whereby perishables were cooked, then poured over with hot oil and sealed with a tough crust. As coinage was frequently scarce throughout the Empire, salt, an essential preservative, was often used as barter. Legionnaires often received their pay in salt; in fact, our modern word "salary" comes from the Latin word for salt, "salarie." By the 17th Century, certain foods were heated in bottles and sealed with corks.

Canning was the invention of the Frenchman Nicholas Appert in 1809, who was commissioned to come up with an improved technique for preserving food for Napoleon's campaigns. By the mid 19th Century canning was widespread, although the lids were sealed with a cumbersome hand-soldered method. In 1856 Gail Borden of Brooklyn, New York, patented a process for evaporated canned milk. Louis Pasteur provided the scientific understanding of sterilization to destroy microbes, and by the 1880's canned foods had an important place in America's food supply.

Refrigeration dates from at least 1000 B.C. when the Chinese stored natural ice in ice cellars. Even earlier, the Egyptians understood that vaporizing water produces ice, that water in porous clay vessels left overnight in holes in the ground would freeze. From very early on, ships brought ice from frigid regions to sell in the ports of the world. Ships that called at Crandall, my paternal ancestor's saw-mill settlement on the St. Mary's River in Florida, brought northern ice which the families kept in ice houses well insulated with saw-dust.

The first American to patent a design for refrigeration by the compressed air method was in fact a Floridian, Dr. John Gorrie. By the mid-19th Century hardly a town of any size in America was without its ice plant, with its wagons that went from door to door delivering blocks of ice to their customers' oak-and-tin ice boxes. Electric refrigeration became commonplace during the 1920's; the G.E. refrigerator with its condensation coils perched on top like a washtub became a familiar feature of the American home, and by the 1940's, lowly was the household without one.

Many 19th Century cookbooks are replete with recipes for ice cream and ices with the instructions, "Place in the freezer." This puzzled me for a while, since home freezers were then unknown, until it dawned on me that "the freezer" was the hand cranked ice cream churn in which salt is added to ice. It is one of nature's marvelous contradictions that melting ice produces colder conditions than stabilized ice.

SOURCES FOR THE RECIPES

The core of the recipes included herein are from the kitchen of my mother, Dorothy Dosher Hardee. Some of these were passed down from my great-great grandmother, Elizabeth Durant Drew (born 1816), to my great grandmother, Sarah Rebecca Drew Wescott (1847-1932), to my grandmother, Alta Wescott Dosher (1886-1963), thence to my mother (born 1915) and her descendants. Contributions of many cousins, particularly Brooks Newton Preik and Vivian McKeithan Jones, aunts and friends are also included. Altogether, six generations are represented in this book.

I have further drawn upon cook books compiled and published over the years by Southport churches and civic organizations as fund raisers. The oldest of which I am aware is *Recipes From the Parish of St. Philips in Southport* of 1907, published at Christmastime of that year by the venerable St. Philip's Episcopal Church, which has its origins at Old Brunswick Town of Colonial times.* Theirs is a charming booklet of thirty-two pages plus an index, with ninety-seven recipes and entries. The credit reads, "Crumbs Swept Up by Mrs. J. A. Bell and Mrs. Dunbar Davis." In 1913, Southport native Annie May Woodside (1892-1981) compiled a cookbook based on recipes she had collected; I have referenced it as if it were a published work, which it deserves to be.

Southport's Favorite Recipes, compiled in 1950 by Southport historian Susie Sellers Carson for the Women's Missionary Union of the Southport Baptist Church, was invaluable, both for the menus in vogue a half century ago and for the recipes. Also very useful were *Southport's Treasure of Personal Recipes*, published in 1952 by the local chapter of the Daughters of America; *Brunswick Potluck Cookbook*, published during the 1960's by the Southport Junior Woman's Club; *Our Favorite Recipes,* produced by the Live Oak Chapter of the Eastern Star in 1974; *Finger Pickin's* printed during the 1990's by the Southport Woman's Club; *The Proverbial Church Cookbook*, put out in 1991 by Trinity Methodist Church; and *Coastal Cuisine. A Century of St. Philip's Favorites* of 2000, in which sixteen recipes from their 1907 cookbook have been reprinted.

---

* "St. Philip's" was spelled without the apostrophe in their 1907 cookbook.

5

I have also drawn upon a number of antique cookbooks known to have been used in Southport. *Hood's Practical Cook's Book* (1897) and *Key to the Pantry* (1898), compiled by "Ladies of the Church of the Epiphany," Danville, VA, were used at the Stuart House. This famous inn on the Southport waterfront was founded by Mary Elizabeth Bensel Stuart, but was most associated with her daughter, Miss Kate Stuart (1844-1929), "the Grand Old Lady of North Carolina," who ran it for many years. Each book is stamped "Stuart House" throughout. Hood's book was loaned to me by Susie Carson, and *Key to the Pantry* by Brooks Newton Preik, Miss Kate's grand niece. Fanny Merritt Farmer's cookbooks, which first appeared in 1896, have long been used in Southport. *The Rumford Complete Cook Book* of 1908 and in later editions was popular in Southport kitchens, as was *The Art of Cooking and Serving* (1928), by Sarah Field Splint. *Fish Facts* (1930) has been used in my family for many years and has been helpful; this booklet was distributed by the Anderson & Price Fish Corporation of Fulton Fish Market, New York City, to my father and other Southport seafood dealers.

A few cookbooks specific to North Carolina have been informative: *Favorite Recipes of North Carolina* was published about 1944 by the State Department of Agriculture to answer the need for "a recipe book with an Old North State flavor." A much-used copy belonging to our friend and neighbor Mrs. Ina Norment was loaned to me by her granddaughter, Pat Marlowe. *Seafood Cookery in North Carolina* of 1960 was published jointly by the N.C. State Department of Conservation and Development and the Agricultural Extension Service of North Carolina State College. The N.C. Department of Natural and Economic Resources and other state agencies contributed recipes for *Coastal Carolina Cookbook* (about 1960).

Of indirect influence on Southport was *The Cook's Oracle,* published in 1817 in London, of which some of the early 19th Century Southern cookbooks made good use. Mary Randolph's *The Virginia House-wife* (1824) was a most popular cookbook for the first part of the 19th Century and widely circulated in the South. *The Carolina Housewife* (1847), another popular cookbook, was published anonymously by "a Lady of Charleston." The lady, it was later determined, was Sarah Rutledge, the daughter of Edward Rutledge, a signer of the Declaration of Independence, who apparently considered it unladylike to engage in a publishing enterprise. But her recipes are clear and understandable, and I have quoted some in this book. *Confederate Receipt Book,* published in Richmond in 1863 as the Civil War raged, yielded a few recipes. *Mrs. Hill's New Cook Book* of 1870 by an enterprising aristocrat trying to make ends meet during Reconstruction, reprinted in 1872 *as Southern Practical Cookery and Receipt Book,* is clear in its instructions; it provided a number of recipes. *The Southern Cook Book of Fine Old Recipes* of 1939 exploits the nostalgia for the "Old South," but yielded useful information and a few recipes.

Altogether these sources provide a fair view of Southport's cooking—it was more than just fried fish and grits. While the typical family made do with plain fare, there was also a remarkable variety and sophistication. Many cooks knew how to cure a ham, to keep eggs fresh through the winter, how to make souse and hog's head cheese and beef jerkies, and how "To Corn Beef for Winter Use." But many knew how to make Oyster Fricassee, a Newburg sauce, Fish Soufflé, Beef à la Flamade, Fricassee of Veal, Hollandaise Sauce, Peach Trifle, Fruit Blanc Mange, how "To Blanquette Chicken," how to make "Tomato Pillau" (nowadays spelled pileau), and "Mushroom Sauce." They were familiar with foods you would have thought came much later—curries, soy, French rolls, "maccaroni," [*sic*] vermicelli, Welsh Rarebit, Charlotte Russes, and almond paste. "Good French Brandy" and wines were kept in the dining room sideboard. Their green gardens grew not just "parsley, sage, rosemary and thyme," but sweet basil, chives, mint, and other herbs. Their kitchens were well stocked with spices—the recipes call for allspice, cardamom, cinnamon, cloves, cumin, Cayenne pepper, black pepper corns, ginger, mace, mustard seed, marjoram, nutmeg and turmeric. They used Worcestershire sauce (which they sometimes called "Worcester sauce"), "caviare," anchovies, English mustard, tarragon vinegar and horseradish. They decorated plates with parsley, lemon slices or celery, their salads with edible flowers.

So, fine Southport cooking extends back many, many years. Certainly, by the mid 19th Century, its cooks were familiar with a wide variety of subtle and worldly dishes. And what's more, they knew how to make them from scratch, starting with the lopping off of the head of the turkey or the butchering of the hog. How many modern cooks could claim such?

The above caveats aside, the intrepid will be rewarded with delicious and delightful dining, and the joy of Classic Southport Cooking.

7

Views of the Southport waterfront early 1950's. Photos by Art Newton.

Some of the many piers that once thrust out into the Cape Fear River. The large building upper left is the old Miller Hotel. Mack's Cafe, the old Pilot Tower, and Dan Harrelson's grocery store are center, on the waterskirt. The vessel in the left foreground was abandoned by Estonian refugees fleeing Communist rule.

1..

Long, Long Ago
Old Southport Unto Itself

Let me take you back in time half a century to the days when Southport was a major shrimping and fishing port. The town I knew during the 1940's and 1950's is a greatly different place than you see today, still salty and uniquely Southern, and very much Old Southport and unto itself. There is a sense that time has stood still, with very little changed since the Civil War when much of the South froze in time. Even as a child I recognized that. There is one road in, the same road out. Howe Street has a narrow strip of Model-T era paving down to the waterfront; Moore Street, a principal business street, is paved about a block in each direction from Howe. Perhaps half the houses have not seen a coat of paint in half a century. Some of our relatives and friends still cook on wood stoves, light their houses with kerosene lamps, draw water from pumps on the back porch, and use privies in the back yards.

The waterfront is lined with piers and shrimp houses, one after the other jutting out into the Cape Fear—sheds, marine runways, shrimp trawlers sitting in cradles, still under construction. The shrimp houses are where the shrimp are processed for market—ramshackle buildings, some of tin, a few of wood, creaking and swaying in the wind and tide. Sea gulls sit atop their roofs and perch on the black, creosoted pilings, facing the wind. (You can always tell the direction of the wind from the gulls— they always face the wind.) Impatiently they await the return of the shrimp boats from the sea in the afternoon, hungry for the feast of scraps the shrimpers will throw overboard.

At the north end of town is the pogy dock where the big menhaden boats moor for the night. At Kingsley Street is the Fodale dock. At the foot of Atlantic Avenue are Bill Wells' dock and marine railway and Wiley Wells' dock. The Government dock in front of the Fort Johnston Garrison is for the Coast Guard cutter. Near Dry Street are rows of palmetto tree pilings, harvested years before at Baldhead Island, now abandoned and forlorn, lapped by the timeless currents of the river, all that is left of what had earlier been Bingo Burris's shrimp house.

Between Dry and Howe Streets, a cluster of buildings and docks crowds the water skirt. My father's tool shop and huge, make-shift tin shed with its sagging roof houses the *Sea Belle,* perched high in the air, still under construction. The shed is an eyesore and blocks the view from

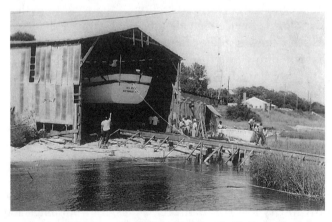

Three scenes by Art Newton, early 1950's. Top: Lewis Hardee's Dock is center; Dallas Pigott's is right. Center: the old Whittler's Bench at the foot of Howe Street, and the Hardee dock in the distance. Lower: Lewis Hardee's *Sea Belle* is about to be launched.

Rudolph and Mary Mintz's porch; they are not a bit happy about it, but my father assures them that the minute the last of the new fleet is launched he will tear it down. Ledrew Sellers' grocery store is immediately next. Then you see Dallas Pigott's shrimp house, its long pier extending far out in deep water, where Mr. Rob Thompson has his marine service station. Dan Harrelson's grocery is here as well.

At the foot of Howe Street is my father's shrimp packing plant with its red roof, at the end of a long pier jutting far out into the river. Before he turns to real estate and banking, my father will own thirty of the finest shrimp trawlers you ever saw. The three-story wooden base of the old pilot tower rises at the end of Howe Street like a Holland windmill, its tower torn off by a hurricane. Mack's Cafe is only a few feet away. Not far beyond are the shrimp docks of Capt. Church and Jim Arnold. At the foot of Lord Street sits *The Finest Kind,* still all ribs rising from the keel; but when completed, Herman Sellers' trawler will be the largest yet built in the area. What pride is manifest in these fine boats of the Southport fleet! What rightful pride, and skill, and art! A little farther away is James Fraser's marine railway. Now you are at the Old Yacht Basin. No bulkheads or buildings yet line its banks; the shrimpers have thrown planks across the marsh to reach their boats that tie up here.

The menhaden boats and dozens of shrimp trawlers have been out riding the ocean since before daybreak. The menhaden crews will be lowered from the mother ship into their small "purse" boats, surround a school of menhaden and snatch them up like coins in a pinch-purse, then haul the catch aboard. Menhaden are a smelly, oily and bony fish, used for making fertilizer.

The trawlers toss their small "try nets" over the side to see if the shrimp are running. If they come up good, they'll lower the big nets over the side and begin trawling. These have heavy wooden "doors" the size of regular house doors, reinforced with iron to weight-down the big funnel-shaped nets and keep them open as they drag along the ocean bottom.

My father's Hallicrafter shortwave radios, one beside his bed and one in his upstairs office on the dock, are on all day. Through the crackle of the static, you can hear the shrimpers swapping information on where the shrimp may be found. One of them asks,

"Come in, Sandy. Where you at and what you doing? Over!" he calls. "Sandy, where you at?" he repeats. "Where you at and what you doing. Over!" Capt. Sandy Simmons hears him and answers back. With plenty of shrimp to be had, there is a gracious and goodly lack of greed among the shrimpers. The ocean is their competition.

Top: Menhaden boat, with purse boats at its stern. Center and lower: two scenes by the author, shrimp pickers and workers at Hardee's dock, early 1950's.

Shrimp pickers at Lewis Hardee's dock. 1950's. Mary Mims is seen at right.
Photo courtesy of Marjorie Clemmons.

Late in the afternoon the "pickers" begin to drift down to the docks. These are the colored ladies who "head" the shrimp, separating the heads from the tails. Some are industrious, seldom idle, and bring along sewing or knitting. For others it is a social hour; they straddle wooden shrimp boxes and play cards with a set of dog-eared and well-worn kings and queens and jacks, spades, diamonds, clubs and hearts, slapping them onto the shrimp box with a fury, still trying to get a pop and a snap out of them. A curious antagonism plays among them, although they are mostly friends and go to the same churches.

"I wish I *was* at you," calls one. "I'd box your ears!"

"Yeah? I wish I was at *you!*" calls the other. If they really meant it, they'd only have to take a few steps and go at it.

The fleets begin to appear across the bar. The menhaden boat *John M. Morehead* gives three thundering blasts of its whistle loud enough to be heard miles away, a salute to the city and an alert to the pogy plant waiting to receive its catch. The entire population stops dead in its tracks. Even people not connected to the pogy boats stop to listen. Cars stop, people turn off their radios, hush the kids and do not move a muscle. After a pause the *Morehead* gives more blasts. This lets folks know the size of its catch. Today there are three long and one short—it is steaming up the Inland Waterway to the pogy plant with three hundred fifty thousand pogies aboard. This is good news, and the wives will feel easy about buying a little something extra for dinner.

The shrimp boats are now headed in. Most belong to the major operators, but many more belong to the independents. They name their boats after their girl friends, mothers, grandmothers, or after things and people that just make them feel good. Capt. Merritt Moore runs the *Penny,* named after his daughter. Dallas Pigott and my father together own the *Gen. Douglas MacArthur.*

The *Sea Ranger* pulls up at my father's shrimp house. Capt. Sandy has made a last drag just off the bar and the catch is still in the net. The rope groans and squeals in the winch as he hoists the tail high into the air, the mouth opens, and the bottom of the sea spills onto the deck. These nets are like whales, swallowing up everything in their path. It's a sight to see—shrimp snapping about, crabs scrambling to escape overboard, flounders floundering, croakers croaking. Sometimes there are sharks hoping to murder you or take off a leg. Conchs and a tennis shoe just lie there.

Capt. Sandy and his mate cull the shrimp from the "trash"—fish and creatures of insufficient quantities to be sold commercially. When they have enough shrimp tossed into the heavy, wire bushel baskets, Prim Ray, my father's right-hand man, and Boots, his helper, hoist them up with the crane out front of the dock and dump them onto the picking tables. The colored ladies pass their baskets down to Sandy's mate who fills them with croakers, squid, crabs, and other creatures that won't sell. And little boys tie them on a string to go around town selling them for twenty-five cents a string. Southport is poor, very poor. But nobody starves. We think we are rich because we have a 1942 Chevrolet coupe.

Daddy has two "picking tables," each about five feet wide and twenty long, on the top of which is a shallow trough about six inches deep, lined with tin, as long as the tables. On each side of the tables where the pickers stand is a narrow slot where they drop the shrimp heads straight to the river. If the tide is ebbing, they wash out to sea; on a rising tide they wash ashore by the ton, and Lord Help Us. Rotten shrimp don't smell any too good.

The tables are now piled high with shrimp; one is full from end to end, the other only partly so. There are times when both are filled and Daddy doesn't get home until daylight.

The pickers begin to take their places beside the tables. There is a protocol among them as strict as that of an embassy. White haired "Aunt" Mary Mims has seniority and the place of honor at the end of the table closest to the double doors, the first to be loaded up with shrimp. Her daughter Lily has the station just opposite. The other women take

14

their places in descending order of rank away from Aunt Mary. Some who are not regulars roll tiny rubber thimbles onto their tender fingers.

My father will not allow anyone to start until the entire catch is upon the tables. No one will be allowed an unfair head start. Now he nods and gives the signal. Each of the pickers has a lard can or two and an old auto license plate or wooden paddle to shuffle the shrimp about, which they store overnight on nails overhead. They form a little well in the pile of shrimp, and then begin a swift hand-over-fist movement like pistons, snatching up a handful of shrimp with the right hand then the left. They grasp the tails in their hands, snap the heads off into the slot and down to the rover, and stuff the tails into the lard cans.

Aunt Mary's lard cans are filled and hard-packed with headed shrimp. She turns them into a five gallon galvanized bucket the house provides—most gently and as fluffy as possible, for the pickers are paid by the bucket, not the pound. She waddles to the big steel vat filled with ice water, dumps a bucket of her work in and collects her pay. That's my job, to hand out the pay—20 cents a bucket.

(Once, Daddy became very suspicious of one of the pickers. She wasn't a regular, but seemed to be a very fast picker indeed. He noticed that when she tossed the shrimp into the vat she quickly tucked her bucket upside down under her arm. "Let me see that bucket," he said. It was lined with a false bottom of tarpaper.

"What did you do?" I asked.

"I said to her," he answered, "Get off my dock and don't come back until you can behave yourself." The shrimp were running and her friends were making good money. In a week, she behaved herself.)

Prim and Boots begin churning the shrimp in the vat to wash off the sand. They pack them in rough-cut pine shrimp boxes that hold 100 pounds, made in Daddy's shop. I weigh and count a pound of shrimp and mark it down, 26 to 30 per pound—a good size. Boots shovels a layer of ice onto the bottom of the box, and then a layer of shrimp, another layer of ice, another layer of shrimp, spreads ice on top, and nails the lid shut. I tack cardboard tags supplied by the broker to show its destination—John Feeney, Fulton Fish Market, New York. Prim and Boots stack the boxes on the platform wagon that runs on steel rails and push it from the shrimp house down the middle of the pier to the shore where a big truck is waiting. The driver is in Mack's Cafe finishing his coffee. Soon he'll be on his way up U.S. 17 headed to Fulton Fish Market. Today's catch has been good. My mother has closed the kitchen long ago, so Daddy takes me to Mack's.

"No, you can't have the steak," he says. But he lets me have a hamburger and French fries. Mack makes good hamburgers.

15

Bringing Home the Bacon:
How You Got Your Groceries in Old Southport

During the 20th Century there was a surprising number of grocery stores scattered around town for a population of about fifteen hundred. From about 1910 into the 1930's, Northrop's, with its second floor balcony the largest grocery business in town, operated on Moore Street. It is now Northrop Mall. In mid-20th Century Howe Street was lined with various well-stocked grocery stores. Lancaster's, Mrs. Hettie Arthur's and Joel Moore's were a block from the river on the east side of Howe; Carlton Price's Superette was opposite the water tower; Dolly Evans's store was a few blocks north at the northwest corner of Howe and St. George; and Alex Fox's was at Howe and Owen. Gracie Ford's, Mary Temple's and a few other small stores catered to their neighborhoods. Dan Harrelson's operated on the waterfront at the foot of Howe Street until October 15, 1954, when Hurricane Hazel demolished the waterfront; he then relocated at the northeast corner of Howe and Nash in what had earlier been Lancaster's. Mr. Ledrew Sellers ran a grocery on the waterskirt where the Waterfront Park is now located, from the late 1930's until the 1950's when he relocated at the Old Yacht Basin. Cronley Ruark's on East Moore Street across from the old Episcopal Church was a major general store until it burned in the 1950's. At the fire sale, our neighborhood gang bought pogo sticks for 50 cents each and happily bounced around town, joyfully released from earth's gravity like astronauts frolicking on the moon until the springs wore out.

Mr. Willie Fullwood's deserves special mention. Until he closed his store in 1969, Mr. Willie was for decades the main supplier for many of the households in Southport. He'd call at your back door in the morning with his pencil and pad, take your order, and return later with your groceries in the trunk of his little coupe. His store on Howe Street was sandwiched between the old barber shop and Joel Moore's. Fullwood Grocery was a flat-roofed lean-to, painted as bright red as the Royal Crown Cola sign under the window. It was so narrow Mr. Willie hardly could have stretched out in it crosswise. It stocked little more than a hundred items, if that. There was one brand of flour and one of canned milk. But it sufficed; if you wanted something exotic, he got it from Dan's or sent to Wilmington for it. My brother Mikael remarked,

"I doubt there was room enough in Mr. Willie's store for the choice of potato chips alone you see at supermarkets nowadays."

Willie Fullwood standing before his store
on the last day of business in 1969.

The bright red façade of Fullwood Grocery has been preserved
thanks to Southport native Thomas Harrelson. After Fullwood's closed,
it was removed and relocated next door within Harrelson's Grocery.
When Harrelson's closed, Tommy had it taken across the street where
David Watson stored it in his garage. It is now on permanent loan to the
Southport Maritime Museum; a 5 cent cigar ad can still be seen on its
window. (This is not the only effort at historical preservation by the
Harrelson family. Some years ago the Southport Fire Department
purchased a new fire truck and was about to dispose of the 1920's
vintage model that had served the City faithfully for many years. Dan
Harrelson stored it until a few years ago when our community had grown
more preservation minded. He returned it to the Fire Department which
raised a large sum to have it restored. It is today a town treasure.)

Roscoe Davis gives his picnic. Early 1950's.
Photos courtesy of Thomas Harrelson.

Roscoe's Picnic

Harrelson's Grocery didn't make house calls to take your order, but if you telephoned or sent word it would make deliveries. Roscoe Davis, Dan's right-hand-man for many years, would deliver to the customers and if you weren't home, he'd put the milk in the refrigerator for you.

You had a friend in Roscoe Davis. He and his wife Bertha were active members in the St. James A.M.E. Zion Church. Roscoe was one of the most beloved men in our town. He never looked at people as white or black, but as people. Dan Harrelson's son, Tommy, said,

"I think he did more in a subtle, quiet way toward helping the transition to integration in Southport than any other person."

A certain local boy had a difficult home life; Roscoe knew this and gave him special attention. He did well in life, and from time to time would fly back in a private plane and take Roscoe up for a ride.

Election time came around one year and no one had filed for constable. Dan Harrelson and Ormand Leggett had such regard for Roscoe that they collected signatures and Roscoe won the election with a write-in vote.

He had character without being one of those persons you would refer to as "a character." He liked to joke with the children whose parents

18

came into the grocery store. He'd say,

"I'm building you a wheel barrow."

"Can I get one?!" we asked.

"All you kids are going to get one. Everybody's going to get one. And when they're done we're going to have a big parade, and I'm going to ride you all around town." He stuffed our heads with dreams, which, of course, were his own dreams.

"Where's my wheel barrow, Roscoe?" we asked over and over.

"I'm missing a part that I ordered, to come in on the bus. It'll be here soon." Or he'd say, "Well, the paint isn't dry yet."

I'm still waiting for a ride in my wheel barrow.

Dan gave him his own key to the grocery store, and if you needed something on Sunday when it was closed, he'd go in and get it for you and mark it down on your charge account.

Roscoe had terrible asthma, and someone told him that if you kept a Chihuahua in the house it would cure it. So he got a Chihuahua and kept it in the house. It didn't cure his asthma, but he had a nice pet.

"One of these days soon," Roscoe teased, "we're going to have us a picnic. I'm going to round up every one of you children and we're going on a picnic and have us a good time." And for a long time the kids kept asking,

"Roscoe, when are we going to have our picnic?"

"Real soon. Any day now!"

Dan's wife, Lib, had enough of this.

"Dan, *you've got to do something about that picnic.* Roscoe is driving the children crazy." So Dan said,

"Now Roscoe, you've strung along these kids long enough. Go into the store and get whatever you need for a picnic. *But go have that picnic.* You can take the truck." And sure enough, on his afternoon off, he rounded up the kids—I think there were eleven of them, maybe a dozen—and off they went out to the old ball park off Leonard Street for their picnic, their little legs hanging off the back of the truck. There he sat upon a Pepsi Cola crate passing out sandwiches and cookies, with the children at his feet like little disciples.

Dan Harrelson, a prominent grocery merchant
and civic leader, on his 90th birthday in 2000.
Photo courtesy of Thomas Harrelson.

A word about the intimacy of the town at the time: During the late 1950's a classmate at Chapel Hill tried to telephone me at my parents' in Southport, but misdialed and reached Harrelson's, whose telephone number was one digit different than ours.

"No, Lew Hardee isn't here," they informed him. "This is Dan Harrelson's. But I can tell you he's not home either. He's gone to New York."

The Southport waterskirt about 1910 showing two of the popular inns.
The Brunswick Inn, still standing, is seen at the far left, the Stuart House,
demolished in Hurricane Hazel, is on the right.

Eating Out: The Old Boarding Houses

Often in Southport's history, the only place for a visitor to find a meal
was in one of the numerous boarding houses that lined Bay Street or
Moore Street. In 1838 Mary Elizabeth Garland Bensel came to Southport
from Tennessee and opened a "waterskirt" inn, renamed the Stuart House
in 1842 after her remarriage to Charles Henry Stuart. Their daughter
Kate eventually took over the operation and ran the inn for many years.
The Stuart House was long a town landmark, a large, elegant, two storied
building in the Bahama style, situated so close and intimate to the Cape
Fear you could hear the river lapping at its piazza. During her lifetime
Miss Kate maintained a bulkhead at water's edge.

In 1859 Thomas D. Meares purchased the former residence of
Benjamin Smith, the town's founder, and built the handsome Brunswick
Inn which still stands at the southeast corner of Atlantic Avenue and Bay
Streets. During the late 19th Century the Bell-Clemmons House on East
Moore Street operated as a boarding house. During the mid-20th Century
Helen Niernsie Bragaw welcomed guests at the Camellia Inn at the
southwest corner of Moore and Atlantic in the former residence of Dr. J.
Arthur Dosher, guiding force of what became Dosher Memorial
Hospital. Helen Bragaw tired of her male guests ruining her bathroom
floor, and posted a sign, "STAND STILL AND AIM STRAIGHT."

The Grimes House was the last of the old boarding houses on Bay Street. Writers would come and spend the summer, and at noontime the local folks would show up for lunch, mostly the unmarried or divorced, or those who didn't cook. You might say it was a gathering of town characters. It was run by old George Grimes and his daughter Beth, the one-armed cook and waitress. Miss Grimes had been a stenographer, but lost an arm to a hit-and-run driver in Whiteville. She always wore black capes in a futile effort to hide the missing limb, and had orange hair which she dyed herself. Beth, whom I knew from the 1940's until her death in 1964, was herself quite a character. She was librarian of the Southport Public Library when it was located in a dank and dreary wing of the Government Building on the Garrison stocked with musty old books, mostly donated. Beth was a curious, high strung, distressed figure, and fell in love with the glamorous Hollywood beauty, Grace Kelly. I can't recall if her voice was that of a crow or a powder-puff, but it was distinctive. I do remember her exiting Leggett's Drugstore one day clutching an armload of magazines featuring Kelly, one with her picture on the cover. "I collect every word written about her," she told me with great pride.

Business woman and civic leader Bette Leggett married into a household that didn't cook and often took its meals at the Grimes'.

"I wish you could have been there," Bette recently recalled. "They had great food—fried chicken, stewed chicken, fried fish, baked flounder with dressing, and the best baked beans you ever had."

Bette Leggett has her own stories about Beth Grimes and the Grimes House customers. Bette came to Southport during the 1940's as a technician at Dosher Memorial Hospital. Once Beth came to Dosher for blood work.

Mary Lee Norment.

"I hate to tell you," said Bette, "but these tests show you have diabetes." Beth grew furious and accused Bette of giving it to her.

"I'm sorry," protested Bette, "but I didn't have anything to do with it."

"Well, I didn't have it when I came in here!" snapped Beth.

Among those who took board at the Grimes House was Mary Lee Norment, a school teacher who owned the first grade—it was taken for granted that the first grade was hers. Her life was teaching her students, and she would allow no one to disrupt her class for any reason, including the principal. I recall tiptoeing past her classroom door on the way to the boys' room so as not to incur her wrath. She scared the daylights out of the kids. One of her students passed Leggett's one day after school in tears. Mary Lee had warned the class that if they failed to do their assignment, *"There will be consequences!"* But no child left her grade without knowing how to read and write. Mary Lee had her quirks, and insisted on eating her dessert first. She'd sit and sulk and wouldn't eat until they brought her dessert. And she refused to touch pocket change. She'd open her change purse and let the salesperson remove the coins to pay for something.

"I'm not about to touch it," she said. "No telling where it has been. It might have been in somebody's shoe—or mouth!"

Bette's husband, Ormand (1916-1977), ran Leggett's Drugstore on Moore Street. He was a long time Chief of the Southport Volunteer Fire Department, a position of great honor, ranking above the Mayor, the City Aldermen, and the County Commissioners.

He had a great sense of humor. Bette came to Southport from Baltimore, which he considered the North, and called her his carpetbagger.

Back in the 1940's and early 1950's he also ran an appliance store. One day a farmer from out in the county came in and said, "Ormand, I want you to order me a radio and record player. I want the very best there is. Don't mind the money. I got the money." So Ormand ordered a free-standing Philco, top of the line. It arrived, he put it in his truck, drove to the man's house and took it into the living room. "Where is the electric outlet?" he asked. "I can't seem to find it." The farmer looked at him in a funny way and replied,

Ormand and Vienna Leggett, 1940's.

"Now Ormand, you know I ain't got no electricity!"

One Sunday at the Grimes House as they were finishing lunch, Ormand spied a single biscuit remaining in the basket.

"He wanted it *the most!*" said Bette. As he reached to pick it up, Vienna said,

23

"Ormand, pass those biscuits."

"I forgot to tell you, mother," replied Ormand. "I petted the dog and forgot to wash my hands." Ormand got his biscuit.

The surveyor Mark Farguson (1865-1961), who also took his meals at the Grimes house, lived close by in an eccentrically shaped house full of cats. When he died they found a small wooden coffin nailed to a floor in one of the rooms with the corpse of a cat in it.

Another steady customer was Percy Canady, who wouldn't enter or exit a room without turning around three times to avoid a hex, nor would he step off a curb or back onto it, nor open his mail box without going through this queer little ritual.

Eating Out: The Restaurants

Over the years a number of "eating places," as they were often referred to, served the public. Susie Carson tells us that "In 1839, Mrs. Mary Duffy of Smithville was operating an 'eating house' on the waterskirt— we do not know exactly where. This was a very popular place with residents and visitors alike. She liked children and kept them supplied with little tea cakes or sugar cookies which the children called Duffy Cakes."

During the 1920's, "Jimmy the Greek" Xanthos of Wilmington operated a restaurant at what was referred to as "monkey wrench corner," for reasons obscure, at the northeast intersection of Howe and Moore Streets. Susie Carson remembers that in the evening, men would send the wives and the children to the Amuzu "picture show" and gather at Jimmy's to gossip "and do whatever men do when they get together."

A story goes that a town drunk got dressed up in his brand new Easter suit, went in, sat down and ordered a steak. His wife came in on the warpath looking for him and demanded that he go home instantly. He shoved the steak in the pocket of his new suit and did as he was told.

Upstairs over Jimmy the Greek's was the old Bell Telephone Company exchange where my great-aunt Edna Dosher was an operator. In the 1920's and into the 1940's, the Miller Hotel at the southeast corner of Howe and Bay Streets operated a dining room and soda fountain. When my father first arrived in Southport in 1934, he rented one of the hotel's seven rooms. One night half of the plaster ceiling collapsed onto the floor next to his bed. Mrs. Anna Miller who ran the hotel heard the noise, came running upstairs and offered Daddy another room. He politely declined, slid the bed over the plaster and slept well the rest of the night, knowing there was no more plaster overhead to fall on him.

Mack's Cafe, southwest corner of Howe and Bay Streets, 1930's.
Photo courtesy of Betty McGlamery Cochran.

Quack's Sea Shack, and Ledrew Sellers' grocery, destroyed by Hurricane Hazel.

And in the 1950's Harry "Quack" Sanders, principal of Southport High School, opened a popular little cafe down near the Old Yacht Basin. Quack's Sea Shack was destroyed October 15, 1954, by Hurricane Hazel, an event still used to reckon time in Southport.

G. W. "Mack" McGlamery and Mary Swain, foreground;
Elizabeth Watson and "Fat" Marr, in front of Franklin Square Park, 1930's.
The Southport Baptist Church is seen in the background.
Photo courtesy of Betty McGlamery Cochran.

Mack's Cafe

During the Great Depression, G.W. "Mack" McGlamery came to
Southport with Roosevelt's C.C.C. (Civilian Conservation Corps).[*] He
married Mary Swain, a local belle, and in 1936 opened a cafe on Moore
Street; two years later he leased a former ship's chandlery at the foot of
Howe Street on Bay Street and opened what became for years the
principal eatery in town. Mack's was totally lacking what in those days
people called "atmosphere"—seductive blue neon signs announcing
"Cocktail Lounge," fake palm trees, vaguely Spanish or Bavarian
décor—but an honest reconstruction of it would have more "atmosphere"
than a Hollywood set-designer could invent. It was a bare-bones place
with plain wooden booths. A Wurlitzer jukebox played Dorsey and
Lombardo. Cases of Budweiser and Schlitz beer were stacked to the ceil-

---

[*] An account of the Civilian Conservation Corps and some of the men who later settled in
Southport appears in Susie Carson's *Joshua's Dream*. Mack's Cafe, remodeled, is today
the Ship's Chandler Restaurant, so named by Leila Pigott who knew its history.

Mack's Cafe on Bay Street at the foot of Howe, after its
remodeling in the 1950's. It was often Southport's only restaurant. Closed Thursdays!
The old Pilot Tower is seen to its rear, the Whittler's Bench to the left.
Photo by Art Newton.

ing. They served breakfast, dinner and supper, except for Thursdays
when it was closed. Coffee was served in heavy, thick-lipped white
mugs; iced tea came in thick, beer-barrel shaped glasses. In summer, a
single oscillating floor fan with blades the size of B-27 bomber
propellers roared, with about their equal in decibels. We felt quite
"uptown" when he later remodeled and installed individual juke boxes in
the booths. Out back of the cafe beside the river they killed chickens,
dressed fish and chopped vegetables. Mack's turned out good short-order
cooking, steaks and chops, classic Southern cooking and seafood. (The
instructions for Mack's famous fried flounder may be found on page
218.) Stew beef was on the menu regularly every Monday, with specials
during week days when people from out in the county came to town on
business or for Court. Local delicacies such as pogy roe were served up
in season. Mack was known for serving fresh country vegetables. Lawyer
Dwight McEwen ordered string beans which were out of season. Mack
knew how to fix up canned beans, and Mr. Mac never knew the
difference. (See the recipe for canned string beans on page 170.)

Mack understood people.

"If you'll let people think they know more than they do," he said, "they'll eat out of your hand."

The McGlamerys were hard workers and put in long hours. At noon on Sundays there would be a line of church goers waiting to be seated for the Sunday special. Their hard work paid off. In 1966 Mack went out the road to Clewis's Chrysler dealership and bought himself a brand new, swanky sedan in his favorite color, blue. But Mary wouldn't hear of him riding his dogs around in the new car. "Not in a *light blue* car! It'll get ruined!" So Mack went back out the road and bought another Chrysler sedan. And the McGlamerys had a pair of brand new sedans, powder blue for Mary, brown for Mack and the dogs.

Mack's was one of the few places that fun seekers could go for a little amusement. Once such a crowd gathered around a table having coffee and cigarettes when the topic turned to a woman who was "running around." A town dowager known for getting her phrases wrong, exclaimed, "Ah ha! I suspected it was about time for sex to rear its ugly *thing!*"

Miss Annie May Woodside

Miss Annie May Woodside (1892-1981) was a family friend, part of my world for as long as I can remember. It shames me now to think how casually I took her friendship and love, assuming that all people were as good and kind as she. Certainly, I did not appreciate her accomplishments, which were extraordinary—she ranks among the most distinguished women of Southport, and North Carolina as well.

Schooled at the old Southport Academy, she continued her education at State Normal and Industrial College in Greensboro, now U.N.C.-Greensboro. During 1930-1935 she served as Assistant Superintendent of Brunswick County Schools, then as Superintendent until her retirement in 1947, the first woman in North Carolina to hold such a position. She was active in civic affairs and was treasurer for the Southport Baptist Church. The bell tower in front of the Baptist Church was her gift.

On summer outings to our cousins' place on Walden Creek, which I write about in Chapter 12, she was always included like family. Once at her home down on Bay Street, trying to avoid her pesky Pekinese yapping at my ankles, I admired a little blue china dish in the shape of a boat she had brought back from a trip to Holland.

Miss Annie May Woodside at a night honoring her at the Southport Baptist Church, January 11, 1976, for her extraordinary service to the church and community. She was the first woman to serve as a County Superintendent of Schools in North Carolina, and one of the first in Southport to compile a cookbook. Photo courtesy of Susan S. Carson.

"Would you like it?" she asked.

"It's wonderful," I stammered.

"Here," she said, and took it from the shelf and gave it to me. I have it to this day.

Above I have mentioned her cook book of 1913, a skillful compilation of recipes and etiquette, carefully written out in a graceful longhand on seventy-five pages of a lined notebook. It contains over a hundred recipes of many kinds, from salads to breads to entrees to desserts, along with information on nutrition, percentages of water, protein, fat and calories in beef, and etiquette. So, North Carolina's first woman to serve as a Superintendent of Schools also wrote one of Southport's first cook books.

The Amuzu Theater, 1950's. Photo courtesy of *The State Port Pilot.*

2..
Snacks and Appetizers

The Amuzu and Mary Johnson's Popcorn

For years, the principal place of amusement was the Amuzu movie
theater, or picture show, as we called it, downtown on Howe Street.
When a good Gene Autry or Roy Rogers movie played, outside there
would be a long line on the sidewalk waiting to get in, and inside, a full
house and standing room only. The Amuzu was opened in 1913 by Mr.
Price Furpless (1869-1959) who ran it with his wife Lillie (1877-1945).
In the days of silent movies, he hired John Boyd Finch to play the violin
and Jim Hood to accompany him at the piano.

Lillie was, shall we say, a woman of character. If her dinner ran
late, she'd keep people waiting outside the theater until she got there. She
put up little bags of peanuts which she sold to the customers for a nickel.
When the kids had eaten their peanuts, they'd blow up the bags and pop
them, much to the annoyance of the adults. Lillie solved this problem by
cutting holes in the bags so they couldn't blow them up.

She was also a pinch-penny. Archie Johnson had a pig he was
about to cure, and she wanted one of the hams.

"No, I'm not interested in selling," he told her. She kept
pestering him until he finally consented to sell her a shoulder.

"No, I want a ham," she insisted. He held firm, and finally she
agreed to buy a shoulder. Then she told him,

"I don't have any money with me, but go see Price and he'll give
you some movie tickets."

"Hand me back my shoulder," replied Archie. "I can't eat movie
tickets."

Price eventually turned over the business to his son and
daughter-in-law, Bremen and Cora Lee. Admission in the late 1940's
was nine cents until you turned twelve, then fifteen cents. Bremen let you
in free on your birthday so he could learn when you turned twelve and
had to start paying the adult fare. Mary Johnson, Archie Johnson's sister,
was his all-around assistant, and their brother John Henry ran the
projector. If the movie had boring kissing scenes and the kids grew
rowdy, Bremen would have John Henry stop the projector and send Mary
down the aisle and tell them to shut up. If they started up again Bremen

31

would come down front, but we knew he was too nice and we weren't scared of him. We paid more attention to Mary than Bremen. She'd point that flashlight in your face and snap her finger and you'd shut up all right. If all else failed, they'd send in the Big Gun, old Mr. Price. He was by now white-headed, but still tall and erect and commanding as General MacArthur wading in at the Philippines. As Mary Johnson said,

"Mr. Price would simply walk down the aisle, cross over without saying a word—would just look at them, walk back the other aisle, and you could hear a pin drop."

But Bremen sold no popcorn and I can't enjoy a movie without popcorn which I adore. I can get up from a steak dinner, smell popcorn cooking, and get hungry all over again. It's one of the great snacks. I can devour great quantities just as is, or loaded with salt and butter, or coated with toffee or butterscotch. So, I longed for the day when the Amuzu would sell popcorn like the Manor or Bijou or Carolina in Wilmington— really big time. One night, Bremen was at the little wooden, drop-leaf ticket desk. I handed him my dime and said,

"Bremen, why don't you put in a popcorn machine?"

"Well, thank you, son. But I doubt it would pay."

"But people love popcorn," I argued. He gave me my penny change and said,

"Enjoy the picture! By the way, don't you have a birthday coming up soon?"

Ma-Ma, my grandmother Alta Wescott Dosher, had an old 1930's popcorn machine. It was a square contraption of chrome with a glass top and a cloth-covered electric cord, and could handle about a quarter cup of kernels at a time. These you stirred until they popped by twisting a little black, wooden knob at the top. Dan Harrelson sold me some small paper bags, popcorn and oil. My friend Neil Lewis came over and we set up business in Ma-Ma's kitchen, then peddled the bags of popcorn to the customers lined up outside the Amuzu. This went on for a few weeks and we made a little pocket money. But one night we arrived, and what should we find standing there in the little vestibule that opened onto the sidewalk—a big, shiny, chrome and glass popcorn machine. And behind it stood Mary Johnson filling red and white popcorn boxes.

The shameful unfairness of this was staggering: Taking away a child's livelihood! But I paid Mary for a box, and all was forgiven. It was the best popcorn I ever had, before or since.

"We sold it for a dime a box," she recently reminded me. "We had a special popcorn salt. And we used coconut oil. It came in cans like lard, and in winter was so hard I'd have to crack it into pieces with an ice pick. Then it'd melt in the popper. One time we ran out of it, and Bremen went to the store and bought some peanut oil. It tasted terrible."

Coconut oil! That was the secret. Today the American Heart Association would close you down. But I'd risk clogging every artery in my body to have some of that great Amuzu popcorn again, Mary Johnson standing behind the popper, popping away.

ABOUT POPCORN

Popcorn is an ancient, native American food. Benjamin Franklin noted that some nomadic native tribes used it as a lightweight portable food. Archaeologists in New Mexico unearthed some thousand-year-old kernels that still popped.

For a good bowl of popcorn, simply coat the bottom of a large saucepan with a little oil, pour in a single layer of popcorn kernels, cover, and heat, shaking as the popping begins to prevent burning. Salt and pepper, and drizzle on a little melted butter if you like.

ABOUT PEANUTS

Peanuts are actually not nuts, but legumes that grow on the roots of a vine. In our parts they used to be called ground peas. The large variety is called goobers; Spanish peanuts are small with red skins.

ROASTED RAW PEANUTS
Contributed by Vickie Hardee

Vickie's grandparents had a farm in Columbus County. So she has first hand knowledge of preparing peanuts.

Peanuts can be roasted in the shell or unshelled. In both cases set the oven at 350°.

Place peanuts in the shell in a shallow baking pan one or two layers deep. Roast for 25 to 30 minutes, stirring occasionally. Sample a few for doneness before removing from oven.

Shelled peanuts should be placed in a shallow baking pan one layer deep and cooked for 15 to 20 minutes, until golden brown. If you wish, pour melted butter over the peanuts and salt lightly.

BOILED PEANUTS
Contributed by Vickie Hardee

5 pounds green (raw) peanuts
½ cup salt
Water to cover

Wash peanuts well. Use filled-out green peanuts. Place peanuts in an 8-quart pot and cover with water. Add ½ cup salt across the top. Do not stir. Bring to a medium boil. Let the peanuts boil for one hour. Taste test and when the peanuts are tender turn off. Let stand until desired concentration of salt is absorbed, about 15 to 30 minutes. Do not let them sit too long or they will be overly salty. Drain off water and keep cool. Start eating while hot! When they are cooled, you may freeze them in plastic storage bags. They will keep up to a year without turning dark.

FRIED PORK SKINS

Fried pork skins are fatty, but enjoy them now and then. They are fun to cook. Just take pieces of pork skins, dried off well, and drop into hot deep fat. After a few minutes they will inflate like life preservers and become fluffy and crispy.

SHRIMP COCKTAIL

Follow directions for boiling and preparing shrimp in Chapter 11. Line cocktail cups with crisp lettuce. Arrange 6 medium sized shrimp in each. Top with cocktail sauce, which may be store-bought, or made with the recipe on page 152.

TRADITIONAL CRABMEAT COCKTAIL

1 pound of crab meat, cooked	Cocktail sauce
Lemon juice	Lettuce leaves

Sprinkle the crab meat with lemon juice and toss lightly. Line cocktail cups with crispy lettuce leaves. Spoon in about ¼ cup cooked crabmeat for each serving. Top with a spoonful of the cocktail sauce, page 152. Serve with crackers.

FANCY CRABMEAT COCKTAIL

This is a delicious, delicately flavored variation. This recipe makes about 6 to 8 servings.

1 pound of crabmeat, cooked
2 cups iceberg lettuce, chopped
   to the consistency of slaw
¾ cup celery, minced
¼ cup sweet green or red bell
pepper, minced, or a
   combination thereof
Extra lettuce leaves for lining the
   cocktail cups

The dressing

½ cup mayonnaise
½ cup tomato ketchup
1 teaspoon celery seed
1 teaspoon celery salt
1 teaspoon lemon juice
Dash of Tabasco sauce
½ teaspoon pepper

Mix the ingredients for the dressing, and toss lightly with the crabmeat, chopped lettuce, celery and pepper. Line the cocktail cups with crisp lettuce leaves. Fill each with the crab cocktail mixture.

IRMA CAROON'S CRAB SALAD

1 pound Backfin crabmeat
¼ cup diced celery
3 hardboiled eggs, diced
¼ cup sweet pickles, diced
2 tablespoons mayonnaise
2 tablespoons sweet pickle
   vinegar
1 teaspoon Worcestershire sauce
1 tablespoon lemon juice
Salt and pepper to taste

Toss gently to avoid crushing lumps. Serve on lettuce leaf. Garnish with paprika.

IRMA CAROON'S CRAB SUPREME

1 pound Backfin or Special flaked
   crab meat
6 tablespoons water
2 tablespoons vinegar
2 tablespoons butter
Salt and white pepper

Steam in covered dish over low heat for 5 minutes. Serve with crackers.

SWEETHEART'S MARINATED SHRIMP

1 ½ pounds cooked shrimp   ¼ cup salad oil
½ cup vinegar   1 teaspoon salt

Place ingredients in quart jar. Shake well and store in refrigerator for 24 hours, shaking every now and then. Serve with toothpicks.

CLAMS OR OYSTERS ON THE HALF-SHELL

Refer to "About Oysters," on page 237, or "About Clams," on pages 240-241, regarding safety precautions for raw seafood. Clams or oysters are great served on the half-shell. Scrub the shells well with a stiff brush and wash. Open with an oyster knife. Cut the flesh loose from the tough stem that attaches to the shell. Serve in a half shell on a bed of crushed ice with cocktail sauce, lemon wedges, Tabasco, a sprig of fresh parsley for decoration, and saltines.

BAKED CLAMS ON THE HALF-SHELL

6 clams per person   Bacon
Chopped chives   Butter to drizzle
Chopped parsley   Lemon wedges
Herbed bread crumbs

Cut the flesh loose from the tough stem that attaches to the shell. In pie-tins spread a layer of rock salt to keep the clams from rocking about. Place the half-clams on the salt. Sprinkle each with the chives, parsley, garlic, and bread crumbs. Drizzle each with a little butter. Lay on each a 1-inch slice of bacon. Bake on the top shelf of a preheated 425° oven until the bacon is crisp. Serve with a lemon wedge and have a bottle of Tabasco sauce for those who like a little kick.

OYSTERS ROCKEFELLER
(BAKED OYSTERS ON THE HALF-SHELL WITH SPINACH)

This delicious and attractive hors d'oeuvre is made in different ways, but this is my favorite.

1 ½ pounds cooked shrimp   Sour cream
½ cup vinegar   Melted, clarified butter to drizzle
Spinach leaves   1 teaspoon salt

Drain the oysters, saving the liquid for stew or some other dish. Arrange spinach leaves in each oyster shell, about 3 to 4 leaves deep. Spread on a shy teaspoon of sour cream. In each shell place an oyster. Drizzle with melted butter, sprinkle with salt and pepper. Place in a baking pan and bake in preheated 350° oven 10 minutes. Use care when removing to individual serving dishes as the oyster shells will be hot.

SAUSAGE CHEESE BALLS
Dorothy Hardee's Recipe Files

3 cups Bisquick
1 pound grated Cheddar cheese, sharp
1 pound hot Jamestown sausage or similar

Mix thoroughly. Will form gummy dough. Roll into small balls about 1-inch in diameter. Bake in 350° oven for 12 to 15 minutes. Dough may be frozen, thawed and baked later.

CHEESE STRAWS
Favorite Recipes of North Carolina (1944)

2 cups flour
2/3 cup Natural American
   cheese, grated
2/3 cup butter

1 teaspoon salt
1/3 to 1/2 cup ice water
Paprika

Sift flour and salt, cut in butter, add sufficient water to hold together. Turn onto lightly floured board and roll in oblong shape. Sprinkle half the dough with a portion of the cheese and paprika. Fold over two or three times and roll out. Repeat until all cheese is used. Roll slightly thinner than pie pastry. Cut into tiny circles or 4-inch cheese-stick lengths. Bake on ungreased cookie sheet in 425° oven 7 to 10 minutes. [The adventurous may add cayenne instead of paprika.]

VICKIE HARDEE'S SHRIMP MOLD DIP

My sister-in-law is a great cook, adapting many of the traditional recipes of the region to modern ways. You will see this recipe here and there with variations. I like Vickie's best. It is a party favorite.

1 pound shrimp	1 medium bell pepper, chopped
1 8-ounce package of cream cheese room temperature	1 can tomato soup
	3-ounce lemon gelatin mix
1 mild, medium onion chopped	1 cup mayonnaise

Vickie says, "Head, peel, split the shrimp down the back and remove digestive track, chop into small pieces, and boil for 7 minutes, reserving a few whole shrimp for decorating. Mix soup, cream cheese and mayonnaise until smooth in large bowl. In another bowl dissolve gelatin mix in ½ cup of boiling water. When the sugar in the gelatin mix is dissolved, fold into the bowl with the soup mixture and mix well. Add the chopped onion, pepper and shrimp. Pour into molds, cover with handy wrap, and refrigerate overnight. If you plan to turn out of mold, then line mold with handy wrap first. This dish looks good in a lobster mold turned out onto a glass or silver plate and surrounded by your favorite crackers or slices of good breads. For added effect lay a few whole boiled shrimp across the top before serving. This recipe will make at least two molds and will last in the refrigerator up to a week. Excellent flavor, and lots of calories and cholesterol and fat grams. Must be eaten in excess."

SIMPLY SCRUMPTIOUS SHRIMP SPREAD
Contributed by Brooks Newton Preik

2 cups or more boiled shrimp, cut into small pieces	1 small onion, finely grated
	½ cup mayonnaise
1 8-ounce package cream cheese	¼ cup ketchup
2 tablespoons horseradish	2 tablespoons lemon juice

Blend all ingredients together, add shrimp and refrigerate for 24 hours. Serve with crackers. Buttery crackers go well with this.

EASTERN NORTH CAROLINA CUCUMBER SANDWICHES
Contributed by Margaret Connaughton

Peel and score cucumbers with a fork and slice thin. Put in ice water until ready to use on sandwiches. Dry on paper towels, when ready to make sandwiches. Use soft, white bread cut into rounds with biscuit cutter. Mix desired amount of mayonnaise (Best Food preferred) with garlic salt to taste, add dash or two of red cayenne pepper. Spread mayonnaise mixture on bread rounds, add cucumber slices. Place on attractive tray. Add a gentle dash of garlic salt and pepper over the sandwiches. Serve immediately. Cucumber sandwiches are best when cucumbers are still crisp.

HOT PEPPER JELLY & CREAM CHEESE

Place a dish of Dovie White's Hot Pepper Jelly on a plate with a block of cream cheese and crackers. Let the guests help themselves. See Dovie White's recipe on page 146.

DEVILED HAM SPREAD

1 cup cooked ham, ground
4 tablespoons grated onion
2 tablespoons mayonnaise
2 tablespoons sweet and sour
    mustard

Coarse black pepper
1 tablespoon horseradish
    (optional)

Mash ingredients together and spread on toast or crackers.

HOT CHEESE PUFFS

2 egg whites
½ cup grated sharp American
    cheese

½ teaspoon baking powder
¼ teaspoon paprika
¼ teaspoon salt

Beat the egg whites until stiff. Beat in the baking powder, salt, and paprika. Fold in the grated cheese. Spoon onto toast rounds. Broil about 5 minutes, until just brown.

HOT CRAB MEAT PUFFS

2 egg whites   1 cup crabmeat, flaked
1 cup mayonnaise   Paprika to sprinkle

Whip the egg whites until stiff. Fold in the mayonnaise and the crabmeat. Spoon onto toast beds and sprinkle with paprika. Broil about 3 minutes until puffed and brown.

HOT CRAB DIP

½ pound fresh crabmeat   ¼ cup dry white wine
1 8-ounce package of cream   2 teaspoons sugar
    cheese, softened   1 teaspoon ground mustard
¼ cup grated Parmesan cheese   4 medium green onions,
¼ cup mayonnaise   sliced thinly

Mix all ingredients, adding the crabmeat last to avoid breaking. Place in a shallow 1 quart casserole dish. Bake in preheated 375° oven 15 to 20 minutes, or until bubbly. Serve with crackers or sliced raw vegetables.

WATER CHESTNUTS AND BACON

This recipe has become very popular in recent years. Drain a can of water chestnuts. Wrap each chestnut with a half slice of uncooked bacon and fasten with a toothpick. Marinate for an hour in soy sauce. Bake about 15 minutes in a 350° oven, until the bacon is nicely browned, basting occasionally.

CORN CRISPS

These go great with drinks, soups or salads.

½ cup corn meal   1 teaspoon salt
¾ cup boiling water   Celery seed or poppy seed
2 tablespoons butter

Mix corn meal with salt. Melt the butter in the boiling water, and mix with the corn meal and salt. Drop by spoonfuls on ungreased cooky sheets, leaving room for spreading. Bake in preheated 425° oven about 8 minutes until lightly brown. Will make about 48 2-inch wafers, so this may take more than 1 baking.

CANAPÉS

The open-faced canapé has long been very popular. Various fillings are spread on crackers, or sandwich bread cut into attractive shapes. Use a cookie cutter to make circles, a knife to make rectangles or diamond shapes. Then spread onto the open face little sandwiches one of many fillings, such as cream cheese and olives, chicken salad dusted with paprika, or ham spread. Rolled sandwiches make an attractive offering. Remove crusts from thin slices of bread, spread with topping, and slice crossways like a miniature jellyroll. Toothpicks help to keep them from coming apart.

HOT SALMON CANAPÉS

1 small can salmon, drained
1 tablespoon finely minced onion
2 tablespoons mayonnaise
2 tablespoons bread crumbs
1 tablespoon sherry wine
1 tablespoon Parmesan cheese, grated
Salt and pepper

Mix ingredients well and let stand for several hours, or overnight. If mixture separates slightly, drain excess liquid and add a little more bread crumbs. Spread on crackers, sprinkle on a little more Parmesan cheese. Bake in preheated 425° oven about 5 minutes, until brown, and serve immediately.

HOT SEAFOOD CANAPÉS

Follow instructions for Hot Salmon Canapés, but use cooked and chopped clams, lobster, or shrimp.

CHEESE SPREAD WITH SHERRY

½ pound Cheddar cheese, finely ground
3 tablespoons sherry
2 tablespoons butter, creamed
1 tablespoon prepared mustard
½ teaspoon salt
Dash of cayenne

Mix well and let stand a while, or overnight. Serve with crackers.

Ma-Ma (Alta Wescott Dosher) at Mammie Dozier's punch bowl, about 1950.

3..
Beverages

Mammie Dozier's Punch Bowl

One of my great aunts, Margarette Dozier, whom we called Mammie, owned the biggest pressed-glass punch bowl in the county so far as was known, kept like a trophy in her dining room cabinet. She had visions of giving fancy parties and pouring from her prized bowl, but the closest she got to that was entertaining the church circle meeting. I doubt it had been used more than a dozen times in her life. Even that came to an end. One year, Mammie decorated the Baptist church for the Christmas Eve service, hauling in holly and yaupon branches and candles and slaved over it, never one to do things by halves. When she went home to dress for the service, one of the deacons declared the candles in the windows a hazard and had them taken away. When she returned to find her elegant decor removed and the candles gone, she was heartbroken, hurt and humiliated. She went into a fury and vowed never again to enter the church, a promise she kept except for a few funerals and that of her own.

The giant bowl mostly remained on the shelf collecting dust. For years my mother coveted it, and one day Mammie realized she had grown old and was never going to be a grand lady, and presented it to her. It really is a handsome piece. Any lady would feel very important pouring from it.

The Four Sisters

In Franklin Square Park are four giant oaks which are joined together at the roots and are called The Four Sisters. In my family were also my very own four sisters—four of my great-aunts—who were very much a part of Old Southport, and to my memory were also giants, with common roots. They were the children of my great grandfather, George Dosher, raised in his house that still stands at the northeast corner of Caswell and West Streets. Edna (1888-1974) was the eldest, full sister to my grandfather, Harry Lee Dosher. Three of her half sisters by George Dosher's second wife, Georgianna Cumby, were Margarette (1893-1966), Lillian (1896-1958) and Gladys (1904-1964). Seldom were they ever called by their legal names. Harry Lee Dosher (1886-1943) was called Pa-Pa, Edna was Ted, Margarette was Mammie of whom I have

43

Children playing in the Four Sisters Oaks at Franklin Square Park:
Paul Merritt Moore, Penny and Jimmy Moore, late 1940's.
Photo courtesy of Jimmy Moore.

referred to above, Lillian was Bitsie, and Gladys was Auntee. (There
were other siblings whom I will mention in passing.) I'll first tell about
Auntee, Mammie, Ted, and in a later chapter tell about Aunt Bitsie.

Three of the Four Sisters. Gladys "Auntee" Dozier, launching the *S. S. Charles D. McIver* at the Wilmington Ship Yard, 1943. Edna "Ted" Dosher is center, in a white hat; a proud Margarette "Mammie" Dozier is seen, right.

Auntee

Gladys Dozier Miller was the youngest of my great aunts, the Dosher/Dozier sisters. She liked for us to call her Auntee as it made her feel genteel, which she was. She was a beautiful woman, slender, sleek and sophisticated, who dressed stylishly and had elegant china and silver and furniture. She wanted everything always to be perfect. I delighted in her company; but underlying her grace and elan was an ever present current of dissatisfaction, for nothing is perfect and she craved perfection. Mammie and Ted doted on her, idolized her. During World War II she won a raffle, the prize of which was the privilege of christening the *S.S. Charles D. McIver,* one of the many Liberty Ships constructed at the Wilmington Ship Yard.

Years ago she came under the spell of a genealogist who convinced her the family name should be spelled Dozier, not Dosher. Auntee and Mammie aspired to gentility, liked the fancier French spelling, and legally changed their names. Pa-Pa and Ted considered the names they were born with were good enough and would have no part in this nonsense. Today in Northwood Cemetery you will see brothers and sisters lying side by side with different surnames.

45

The George Dosher House, northeast corner of
Caswell and West Streets, about 1920.

Auntee married Hal Y. Miller, an engineer with the N.C.
Highway Department. They adored each other and were a handsome
couple. In his Jodhpur boots and tweeds, Uncle Hal seemed to have
stepped out of *Gentlemen's Quarterly*; in her stylish dresses, Auntee
seemed right out of *Bazaar*. They drove a fine Cadillac sedan they called
"Betsy," purchased a large lot behind Great Grandfather Dosher's on
Lord Street, and laid plans to built a house of their own. They had no
children—their dog Blackie was their child, and a spoiled one.
Something then occurred that seemed an omen of bad things to come.
One Sunday afternoon they were pleasure driving out in the county when
Blackie darted from the car and vanished. Day after day they returned to
the same spot, hoping desperately to find their beloved child-pet, but
never did. Not long afterwards, in 1954, I received word that Uncle Hal
had suddenly died of a heart attack. He was only fifty-three years old;
Auntee was devastated.

She moved to Columbia and took a job in the Governor's office.
During my Army days at Fort Jackson, I visited her on weekends at her
apartment in Cornell Arms, a modern high-rise and a very proper
address, but which she ruefully referred to as "Widow's Arms." An
Army buddy of mine from Tennessee went with me for a visit one
weekend. You would have thought we were visiting-royalty. Everything
was sparkling. She had had a maid come in and polish the silver and the
Drexel mahogany furniture. She had gone to the library and brought
home some books to read up on the State of Tennessee so she could
make interesting conversation with my buddy. After treating us to lunch
in a hotel restaurant downtown, she had us up for coffee.

46

"I hope you can drink it," she said apologetically. "I never seem to make good coffee."

"It's fine!" we protested, finding welcome relief from Army brew. "Your mother makes such fine coffee," she said, "I don't know how Dorothy does it! I wish you'd find out and let me know. Mine always tastes like aluminum!"

Mammie Dozier

Margarette Dozier was a remarkable person, a big-boned woman of peasant proportions who bore herself with dignity and grace. Like her half-sister, Ted, she remained a spinster; they lived their lives in their father's house on West Street. Mammie was lovable but dominant and controlling; Ted was passive. How many times did I hear Ted say, "Well, we'll have to go ask Margarette."

Mammie had a keen sense of beauty and coveted nice things. Photographs I have seen in an old 1930's etiquette book could have been taken in her dining room. The mahogany veneer table and chairs gleam with polish, the starched linen napkins and silverware are lined up and down to the quarter-inch according to adamantine law. There was never enough money to turn her back yard into the English garden of her dreams, but she came close. Azaleas lined the fence, wisteria grew up on a trellis into the trees and in the spring was a shower of lavender. Boulders, alien to our parts, encircled a lily pond.

She was a self-taught secretary and worked for lawyer Rob Davis, then for lawyer Dwight McEwen; some said she knew as much about lawyering as they did. When her sister Dewey died in 1941 leaving six boys, Mammie closed her house and moved a couple of doors away into Aunt Bitsie's big two-story house on W. West Street, where she and Ted raised the boys to manhood. The boys' father was away most of the time as captain of a dredge, and would send money home for their keep. But a dredge boat captain's pay did not go far with six growing boys, and every Christmas, Mammie would go to the bank and see Prince O'Brien to take out a loan for presents. He never questioned her ability to repay, but would peer out from over his bow tie and ask,

"Well, Miss Margarette, how much will it be this year?"

She loved children, and after the boys were raised and moved away, focused her attentions on me in particular. On Sundays she would hire a man to go to the Yellow Hole, a sandy beach near a creek in the woods, for a wheelbarrow load of clear sand, just so I could play with my shovel and pail on her sidewalk. Little wonder I grew up thinking myself a young lord.

She had the determination of a Caterpillar diesel, and was acquisitive. She once asked my friend Neil Lewis and me to drive her to pick up a desk she wanted to buy from Aunt Bessie, the widow of her deceased brother, Edwin. I drove Daddy's old 1938 Chevy truck up in front of Aunt Bessie's house.

"Here's the money," said Mammie, handing me two ten-dollar bills. I walked onto the porch and knocked on the door. Presently Aunt Bessie appeared from the back of the house, a willowy specter of a woman who never left her house.

"We've come for Uncle Edwin's desk," I announced. Bessie remained behind the screen door chewing on a thumb, and said,

"You tell Margarette I don't know where that desk is." I returned to the truck and conveyed the message to Mammie, who scrooched up her face like a rhino.

"You go tell Bessie a bargain's a bargain. Here's cash money, and I've come for Edwin's desk. She knows exactly where that desk is— out back in the garage. She's not using it. It's of no earthly use to her. It just sits there. You tell her she agreed to sell, and she can't go back on her word. Now you go tell her that!" Neil stared ahead motionless and wordless, wanting no part of this cat fight. Once again I returned to the door, knocked, and Aunt Bessie appeared from the shadows.

"Honey, you go tell Margarette I've decided I'm not ready to get clear of it."

My great-aunt did not take this news well. As we drove away she clinched her fist and a ferocious look came upon her.

"She's from out in the county," she muttered. "They're all like that!" And shaking her fist declared, "I'll get that desk yet!"

Neil, transfixed, stared ahead into space, not saying a word.

Later in life when she was bedridden, lawyers and clerks in search of some legal document or other would call at her bedside.

"If you'll go to the back room upstairs at the Court House," she'd say, "and look in the top drawer of the second file cabinet, you'll find it."

Ted

She was a slow moving, well shaped woman with fine features and long, strawberry blonde hair that nightly she unpinned and brushed. She had a weak left eye that "traveled" outward as she grew older. Unkind people made fun of her.

In the days before dial phones, Ted was an operator with the Bell Telephone Company downtown on Moore Street. Capt. Ikey Davis annoyed her. He would ring, and in a grand, imperious manner announce, "Central! I wish you to connect me to..." She grew tired of this and one day when he called said, "Now Ikey Davis, you know perfectly well my name is *not* 'Central.' It's Edna Dosher. And in the future I wish you'd start calling me *Edna Dosher*."

There was a sweet naiveté about her. She would say, "You know what I'd like? I'd like to wake up Christmas morning and find a shiny, brand new Chevrolet out front, with a big red ribbon around it." It was a useless fancy, of course; neither she nor Mammie ever learned to drive.

One hot summer afternoon I parked my bicycle out front and she brought to the kitchen table a pitcher of ice water which I lapped up.

"Wow!" I exclaimed. "I drank three glasses!"

"Why don't you make it ten?!" she replied with glee.

She was always in the shadow of Mammie, who more or less called the shots. But Ted did odd little things to assert herself. A photograph taken during World War I shows her dressed up in Pa-Pa's doughboy uniform—he had served in the War. Someone killed an enormous rattle snake of record length which she preserved in a big pickle jar and used as a door-stop. This coiled monster with its greenish-brown scales set a solemn tone to the house as you entered.

Ted would have a little glass of wine with dinner every now and then, and dared Mammie to say anything about it. She held her teacup with the pinkie of her right hand curled high in the air ever so daintily as if to prove to Mammie she was the more lady-like. When everyone was having iced tea, she'd make herself a glass of iced coffee. Few in town drank iced coffee, but Ted did. I can see her now, sitting at her place at their dining room table, white cream drifting down into the tall glass of dark coffee like patterns in marble.

On a summer's day I'll enjoy a glass of iced coffee on my porch and conjure up sweet memories of Ted and her dear half-sisters, still deep in my heart, many years after their passing.

SIMPLE SYRUP

Simple syrup used to be kept on hand for sweetening beverages, foods, and for use in canning. Basic simple syrup is sugar boiled and dissolved in water for 5 minutes, according to the following proportions. Honey or corn syrup may also be used.

> Thin syrup: 3 cups water to 1 cup sugar
> Medium syrup: 2 cups water to 1 cup sugar
> Thick syrup: 1 cup water to 1 cup sugar

GOOD COFFEE

Nutritionists recently announced that just smelling a good cup of freshly brewed coffee gives health benefits. But haven't we known this all along? I do know it makes you feel better, even as you lift the cup to your lips. There's nothing like it to start the day.

Start with a clean pot! Do not use steel scouring pads, but clean with soap and hot water and rinse well after each use. Grind your coffee beans just before brewing for the best coffee. Certainly, use fresh grounds if you do not grind your own. Start with fresh, cold water. The rule of thumb:

Regular strength, use 1 level tablespoon of ground coffee for each ¾ cup water.

For strong coffee, use 2 level tablespoons of ground coffee for each ¾ cup water.

Coffee dies and becomes bitter if left on the heat for very long.

ICED COFFEE

Brew a good cup of coffee. Pour it over ice in a chilled glass, and drizzle down cream or canned evaporated milk.

TEA

Nowadays we use instant teas so often we can forget how brisk and wonderful freshly brewed tea can be. A few hints from the old timers: Heat a spotlessly clean, non-metallic teapot with hot water, then pour out. Boil freshly drawn cold water in a kettle. Add tea to the warmed teapot, 1 tea bag for each ¾ cup water, and pour the furiously boiling water over them. Let it steep 3 minutes for weak tea, 5 for strong.

ICED TEA

Iced tea is probably the most popular drink in town, served year 'round. Our kitchen is seldom without pitchers of it, one unsweetened, and one sweetened. (Or, as Theresa Moore, our beloved cook for many years, would say, "Mrs. Hardee, do you want this tea adulterated?")

Follow directions above for the basic tea. Before storing in refrigerator, allow to cool to room temperature to prevent its becoming cloudy.

MAMMIE DOZIER'S HOT CRANBERRY PUNCH

2 cups cranberries
2 cups sugar
2 cups water
Rind of 1 orange

Rind of 1 lemon
1 16-ounce can pineapple juice
Juice of 6 oranges
Juice of 4 lemons

Peel the orange and lemon rinds, taking care not to cut into the bitter white membrane. Cook all ingredients together until berries pop. Remove rinds and strain remainder through potato ricer or colander. Add the orange and lemon juices. Heat and pour into your fanciest punch bowl. Serve in pretty punch cups. Delicious and festive!

GRAPE PUNCH
Southport's Treasure of Personal Recipes (1952)
Contributed by Clayton Hickman

Clayton was one of Southport's renowned cooks, and for a number of years ran the Southport High School lunch room.

4 teaspoons loose tea leaves
2 cups boiling water
1 pint grape juice
½ cup sugar

1 12-ounce bottle ginger ale
Juice of 4 lemons
Juice of 2 oranges

Make double-strength tea by pouring 2 cups boiling water over the tea leaves. Seep 5 minutes. Strain. Add the sugar and stir to dissolve, then remaining ingredients. Chill. Pour over ice cubes in punch bowl.

ORANGE-LEMON PUNCH
Southport's Treasure of Personal Recipes (1952)
Contributed by Mrs. Leila Jane Sellers

2 teaspoons tea leaves
2 cups boiling water
1 cup sugar
1 cup orange juice

½ cup lemon juice
½ cup cold water
1 quart ginger ale, chilled

Pour boiling water over tea leaves. Cover and allow to seep 3 minutes. Strain. Add sugar and stir to dissolve. Add juices and cold water. Chill. Pour over ice in punch bowl, and add ginger ale just before serving.

The FF Club, 1920's. L-R, top row: Mary Dosher Bussels, Ada Morse, unidentified; front row: Ida Potter Watson, unidentified, Minnie Butler, unidentified, Annie Kay Harper Vitou. Some of their recipes are included in this book. Photo courtesy of Elizabeth Watson Griffin.

The FF Club

Whatever passed for Southport "society" in 1922 centered in the informal FF Club, founded in that year by a select set of ladies to play canasta, socialize, and discuss civic affairs. It continued into the 1950's. Among its members were Ida Potter Watson, "Miss Minnie" Butler, Annie Kay Vitou, Mrs. Mary Dosher Bussels, "Miss Eva" Ruark and others. Of them, only Mary Bussels and Eva Ruark were business-minded; "Miss" Mary built four tourist cabins on Bay Street (later replaced by the Riverside Motel). "Miss" Eva Ruark operated a major general merchandise store with her husband Cronley at the northeast corner of Moore and Dry Street. Mr. Cronley was a crochety old somebody, but "Miss Eva" was a sugar plum. When their store burned uninsured in the 1950's, they relocated with a reduced store on Howe Street.

What "FF" stood for is not clear. Jealous outsiders not admitted to their circle referred to them sarcastically as the First Family Club. With good natured self-deprecation, they insisted that FF stood for "Fat and Forty." My mother remarked, "There were some who would have given their eye teeth to get in, but weren't allowed." But these ladies had in common a sense of fun and good will toward men. They personified Faith, Hope and Charity, Southern refinement and gentility. I often thought that had the Queen of England called, they would have received her with dignity and ease.

"MISS EVA" RUARK'S RUSSIAN TEA
The Proverbial Church Cookbook (1991)
Contributed by Mrs. Margaret Harper

1 ½ cups sugar	Juice of 1 lemon
5 cups water	2 quarts of tea
Grated rind of 1 orange	Cloves
Juice of 4 oranges	

Boil water and sugar and mix with rind of orange and the citrus juices. Add tea at the last minute, reheat and serve in hot teacups with 1 or 2 cloves in each cup.

SUMMER LEMONADE

1 cup sugar	1 cup lemon juice
5 cups water	Rind of 2 lemons, cut into pieces

Dissolve sugar in 1 cup water over low heat with the lemon rinds and boil 7 minutes. Cool and add the lemon juice and 4 cups of ice water.

LIMEADE OR ORANGEADE

Follow the Summer Lemonade recipe, but use limes instead. For orangeade, use the Summer Lemonade recipe, but instead of the lemon juice, use 2 cups of orange juice and ¼ cup lemon juice.

Mammie Dozier's Tea Cart

Mammie Dozier passed this tea cart on to my mother. It is set with a tea service my cousin Jack Dosher, who was in the merchant marines, brought back from Kobe, Japan, shortly after World War II. The tea carts that one sees today in some of the old Southport homes speak of a time when the afternoon tea was a familiar social event. With its small front wheels and large, spoke rear wheels, the tea cart would be rolled in from the kitchen bearing the teapot, fancy China tea cups, and a plate of canapés and sweets. Nowadays the tea cart is more likely to be found sulking in a corner somewhere as a stand for a vase of flowers or the telephone book.

ROOT BEER FLOAT

Every now and then pamper yourself with this old fashioned classic, a root beer float. Pour cold root beer over ice, and add a scoop of vanilla ice cream. Serve with a straw and an ice tea spoon.

GINGER BEER
Confederate Receipt Book (1863)

"One pint of molasses and two spoonfuls of ginger put into a pail, to be half filled with boiling water; when well stirred together, fill the pail with cold water, leaving room for one pint of yeast, which must not be put in until lukewarm. Place it on a warm hearth for the night, and bottle in the morning."

METHODIST CHAMPAGNE
The Proverbial Church Cookbook (1991)

1 cup sugar
1 cup water
1 cup unsweetened grapefruit
 juice

½ cup orange juice
1 quart ginger ale, chilled

Boil sugar and water 5 minutes. Remove from heat and let cool in refrigerator several hours. Stir in cold ginger ale before serving. Makes 13 4-ounce cups.

HOT SPICED CIDER

2 pints cider
1 teaspoon whole allspice
1 stick cinnamon
4 cloves

¼ cup lemon juice
2 tablespoons orange juice
1 orange sliced crosswise

Simmer all ingredients except the lemon and orange juice. Strain to remove the spices. Add the lemon, orange juice, warm, then add the orange slices and serve.

HOT CHOCOLATE

Instant mixes are so easy to fix these days that we seldom bother with making hot chocolate from scratch. But if you want to be reminded of how good hot chocolate can be, try this:

3 ounces unsweetened baking
 chocolate
2 cups milk or half & half

1 cup water
1/3 cup sugar
Dash of salt

Heat the chocolate and water until the chocolate is melted. Add the remaining ingredients and heat almost to the boiling point, but do not boil as it will form a skin. Beat with a hand or electric beater until foamy and smooth.

The Soda Fountain

For more than a hundred years the soda fountain was a familiar feature across the U.S.A., and sorry was the town without one. In fact, cookbooks such as *Southport's Favorite Recipes* of 1950 contained a Soda Fountain or Restaurant diet "for the benefit of those who are unable to eat at home." Here the folk would gather to hear the latest news and gossip, and get the soda jerk to stir up a Coke or ice cream soda or banana split. The drinks were made to order with crushed ice with a few squirts of syrup and a fierce stream of carbonated water from the fountain faucet. Alas, nowadays you feed coins into a slot and out drops your canned drink with a clunk.

We had three choices, Leggett's Drugstore, Watson's Drugstore, and Willie McKenzie's Confectionary. Leggett's and Watson's glared across at each other on East Moore Street. McKenzie's was out the road a few blocks on Howe Street. Each had a soda fountain where you could get a great Coke with lots of crushed ice, a Cherry Coke, a Vanilla Coke, Cherry Smash, or a Root Beer Float, then sit at one of their little hard-bottomed ice-cream chairs and enjoy it. If one of the town ladies was feeling a little peaked, she'd look to see that none of her friends was looking, sneak into Watson's and order an ammonia Coke.

Leggett's Drugstore early 20th Century. P.O. Leggett is to the left, Ed Weeks is behind the soda fountain. Note that all employees wore white shirt and tie. Photo courtesy of Bette Leggett.

Leggett's Drugstore, 1930's.
Photo courtesy of Bette Leggett.

Bette Leggett, civic leader, business woman, artist,
who married into a household that didn't cook.

57

Vienna Mae O'Quinn Leggett,
in her 1940's Buick.
Photo courtesy of Bette Leggett.

The Duchess of the Evening In Paris

Despite my praise of Southport's cooks, Vienna Mae O'Quinn Leggett (1891-1964) never cooked a meal in her life. She was the owner of Leggett's Drugstore, run by her son Ormand. P.O. Leggett, her husband, had died before my time. She was as elegant and Rococo as her namesake, Vienna, Austria. Her uncle happened to be in Vienna when she was born and sent word that the child should be named Vienna, and so she was. It never occurred to her to join the select FF Club; her own universe was quite sufficient unto itself, thank you. The women of the FF Club *did their own cooking and washing, for Lord's Sake!* Vienna never did a hand's turn. She lived directly across the street from the drugstore with her son and his wife Bette in a classic white Southport two-story house with a banistered front porch upstairs and down. By the time she stirred in mid-morning, most of the women in town had done a day's work. She'd devote all morning to her toilette, and in mid-day or early afternoon would emerge within a cloud of bath powder and perfume from her house and cross Moore Street to the drug store, as regal as a duchess making her progress to court. Compared to Vienna, The Duchess of Windsor was a weak sister.

Her hair was perfectly set in beauty-parlor jet black; some rude gossips insisted she used shoe polish to keep it black, but this was untrue—it remained naturally black for all of her life. Her face was white with talcum, her cheeks were rouged, her lips ruby red, and her dress exquisite and fine. Earrings in those days were considered inappropriate for everyday wear, but Vienna's sparkled year-round in the mid-day sun, as she sparkles in memory.

On the right as you entered Leggett's were the magazine racks and the splendid white marble soda fountain fit for a Hapsburg palace. On the left were the ice cream parlor tables. Just behind sat Vienna's throne: an ice cream chair positioned in front of the Evening in Paris perfume showcase. What an enchanting sight it was!—little midnight-blue bottles of perfume with silk tassel tops, heart shaped bottles of cologne, eau de toilette, and plump boxes of dusting powder, each resting upon a pillow of blue taffeta, exotic and mysterious. It was a place of magic. And here, Vienna Leggett would hold court. I'd come in, eyeing the new magazines that might hold some wicked pictures, some mischief, but dared not part their covers, for the Duchess stood guard.

"Young man," she'd say, "Aren't you going to speak to us today?"

Watson's also sold magazines and cokes, but the glory days when it was run by old Doc Watson were behind it. By comparison, it was slightly plebian—they carried Rexall stuff and had 2-for-1 sales. But its most serious shortcoming was the absence of the Evening in Paris counter and the Duchess who daily took up residence across the street, holding court in an ice cream chair throne before her treasury of midnight blue.

Vienna did cook, at least once in her life. Ormand came into the kitchen and was startled to find her standing before the stove.

"Mother, what are you stirring up?" he asked.

"I don't know," she replied." Can you make out what it is?"

And she never told her age.

"Any woman who will tell her age will tell anything!" she said. As the years went by, she kept getting younger and younger, until someone quipped that she was younger than her son. When she had a fall and was taken to the hospital, Dr. Landis Brown determined her hip was broken.

"Now, Mrs. Leggett," he said, "we have to send you to Wilmington to have some surgery and they'll want to ask you a few questions. They'll want to know your age. How old are you?" Vienna turned her head to the wall, and never said another word. Dr. Brown never got her age, but he did get a lot of chuckles telling the story.

Willie McKenzie, as I remember him. Photo courtesy of Yvonne McKenzie Adams.

Mr. Willie McKenzie

Mr. Willie McKenzie's ice cream parlor was a town institution. If ever a good, kindly man lived, it was he, and one of the most highly respected men in both the black and white communities. We kids never once called him Willie; it was "Mr. McKenzie." For some years he ran a dance hall in a building adjoining his confectionary, but a shooting there one night so distressed him that he never opened it again.

Mr. McKenzie's Lime Sherbets and a Near Tragedy

Neil Lewis remembers the date, August 10, 1951, even if I can't. I have a way of forgetting bad times. Ma-Ma was watching out for us, as it was a Friday and my mother was over at the beach with her bridge club. Somehow my mother was always away somewhere when something bad happened and poor old Ma-Ma had to deal with it.

We wanted a sherbet, or sherby, which is what we called snow cones, and set out for Mr. Willie McKenzie's ice cream parlor.

"Don't forget *mine!*" cried my four year old baby brother, Don.

"We won't."

"Yes you will," he fretted. *"You forgot it last time!"*

It was a hot, black, moonless night. A thunder storm was rumbling in the distance, so we piled on my shiny red Schwinn bicycle, clad only in our dungarees, shirtless. Neil hopped on the handlebars, Dickie Marlowe straddled the back carrier. I pedaled, and we sped away.

As the summer was winding down, we had long since worked our way through the usual flavors of syrup for our sherbets—cherry, strawberry, orange, vanilla, lemon, grape and Pepsi.

"Mr. McKenzie, don't you ever get in any new flavors?" I asked. To my surprise he answered,

"Lime. I got in some lime." What a treat! How happy my little brother will be to have a lime sherbet! We ordered four, not forgetting Don. Mr. McKenzie chipped a block of ice and dropped it into his shiny metal grinder. Sherbets were 5 cents each; we placed the 20 cents on his white marble counter, and were on our way, Neil and Dickie triumphantly holding our prizes.

Thunder rumbled loudly. The whole town shook. A chill was in the air, and lightning lit up the place like daylight, so I pedaled as fast as I could. The next thing I knew, I saw stars. The world reeled about as if I were on a wild carnival ride. A man in a pickup truck ("drunk as Cooter Brown," as he would later admit), had hit us. I picked myself up from the sandspur patch where I had been hurled and hobbled home in a daze.

The rain began to pour in torrents. As they were about to take us to the hospital, Don came hurrying in from the kitchen with a very distressed look on his plump little baby face.

"Did you spill it?!" he demanded. *"Did you spill my sherby?!"*

"Yes, Don," I said miserably, once again having failed my baby brother. "We spilled your sherby."

But we all survived, thanks to Dr. Brown and Dosher Memorial Hospital.

Dolly Evans.

Dolly Evans

Dolly Evans was a savvy, industrious woman, beautiful inside and out, with the face of an Indian princess, which she may have been, denied her birthright. She was a leader in the St. James A.M.E. Zion Church, generous to those in need, and had boundless energy. She drove the first modern automobile in her community. Besides running her store at the northwest corner of Howe and Brown Streets with her sister Mim, she had a dance hall upstairs, made Brown Dogs candy to sell, and ran a sawmill operation out front of her store for cutting pine slab for cooking and heating. She knew politics, and if you wanted the black community to vote for you, you'd have to clear it with Dolly. She'd tell you what you had to do to get elected, but she wouldn't tell you their recipe for Brown Dogs.

Her store had no soda fountain, but it did have the best variety and the coldest bottled drinks in town. Drinks were a nickel. You'd plunge your hand into the stinging, freezing ice water and pull up a Coca Cola, Pepsi, R.C. Cola, Dr. Pepper, NEHI, or Grape drink or a Pal Ade— an orange drink with a peculiarly bitter taste that provided a change from the more predictable drinks. Orange Crush was the best of the orange drinks, with tiny flakes of real orange. It poured out almost clear and not a bit orange, disguised in dark brown bottles as if ashamed of its purity. The new version is doctored up with orange coloring and tastes like orange syrup. We were at Dolly's a lot, for on a hot summer day you could never quite quench your thirst.

The Road to Perdition

Alcohol was for many years virtually unknown to Southport tables. Even after Roosevelt legalized drinking in 1933, it was slow coming around, forbidden to all but the Whiskeypalians and Catholics. When Petesy Bill Larsen started selling beer at his cafe out the road, the Baptist deacons paid him a call and told him he had to choose between beer or the church. He chose beer. In the late 1940's or early 1950's the Catholics put on a spaghetti dinner fund raiser and served wine. It was the talk of the town. But a sell-out crowd showed up to buy tickets—at a time when there were hardly more than a dozen Catholics in the congregation.

COCKTAILS

The most popular mixed drinks in these parts are the Bloody Mary, made with vodka, tomato juice and lime juice, Tabasco and Worcestershire sauce. (If made without the vodka, it's a Bloody Shame); the Daiquari, made with rum, sugar and lime juice; and the Screwdriver, of vodka and orange juice. Of the so-called Long Drinks, the most popular are the Tom Collins, of gin, rum or vodka, with soda water, sugar and lemon or lime juice, and Gin or Vodka and Tonic, made with liquor, lime or lemon and quinine water.

The Mint Julep

The legendary mint julep is the official drink in Louisville for the Kentucky Derby, but today is actually a rarity throughout much of the South. It is seldom served in Southport except on Derby Day, and then only for the novelty. In old Southern cookbooks it's easier to find a remedy for Camp Itch or how to Destroy Warts than to find a recipe for a julep. There is no definitive recipe for a mint julep, and few agree on what makes a good tasting julep. The English naval officer and diarist Captain Frederick Marryat, in his *A Diary In America* of 1837-1839, disputed the claim by Virginians that they had invented the julep, noting that two hundred years earlier Milton had written,

"Behold the cordial julep here, which flames and dances in its crystal bounds with spirits of balm and fragrant syrups mixed."

During his sojourn in Virginia, Marryat overheard a lady say to her friend,

"Well, if I have a weakness for any one thing, it is for a mint-julep."

Marryat wrote,

"A very amiable weakness, and proving her good sense and good taste."

The Captain gives us the recipe for a good julep he picked up in Virginia: "Put into a tumbler about a dozen sprigs of the tender shoots of mint, upon them put a spoonful of white sugar, and equal proportions of peach and common brandy, so as to fill it up one third, or perhaps a little less. Then take rasped or pounded ice, and fill up the tumbler. Epicures rub the lips of the tumbler with a piece of fresh pineapple, and the tumbler itself is very often incrusted outside with stalactites of ice. As the ice melts, drink."[*]

Other recipes insist that you pack a tumbler with mint—"bruise it"—then pour over Bourbon or brandy. Let it stand a bit. Then discard the mint. ("It is a sacrifice.") Add heavy sugar syrup to taste, pour over crushed ice, and serve very cold in frosted glasses decorated with a fresh sprig of mint.

BLACKBERRY WINE
Confederate Receipt Book (1863)

"Measure your berries and bruise them; to every gallon add one quart of boiling water, let the mixture stand twenty-four hours, stirring occasionally, then strain off the liquor into a cask; to every gallon add two pounds of sugar, cork tight, and let it stand till following October, and you will have wine ready for use without any further straining or boiling, that will make lips smack as they never smacked under similar influence before."

EGG NOGG

Mrs. Hill's Southern Practical Cookery and Receipt (1872)
Mrs. Hill includes this recipe in her chapter "Cookery for Invalids."

"To the yolk of each egg add a tablespoon of loaf [confectioner's] sugar; beat well together; add two tablespoonfuls of good brandy or three of Madiera wine. Beat the whites to a solid froth; put them to the yolks, and to every three eggs add a wineglass of thick rich cream. Stir lightly into the yolks. The cream may be omitted, if not liked. It injures the egg-nogg if not very thick and rich. This is excellent for persons suffering from bad colds and coughs."[†]

---

[*] Frederick Marryat, *A Diary in America*, pp. 386-387.
[†] In her book, Mrs. Hill spells it "egg-nogg," not "egg-nog" as is usual today.

The Silk Hill Boys Discover a New Drink

Late one fall, Norman Holden and I decided to row up the Cape Fear and scout for our Christmas trees. We knew of some cedars growing beside the river that might do. We packed a lunch, climbed down the ladder off Daddy's dock into his skiff bobbing up and down, and sped up the river with the swift, incoming tide.

The little grove of cedars was on a nice, sandy little white beach littered with interesting pieces of driftwood; these might make nice lamps and make us some money—we were always dreaming up something.

I poked around under a clump of cedars when something caught my eye—a pile of gunny sacks filled with Mason jars.

"Hey, Norman! Look what I found. Bottles of water!" Norman, always far more worldly than I, took one look and said,

"Don't you know what that is?! That's not water. That's white lightnin'!" What in the world was "white lightning?" I had never heard of such a thing.

"It's a drop-off!" he exclaimed. "Moonshiners dropped it off here for somebody to pick up. We'd better clear out of here fast. If moonshiners catch you they kill you!"

The tide had gone out and the skiff was marooned high up on the beach. Terrified, we somehow shoved it into the water and rowed like a Fury, past the pogy dock, under the Wells' docks, past the Government Dock, Mr. Rob Thompson's place, back to Daddy's dock, all the while keeping an eye out for the wicked bootleggers. We clambered up the ladder, found Daddy in his upstairs office, and breathlessly blurted out our story. An amused look came across his face.

"Well, what do you know about that!" he said, and returned to his bookkeeping.

Good vigilantes that we were, Norman and I sought out Chief of Police Otto Hickman and told him of our discovery. He drove us in his car to the edge of town.

"Now, just where is this moonshine?" he asked. We pointed across the marsh to where the evil cedars could be seen from a distance.

"Well, thank you, boys," said Otto as he drove us home. "I'll sure look into it."

For weeks we eagerly searched the papers for the story of a big moonshine bust and the brave young boys responsible. Christmas came; we bought our trees from Dan Harrelson's grocery. And that's as close as we ever came to playing Elliot Ness and setting straight this outrageous miscarriage of North Carolina justice.

Harry and Mercedes Sell. Photo courtesy of
Harry D. Sell.

Harry Sell's Scuppernong Vineyard

I'm going to tell you about Harry Sell's vineyard and his wines, but first I must tell you a little about the man himself. Our neighbor lived across from us on Leonard Street with his wife Mercedes, his son, his father, Cader "Sparky" Sell, and his mother under some of the largest live oak trees in town, in one of the tiniest house trailers five people ever did inhabit. It was hardly ten feet long, a bent oval of plywood shaped like half of a mail box, constructed by Harry himself. His son, Harry D., told me,

"We went to bed in layers. The last person laid a plank with a mattress on the back of a chair or the little couch."

Harry was tall and very handsome, with the squared, swarthy face of a proud Indian chief, and wore a mustache. The pious were suspicious of him, as he was an independent thinker, didn't go to church, and liked classical music. He studied pre-med at Wake Forest for two years, but Sparky had financial problems and he had to come home and go to work. He was sometimes employed by the Brunswick Navigation Company keeping their electrical things going. He was a maverick, a tinker and an inventor, and could make anything he set his mind to. He loved to build boats, including a small cabin cruiser modeled after a menhaden "purse boat," then gave them away. For three days after Hurricane Hazel roared through in October 1954, Harry, with his Briggs and Stratton generator and ham radio set, was the town's sole link to the outside world.

66

For reasons I never understood, our part of town was called Silk Hill, odd, since there was no silk and no hill. You understand that our neighborhood was full of boys, mostly the same age, and we were sometimes called the Silk Hill Boys. One languid August as the summer droned on, we took to dividing up into gangs and fighting among ourselves like savages, for no reason whatsoever that I can recall, except that we were bored and school needed to start. We'd awaken happy and safe in our separate homes, eat our parents' breakfast, and by mid-afternoon were fighting and miserable. One afternoon, Harry summoned us all, made us sit in a circle under one of his oaks, and gave us a talking to. Many children have no childhood, he reminded us; they pass straight from being babies to working in the fields or mines. We boys were all really friends, but here we were, in-fighting and squandering a precious gift—the miracle of growing up, of summer in Southport. The exact words he used have long since flown away, but the moment and the sentiment have not. We felt ashamed, gave up our quarreling, and went back to being friends and playing Cowboys and Indians. Would that the nations raging so furiously together had a man like Harry Sell to sit down and give them a good talking to.

Harry also had a little home-made trailer-cart hitched to his car for hauling things about. On Sunday afternoons he'd round us up. We'd climb into his trailer-cart and ride out to Price's Creek Range Light up the Cape Fear River to gather up bricks from the old light keeper's house, abandoned and collapsed years before. These he used to build a new house. Mercedes paid us off in peanut butter and jelly sandwiches and Kool Ade. The first floor of the house at the southwest corner of Leonard and Atlantic is made from these bricks, and Harry laid every one of them himself, with a little help from Sparky and the Silk Hill Boys.

Wine making—a radical notion in these parts at the time—interested Harry. He bought land out on the Fish Factory Road on the mainland not far from the Oak Island bridge, built himself a spacious, two-story home, and planted a scuppernong vineyard. The scuppernong is the only grape that grows well around here; however, its grapes do not grow in clusters, but are scattered and secreted among the vines and must be picked one at a time by hand, making it uneconomical to harvest. Harry's scuppernong vineyard of forty acres was the largest in North Carolina at that time. (At that time there were no more than a hundred fifty acres total.) A $150,000 harvesting machine tested on scuppernongs squashed the grapes to smithereens and was a total failure.

Harry Sell seated in his scuppernong grape harvester, 1950's.
Elmer Sellers, left, and Harry D. Sell, right, help with the harvest.
Photo by Boyce Spencer, courtesy of *The State Port Pilot.*

"Yep," said the wags. "I always thought Harry was a bit of a queer duck."

But Harry had figured out a solution. He trained his vines not onto overhead trellises in the traditional manner, but in long, low rows like a rail fence. He designed a machine to harvest the grapes, an old Ford pickup raised high on spider legs much like a lumber carrier. The contraption would straddle the vines and ride up and down with special brushes underneath that slapped back and forth to dislodge the grapes.

On the first fall that the vines reached maturity, the harvest was ripe, but without a harvester, for the brushes failed to arrive. Undeterred, he went downtown and bought every broom he could find, sawed off the handles and rigged them up. This was said to be the first practical machine for harvesting the scuppernong grape; certainly, it was among the first.

Harry experimented with making various types of wine in a little laboratory in his house and shared some samples with us. Scuppernong wine is naturally sweet and musky, aromatic as honey from ancient Persia, a delicious dessert wine. Scuppernong wines were scorned at the time; Harry perfected his, entered it in a competition in New York and came away with Second prize. Since Harry's time, vineyards have sprung up all over Southeastern North Carolina, and you can find their wines on the shelves of supermarkets. But so far as I know, Harry got there first.

He never made any money from his harvester. As a matter of fact, a man stole the design and ran off to Australia, manufactured the harvester, planted a vineyard and set up a winery. But Harry always seemed more interested in doing what he liked than making money. And who can fault that?

Vickie White Hardee starts a dinner off with a salad
decorated with green pepper rings. 2005.

4..
Salads & Salad Dressings

ABOUT COLESLAW

Coleslaw appeared in literature at least two-hundred years ago. Its name is of Dutch origin, from two words combined, *kool,* meaning cabbage, and *sla,* meaning salad. Coleslaw and Cold slaw can both be found in respectable books. Slaw goes well with just about everything. It can be used on sandwiches, as a salad dish, or as a side dish served with the entrée.

COLESLAW

½ head cabbage, finely shredded
½ cup mayonnaise, or coleslaw
   dressing. (See recipe on
   page 82.)

1 carrot, finely shredded,
   optional
Salt and pepper

Combine ingredients and mix well.

TANGY COLE SLAW

1 cup Mayonnaise
4 chopped scallions
2 teaspoons vinegar

1/8 teaspoon Worcestershire sauce
1/4 teaspoon sugar
Salt and pepper to taste

Mix ingredients and add to shredded cabbage, salad greens and carrots.

CACTUS PEAR SALAD

The cactus we called "pear pads" is one of several cacti around the world that bear edible fruit. They used to grow wild in some abundance in the vacant lots around town. Due to development, these pretty little pink fruits are seldom seen today, but if you find some, you are in for a treat. Slice either crossways or length-wise. Serve on crisp lettuce and top with mayonnaise or Russian dressing.

SWEETHEART'S CHERRY-RASPBERRY CONGEALED SALAD

This recipe works equally well with regular flavored gelatin, or with the sugarless kind. As the vegetables and nuts rise to the top and tend to turn brown if not used immediately, this method seals them within the middle of the dish with a nice layer of gelatin. Goes nicely with the entrée, or topped with whipped cream, doubles as a dessert.

1 package cherry flavored gelatin	1 cup boiling water
1 8-ounce can whole cranberry sauce	1/2 cup diced apples
	1/2 cup diced celery
¾ cup pineapple juice	1/3 cup chopped nuts

Dissolve the gelatin in boiling water. Add pineapple juice and cranberries. Pour half of the liquid mixture into an 8-inch pan or casserole, or in individual molds, reserving the other half of the mixture. Stir in the diced apples, celery and nuts and chill for about 2 hours. Pour on the remaining liquid mixture and chill another 2 hours until well set.

FRESH CRANBERRY SALAD

1 pound fresh cranberries	1 package raspberry gelatin mix
1 ½ cups sugar	1 package plain Knox gelatin
1 cup finely chopped celery	(optional)
1 cup chopped nuts	2 cups boiling water

Bring berries to boil until they pop. Let stand and cool until almost firm. Dissolve 1 package raspberry gelatin mix in 2 cups boiling water. Add the celery and chopped nuts. Chill until firm. To be sure of firm jelling, add the plain gelatin to the mixture along with the raspberry gelatin mix.

WALDORF SALAD

1 cup apple, peeled, cored and cubed	½ cup walnut or pecan meats
	½ cup raisins
1 cup celery, diced	¾ cup mayonnaise

Mix ingredients and serve on crisp lettuce

PERFECTION SALAD
From Dorothy Hardee's Recipe Files

1 6-ounce package lemon gelatin
3 1/4 cups boiling water
1/3 cup white vinegar
2 tablespoons lemon juice
3/4 teaspoon salt

2 cups shredded cabbage
1 cup chopped celery
½ cup chopped green pepper
¼ cup sliced pimento-stuffed
olives

Dissolve gelatin in boiling water. Stir in vinegar, lemon juice and salt. Chill mixture until partially set. Fold in cabbage, celery, pepper and olives. Turn mixture into a 5 ½ cup mold or muffin tins. Chill until firm.

For a festive presentation, use an extra 3-ounce package of lemon gelatin. Pour a little onto the bottom of the muffin pans and put ½ stuffed olive in the center of each, and if you wish, pimento strips. Chill until set. Then pour over the mixture from the main recipe, above.

TOMATO ASPIC
Brunswick Potluck Cookbook
Contributed by Mrs. Bobby Spencer

4 cups tomato juice
¼ cup chopped celery leaves
1 teaspoon cloves
1/4 cup cold water
3 tablespoons lemon juice
1/3 cup chopped onion

2 tablespoons brown sugar
2 small bay leaves
4 whole cloves
2 envelopes unflavored gelatin
1 cup celery, finely cut
Salt to taste

Combine tomato juice, onion, celery leaves, sugar, salt, bay leaves and cloves. Simmer 5 minutes and strain. Soften gelatin in cold water. Add to hot tomato mixture. Add lemon juice. Chill until partly set. Add celery. Pour into ring mold and chill until firm. Unmold and fill center with slaw, tuna salad, cottage, etc.

Leila Hubbard Pigott at the piano, as usual,
with her friend Lois Jane Bussels Herring, 1940.

Leila Hubbard Pigott

Following in the steps of the FF Club was a very special generation of up-and-coming young civic leaders. They were bright, sophisticated, energetic, and they were beauties, dazzling as Hollywood starlets. Among them was Leila Hubbard Pigott. She would show up at a prom or a dance looking like a million dollars in a dress she had made herself, sometimes held together with safety pins. She half raised me and once threatened that if I didn't learn how to swim, she'd throw me into the river—"You'd swim then!" she declared. I learned to swim.

Leila is one of life's enthusiasts, and expresses everything in superlatives. When the song "Far Away Places" was popular, she exclaimed,

"That is *the most beautiful* piece I ever heard! *Absolutely beautiful!"*

She was a natural born musician. She read music and played anything by ear. She'd say unblushingly,

"Yes, I play the piano. And I've got curly hair!"

Her repertory was huge. A tune was driving me crazy, so I asked,

"Leila, who wrote 'It's spring again and birds on the wing again?'"

"'I Love You' by Cole Porter," she replied without hesitation. She conducted the Methodist choir, and when there was no money for music in the high school, started a glee club. During the Key West years of the 1950's when the shrimp boats were working out of there, the Southport couples would sometimes take in a night club. She'd shoo the pianist from the bench and amaze the audience by playing anything they wanted to hear, from Broadway to classical to pop.

As a child she had moved to Southport with her family from South Carolina, but no one loved Southport more than Leila. She has often said,

"I love every tree, every blade of grass, every grain of its sand." She was a leader in civic affairs and a Town Crier, regularly sounding off to the *Pilot,* the radio or TV, or to whomever would listen to her. No meeting of the Board of Aldermen opened without Leila in attendance, ready to give them a piece of her mind and set things straight. She was the founding president of the first Little Theatre in Southport. When the new River Road was laid down in the 1950's to by-pass Sunny Point Army Terminal, she personally collected pledges from the landowners en route to keep it natural and not allow billboards. That is why it remains so pristine today. After her husband Dallas took ill, she ran his United Shrimp Company until she discovered she could make more money selling shells caught in shrimp nets than the shrimp itself, and turned the place into a shell shop.

Her friends said Leila didn't know where to locate the kitchen in her own house, so seldom did she cook. But when shamed into providing something for a Garden Club luncheon she made a classic Southport chicken salad.

LEILA PIGOTT'S CHICKEN SALAD

1 hen
½ dozen hard boiled eggs,
    chopped
1 cup finely diced celery

1 cup mayonnaise
½ cup sweet pickle salad cubes
Salt and pepper to taste

Boil the chicken until tender. Remove and discard the skin and pick the meat from the bones. Chop finely. Mix chicken and remaining ingredients in a bowl. Chill. Place on a bed of lettuce and serve.

EGG SALAD

Egg salad is delicious spread on bread for a sandwich, or served up on crisp lettuce as a salad dish. But use it promptly; it does not keep well.

6 eggs, hard boiled, and chopped
½ cup mayonnaise
¼ cup sweet relish or salad cubes

1 teaspoon salt
½ teaspoon pepper

Combine ingredients and mix well.

PINEAPPLE CHEESE SALAD

2 medium cans crushed pineapple
2 envelopes plain gelatin
1 cup sugar
½ cup lemon juice

2 small packages cream cheese
1 cup grated yellow cheese

Heat pineapple, sugar and lemon juice, and then add cream cheese and gelatin which has been soaked in pineapple juice. Cool. Then add grated cheese. Cool in refrigerator until firm—several hours.

MRS. FRED FULFORD'S TUNA FISH SALAD
Southport's Favorite Recipes (1950)

1 6-ounce can tuna fish, flaked
3 hard cooked eggs
2 small sweet pickles

1 small onion
1 sweet pepper
3 tablespoons salad dressing

Dice eggs into small pieces. Chop onion, pickles and pepper. Then put in the flaked tuna and mix well with the salad dressing. Serve as a salad on lettuce, or spread on crackers, or spread on bread for a sandwich.

SWEETHEART'S SHRIMP SALAD

Some stretch their shrimp salad with pasta elbows, but most Southporters use potatoes. As you can see, this is real *shrimp* salad, not shrimp flavored. Make this shrimp salad some hours ahead of time and let sit so the flavors have time to meld. The shrimp are boiled with the shells on to preserve their flavor. This recipe will serve a crowd.

5 pounds shrimp, headed	2 hard boiled eggs
1 pound potatoes	1 green pepper, diced
4 stalks celery, minced	1 cup mayonnaise
1 cup sweet pickles, cubed	Salt and pepper to taste

Boil shrimp, peel, de-vein, and cut into bite-sized pieces. Peel and dice potatoes into ½ inch cubes and drop into boiling salt water. Boil until done, but don't allow them to overcook and become mushy, keeping them on the firm side. Place in a colander and wash with cold water to stop the cooking. Mix all well with the mayonnaise, salt and pepper to taste.

Cousin Annie Lou Knox Newton

Cousin Annie Lou Knox Newton (1900-1985) was an absolutely lovely person, with auburn hair and a beautiful face like a perfect Carolina peach, one of those persons who made you feel good just being in her presence. She had a keen mind and a reputation as one of the town's best cooks.

For years she resided with her family in the big Queen Ann style house with the wrap-around porch at the northwest corner of Lord and West Streets. Jobs were scarce in Southport, so her husband Ed was away in Raleigh much of the time to make a living, and it mostly fell on her to raise their four sons, Ed, John, Lou and Jack, and daughter, Brooks. Each was college educated and successful in life.

Some years ago Brooks went with Jimmy Harper, Sr. (Editor of *The State Port Pilot),* and others to a series of Methodist meetings to which they had to take their own box lunches. Jimmy knew that the paper bag lunch Annie Lou put up for Brooks was better than his.

"He'd hardly sit down in the car and shut the door," Brooks told me, before he'd say, "Want to swap lunches?"

Throughout this book appear Annie Lou's recipes, including her unbeatable potato salad on page eighty-one.

A Genealogy of Notable Southport Cooks

ELIZABETH BENSEL STUART
1795-1884
Came to Southport in the 1820's
Established an inn on Bay Street in the 1830's,
Named The Stuart House in 1842

Among her children were

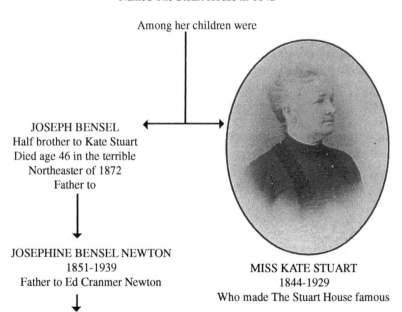

JOSEPH BENSEL
Half brother to Kate Stuart
Died age 46 in the terrible
Northeaster of 1872
Father to

JOSEPHINE BENSEL NEWTON
1851-1939
Father to Ed Cranmer Newton

MISS KATE STUART
1844-1929
Who made The Stuart House famous

Ed Cranmer Newton ←→ married ←→ Annie Lou Knox
1890-1968   1900-1985

Among their children

Brooks Newton Preik
1938-

Southport High School 1922-1969.
Presently the site of the Southport Post Office.

The Southport High School Lunch Room

Our school had no lunch room. They called it the Southport High School, but it was for all grades, one through twelve, with one teacher per grade. The 1940's were poor times, and the State did not just hand out money. So the P.T.A. began raising money for a lunch room by putting on pie and cake sales and Halloween Carnivals in the old gym. Clubs and churches joined in. Someone donated or sold cheap an old gas stove and a refrigerator. Volunteers installed a sink and a counter in one of the classrooms and we had a lunch room.

Annie Lou Newton was hired to run the lunch room. Tickets were fifteen cents. That wouldn't go far, so the ever resourceful Annie Lou would go down to the docks and sweet-talk the fishermen into donating, or giving her a good deal, on some croakers or spots or other small fish they couldn't sell commercially. With her helpers, all superb cooks, they'd roll the fish in meal and fry them up in huge cast-iron skillets, bone in—we were expected to have brains enough not to choke on a fish bone. They served them with grits or Annie Lou's potato salad, canned green beans fixed up, or red beans with ham hocks and collards. There was always a dessert, even if it was Jello. But often it was chocolate pudding or cherry cobbler or some other wonderful thing. I will tell you, the food that those women served up in that converted classroom was as good as anything you ever ate—except the government surplus spinach, which came from gallon cans and tasted like algae.

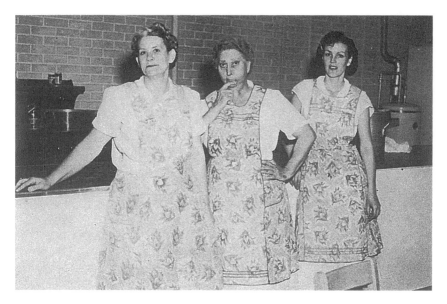

The Southport High School Lunch Room Staff. 1954.
Clayton Hickman, Marion "Mammy" St. George, Doris Hickman.

ANNIE LOU NEWTON'S POTATO SALAD
Brooks Newton Preik's Recipe Files

6 to 8 medium sized potatoes, red or white, whatever is in season, peeled and diced into ½ inch cubes
½ cup celery, finely chopped
¼ cup bell pepper, finely chopped

¼ cup onion, finely chopped
½ cup mayonnaise
1 tablespoon prepared mustard
½ cup salad dressing
Seasoning salt
Salt and pepper

Boil potatoes in slightly salted water until tender but not mushy. Place in cool water to stop cooking process, or they may be ready for mashed potatoes. Mix other ingredients in large bowl. Turn in potatoes and serve.

ABOUT SALAD DRESSINGS

Until the second quarter of the last century, most salad dressings were scratch-made in the home. Most are made by one of two methods. Uncooked dressings such as mayonnaise are created by slowly adding oil, olive or vegetable, in a matrix of egg yolks flavored with vinegar or lemon juice and seasonings, and beaten to form an emulsion. Cooked salad dressings are similar to mayonnaise except that less oil is used, and a cooked, starched base is added.

BLUE CHEESE DRESSING

½ cup mayonnaise
¾ cup crumbled blue cheese

1 3-ounce package cream
   cheese
1/3 cup half & half

Mix the mayonnaise, cream cheese and half & half. Crumble in the blue cheese. Optional: substitute ½ cup sour cream for the cream cheese and half & half.

COLESLAW DRESSING

½ cup white vinegar
¼ cup vegetable oil
½ cup sugar
½ teaspoon salt

1 tablespoon mustard
¼ cup cream
2 tablespoon sour cream

Combine ingredients and mix well.

FRENCH DRESSING

1 cup vegetable oil
¼ cup cider vinegar
¼ cup lemon juice

½ teaspoon salt
½ teaspoon ground mustard
½ teaspoon paprika

Mix ingredients, drizzling in the oil last and whisking to form an emulsion.

RUSSIAN DRESSING

To the recipe for French Dressing above, add 2 tablespoons chili sauce, a tablespoon red or green pepper, finely chopped, and a few drops of onion juice.

SOUR CREAM DRESSING

1 cup sour cream
2 tablespoons vinegar
1 tablespoon lemon juice

1 teaspoon salt
1 teaspoon sugar
Dash of cayenne

Combine lemon juice, vinegar, salt, sugar and cayenne. Add the sour cream and beat until thick.

GREEN GODDESS DRESSING

This absolutely delicious dressing is also great as a spread for crackers, or a dip for crudités. It has a slightly sweetish flavor, and is perfect for a salad of early spring dandelion greens, or other bitter greens such as chicory or Belgian endive. Do not add water. The pulverized vegetables will provide enough liquid. Nor should you add salt, as the anchovies provide salt aplenty. Prepare only as much as you will use in a day or two, for the crushed parsley and onion will not keep.

½ cup mayonnaise
½ sour cream
¼ cup onion, chopped
1 cup fresh parsley, well
washed, packed hard

2 tablespoons anchovy paste,
or 1/2 to 1 can anchovies in oil,
to taste
1/8 teaspoon cracked pepper

Pulverize in a blender, or otherwise chop and mix very finely.

ITALIAN VINAIGRETTE DRESSING

1/4 cup mild cider vinegar
1/8 cup olive oil
1/8 cup vegetable oil
1 tablespoon water
1/2 teaspoon salt

1/2 teaspoon sugar
1/8 teaspoon pepper
1/8 teaspoon dry mustard
1 tablespoon Italian seasoning

Mix ingredients except for Italian seasoning, adding the oils very slowly at the last while beating with a wire whisk to form an emulsion. Then add Italian seasoning and allow to stand a while for the flavors to meld.

COOKED SALAD DRESSING
Annie May Woodside's Cook Book (1913)

1 tablespoon butter, melted
¼ cup vinegar, heated
2 eggs
½ teaspoon salt

1 teaspoon sugar
½ cup milk
½ teaspoon celery salt
Cayenne to taste

"Beat the eggs, add milk, salt, sugar and cayenne. Pour the hot vinegar over the mixture and return too the stove. Cook very, very slowly, or the mixture will curdle. This is an excellent dressing for lettuce, tomatoes, or potato salad."

ABOUT MAYONNAISE

Mayonnaise is first noted in an English language cookbook of 1841, but is a very old dressing of French origin, the exact origins of which are in dispute. The French often claim that it dates from a victory of the French over the British (naturally), in 1756 in the Balearic Islands at the port of Mahon, from where, they say, the word "mayonnaise" takes its name. The origins were likely much earlier. Possibly "sauce Mayonnaise" was named for Duke of Mayenne of northwest France in the 16th Century; or it could have been invented by any of a number of chefs, derived from the French word "manier," meaning, to handle, or to stir or blend.

The first commercially produced mayonnaise in America was sold in Richard Hellman's deli in New York, made from his wife's recipe, and in 1912 was mass-marketed as Hellman's Blue Ribbon Mayonnaise. Not long afterwards, Mrs. Eugenia Duke of Greenville, South Carolina, began distributing her own mayonnaise that also became very popular in the South.

Since homemade mayonnaise contains raw egg yolks, there is the danger of salmonella poisoning. Commercial producers pasteurize or freeze the yolks. Either use pasteurized eggs which are available at some stores, or coddle the eggs in 170° water and remove the hot yolks from the whites which will have partially cooked. Refrigerate homemade mayonnaise no more than 3 or 4 days.

MAYONNAISE

1 whole egg	2 tablespoons vinegar or lemon
1 tablespoon sugar	juice, or mixture of both.
1 teaspoon salt	2 cups Wesson oil
1 ½ teaspoons dry mustard	Dash of paprika

Mix all ingredients except the oil. Mix with wire whisk or, beginning on slow speed, mix with electric beater, pouring in the oil, then on high. When nearly thickened, add 2 more tablespoons vinegar or lemon juice. For a thicker mayo, put 2 tablespoons vinegar in at the beginning and at the last add 1 tablespoon.

THOUSAND ISLAND DRESSING

1/3 cup salad oil
4 tablespoons orange juice
3 tablespoons lemon juice
1 teaspoon salt
¼ teaspoon paprika
¼ cup sweet pickle relish

¼ cup stuffed olives, chopped
1 teaspoon onion juice
1 teaspoon Worcestershire sauce
¼ teaspoon dry mustard
1 tablespoon parsley, chopped

Mix well and serve on salad greens.

WHIPPED CREAM DRESSING
Annie May Woodside's Recipe Files

1 tablespoon mustard
1 tablespoon flour
1 tablespoon sugar
1 tablespoon salt
1 cup vinegar

4 eggs
2 to 4 tablespoons butter
Cayenne to taste
½ tablespoon whipped cream

Mix dry ingredients to a paste. Heat the vinegar, add the paste and the butter, stirring constantly until thick. Beat the eggs in a separate bowl, then pour into the hot vinegar sauce over the eggs. Return to the stove and cook slowly until sooth. When cool add the whipped cream. If used for meat salads, less sugar should be used.

Ressie Robinson Whatley (1910-2001) baking bread
to raise funds for Dosher Memorial Hospital.
Photo by Jim Harper, 1999, courtesy of *The State Port Pilot.*

5..
Breads, Dumplings & Stuffings

Few persons can remember growing up in Southport without some kind of bread on the table, even if it was "light bread," which is what they called plain white Merita or Wonder Bread. Biscuits, hot or cold, were what you were served most. On Sundays and special occasions there would be hot rolls or homemade yeast bread. Corn bread of some sort was the staple with seafood or greens

Ressie Whatley

Ressie Robinson Whatley was a very dear friend. For years she was Auditor for Brunswick County, so you know how clever she was to hold onto that prized political plum in Brunswick County. She was a pillar of the Baptist Church and gallantly sang in the choir. She served as Treasurer for *Revolution!,* our bicentennial out-door musical, wisely managing its funds. She had a lively sense of humor. During my college years, when she attended meetings at the Institute of Government in Chapel Hill, we'd meet and have dinner. A cocky young man once jay-walked in front of her car on Franklin Street. Ressie drove gaily by him, and said, to no one in particular,

"Stick it out there again and I'll stamp Dodge on it."

Another time we were discussing a certain fertile Southport woman who was having yet another baby.

"Is she pregnant *again!"* I asked.

"Oh yes," answered Ressie. "She pulps 'em like grapes."

Ressie was also a fine cook, and for years baked bread to raise funds for Dosher Memorial Hospital. I include some of her recipes.

Biscuits

I've never had a bad biscuit in Southport, except for Ballard's. They always smelled like bad breath, and came canned from the grocery store refrigerator, made God Knows Where. There are as many different biscuit recipes and styles as there are cooks. Mammie Dozier used a cookie cutter to turn out the daintiest, most uniform biscuits you ever saw, each like a rouge compact. Ma-Ma's were more of the country fashion. She'd roll the dough into a ball the size of a golf ball and punch them down a bit with the heel of her wrist, and they'd come out looking like powder puffs. With an arched eye Mammie would say,

"Of course, Alta rolls her biscuits. Some people have *dropped* biscuits, heaven forbid. They taste fine, of course, but I never approved of dropped biscuits." Ma-Ma would say, with the satisfied air of one having exposed snobbery,

"Margarette always cuts her biscuits."

One day we were out in the county at Aunt Wren's Antiques barn plundering. Aunt Wren (no kin to us) was a nice old lady, I suppose, and sharp as a razor when it came to business. I found a pair of overpriced brass lanterns, but I wanted them, and went to the house to pay. On her kitchen table was a plate of big, plump biscuits, looking and smelling like I remembered from my youngest days. I *knew* they were delicious.

"Of course, you can have one. Here, put some butter on it. Take two," she said. Being polite, I only took one, buttered. And yes, it *was* as good as they get.

"Ummm!" I exclaimed. "How *do* you do it?!"

"Just flour and baking powder and cut it into your lard. Add a little buttermilk." She answered. *Lard!* That was it. Nutritionists have long convinced us that if we walked past a pound of lard we would drop dead of a heart attack. But occasionally I will sneak some into the house and cook up a pan of lard biscuits. There's nothing like them.

ABOUT SELF-RISING FLOUR AND MEALS

Self-rising flour and meals are widely available in the South, but many careless parts of the country don't stock them. If this is the case, you'll have to go to the trouble of adding 1 ½ teaspoons of baking power and a pinch of salt to each cup of regular flour or meal.

SOUR MILK—MOCK BUTTERMILK FOR COOKING

Some old recipes call for "sour milk." This does not connote whole milk that has soured, and which will make you sick if consumed; rather, it is whole milk, room temperature, to which vinegar has been added to make it curdle. If you're caught short without buttermilk for your biscuits or another recipe, add a tablespoon of strong vinegar to a cup of whole milk. Let it sit for fifteen minutes. It will curdle and give your recipe a taste that's hard to tell from real buttermilk.

MA-MA'S BUTTERMILK BISCUITS

2 cups sifted flour
1/2 cup shortening such as Crisco,
   or if you really want to have
   the old-time biscuit, use lard.
2/3 cup buttermilk

3 teaspoons baking powder
1 teaspoon sugar
½ teaspoon salt
¼ teaspoon soda

Mix dry ingredients. Cut in shortening with a fork and blend. Add buttermilk and mix. Roll into golf sized balls and punch down a bit with the heel of your wrist, and place on cookie sheet. Bake 12 to 15 minutes in hot preheated 450° oven until golden brown. Should yield 12 biscuits. For richer biscuits, dip each biscuit in melted butter before baking. For fluffier biscuits, substitute evaporated milk or light cream.

Waking Up to Cinnamon Biscuits

What a joy to wake up on a cold winter morning to the aroma of Ma-Ma's cinnamon biscuits wafting from her kitchen!

A memory: I am lying in the warm cocoon of the feather bed in my bedroom, dreading to get out of bed and touch the icy floor with my feet and get to Harry Sanders' algebra class. Except for the kitchen and dining room, the house is freezing cold. Ma-Ma has been awake for an hour, has lit the fire in the Franklin Stove in the dining room. She is very proud of the Franklin Stove; it is the Cadillac of stoves—a cast iron stove with an open hearth like a stand-alone fireplace.

And the coal stove in the kitchen is going, so the back part of the house is warm and cozy. Ma-Ma places before me a plate of her cinnamon biscuits, luscious and steaming and dripping in their own syrup—dessert for breakfast!

MA-MA'S CINNAMON BISCUITS

2-day-old leftover Ma-Ma's
   Buttermilk Biscuits, above
½ cup sugar
2 tablespoons water

2 tablespoons butter or margarine
2 teaspoons ground cinnamon
Dash of salt

Melt butter or margarine in skillet. Add sugar, then cinnamon, water and salt. Heat to form a syrup. Split the biscuits, place cut side down and simmer in the syrup, drizzling some over them. Let cook until syrup is thickened and almost candied.

Dot Watts Schmidt

Dorcas Ann Watts Schmidt (1932-2004), whom we called Dot, was a very special person, intelligent, hard working and civic minded. She compiled *The Cemeteries of Southport (Smithville) and Surrounding Area*, an essential tool for historical research. For years she ran the Shell Shoppe down on the Old Yacht Basin, and built it into a substantial business. She was private and hid her many talents and virtues under a basket. She had an infectious humor, and loved a good story. Her father, Hulan Watts, ran a successful party boat operation, and after his death, her mother Annie Mae took over.

Dot enjoyed telling this anecdote: In 1961, the battleship *U.S.S. North Carolina* passed through on its way up the Cape Fear toward its present location in Brunswick County across from Wilmington. Sometime later, Hulan said to his daughter,

"I'll swear, we ain't had a drop of rain since The Raleigh came through!" This gave Dot a big chuckle, since the cruiser *U.S.S. Raleigh* had called at Southport in the early 1930's. She went to Annie Mae and said,

"Mother, you know what Daddy said? 'We ain't had a drop of rain since The Raleigh came through.'"

Annie Mae replied,

"Well, ain't it the truth!"

DOT WATTS SCHMIDT'S CHEESE BISCUITS
The Proverbial Church Cookbook (1991)

1 ½ pounds New York sharp cheese
1 ½ pounds margarine

1 ½ pounds flour
Pecan halves

"Preheat oven to 350°. Partially melt cheese and margarine; gradually add flour until of adequate consistency to use in a cookie press. Press out cookies, place a pecan half on each, pressing gently into the dough. Bake for approximately 10 minutes. Carefully observe to not overcook on the bottom."

MRS. J. J. LOUGHLIN'S CURRANT BISCUITS
Southport's Favorite Recipes (1950)

Mrs. Loughlin was Susie Carson's mentor. Susie: "I was president of the organization that put the book together *Southport's Favorite Recipes* from recipes gathered by the members. Mrs. Loughlin told me that she had been using the recipe for at least fifty years at that time. She and her family moved to Southport sometime before 1912. I bake these often and for my oven, the best temperature is 400°. I also brush them with a mixture of egg and milk. I do not measure this—just guess at the amount based on how many biscuits I make. Also, I seldom use as much sugar as her recipe calls for. Makes it easier to handle."

3 cups all purpose flour
1 cup sugar
4 tablespoons shortening
1 cup currants, washed and
    drained

Milk
3 teaspoons baking powder
1 teaspoon salt

Sift together the flour, baking powder, salt and sugar. Add currants and mix thoroughly. Cut in shortening. Add a sufficient amount of milk to make a soft dough. Mix well. Turn out on a floured board and roll to ¼ inch thickness. Cut with a biscuit cutter and place in pan to bake. Bake 15 minutes in 400° oven. Serve hot with butter.

APPLE BREAD
Brooks Newton's Preik's Recipe Files

This very old recipe was passed down to Brooks from her great grandmother. It makes an excellent coffee cake, and has a genuine old-time flavor.

½ cup shortening
1 egg, beaten
½ teaspoon cinnamon
2 cups flour
1 teaspoon baking powder
1 teaspoon soda

1 cup sugar
½ cup milk
1 cup apples, cored, peeled and
    chopped
½ teaspoon salt

Cream shortening with the sugar. Add the egg and milk. Sift the dry ingredients into the liquid mixture and add the chopped apples. Stir. Mix thoroughly. Bake in a greased loaf pan in a 350° oven for 50 to 60 minutes. Sprinkle extra sugar and cinnamon on top before baking. Bake in a shallow pan and serve warm.

SCONES

This classic English biscuit was served for late afternoon teas. Serve with butter and homemade jellies.

2 cups flour, sifted
1 tablespoon sugar
4 teaspoons baking powder
½ teaspoon salt
4 tablespoons cold shortening

1/2 to 2/3 cup milk
1 egg, well beaten
Melted butter
Sugar for dredging

Sift together the dry ingredients together and cut in the shortening with a fork until the consistency of very tiny beads. Add milk to the beaten egg, then add to flour mixture gradually. Knead lightly onto a floured surface. Roll to ½ inch thickness. Cut into wedges, place on greased baking sheet. Brush lightly with melted butter and dredge with the extra sugar. Bake in hot 400° oven 15 minutes. Makes about 15 4-inch scones.

SHORTCAKE

2 ½ cups all-purpose flour
1 tablespoon baking powder
½ teaspoon baking soda
½ teaspoon salt

¼ cup sugar
1 cup buttermilk
1 stick butter, cold, and cut up
1 large egg separated

Sift together the flour, baking powder, baking soda, salt and sugar. Cut in the butter with a fork. Beat the egg yolk with the buttermilk. Stir into the flour mixture. Flour your hands. On a floured surface knead the dough 6 to eight times, and pat into ¾ inch thickness. Either cut into 8 individual shortcakes with a biscuit cutter, or bake whole for a family-style dessert. Beat the egg white and brush on the shortcake or cake. Bake on a cookie sheet in preheated 425° oven. Split the cakes and spoon on sweetened strawberries or other berries, then sweetened whipped cream. Place on the tops of the cakes, and spoon on more berries and whipped cream.

ABOUT SALLY LUNN

The popular Sally Lunn cake was brought from England to Virginia in the earliest days of our country. According to legend, it was named "Sol et Lune," meaning "sun and moon," by an English girl who sold it on the streets of London. The top of the bread is golden like the sun and the bottom white like the moon. The Sally Lunn can be made with either the baking soda method or the yeast method.

SOUTHERN SALLY LUNN LOAF, SODA METHOD
Brunswick Potluck Cookbook
Contributed by Mrs. Gertrude Blake

2 cups plain flour	¼ cup melted shortening
2 eggs	½ teaspoon salt
½ cup sugar	1 cup buttermilk
¾ teaspoon baking soda	1 teaspoon cream of tartar

Sift dry ingredients, add beaten eggs, milk and shortening. Stir just enough to moisten. Bake in loaf pan in hot oven 400° for 25 minutes. Serve hot.

SALLY LUNN, YEAST METHOD
Key to the Pantry (1898)

"Two teaspoons sugar and 1 of salt, 3 eggs (beaten separately,) a quart of flour, a piece of butter a little larger than a turkey egg. In summer make up your Sally Lunn about eleven o'clock, in order to have it for an early tea. To the beaten yolks add a teacupful of milk and to this the beaten whites and flour alternately, until all are well mixed. To this add a cup of good yeast, and last, add the butter. If the batter is still too stiff, pour in more milk until it is of proper consistency. Make a very stiff batter and beat it until it blisters and pops. The Sally Lunn rises and bakes much better, and the grain is finer, when it is stiff. Pour into a greased jar or bucket; set in a warm place to rise. About one and a half hours before it should go into the oven, it should be well beaten and poured into a greased shape or mold to rise. Allow it fifty or sixty minutes for baking, as it should be done slowly."

JOHNNY CAKE, or JOURNEY CAKE, MADE WITH MEAL

The very, very old staple, Johnny Cake, also travels under the alias Journey Cake, as it was convenient to travel with. It was made in many fashions, with meal, flour, or rice. My mother tells me that when she was young, Johnny Cakes were sold in just about every grocery store in Southport. You'd have them with a pickle from a big pickle jar or barrel. For a sweet Johnnycake, add a little maple syrup to the batter.

½ cup white corn meal	1 cup scalded milk
1 teaspoon salt	

Mix the ingredients and pour into a buttered skillet. Bake in a 350° oven until crisp.

JOHNNY CAKE, or JOURNEY CAKE, MADE WITH RICE
The Carolina Housewife (1847)

The *Confederate Receipt Book* has a similar recipe, but without some of the detail shown here in Sarah Rutledge's book.

"Half a pint of soft boiled rice, with just rice flour enough to make batter stick on the board. Salt to the taste. Spread it on the board thick or thin, as it is wanted. Baste it with cream, milk or butter, cream is best. Set it before a hot fire, and let it bake until nicely browned. Slip a thread under, to disengage it from the board, and bake the other side in the same manner, basting all the time it is baking."

Don Frink. A recent photo, courtesy of Don Frink.

Don Frink and
"Foods That Got Us Through"

Don Frink is a monument salesman, and "just an old resident of Southport," he says. He is a loyal member of the St. James A.M.E. Zion Church. He graciously shared with me a number of his family menus and recipes, and delivered them in an envelope marked, "Foods That Got Us Through. p.s.: And we still like them."

94

Foods That Got Us Through

Fish roe with grits
Fried fish with grits
Shrimp with gravy and grits
Conch soup
Fish cakes, homemade
Stewed pig feet with potato salad
   and greens
Chitterlings served with rice or
   potato salad and greens
Homemade fried chicken
Pork neck bones with rice
Homemade beef stew
Fried mullet served with whole
   baked sweet potatoes
Oysters/clam fritters
Terrapin stew with potatoes
Corn meal mush with fried fatback
   and molasses
Cracklings with whole baked
   sweet potatoes
Liver pudding with buttered grits

Collards or cabbage with drop
   dumplings on top
Rutabaga turnips with pork backbone
Shrimp pileau
Shrimp salad
Boiled crabs
Patty bread (turn over bread, fried)
Lima beans wit ham hock
Black eyed peas with ham hocks
Salted fish (preserved in heavy brine)
Homemade ice cream made in a
   bucket
Blueberry duff (cooked in a cheese
   cloth)
Sweet potato pie
Bread pudding with raisins
Cracker pudding
Homemade brown dogs made with
   sugar and peanut
Homemade fudge
Yalla gal (home brew)

SWEET WATER BREAD
Contributed by Don Frink

8 to 9 slices store-bought
   light bread
3 tablespoons sugar

1 ½ cups water
Lard for frying

Dissolve the sugar in the water. Dip slices of bread in the sweet water and brown on both sides in the fat.

HOE CAKE
Contributed by Don Frink

½ cup corn meal or flour
Enough scalding water or
   Milk to moisten

Salt
Grease to fry

Mix and allow the batter to stand for an hour. Heat 2 or 3 teaspoons of grease in a skillet. Smooth out the stiff batter to make cakes and brown on both sides. This first cousin to Johnny Cake goes well with sausage.

ABOUT MOLASSES

Molasses figures in many Southern recipes, and is delectable in itself for spreading on hot biscuits or rolls. It is a sweet syrup, a by-product of refining sugar, extracted from each of usually three boilings of the sugar cane. The first produces a very sweet molasses, the second produces a less sweet, dark molasses, and the third yields the bittersweet "blackstrap" molasses which is used for industrial processes such as in the manufacture of alcohol, principally rum.

MOLASSES BREAD
Contributed by Don Frink

3 cups plain flour	1 cup molasses
2 cups sugar	1 teaspoon salt
¾ cup lard	1 teaspoon cinnamon
3 eggs	1 ½ cups water
1 teaspoon baking powder	

Cream sugar and lard and molasses together. Add eggs and remaining ingredients and mix. Bake at 350° for an hour or until done.

OVEN STEAMED MOLASSES BROWN BREAD
Dorothy Hardee's Recipe Files

Wash, dry and save 5 10-ounce soup cans, or similar cans, for cooking the bread. This is a delicious bread, a real treat especially at winter holidays. Serve with whipped cream cheese, open faced or closed. This bread freezes well for use later.

1 cup all-purpose flour	1 cup molasses (Grandma's
1 teaspoon salt	Molasses style)
1 teaspoon baking powder	2 cups buttermilk
1 teaspoon baking soda	1 cup chopped pecans
1 cup whole wheat flour	1 cup yellow raisins
1 cup yellow cornmeal	

Sift all-purpose flour with salt, baking powder and baking soda. Combine all dry ingredients. Beat in molasses and milk. Fold in nuts and raisins, mixing thoroughly. Spoon batter into the 5 soup cans, filling them ¾ full. Cover cans tightly with small pieces of aluminum foil. Place cans on a cookie sheet in preheated 350° oven. Bake 1 hour. Let bread cool in cans until lukewarm. Cut bottoms with can-opener and with bottom lid push the cooked bread through. Cool thoroughly before cutting into slices.

MUFFINS

2 cups flour, sifted
3 tablespoons sugar
¾ cup milk
½ cup butter, melted
1 egg, well beaten

3 teaspoons double-acting baking
   powder
¾ teaspoon cinnamon
¼ teaspoon salt

Measure 2 cups sifted flour. Combine with the baking powder, sugar, salt and cinnamon and sift again. Add the milk and beaten egg and mix with the flour mixture. Add the melted butter and mix thoroughly. Fold in the blueberries. Spoon into buttered muffin tins 2/3 full. Bake in 400° oven about 25 minutes, until brown and plump.

BLUEBERRY OR OTHER BERRY MUFFINS

To the basic muffin recipe above, add 1 cup of berries.

CORN MUFFINS

1 egg
1 ½ cups buttermilk
½ teaspoon soda
½ cup sifted all purpose flour
1 ½ cups corn meal

¼ cup soft shortening
1 teaspoon sugar
3 teaspoons baking powder
1 teaspoon salt

Beat the egg. Beat in the remaining ingredients. Spoon into generously buttered muffin cups. Bake in pre-heated 425° oven 20 minutes.

OATMEAL MUFFINS
Favorite Recipes of North Carolina (1944)

1 cup milk, scalded
2 tablespoons butter
¾ cup oatmeal, uncooked
3 tablespoons sugar

½ teaspoon salt
1 egg, well beaten
1 ½ cups flour
4 teaspoons baking powder

Melt butter in hot milk, pour over oatmeal, let stand 3 minutes. Add sugar, salt and egg. Add sifted dry ingredients, mixing just enough to moisten. Bake in buttered muffin pans in a hot 400° oven 20 to 25 minutes.

SOUTHERN PANCAKES

1 egg
1 ¼ cups buttermilk
1 ¼ cups sifted all purpose flour
2 tablespoons shortening, softened

1 teaspoon baking powder
½ teaspoon soda
½ teaspoon salt

Beat with rotary beater until smooth. With large spoon, ladle the batter onto hot, greased griddle or skillet. The pancakes will become puffed and full of bubbles. Turn immediately before they break, and brown on reverse side. For thicker cakes add a little less buttermilk; for a thinner pancake make the batter a little thinner by adding a little buttermilk. Top with butter, maple syrup, or jellies or jams. For variation, add a cup of blueberries, or chopped pecans before grilling.

SOUTHERN WAFFLES

2 cups flour, sifted
1 tablespoon sugar
2 eggs, separated
1 tablespoon sugar

1 ½ cups buttermilk
1/3 cup oil or shortening, melted
3 teaspoons baking powder
1/2 teaspoon salt

Sift together the dry ingredients. Beat egg yolks and add milk and melted shortening and add to dry ingredients. Beat the egg whites until stiff but not dry, and fold into the batter. Pour onto middle of hot waffle iron to one inch from edge. Bake 4 to 5 minutes. Serve with butter and real maple syrup.

BUCKWHEAT CAKES
Annie May Woodside's Cook Book (1913)

1 pint lukewarm water
½ pint lukewarm milk
1 cup flour
3 cups buckwheat flour

1 tablespoon molasses
1 cake yeast
1 teaspoon

"Make water or milk lukewarm and add salt, molasses, yeast, flour and buckwheat. Sit in warm place to rise. When light, fry in hot greased pans. (if set overnight, ½ cake of yeast is sufficient.)"

Georgianna Cumbee Dosher, second wife of my maternal great-grandfather, George Dosher, mother to Margarette "Mammie" Dozier and others in this narrative. Their home at the northeast corner of Caswell and West Streets, seen in the background, still stands.

GEORGIANNA CUMBEE DOSHER'S DO-NUTS
Southport's Favorite Recipes (1950)

¾ cup sugar
1 cup whole milk
1 teaspoon shortening
    such as Crisco
4 cups enriched flour
1 egg

1 teaspoon vanilla
1 teaspoon lemon extract
½ teaspoon cinnamon
½ teaspoon nutmeg
4 teaspoons baking powder

Sift together the flour, cinnamon, nutmeg and salt. Cream shortening and sugar. Add well beaten egg. Mix thoroughly. Add lemon and vanilla. Add alternately the milk and sifted dry mixture. Roll onto well-floured board about 1/3 inch thick. Cut with doughnut cutter, or with 3-4 inch round cutter, then cut out center with smaller round cutter. Handle dough as little as possible. Lift up with wide spatula and slide into 3 to 4 inches of fat heated to 390°. Fry for about 3 minutes. Lift from fat with long fork, without pricking doughnuts. Drain on absorbent paper. Sprinkle with powdered sugar.

RAISED (YEAST) DOUGHNUTS

2 ½ cups flour, sifted
½ cup plus 2 tablespoons milk,
    scalded
½ package yeast
1/8 cup salt

2 small eggs
1/3 cup sugar
3/4 teaspoon cinnamon
1/8 teaspoon nutmeg
Pinch of mace

99

Blend shortening, milk and salt and cool to lukewarm. Add the yeast and let stand 5 minutes. Add the flour and beat until smooth. Cover with a damp towel and allow to rise to the bubbly state. Add the eggs, sugar and spices and mix well. Add enough flour to make a dough that can be kneaded. Knead until smooth. Cover again and let rise until double in volume. Roll out ½ inch thick and cut with doughnut cutter. Fry a few at a time in hot 375° deep fat 3 minutes, turning once. Drain on paper towels.

POPOVERS

What a glory—popovers served with good, room-temperature butter, apricot or strawberry preserves, or whatever you like, with hot coffee on a Sunday morning! A successful popover is crisp and brown on the outside, hollow and tender and moist within. They must be thoroughly cooked before removing from the oven or they will collapse.

2 eggs	1 cup all-purpose flour
1 cup whole milk	¼ teaspoon salt
1 tablespoon melted butter	

Preheat oven at 450°. In a bowl beat the eggs, then add the remaining ingredients. Avoid creating air bubbles. The batter should be the consistency of heavy cream. Pour into greased muffin tins, or glass custard cups 2/3rds full. Bake on center rack of oven 15 minutes, then reduce temperature to 350° and bake another 20 minutes. *Do not open door while baking.*

ABOUT CRACKERS

When it comes to groceries, I confess I'm not very frugal. If I want something, I toss it into my shopping cart and head for the checkout line. But a few years ago my grocery bill was so unexpectedly high I thought that surely the clerk had made a mistake. On checking the receipt, the culprit was not the under-paid clerk, but the crackers. A few boxes had driven the cost out of sight. How much can these cost to make?! They're just flour and water. I'll bake my own. To my surprise, not a single recipe for made-from-scratch crackers was to be found in any of my numerous cookbooks. I concluded that commercial bakeries have made it so easy it's not worth the bother any more to bake your own.

During the preparation of this book I acquired a number of antique cookbooks. Mrs. Hill came to the rescue, with no fewer than four, which I reprint here. I had great fun with these, experimenting by adding grated Cheddar cheese, or sesame or caraway seeds to some, with good results. They can be cut into rounds or squares, pricked with a fork for an interesting look.

MADE-FROM-SCRATCH CRACKERS
Mrs. Hill's Southern Practical Cookery and Receipt Book (1872)

No. 1
"Rub six ounces of butter into two pounds of sifted flour; dissolve a teaspoonful (level full) of soda in a wineglass of buttermilk; strain this through a fine sieve to the flour; add a teaspoon of salt; beat well; roll thin; bake. If not crisp when first baked, put them again into a slack oven, and merely heat over."

No. 2
"One pint of flour, the yolk of one egg; beat this to a dessert-spoon even full of fine sugar, one teaspoonful of butter, salt to taste; the same of lard, mixed together; wet with sweet milk to a stiff dough; beat well; cut with a wineglass; bake in a moderately hot oven. These are excellent if well made."

No. 3
"One quart of flour, two ounces of butter, half a teaspoonful of salt, a level teaspoonful of soda dissolved in warm water, sweet milk enough to make a stiff dough; beat well with a pestle. Cut with a wineglass after rolling the dough thin."

No. 4
"One teacup of sweet milk, half a teaspoonful of soda, one of cream of tartar, one tablespoonful of the white of an egg, first measuring and then beating it; a tablespoonful of butter, a little heaped teaspoonful of salt; mix very stiff; beat well; roll thin, and bake. Make these with arrow root flour, instead of flour."

CHEESE CRACKERS

To the recipe for Made-From-Scratch Crackers No. 1 above, mix in 3 ounces of grated sharp Cheddar cheese for each ½ pound of completed dough.

HARDTACK
(SAILORS' BISCUITS)

This famous bread was familiar to the sailors on the ships that called at Southport, and also to the soldiers and sailors, North and South alike, who warred between the States. They were made in various ways, some with honey and vegetable oil and brewer's yeast, but most were so indestructible they were called "sheet iron crackers."

Rye flour, enough to make a thick
    dough when mixed with the
    other ingredients
1 pint buttermilk

½ cup shortening, melted
½ cup sugar
1 teaspoon salt
1/8 teaspoon baking soda

Mix ingredients into a thick dough. Shape into small balls, drop into flour, then flatten until very thin with a rolling pin. Prick all over each with a fork or other barbed instrument. Bake on a cookie sheet in hot 425° oven about 15 minutes, until browned. They should be crisp and tender.

CORN PONE
Southport's Favorite Recipes (1950)
Contributed by Mrs. Gracie Ford

2 cups yellow corn meal
1 cup flour
2 cups milk
2 eggs

2 tablespoons melted shortening
1 teaspoon salt
3 teaspoons baking powder

"Sift the flour, corn meal, salt, sugar and baking powder into bowl; add the milk, melted shortening and well beaten eggs. Mix well. Brush shallow pan with a little shortening, pour in the mixture and bake in a hot oven for about 20 minutes."

BASIC DUMPLINGS

Use Ma-Ma's recipe for buttermilk biscuits on page 89, but add additional milk to make a dough moist and fairly soft. You should be able to drop it off a spoon. Drop them onto the surface of a bubbling chicken stew or other stew, or on top of a pot of collard greens. Cover, and cook about 10 to 18 minutes, or until done, depending on the size of the dumplings.

FEATHER DUMPLINGS

2 cups flour
4 teaspoons baking powder
½ teaspoon black pepper

1 egg, beaten
3 tablespoons melted butter
About 2/3 cup milk

Sift dry ingredients together, add egg, melted butter and milk. Drop by teaspoons in boiling liquid. Cover tightly for 10 to 18 minutes, or until done, depending on the size of the dumplings.

EASY FEATHER DUMPLINGS

1 cup Bisquick mix
1 egg well beaten

2 to 3 tablespoons milk
1 teaspoon baking powder

Beat the eggs in a mixing bowl. Add 2 tablespoons of the milk and the baking powder. Mix. Add the Bisquick mix and stir. Add just enough of the remaining milk to milk to make a stiff dough. Drop by spoonfuls onto hot broth, a chicken stew or greens in broth, or whatever you like. Cover and cook 15 minutes. Remove from heat and let stand 10 minutes or so. Makes 8 to 10 dumplings.

CORNMEAL DUMPLINGS
Contributed by Don Frink

2 cups corn meal
½ cup all purpose flour

½ cup to ¾ cup water or broth
    (chicken, or from collards)
3 tablespoons lard for frying

Mix dry ingredients, then add broth until mixture is stiff enough to drop off of a teaspoon. Lay out on top of greens and let cook until done—about 15 to 20 minutes.

HARD CORNMEAL DUMPLINGS

1 cup corn meal
1 teaspoon salt

Enough water to form a heavy
Dough

Mix together, form into small balls in your hand, press flat, and lay atop collards, other greens, or stews.

SPOON BREAD

Spoon bread may be served at breakfast with maple syrup and butter, or at dinner as the starch with the entrée.

1 cup boiling water	1 tablespoon butter, melted
½ cup white corn meal	2 eggs, well beaten
½ cup milk	½ teaspoon salt
1 ½ teaspoons baking powder	

Pour the boiling water over the corn meal. Beat in the salt, baking powder, melted butter and eggs. Butter a casserole pan or dish, pour in the mixture. Bake in preheated 400° oven for 20 to 25 minutes or until set. Serve hot from the pan. Serves 4 to 6.

YELLOW CORN BREAD

1 cup yellow corn meal	1 teaspoon salt
1 cup sifted flour	¼ cup soft shortening
¼ cup sugar	1 cup milk or buttermilk
3 teaspoons baking powder	1 egg, beaten

Combine meal, flour, sugar, baking powder and salt, and then cut in shortening. Mix egg and milk together and add to the dry ingredients, beating as little as possible. Bake in preheated 425° oven in a 9x9-inch pan for 20 to 25 minutes, until nicely brown.

SWEETHEART'S FRIED AND BAKED CRUSTY CORN BREAD

This is a recipe handed down in our family for generations and perfected by my mother. It is an unbeatable cornbread with crusty bottom and top.

1 ¾ cups self-rising yellow corn meal	1 ½ cups whole buttermilk
	1 teaspoon bacon drippings
½ cup self rising all-purpose flour	1 teaspoon sugar
1 large egg	½ teaspoon salt

Preheat until hot a 10-inch cast iron skillet generously covered with bacon drippings. Preheat oven to 450°. Beat egg, buttermilk, sugar and salt in mixing bowl. Stir in corn meal and flour. Pour batter in hot skillet—it should sizzle a bit. Let fry for about 1 minute. This gives the bottom of the cornbread a nice crust and rich taste. Then immediately transfer to top shelf of oven and bake 20 minutes or until golden brown.

CORN BREAD WITH BACON OR OTHER VARIATIONS

To the recipe for Yellow Corn Bread, or Sweetheart's Fried and Baked Crusty Corn Bread, on page 104, add ½ cup crisp bacon broken up, and bake. Or add 1 cup minced onion; or green scallions; or a combination.

INA NORMENT'S CHEWY, COUNTRY CORN BREAD

Our neighbor served up a wonderfully rustic, chewy cornbread baked in a skillet. You'd just tear off a piece and eat it.

1 cup cornmeal	Bacon drippings to cover the
½ cup water	skillet well
1 teaspoon salt	

Mix, pour over drippings in a skillet and bake in 400° oven until browned.

CORN STICKS

Use the recipe for Corn Muffins. Turn into buttered corn fritter molds and bake 15 to 20 minutes. Makes about 14 sticks.

ABOUT FRITTERS

Fritter is the English word for a light batter to coat some meat, fruit, fish or vegetables, then fried.

FRITTERS – BASIC BATTER

2 eggs	1 teaspoon salt
½ cup milk	1 teaspoon melted fat or cooking
1 cup all purpose flour, sifted	oil
1 teaspoon baking powder	Fat or oil to fry

Mix together. Drop by spoonfuls onto 375° hot grease, flatten slightly, and cook until brown and done. Add vegetables, seafood, or meat as desired. Makes 12 to 15 small fritters.

CLASSIC CORN FRITTERS

To basic corn fritter batter on the following page, add 1 cup whole fresh corn kernels, or 1 can drained kernels, or 1 box frozen kernels.

MARY TOMLINSON'S SPICY CORN FRITTERS

Our neighbor Mary is a terrific cook, and leans toward spicy things. Her corn fritters are nothing short of delicious.

2 cups white corn meal
1 cup flour
1 egg slightly beaten
½ cup milk
1 small can niblet corn
½ cup spring onions

¼ cup green, or red bell pepper, or
    combination of the two
Garlic powder to taste
Salt and pepper to taste
Cooking oil

Mix and fry in skillet until browned.

HUSH PUPPIES

It was said that hunters would throw their whining, hungry dogs bits of corn patties to keep them quiet, yelling, "Hush, puppies!" I don't know of a local seafood restaurant that doesn't do the same for their customers. This basic recipe may be varied according to taste according to the suggestions below.

1 pound corn meal
½ pint buttermilk
1 egg
2 tablespoons sugar

¾ pint water, more or less
1 tablespoon salt
Pinch of salt

Mix, adding water gradually to make thick consistency. Drop by small spoonfuls in deep fat at 375°. Drain well and serve.

Variations:

* Reduce the amount of sugar and add minced onions or chopped parsley, or both.

* For fluffier hush puppies, use ½ pound flour and ½ pound cornmeal, and add 1 teaspoon or more baking powder.

* For a sweeter puppy, increase the sugar and when fried, sprinkle with confectioner's sugar.

SWEETHEART'S CORNMEAL STUFFING

This goes well with turkey, baked pork chops, chicken halves and seafood. In the old days, the drying out process of this recipe was by slow cooking for hours on the back of Ma-Ma's coal stove. It will turn out a bit differently every time. Great eating, nevertheless.

½ stick butter
½ cup bacon drippings
6 cups chicken broth, or more
2 to 3 cups chopped onions
3 cups chopped celery
1 cup chopped green or red
   bell peppers
4 cups left over 2 to 3 day-old
   corn bread

4 cups herb seasoned bread
   crumbs
3 tablespoons parsley
3 tablespoons sage
1 tablespoon thyme
1 tablespoon poultry seasoning
1 tablespoon oregano
1 teaspoon salt
1 teaspoon pepper

Melt butter in black cast iron Dutch oven on back burner of stove. Add the chicken broth and simmer on low. In a skillet on another burner heat the bacon drippings and slowly sauté the chopped onions until glossy ("until you can read through them," says my mother), then after a few minutes the celery, and last, the peppers. Crumble the corn bread and seasoned bread crumbs into simmering broth. If you do not have a sloppy mush, add additional broth. Add seasonings. Simmer on back burner at lowest possible temperature, uncovered, for 2 to 3 hours or more. It should dry out enough to hold its shape when scooped out in balls with an ice cream scoop. There are two ways to serve the stuffing:

1. Turn the stuffing 1 ½ inch deep in pans. When ready to serve, brown in a hot oven.
2. Make individual servings by scooping up in balls with an ice cream scoop. Place on a cookie sheet. When ready to serve, brown in a hot oven.

Note: The stuffing stores or freezes well. It can be scooped out in individual servings with an ice cream scoop, frozen on a cookie sheet, placed in heavy plastic freezer bags. Then take out as many as you need to serve, let thaw, and reheat and brown.

OYSTER CORNBREAD STUFFING

Since oysters are commonplace in our area, so is oyster cornbread stuffing.

2 pints shucked oysters in their liquor
¾ cup butter or margarine
1 large yellow onion, chopped
2 large garlic cloves, minced (optional)
1 cup chopped celery
1 green pepper, seeded and chopped, about 1 cup
1 teaspoon dried thyme
1 teaspoon dried marjoram
½ teaspoon dried oregano
½ teaspoon celery seed
6 cups crumbled cornbread, or commercial cornbread stuffing
1 egg, lightly beaten
½ bottle clam juice
Salt and pepper

Drain oysters, reserving liquor. Cut each in half and set aside. Sauté vegetables until tender in the butter or margarine. Add herbs and celery seed and stir well. Beat egg into the oyster liquid and combine with stuffing mix, oysters, salt and pepper. Pour into 2 ½ to 3 quart shallow casserole dish. Add enough clam juice to make the mixture moist. Bake in 400° oven on top shelf until crusty and brown on top.

COUSIN VIVIAN JONES'S YEAST BREAD

1 cup whole milk
1 package dry yeast
3 cups plain flour
¼ cup oil
1 egg
2 tablespoons sugar
1 teaspoon salt

Heat milk to scalding; cool to lukewarm. Put milk and yeast in small bowl and let stand 5 minutes. Beat a little; add oil, egg salt, sugar and beat again. Pour into flour and stir till mixed. Cover and let rise 1 ½ hours. Knead down using flour as needed to obtain a smooth consistency. Shape into loaves, rolls, coffee rings, cheese breads, etc. Let rise again 45 minutes or till doubled. Vivian says, "I use a wet, warm towel with each rising. Bake in oven at 350° till done. The time is determined by what is being baked."

CLASSIC WHITE YEAST BREAD

6 cups of flour	2 tablespoons sugar
2 cups lukewarm milk	1 tablespoon salt
1 cake or package of yeast	4 tablespoons butter, melted

Measure ingredients carefully. Place lukewarm milk in a large bowl and add the yeast, breaking up yeast if it is in the cake form. Add sugar and salt and stir until all are mixed well. Use a mixer with a dough hook attachment at low speed, or mix by hand: Add the flour 1 cup at a time. When you have achieved a smooth dough, add melted butter to the mix. Then add remaining flour and stir until the dough is completely blended. Turn out the dough onto a floured board, cover with an inverted bowl and let it rest for 10 minutes. Dust your hands with barely enough flour to keep the dough from sticking and knead, pressing down with the heels of the hands, rolling the dough back and forth as you press. Continue until the dough is elastic and has a satin sheen.

Place dough in large bowl, cover with a cloth, place it in a warm spot 80 to 90°, and let it rise until double in volume, about 1 ½ to 2 hours. Punch the dough down, and then turn out onto the slightly floured board. Knead for 3 minutes and divide into 2 loaf shaped parts. Place these in well buttered bread pans and let rise again until doubled in size. Bake in preheated 375° oven until brown, about 40 to 45 minutes. This will make 2 loaves.

CLASSIC YEAST ROLLS

Follow the Classic Yeast Bread recipe to make the dough. After the second rising, knead, and then flatten out onto the slightly floured board about a ½-inch thick. Cut circles with a 3-inch cookie cutter and place on a cookie sheet. Cover and let rise for 25 minutes. Brush with melted butter and bake in a 425° oven until brown, about 15 minutes

For clover-leaf rolls, after the first rising, knead, then roll into small balls about 1 ¼-inch in diameter. Place 3 of these in each cup of a muffin tin. Let rise, then bake in 425° oven for about 15 minutes.

COUSIN VIVIAN JONES'S COFFEE RING

1 batch of Vivian Jones' basic
   yeast bread recipe
Brown sugar
Chopped nuts
Cinnamon

Nutmeg
1 cup confectioner's sugar
1 tablespoon margarine
¾ cup Maraschino cherries, cut up
Water

Prepare Vivian's yeast bread recipe, page 108. Vivian says, "Roll out after first rising into rectangle about 10x16 inches. Spread butter or margarine over entire surface, and then sprinkle with brown sugar, chopped nuts, cinnamon and nutmeg. Roll up from long side and shape into a circle. Cut with scissors and shape. Bake at 350° till done, about 20 to 25 minutes. Let cool in pan. I use pizza pans covered with tin foil and greased with Crisco. Transfer the coffee ring to a large plate, drizzle on a mixture of about 1 cup of confectioner's sugar, 1 tablespoon margarine, and a small amount of water. Sprinkle chopped maraschino cherries over the ring."

COUSIN VIVIAN JONES'S CHEESE BREAD

1 batch of Vivian Jones's basic yeast bread recipe from page 108.

For the cheese filling

1 8-ounce package cream cheese,
   room temperature

1 egg yolk
¼ cup sugar

Prepare basic yeast bread recipe. Let rise first time. Roll into a 10x14 inch rectangle. Blend together the cream cheese, egg yolk and sugar, and spread onto a pastry board. Spread the cheese filling over the flattened bread. Roll up, starting at the narrow end, jelly fashion. Seal the edges. Place on greased cookie sheet, sealed edges down. Cut strips at 1-inch intervals along the loaf. Let rise 1 hour. Bake in a 350° oven 20 to 25 minutes.

ENGLISH MUFFINS

4 cups flour, sifted
1 cup milk, scalded
1 egg, beaten
3 tablespoons butter

2 tablespoons sugar
1 ¼ teaspoons salt
1 cake yeast
¼ cup lukewarm water

Mix butter, salt and sugar in the hot milk and let cool to lukewarm. Soften the yeast in water. Add the yeast, egg and 2 cups of the sifted flour to the milk. Stir to blend well, and then knead in the remaining flour until firm and elastic. Let rise until doubled in volume, about an hour, depending on freshness of the yeast and warmth of the room. Roll out on floured board until ¼-inch thick. Cut into 4-inch circles. Cover and let rise again until doubled in size, about 1 hour. Sprinkle with cornmeal. Bake slowly on ungreased griddle or cast iron skillet about 10 minutes or less on each side. Makes about 12 muffins.

MA-MA'S HOT CROSS BUNS

Ma-ma's hot cross buns were always a special Easter treat.

4 cups flour, sifted	¼ cup shortening
¼ cup chopped pecans	1 ½ teaspoons salt
½ teaspoon mace	¼ cup sugar
¼ cup raisins	1 egg, beaten
1 cake yeast	½ teaspoon vanilla
2 tablespoons lukewarm water	¼ teaspoon lemon extract
1 cup milk	

Mix flour, nuts and mace. Wash raisins in hot water, dry, and add to flour. Soften yeast in the lukewarm water. Scald the milk and add shortening, salt and sugar. Add 1 cup flour mixture and cool to lukewarm. Add yeast and the beaten egg. Mix well. Add the vanilla and lemon extracts, and the remaining flour. Knead well and place in greased bowl. Allow to rise to double in volume. Knead again; form into buns and place on greased baking sheet. Cut an X on top of each with a sharp, lightly greased knife. Let rise until doubled in volume. Bake in preheated 400° about 15 minutes. Make a cross on each bun with confectioner's icing.

Confectioner's icing

Confectioner's sugar, sifted	¼ cup cream or milk
¼ cup butter, melted	½ teaspoon vanilla

Melt the butter in a small saucepan, add the cream or milk. Beat in enough confectioner's sugar until smooth and thick enough to spread. Add vanilla.

ICE BOX ROLLS

Ice box rolls, so named as in the days before electric refrigeration the dough was kept in the "ice box" until needed for baking. They remain popular as one batch of dough will do for making freshly baked rolls over several days.

1 cup water	1 teaspoon sugar
½ cup shortening	2 large eggs
1 ¼-ounce envelope active dry yeast	1 teaspoon salt
	5 cups bread flour
½ cup warm (100° – 110°) water	¼ to ½ cup butter, melted

In a saucepan, bring the cup of water and shortening to a boil. Boil 5 minutes. Remove and let stand 30 minutes, or until completely cooled. Stir together the yeast, the half cup of warm water and sugar in a small measuring cup and let stand 5 minutes. Beat eggs at medium speed. Add shortening mixture and yeast mixture. Beat on low, gradually adding the flour. Cover and chill dough 12 hours, or up to 5 days. Take out as much as you will need for a baking. Turn out onto lightly floured surface and roll to ¼-inch thickness. Cut with floured 2 ½-inch round cutter. Crease each across the middle with a knife and fold in half, gently pressing edges to seal. Place rolls on lightly greased baking sheet. Cover and let rise in warm 85° place away from drafts, 1 ½ hours or until doubled in bulk. Brush each roll with melted butter. Bake in 400° oven about 15 minutes or until golden brown. Brush with a mixture of melted butter and sugar.

CITRON BUNS

2 cups milk	1 teaspoon salt
1 package dry active yeast	1/3 cup butter, softened
¼ cup sugar	1 cup raisins
8 cups flour, sifted	4 cardamom capsules
2 eggs	¼ cup chopped citron

Scald the milk and cool to lukewarm, and add yeast. Add sugar and 4 cups of the flour to make a sponge. Beat well. Cover and let rise in warm 85° place until double in bulk, about 1 ½ hours. Add unbeaten eggs, salt and butter and mix until well blended. Sift remaining flour over raisins and citron. Remove cardamom seeds from capsules and crush fine. Add with flour, raisins and citron to first mixture. Work to a smooth, elastic dough. Cover and let rise until doubled in bulk, about 1 ½ hours. Turn onto lightly floured surface and shape into buns. Place on baking sheet 1 inch apart and bake in moderate 350° oven about 20 minutes. Makes about 30 buns.

Ressie Robinson Whatley (1910-2001) baking bread.
Photo by Jim Harper, 1999, courtesy of *The State Port Pilot.*

Great Grandma Mary Allen Jones Davis's soup tureen, and many a meal has been served from it. It is Austrian, and dates from about 1880.

6..
Soups, Chowders & Stews

ASPARAGUS SOUP
Mrs. Hill's Southern Practical Cookery and Receipt Book (1872)

"Boil the asparagus with any kind of fresh meat or fowl, or the broth in which they have been boiled. To a quart of this liquor add heaping teaspoonful of flour stirred into a teacup of cream, added just before serving. A hundred points of asparagus will never answer for three pints of broth; cut them into places two inches long; boil half an hour; salt and pepper to taste."

FRESH BROCCOLI SOUP

1 bunch fresh broccoli	2 cups beef bouillon
¼ cup chopped fresh onion	1/8 teaspoon Tabasco sauce
2 tablespoons butter or margarine	3/4 cup light cream
1 rib celery, chopped	

Melt butter in medium saucepan. Add onion and celery and cook slowly until tender. Wash and trim broccoli, removing leaves, and cut into small pieces. Add broccoli, the bouillon and Tabasco to saucepan. Bring to a boil. Cover and cook over medium heat 20 minutes. Purée in electric blender or food mill. Return to saucepan, add the cream, and heat. Makes 1 quart, 4 to 6 servings.

CREAM OF CHICKEN SOUP

3 cups chicken broth	2 cups hot milk or half & half
3 tablespoons rice	Salt and pepper to taste
½ cup diced celery	

Cook the rice and celery until soft. Strain through a strainer and add to the stock. Add the hot milk and the salt and pepper.

CREAM OF CELERY SOUP
Hood's Practical Cook's Book (1897)

"Wash and cut into inch pieces one bunch of celery, boil it in one pint of salted water, until tender enough to mash, and strain. Melt one tablespoon of butter and one tablespoon of flour together until smooth, and stir into one pint of hot milk or cream; then add to the celery, with salt and pepper, and boil altogether for five minutes. A few drops of onion juice improves this dish for some people. A good and easy way to get onion juice is to rub the onion, after the outside skin has been removed, on a rough grater. Four to eight drops gives a suggestion, without the positive onion flavor."

CORN SOUP
Mrs. Hill's Southern Practical Cookery and Receipt Book (1872)

"To a small hock bone of ham, or slice of good ham, add one quart of water. As soon as it boils, skim it well until the liquor is clear; add one large teacup and a half of grated corn, one quart of sweet milk, and a tablespoonful of butter, into which has been rubbed a heaping teaspoonful of flour; salt and pepper to taste."

CREAM OF ONION SOUP
Recipes From the Parish of St. Philips in Southport (1907)
Contributed by Clara R. Sprague

12 small onions sliced	Salt
1 tablespoon butter	Pepper
1 quart boiling water	Sugar
1 cup cream	Mace
2 egg yolks	

"Fry onions in butter, add milk and water. Cook one half hour slowly. Strain, season to taste. Pour over the well-beaten yolks. Heat quickly, stirring in the cream whipped. Serve at once."

ONION SOUP

1 quart meat broth	½ teaspoon Worcestershire sauce
4 medium onions, peeled and sliced	1 bay leaf
	Salt and pepper to taste
1 tablespoon butter	Grated Parmesan cheese
A drizzle of cooking oil	

Sauté the onions very slowly in the butter and oil. Add the broth, Worcestershire sauce, salt and pepper and simmer at least 45 minutes, until the onions are tender. Ladle the soup into individual oven-proof serving bowls. Serve with grated cheese and toast or rolls.

FRENCH ONION SOUP

Follow the above recipe for Onion Soup. Add 1 to 2 tablespoons minced garlic. After pouring into oven-proof bowls add 1 tablespoon sherry for each serving, and a 2-inch thick slice of French bread. Lay on a slice of Gruyère cheese on each bowl. Place under broiler until the cheese is browned and bubbly. Serve immediately.

PURÉE OF GREEN PEAS
Hood's Practical Cook's Book (1897)

"A puree of green peas is made of two cups of tender young green peas, a quart of chicken broth, a small slice of salt pork, one onion, a carrot, some sprigs of parsley, a branch of soup celery, a bay leaf, a sprig of thyme, two cloves, a teaspoon of pepper, half a cup of rich cream and one tablespoon of butter. Put the salt pork in a pot over the fire, and when it has fried a light brown add the onion and carrot, sliced fine; the parsley, cut fine; the bay leaf, thyme, celery and cloves. Fry the vegetables a delicate brown, drain off the surplus fat and add the chicken broth and the peas. Let the soup cook slowly for a hour. Then remove it from the stove and strain it through a puree sieve. Add the cream, heated scalding hot, and the butter. Serve the puree with little square croutons of fried bread."

CHICKEN NOODLE, OR CHICKEN AND RICE SOUP

In a large kettle make the chicken stock. Place the bones of one hen, with some flesh remaining, 2 or 3 stalks celery roughly cut, 1 medium size onion peeled and roughly chopped, 1 carrot peeled and roughly cut, 2 teaspoons salt, and 4 to 5 quarts water. Simmer for an hour or two. Strain and reserve the stock. After cooling, pick the meat from the chicken bones and add to the stock. Add 1 cup or more chopped celery and onion, and about ½ cup peeled and sliced carrot. Add 1 cup cooked rice or noodles or spaghetti and simmer about 30 minutes; or, ½ uncooked rice or noodles or spaghetti, and simmer for about 45 minutes until rice or noodles are tender. Season to taste with salt and pepper and parsley. A packet of chicken granules may be added for richer flavor.

CREAM OF TOMATO SOUP

3 to 4 pounds tomatoes, stemmed
and roughly cut
1 large onion, roughly cut
2 packets beef granules

½ cup heavy cream, or half and
half, or milk
2 tablespoons butter
Salt and pepper

Place tomatoes and onion in a pressure cooker and cook until they are mush, 15 minutes. If you lack a pressure cooker, steam the tomatoes and onion in a colander over boiling water until they are mush. Process them in a blender or food processor on high speed them until they are liquid. Press them through a colander to strain out seeds and any skin that remain; but this may not be necessary. Pour the tomato and onion mixture into a saucepan, add the remaining ingredients. Heat, careful not to scorch.

TURTLE SOUP
The Carolina Housewife (1847)

"Take the whole of the turtle out of the shell; cut it in pieces, that it may be the more easily scalded. Throw these pieces, with the fins, into the pot, and when scalded, take off the coarse skin of the fins and lay them aside to make another dish. The thick skin of the stomach must also be taken off; under it lies the fat, or what is termed the citron. Thus prepared, it is ready for making the soup. Take a leg of beef, and boil it to a gravy, cut up the turtle in small pieces, throw them into the pot with the beef, and add as much water as will cover the whole about two inches. The seasoning and the citron should be put in when the soup is half done. To two quarts and a half of soup (which will fill a large tureen,) add half an ounce of mace, a desert-spoonful of allspice, a tea-spoon of cloves, and salt and pepper, black and cayenne, to your taste. Tie up a bunch of parsley, thyme, and onions, and throw them into the soup while boiling; when nearly done, thicken with two table-spoonsful of flour. To give it a good color, take about a table-spoonful of brown sugar and burn it; when sufficiently burnt, add a wine-glass of water. Of this coloring, put about two table-spoonsful in the soup, and just before serving, throw in half a pint of Madiera wine."

CREAM OF SPINACH SOUP

1 cup fresh spinach, cooked
  (steamed until collapsed, but no
  more) or 1 package frozen
  spinach, cooked
½ cup minced onions, cooked
1 packet beef granules

2 tablespoons flour
2 tablespoons butter
½ teaspoon nutmeg
½ cup milk or cream, or a little
  more
Salt to taste

This is an easy, modern way of making a delicious spinach soup. Puree the spinach and onion in a blender or food processor. Melt the butter in a sauce pan, add flour to make a roux, then blend in the milk. Stir in the pureed spinach and onions and remaining ingredients. Heat until simmering and serve.

VEGETABLE SOUP

2 pounds uncooked meat bones,
  beef or ham, or a combination.
2 cups onions, chopped
1 cup fresh, or deluxe frozen string
  beans
2 cups celery, chopped
1 cup carrots, peeled and sliced
1 cup fresh or deluxe frozen green
  baby limas
1 cup fresh, or deluxe frozen corn
  niblets

½ cup fresh parsley, chopped
1 bay leaf
½ teaspoon paprika
½ teaspoon rosemary, finely
  crushed
½ teaspoon thyme, finely crushed
Ham or beef bouillon cubes as
  desired, to taste
¼ cup corn meal
Salt and pepper to taste

In a large kettle, cook the meat bones with 1 cup of the onions, with enough water to cover (about 2 quarts) on low heat for about an hour to make a rich broth. Add the remaining cup of onions, bay leaf, salt and pepper and the remaining vegetables and simmer until the vegetables are done but not mushy. Remove the meat bones and discard. Mix the corn meal with about ½ cup of the broth to form a roux and add to the pot, continue to cook slowly for about 10 minutes. Serve with hot corn bread or biscuits.

CREAM OF VEGETABLE SOUP

Use the above recipe for vegetable soup, but substitute 1 cup of half and half for 1 cup of the broth, and add 2 tablespoons butter.

SHE CRAB SOUP

Authentic She Crab Soup is made with the white meat and also the eggs from under the female crab. If unable to obtain "she crabs," then crumble a hard boiled egg in the soup.

2 cups white crab meat and crab
   eggs
1 tablespoon butter
Few drops lemon juice
1 teaspoon flour
2 pints half & half
2 pints heavy cream
1 teaspoon flour

1/8 teaspoon mace
1/8 teaspoon pepper
2 teaspoons Worcestershire sauce
1/2 teaspoon salt
4 tablespoons dry sherry
Parsley or paprika for sprinkling
   on top.

Melt butter in top of double boiler and blend with flour until smooth. Add the milk gradually, stirring constantly. Add the crab and eggs and all seasonings except the sherry. Cook slowly over hot water for 20 minutes. To serve, place 1 tablespoon of warmed sherry in individual bowls and pour in the soup. Sprinkle on the parsley or paprika and serve.

ABOUT CLAM CHOWDERS

Before preparing, see "About Clams" on pages 240-241. Since clams are plentiful in our area, chowders in various styles are very popular. You'll find New England style, which is milk based, and New York or Manhattan style, which is tomato based. Old Southport Style clam chowder uses neither milk nor tomatoes. Note: Local quahog clams are far more flavorful than canned, which tend to be sweet, but bland.

SWEETHEART'S SOUTHPORT STYLE CLAM CHOWDER

2 slices salt pork
2 slices bacon roughly chopped
1 cup chopped clams with juice,
   fresh or canned
1 cup potatoes peeled, cubed and
   par-boiled

2 cups onions, chopped
2 cups water
1 tablespoon soy sauce
2 tablespoons corn meal
1 bay leaf
Salt and pepper to taste

Sauté the pork and bacon until brown. Drain excess oil, leaving enough to sauté the onions until glossy and done. Add the potatoes, water, corn meal and seasonings. Simmer until potatoes are tender. Add the clams and simmer until they are hot. Clams become tough if cooked too long, or at too high a temperature.

MANHATTAN STYLE CLAM CHOWDER

4 slices salt pork or bacon, finely cut
½ cup onions, minced
2 7-ounce cans clams, minced
2 cups potatoes, peeled and cut into small cubes
1 cup or more boiling water

1 16-ounce can tomatoes, diced
½ cup celery, diced
½ cup carrots, diced
¼ teaspoon thyme
2 teaspoons parsley, minced
1 teaspoon oregano
Salt and pepper to taste

Sauté the fat in a kettle until it begins to fry out, add the onion and potatoes and water and boil until tender. Add the remaining ingredients. Simmer for a while to let the flavors meld. Serve with hot cornbread.

NEW ENGLAND STYLE CLAM CHOWDER

2 slices bacon
1 cup onion, finely chopped
2 cups cubed potatoes, or 1 cup each cubed carrots and potatoes
1 pint fresh clams, or 2 10½-ounce cans minced clams

2 cups half & half
2 tablespoons butter or margarine
½ teaspoon Worcestershire sauce
1 bay leaf
1 teaspoon ketchup
1 teaspoon salt
¼ teaspoon pepper

Chop bacon coarsely and sauté in large kettle until almost crisp. Add onion and cook about 5 minutes. Add cubed potatoes, or potatoes and carrots, salt, pepper and 1 cup water. Cook uncovered for 10 minutes or until potatoes are tender but not mushy. In the meantime, drain clams, reserving liquid. Chop clams coarsely. Add ½ cup clam liquid, half & half, and butter. Mix. Heat about 3 minutes but do not boil. Add the clams, heat 1 minute and serve.

CONCH CHOWDER
Southport's Favorite Recipes (1950)
Contributed by Mrs. John F. Potter

¼ pound diced salt pork
1 medium onion, diced
1 cup ground conchs
2 large Irish potatoes, diced

1 cup rice, raw
1 teaspoon pepper
2 quarts water
1 tablespoon salt

"Boil conchs in their shells until tender; remove from shells and grind in food chopper. Place diced pork in pot and brown, add diced potatoes and onions and let steam for 10 minutes, stirring constantly; add ground conchs and water and when it comes to a boil, add rice, salt and pepper. Let boil for 1 hour. Serves 8."

SEAFOOD CHOWDER

Follow the recipe for any style clam chowder above, but reduce quantity of clams and instead add fish, chopped scallops, or any seafood desired.

CRAB BISQUE

½ pound butter
2 tablespoons flour
2 cups milk
¼ teaspoon mace
¼ teaspoon nutmeg

1 pound fresh backfin crabmeat
1 teaspoon salt
¼ teaspoon red pepper
1 cup half & half cream

Melt butter in top of double boiler. Add flour and blend. Add milk and cook, stirring until thickened. Add seasonings and crab. When ready to serve, add cream and heat. Add a splash of sherry wine to top before serving.

SHRIMP BISQUE
Seafood Cookery in North Carolina (1960)

¾ pound cooked shrimp
2 tablespoons chopped onion
2 tablespoons chopped celery
¼ cup butter or other fat, melted
2 tablespoons flour

1 teaspoon salt
¼ teaspoon paprika
Dash pepper
1 quart milk
Parsley

Chop shrimp finely. Cook onion and celery in butter until tender. Blend in flour and seasonings. Add milk gradually and cook until thick, stirring constantly. Add shrimp, heat. Garnish with chopped parsley sprinkled over top. Serves 6.

SEAFOOD IN THE SHELL, IN BROTH

2 slices salt pork or bacon
¼ cup water
1 ¼ cup (8 ounces) clam broth
½ cup onions, chopped
½ cup scallions, chopped
¼ cup carrot, peeled and thinly
   sliced
2 tablespoons crushed garlic
6 clams in the shell
12 fresh mussels

8 shrimp, peeled
4 pieces of firm fish
1 tablespoon corn meal
1 bay leaf
½ teaspoon sugar
½ teaspoon Old Bay or similar
   seasoning
1 cup tomato juice or
   chopped tomatoes, optional
Salt and pepper to taste

Scrub and wash the clams and mussels thoroughly, making sure they are still tightly shut with no broken places. Place the salt pork or bacon and the water in a kettle, cover, and sauté about 15 minutes. Add the clam broth, the vegetables, garlic, bay leaf and seasonings and cook another 10 minutes, until the vegetables are tender. Sprinkle on the corn meal and stir. Add the clams, mussels, shrimp and fish. Cook about 10 minutes, until the bivalves have opened, and the shrimp are pink and the fish is done. Add more clam juice if necessary. Makes enough for four servings if used as an appetizer, or 2 servings if used as a main course. Double or triple recipe if more are expected. Serve in soup bowls with cornbread or corn sticks.

CHICKEN GUMBO

A dish is not a true gumbo without okra. Gumbo is an African word brought over during the days of slavery, and means okra.

1 small stewing chicken
2 tablespoons flour
3 tablespoons butter, melted
1 onion, chopped
4 cups okra, sliced and chopped

2 cups tomato pulp
A few springs of parsley, chopped
4 cups water
Salt and pepper to taste

Clean and dress chicken, and cut into serving portions. Dredge lightly in the flour and sauté in the butter, along with the chopped onion. When the chicken is nicely browned, add the okra, tomatoes, parsley and water. Season with the salt and pepper. Cook on low heat until tender, about 2 ½ hours. Add water if necessary.

SHRIMP OR SEAFOOD GUMBO

2 pounds shrimp
2 cups onions, chopped
2 cups carrots, peeled and sliced
  thin
2 cups celery, chopped
6 slices bacon cut into pieces
½ cup scallions, chopped
2 tablespoons fresh garlic, sliced
¼ cup vinegar
4 cups water
4 tablespoons flour
1 14-ounce can tomatoes,
  chopped or diced

1 8-ounce can tomato sauce 1 bay
leaf
1 2-inch sprig fresh rosemary
2 fresh sage leaves
4 cups okra, fresh or frozen, cut
½ teaspoon sugar
2 to 3 tablespoons Old Bay
  seasoning or similar
Salt and pepper to taste
2 tablespoons Worcestershire
  sauce
Tabasco or other hot sauce to taste

For shrimp gumbo, wash, peel and de-vein the shrimp and set aside, reserving the shells and heads if purchased with heads on. Simmer the shells and heads with ½ cup each of the chopped onion, carrots and celery, vinegar and water, for 20 minutes. Strain, discard the shells and vegetables, reserving the seafood broth. Cook shrimp in the broth for about 4 minutes. Strain through fine sieve, again reserving the broth. Rinse shrimp of frothy residue and set aside. Sauté bacon until done, remove and set aside. Sauté the remaining onions, carrots, celery, scallions and garlic until tender and glossy and set aside, leaving a coating of drippings in the pan. Add flour to make a roux. Then return the sautéed vegetables, add the broth, tomatoes, tomato sauce, salt, pepper, sugar, herbs, and simmer 1 hour. Add okra and simmer 30 minutes longer, adding the shrimp for the last 15 minutes. Adjust consistency with a little more flour if necessary. Add Worcestershire and hot sauce. Serve over steamed rice with a green salad.

For seafood gumbo, substitute crab, fish, or any combination of seafoods, using the shells and bones for the broth.

SHRIMP BOAT STYLE FISH STEW

This fish stew is good for any large fish, such as flounder, king mackerel, red snapper, or sheephead. Fry 2 slices salted fat back and 2 strips bacon in a Dutch oven. Sauté a peeled and chopped onion until glossy. Add about a quart of water. Add 4 medium potatoes, peeled and cut up but not diced. Add about 2 pounds fish, cut to the size of the potatoes. Cook slowly until done. Add salt and pepper.

BRUNSWICK STEW

The origin of this famous dish has never been settled. Some claim it goes back to Colonial times in Old Brunswick Town, Brunswick County, North Carolina, about ten miles up the Cape Fear. Some say Brunswick County, Virginia; some say Brunswick, Georgia. Some say it's not true Brunswick stew without squirrel meat or a pig's head bobbing around in it. You can buy canned Brunswick stew in supermarkets these days. But you may be disappointed—it lacks squirrel meat and a pig's head.

1 3-pound chicken, whole	1 ¾ cups fresh or frozen corn
3 cups water	kernels
1 cup diced potatoes, optional	1 teaspoon sugar
1 ¾ cups frozen or fresh green	1 ½ teaspoons salt
lima beans	½ teaspoon dried or fresh basil
1 ¾ cups tomato sauce	½ teaspoon oregano
1 cup onion, chopped	¼ teaspoon cayenne pepper

Simmer chicken in large pot with water and salt until tender, about 2 hours. Drain off and set aside the broth. If you are fat and cholesterol conscious, remove skin from chicken and discard. Remove flesh from bones and cut or shred into tiny pieces. Pour broth into the big pot and reduce to 2 cups. If you have decided on adding potatoes, add them to pot and cook 10 minutes. Add beans, tomato sauce and onion and cook 20 minutes. Add chicken and remaining ingredients and cook 15 to 20 minutes more, or until vegetables are tender.

OYSTER STEW

1 quart raw oysters	1 bay leaf
¼ pound butter	6 drops Tabasco sauce (optional)
1 quart half & half	1 teaspoon Old Bay or similar
1 teaspoon onion juice or powder	seasoning
1 tablespoon catsup	Salt and pepper to taste
½ teaspoon Worcestershire sauce	

Strain the oysters, removing any pieces of shell, and set aside. Reserve the juice from the oysters. Melt butter in saucepan. Add the oyster juice, and all ingredients except the oysters as they will shrink and become hard if cooked too long. Bring to boiling point but no more. Add the oysters, heat for 2 to 3 minutes and serve.

SUCCOTASH

There's nothing like good succotash made with fresh summer vegetables. Even good quality frozen vegetables will do. Add the vegetables to the pork-broth and cook until tender.

2 cups pork-broth	1 cup okra
1 cup plump, corn kernels	1 cup diced onion
1 cup tender, small green butterbeans	2 cups water
	Salt and pepper

CORNED BEEF STEW

This is another of my favorite dishes. Serve on halves of warm muffins, or on rice, or in a soup bowl with hot, buttered cornbread on the side, and you have some good eating.

1 12-ounce can corned beef	1 ½ cups water
2 cups chopped onion	1 to 2 tablespoons soy sauce
2 cups diced, par-boiled potatoes	1 bay leaf
½ cup chopped sweet bell pepper	Pepper to taste
1 tablespoon bacon drippings or cooking oil	¼ cup cornmeal

Sauté the onions and pepper in the oil until glossy, tender but not mushy. Add the potatoes, water, bay leaf and black pepper. You'll need no salt, as the corned beef is salty. Whisk the cornmeal in the water and add. Break up the corned beef into little pieces and stir in. Simmer about 5 minutes.

POTATO SOUP

Dice the potatoes, reserving 1 cup. Boil remainder of potatoes and onion until mush. Fry out 1 slice bacon, cut into small pieces. Add the potato and onion mush. Puree. Add the diced potatoes and remaining ingredients. Simmer until potato cubes are done but not mushy.

2-3 large Irish potatoes, peeled	2 cups or more chicken broth
1 onion, peeled	1 bay leaf
1 slice bacon	Salt and pepper to taste
1 cup heavy cream	Parsley, chopped (optional)
2-3 tablespoons butter	

Mrs. Sabre Johnson Cooker and her daughter, Juanita Cooker Potter, 1940's.
Photo courtesy of Mrs. Sabre's granddaughter, Annis Cooker Viola.

The Cookers and the Potters

The roots of the Cooker and Potter families are deep in Southport. Mrs. Sabre Cooker was famous for her terrapin stew. Her daughter, Juanita Cooker Potter, had a thriving cottage industry picking out crabmeat, with often a waiting list, as her crabmeat was always the freshest and sweetest to be had, picked cleanly with virtually no shells to annoy the tongue.

TERRAPIN STEW
Southport's Favorite Recipes (1950)
Contributed by Mrs. Sabre Cooker

2 pounds dressed terrapin	2 cups flour, or less
1 pint diced potatoes	2 teaspoons baking powder
½ cup meat fat	1 cup flour
1 good-sized onion	2 tablespoons baking powder
1 tablespoon butter	Salt and pepper to taste

Put terrapin on stove in pan of cold water, about two inches above the meat. Let this boil about 30 minutes and add rest of ingredients except for the flour and baking water and keep about the same quantity of water in the pot. When terrapin is tender and potatoes are done, make a stiff batter of the flour and baking powder. Drop by spoonfuls onto top of stew and sprinkle generously with black pepper. Let simmer about 15 minutes. Do not stir after adding dumpling.

127

Some equipment for canning: a boiler, a stirring spoon, a ricer (or other sieve with pestle to strain fruit for jellies), canning jars, pectin for jams and jellies, and canning jar tongs.

7..
Condiments, Pickles & Relishes, Jellies & Preserves

ABOUT PUTTING UP FOODS

Before attempting to put up foods intended to last a long time, see "About Cooking Techniques" on page 2. Also note that some of the recipes in this book date from the time when people would put up large quantities to get through the winter or share with neighbors, so you may wish to prepare a partial recipe.

ABOUT PICKLING LIME

Some old recipes call for a "tube" of pickling lime, or for "Lily's pickling lime," which may not be available any longer. Pickling lime such as that made by the Ball Corporation that makes the famous Ball jars is available at local supermarkets in Southport, and comes with detailed instructions for its use. You may have to adjust the recipe to accommodate the particular lime you can obtain.

ABOUT JELLING FRUITS AND BERRIES

Making jellies and preserves from fresh fruits and berries is great fun and not difficult, but does require a knowledge of basic techniques. For this it will pay to consult a comprehensive cook book.

Jellies are made from fruit juice, are firm, and are usually clear.
Jams are usually softer than jelly, and contain crushed fruit.
Conserve is a mixture of different fruits, and may contain nuts or
    raisins.
Butters are made by cooking the fruit pulp and sugar to the consistency
    of jam.
Preserves contain pieces of fruit in a transparent, thick syrup.

129

Two Scenes From Old Bethel Community

Above: The old folks at home, about 1900. Standing, Cousin Clara Drew; seated, my great-grandfather, John Wescott, and great-grandmother, Sarah Rebecca Drew Wescott. Below: Old Bethel Baptist Church, 1950.

John and Sarah Rebecca Drew Wescott

My great-grandfather John Wescott (1845-1936) fought for the Confederacy as a foot soldier during the Civil War. After the battle of Bentonville, the last great battle of the War, fought in March 1865 in the central part of the state, men were allowed to surrender their rifles, swear allegiance to the United States, and return home. This has always astonished me. For four years both North and South had fought bitterly; yet, when the guns fell silent, they shook hands and returned to their homes and farms. Contrast this with the murderous retributions that follow so many conflicts around the world, even today, whereby the vanquished are rounded up and executed.

John Wescott and Mr. Pack Tharp walked all the way back to Southport, surviving on the generosity of kind souls along the way. Mr. Pack Tharp opened up a barber shop in Southport downtown near the river on Howe Street. My great-grandfather returned to farming out in Old Bethel Community. He married Sarah Rebecca Drew (1847-1932); they lived out at old Bethel but in later years moved to Southport. Both John Wescott and Sarah Rebecca died before I was born so I never knew them, but photographs show Sarah Rebecca, a tiny, frail woman sitting on the front porch of their house on Atlantic Avenue. My mother remembers her going about the house in an old beacon-cloth housecoat, "about the ugliest house coat I think I ever saw," she told me, "of dark blue and purple and green flannel squares, and a cloth rope around the waist," She kept her head covered with a black satin ruffled maid's duster. For many years, I am told, she enjoyed poor health and being waited on. But I'm glad we have her recipe for tomat-butter.

Ma-Ma kept jars of her mother's tomat-butter in the pantry or refrigerator. My mother does the same. To prepare this recipe or taste a sample will whisk you back in time a hundred years, and will remind you of how cooking was done in the old days. You will notice that the ingredients are measured in pounds. Few households, no matter how poor, were without a scale sitting atop an oil cloth covered table in the kitchen or hanging from the ceiling of the back porch.

GREAT GRANDMOTHER SARAH REBECCA WESCOTT'S
TOMAT-BUTTER

Tomat-butter will take several hours of cooking, stirring ever so often. But you will wind up with a delicious spread, tangy and spicy, almost as if fermented, and dark as mahogany. Spread it on biscuits, toast or crackers. Or serve in a bowl as a condiment with ham, turkey or just about any meat.

4 pounds tart apples   1 teaspoon nutmeg
4 pounds tomatoes   1 teaspoon allspice
A little water   1 tablespoon cinnamon
4 pounds sugar   ½ teaspoon salt
½ teaspoon ground cloves

Weigh, do not measure, the apples, after bad spots have been removed. Cut the apples into quarters. Remove stems only, but not the skins, seeds or the core. Put in a large pot with the tomatoes and just enough water to stew very slowly until very soft. Then mash through a colander, discarding the roughage that does not go through. (A flat-bottomed colander works well. Use a potato masher.) To this, add the sugar and spices. Simmer slowly until thickened, stirring to keep from scorching. Put up in sterilized jars. Makes 12 pints.

APPLE SAUCE

6 medium apples   1/3 cup sugar, or more
½ cup water   Pinch of salt

Peel, core and cut up the apples into quarters. If you don't work pretty fast, drop the pieces in cold water with some lemon juice to prevent their turning brown. Simmer in the water and sugar until they are soft. If the apples are of the sour variety, such as wine sap, you may want to add a little more sugar. Mash with a potato masher, or grind into apple sauce.

Ma-Ma and Pa-Pa

My maternal grandmother, Alta Wescott Dosher (1886-1963), was born and raised in old Bethel Community not far from town. We called her Ma-Ma, with an equal emphasis on both syllables, not Máma, not Ma-Má, but Ma-Ma. She married Harry Lee Dosher (1886-1943), whom we similarly called Pa-Pa, and they had three children, my mother Dorothy, Leighton and Paul. Ma-Ma was a pious woman, always at night with a Bible in her lap reading—"Alta" means "lofty." She was an angel with her feet on the ground. She could chop kindling for her coal stove in the morning, and in the afternoon get dressed and serve punch from a cut glass punch bowl like Mrs. Astor for my mother's Garden Club meeting. She was a mama to all the kids in the neighborhood. Her home was the gathering place for the ladies of the neighborhood who hardly missed a summer afternoon having lemonade or punch on the front porch or side yard, or during cold weather, tea or coffee in the living room.

Every spring we had fresh asparagus from a patch that perennially would sprout up back next to the coal shed, and every fall we had luscious scuppernong grapes from the big overhead grapevine outside the kitchen door. And Ma-Ma made scuppernong jelly. Throughout the winter we had tiny potatoes and sweet potatoes she banked beneath the powdery sand under the house. In winter she kept hard Keiffer pears wrapped under the bed in the cold bedrooms that had no heat.

Pa-Pa was a mechanic and a forward thinking man who built the first modern filling station and garage in this area, at the northeast corner of Howe and Leonard Streets. He was in love with cars, and periodically would go to Wilmington to horse trade and return with a dark green Nash sedan or a two-seated Oakland roadster. He died during World War II, and I have only a few vagrant memories of him; but when I got a little older I was allowed the run of his workshop, a land of wonders—stacks of old *Popular Mechanics* magazines, cartons of dishware salvaged from ships lost off the coast, a box of knives and forks with yellowed ivory handles like piano keys; hammers and saws, drills, axes, planes, paints, brushes, boxes of nails, bolts, screws, stacks of window panes, all to inspire a child's creativity. I built things, a playhouse, and an eight-foot boat with a tin bottom that leaked, and when launched in a rain pond out in the woods promptly sank.

More Generations of Southport Cooks
Whose Recipes Appear in This Book

Elizabeth Durant Drew
Born 1816. Mother to
Sarah Rebecca Drew Wescott

Sarah Rebecca Drew Wescott
1846-1932
John Wescott
1845-1936
Parents of Alta Wescott Dosher

Alta Wescott Dosher
1886-1963
Mother to Dorothy Dosher Hardee

Dorothy Dosher Hardee
1915—
Lewis J. Hardee
1910-1996
Whose children, grandchildren
and great grandchildren continue
to enjoy the old family recipes.

135

MA-MA'S APPLE BUTTER

1 gallon sweet apple cider	1 tablespoon ground cinnamon
7 pounds (about 3 dozen medium)	2 teaspoons ground nutmeg
tart cooking apples, peeled,	¾ teaspoon ground cloves
cored and quartered	Sugar to taste

Bring cider to a boil, cook until reduced to half. Add apples and return to boil. Reduce heat and simmer 4 to 5 hours, stirring frequently, or until mixture is like marmalade. Stir in spices and sugar. Pour hot mixture into hot sterilized jars leaving ¼ inch headspace. Cover at once with metal lids that have also been boiled and screw on tight. Process in boiling water bath for 10 minutes, making sure jars are covered with the boiling water.

HOT PEPPER VINEGAR

Hot pepper vinegar is an indispensable accompaniment to collards and other greens. This basic recipe is easy: Wash four or five hot peppers, red or green, and place in a decanter. Pour in cider vinegar to cover. Let stand for a few weeks.

BREAD & BUTTER PICKLES

3 to 4 young cucumbers	1 teaspoon salt
1 large onion, sliced	¼ teaspoon dry mustard
¾ cup sugar	¼ teaspoon tumeric
¾ cup white vinegar	1 teaspoon mustard seeds

Wash and slice the cucumbers very thin, discarding the ends. Place cucumbers and onions in large pot and add remaining ingredients. Bring to a boil, stirring a bit. Pour into sterilized jars, making sure the liquid covers the cucumbers, and seal. Let stand 3 days.

GREEN TOMATO PICKLES
Recipes From the Parish of St. Philips in Southport (1907)
Contributed by Lilia Williams

This recipe is useful as, unlike many antique recipes, it gives specific amounts and kinds of spices.

1 gallon green tomatoes	1 tablespoonful allspice
4 large onions	2 tablespoonfuls cloves
6 green peppers	3 tablespoonfuls mustard seed
1 tablespoon black pepper	

"Slice the tomatoes (the greener the better), salt them in layers and let them stand over night. In the morning drain well. Slice the onions. Put a layer of tomatoes, then onions, until all are put in. Cut the peppers very fine and spread over the top. Put the spices in a bag and boil in the vinegar till the strength is extracted. Put bag on top of pickles, pour over them enough boiling vinegar to cover. Cover the pickles tightly and let them stand three weeks without opening."

GREEN TOMATO CHOW CHOW
Recipes From the Parish of St. Philips in Southport (1907)
Contributed by Lilia Williams

1 peck green tomatoes	1 cup grated horseradish
6 green peppers	1 tablespoonful cinnamon
4 onions	1 tablespoon cloves
1 cup salt	1 tablespoon allspice
1 cup sugar	

"Slice the tomatoes, peppers and onions, stir in the salt, and let them stand over night. Then pour over the water, put them in kettle, with enough vinegar to cover. Add the horseradish, sugar and spices. Cook till soft."

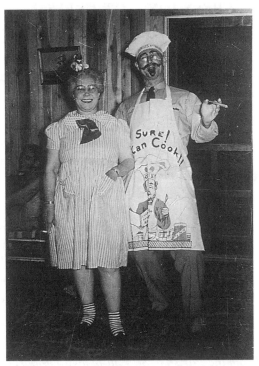

Elizabeth and Roy Robinson at a costume party, about 1950.
Photo courtesy of Leila Hubbard Pigott.

Elizabeth Guthrie Robinson

When famed author Robert Ruark was in town, his first stop was at the home of Elizabeth Guthrie Robinson on Dry Street. It is easy to understand why. Elizabeth was one of the most delightful persons you could meet. I last saw her in 1981 when she was eight-one years old, and still sharp as a tack.

Her father died at age twenty-seven when she was three, and she was raised by her grandfather, Michael Cronley Guthrie, a lawyer and a pillar of the town.

"He looked like a gallon of ice cream," she told me. "Looked enough like Robert E. Lee to be his twin! That's where I get my good looks from."

Like her father, her husband Roy Robinson had also been a mayor of Southport, which gave her the inside story of the town secrets. She knew who was running around, who drank, and who had been kicked out of which church for dancing. And she'd tell you.

138

"I got the talking from somebody, God knows who. I can't stop!" When I asked her to reminisce about certain old-timers she said,

"We'll dig 'em up and bury 'em!" About two feisty women named Kate she said,

"We called them Kate and Duplicate." When I asked her to confirm a certain tale circulated for many years by a lady in town, she said,

"Every thing she said was three-thirds wrong. There's no truth in it. Something somebody made up. She tells it like it's the truth. Actually I think she's told it so much she really believes it." Of a town leader with a shady reputation, she said,

"He was so crooked he'd steal the hairs from the plaster. I know, because I used to work for him."

Elizabeth Robinson was known for her Southport Style Chutney. A close replication appears below.

ABOUT CHUTNEY

Chutney is a delicious comfit that adds a spark to ham, turkey, rice, and many other foods. It's an Indian dish the English brought back to their island during the days of the Raj. There are many varieties, and it can be made with different vegetables and fruits. Major Grey's is probably the most familiar you will find on supermarket shelves.

SOUTHPORT STYLE CHUTNEY

1 cup raisins
1/2 cup brown sugar, packed
3/4 cup pineapple juice
1/2 cup cider vinegar
1 20-ounce can pineapple chunks
  in juice, undrained
1 mango, peeled, cored and
  chopped

2 6-ounce packages of dried
  apricots, coarsely chopped
2 teaspoons ground ginger
1 ½ teaspoons ground mustard
¼ teaspoon cayenne

Simmer all ingredients in 4-quart Dutch oven for 30 minutes, stirring occasionally. Remove cover and simmer for about 15 minutes, stirring every now and then, until mixture is thick. Cool. It will keep in the refrigerator for 2 weeks, freeze for up to 2 months, or properly canned, indefinitely.

SQUASH PICKLES

10 pounds yellow squash	1 ½ tablespoons turmeric
½ cup salt	½ tablespoon ground cloves
10 small white onions	1 tablespoon celery seed
5 cups vinegar	2 tablespoons mustard seeds
5 cups sugar	

Select small, yellow squash, wash and thin slice. Slice onions. Place in container and spread 1 quart of ice cubes over this. Cover and weight down. Soak about 4 hours. Discard the water. Heat the vinegar and seasonings in enough water to cover the squash, and pour over.

GRACIE FORD'S CORN RELISH
Southport's Favorite Recipes (1950)

Mrs. Gracie Ford ran a tiny store on W. West Street. Not long ago it was moved to the Old Southport Village out on Howe Street, where it still survives. Here is Mrs. Gracie's recipe for corn relish:

2 dozen ears of corn	3 cups granulated sugar
1 large head of cabbage	3 pints mild vinegar
5 red sweet peppers	4 tablespoons white mustard seed
3 green sweet peppers	4 teaspoons salt

Boil corn a few minutes until milk is set. Run knife through grains to make them fine, and cut off. Chop the cabbage and peppers. Mix all ingredients and cook about 20 minutes. Put in sterilized jars and seal while hot.

CRANBERRY-PECAN RELISH

4 cups cranberries	1 tablespoon grated orange rind
2 ½ cups sugar	½ cup water
½ cup pecans, finely chopped	1 cup raisins
½ cup orange juice	

Toast pecans 15 minutes in a 350° oven. Pick over the cranberries, removing any stems and poor berries. Cook the cranberries in the water and orange juice in a large saucepan until the berries pop. Simmer about 8 minutes. Add the grated rind, raisins, sugar and pecans. Simmer 20 minutes until mixture thickens. Chill.

FLORIE JOHNSON'S PICKLED PEACHES
Southport's Favorite Recipes (1950)

Florie Johnson lived out on the Southport-Supply road just on the other side of Dutchman's Creek. The ladies of the Baptist Circle enjoyed meetings held at her house because she served home grown watermelon, cantaloupe, or these pickled peaches.

8 pounds Clingstone peaches, firm and ripe	2 quarts vinegar
9 cups sugar	4 long sticks cinnamon
	1 teaspoon cloves

Wash and peel peaches. Boil vinegar, sugar and spices for 5 minutes. Add peaches and cook gently until tender. Let stand in syrup overnight. Drain and cook syrup until thick. Pack peaches in sterilized jars, cover with syrup and seal.

ANNIE WALTON'S CHOW-CHOW
Southport's Treasure of Personal Recipes (1952)

Mince equal amounts of green tomatoes onions green bell peppers cabbage	Salt 1 cup sugar Water Spices to taste

Mix vegetables, salt to taste and let stand overnight. Next morning, drain mixture of salt water and wash well. Press out all the water that you can. Then mix a cup of sugar and a cup of vinegar and spices to taste. Add to above ingredients and cook together about 20 minutes after mixture comes to a boil. Pour into sterilized jars and seal. Yield: about 4 pints.

SWEETHEART'S SPICED BEETS

2 16-ounce cans beets, sliced or small whole	1 cup finely sliced onions
1 cup cider vinegar	½ cup sugar
	½ teaspoon salt

Drain beets and boil juice with all other ingredients except the beets and onions. Simmer juice for about 10 minutes. Alternate layers of beets and onions in a wide-mouthed jar and pour juice over this. Says my mother, "I keep jars of this in the back of my refrigerator year 'round. It goes with any Southern meal."

WATERMELON RIND PICKLES

4 cups watermelon rind
  (about 1 pound)
2 pints cold water
2 pints boiling water
3 cups sugar
½ teaspoon cinnamon

½ teaspoon ground cloves
1 tablespoon whole cloves
1 tablespoon whole allspice
3 sticks cinnamon
1 ½ medium-sized lemons, sliced
Lime water

Trim the tough, outer skin away. Cut the rinds into ¾ inch cubes, leaving just a little of the pink for color. Cover with cold water, add lime water (available in the canning section of your supermarket) according to proportions recommended on package. Let stand three hours. Drain, cover with water and cook on top of stove 8 to 10 minutes. Drain again and put aside.

In a large kettle, combine the boiling water, vinegar, sugar, cinnamon and ground cloves. Tie whole allspice, cinnamon sticks and whole cloves in a piece of cheese cloth with a piece of string, leaving enough string to attach to the cover of the kettle and allow the spices to hang in the liquid.

Boil the liquid for 5 minutes, until the sugar is dissolved. Add the sliced lemon and the rinds. Simmer gently until rind is transparent. Remove the spice bag, spoon into sterilized jars and seal with lids at once. Let stand for 4 weeks. Makes about a pint of sweet, pickled rind. Goes great with roast turkey, ham, or just about any other meat.

SWEETHEART'S SPICED PEACHES

My poor suffering mother always kept spiced peaches and spiced beets on hand in the refrigerator for those many occasions when my brothers or my father or I would show up for dinner with unannounced guests. She always could throw together a good meal as if she had been planning it for weeks.

2 29-ounce cans cling peach
  halves
1 1/3 cups sugar

1 cup cider vinegar
4 cinnamon sticks
2 teaspoons whole cloves

Drain peaches, reserving syrup. Combine syrup with sugar, vinegar, cinnamon sticks and cloves in a saucepan. Bring mixture to a boil and simmer for 10 minutes. Pour hot syrup over peach halves. Chill thoroughly.

PICKLED CRAB APPLES

6 pounds crab apples	¼ cup whole cloves
1 quart white vinegar	1 stick cinnamon
8 cups sugar	1 ½ teaspoons ginger

Wash the apples and remove stems. Prick each apple several times with a fork. Heat the sugar and vinegar to the boiling point, add spices and crab apples. Boil on low flame until the apples are tender. Put up in hot sterile jars, making sure that the syrup covers the apples.

COUSIN MARY MULLING'S RUMQUATS
(Kumquat Preserves)

1 quart kumquats	1 cup water
2 cups sugar	¼ cup Puerto Rican rum

Wash and cut a ¼ inch cross in stem end. Do not cut deep. Place in sauce pan in water to cover and boil gently 5 minutes. Drain water. Add the sugar and cup of water and gently boil 35 to 45 minutes. Add the rum and stir. Put up in sterilized jars. Will keep a year in the refrigerator.

SPICED CRANBERRIES
Annie May Woodside's Cook Book (1913)

3 quarts cranberries	1 tablespoon whole allspice
3 ½ pounds brown sugar	3-inch stick of cinnamon
2 cups vinegar	1 teaspoon whole cloves

"Put the allspice and cloves (both whole) and the cinnamon into a square of cheesecloth and tie them up. Place in a preserving kettle with all of the other ingredients. Let the whole simmer very gently for 1 ½ hour. Turn into a stone jar, or, if preferred into small jelly glasses, and cover closely. The spices can be removed after the cooking is completed."

FRUIT PRESERVES
Annie May Woodside's Cook Book (1913)

"An equal weight of fruit and sugar. Add a little water to the sugar and boil to a syrup. Add fruit and continue the boiling till fruit becomes thoroughly heated through and through. Put away in jars. A little lemon added to apples, pears or figs improves them greatly. Quince is also very nice to add to apples."

Cousin Carl Knox "scrounging" for wild native fruits and berries near the Knox home at Winnabow.

Cousin Carl Knox

Cousin Carl Knox (1902-1964), brother of Annie Lou Knox Newton, was raised out at the Knox homestead on U.S. 17 near Winnabow. The handsome, classic white North Carolina farm house, can still be seen, with the widening of the highway a few years ago relocated a short distance from its original site. Carl spent most of his life in Georgia, but regularly returned to North Carolina. He called himself a "scrounger." "A scrounger on dry land is comparable to a beachcomber on the beach," he said, searching the local woods for native fruits and berries with a thirty-inch long stick with forks at the end that he called "fingers," to pry into briars and undergrowth. The folks would join in to preserve his harvest in jars and cans. June and July were best for wild plums and blackberries at their peak; September and October for the scuppernong grapes. October was also the time for hunting citron, a vine that grows on the edges of fields and whose fruit could pass for a watermelon until you try to prepare it—it's rock hard and must be cooked. It has an enticing ginger flavor and makes a delicious condiment.

COUSIN CARL KNOX'S WILD PLUM PRESERVES

Wash the plums. Use about two cups of water to each gallon of fruit, and boil for 5 to 10 minutes, until the skins crack. Liquefy at low speed in a blender 2 cupfuls at a time, then at high speed for 10 seconds. Push through a sieve and discard the pits. To make the jam:

Method 1: To each 3 cups of fruit pulp add two cups sugar and cook until thick and the juice is jelled when cool.

Method 2: To each 3 cups of seedless pulp, add a half package of Sure-Jell. Boil for about 2 minutes, add 3 ½ cups of sugar and boil for one minute. Skim and put up in sterilized half-pint screw-top jars.

COUSIN CARL KNOX'S CITRON PRESERVES

Citron and sugar, weighed in equal amounts
1 piece of ginger root

To each 4 pounds of citron add 4 pounds sugar and juice and rind of 4 lemons

Choose the ripest you can find. Wash carefully. Split and remove seeds. Then cut into slices. Sprinkle well with salt. Cover with cold water and let stand overnight. Drain. Pare. Heat the sugar, water, lemon juice and rind and ginger to the boiling point. Add the citron and cook slowly until the citron is tinder. Put up in sterilized jars, fill with boiling hot syrup and seal.

CARL KNOX'S WILD PLUM BUTTER

Follow the instructions above for plum preserves, but add a teaspoon of allspice and a teaspoon of ground cinnamon after the heating process is complete.

GRAPE JELLY

4 pounds grapes
Sugar and water as indicated.

Pick over grapes, removing stems, and wash them. Boil on low heat about 3 minutes. Drain through a clean, porous bag. Measure the juice. Cook 3 to 4 cups at a time, with ¾ cup sugar for each cup of juice. Boil on high heat 3 minutes. Test to see if it makes jelly. Too much sugar will make it syrupy; too little will make it tough. Put up in sterilized jars.

145

DOVIE WHITE'S HOT PEPPER JELLY

My sister-in-law's mother puts up just about the best hot pepper jelly you ever had. It goes great with your turkey, ham, pork, venison, lamb, or just about any meat. It's a clear, beautiful green, or red, as you prefer, and dresses up a dull plate. Or, serve as an appetizer on a block of cream cheese with crackers.

12 hot peppers. (Remove seed for spicy, leave in for hot.)
3 bell peppers, medium size, green or red
1/3 cup water

5 pounds sugar
3 cups vinegar
2 bottles Certo
Cake coloring

In a blender liquefy the hot and bell peppers and the 1/3 cup water. In a large pot combine this pepper mixture with the sugar and vinegar. Boil for 5 minutes. Turn off heat. Add color, green or red as desired. Add two bottles Certo and stir for a few minutes. Pour into ½ pint sterilized jars.

HOT PEPPER JELLY WITH FRESH MINT

To ½ cup Dovie White's Hot Pepper Jelly, above, add ½ cup fresh mint leaves that have been washed, dried with a towel, chopped, crushed and pressed down into the measuring cup. Mix well and allow to sit a few hours for the mint flavor to penetrate. This will only keep a day or two, since the mint is fresh and will spoil. But it is sensational with lamb or pork.

BLACKBERRY JAM

Blackberries, Water, Sugar

Pick over the berries, removing any stems, and wash them. Boil in 1 cup of water for each 3 quarts of berries. Strain through clean, porous bag. Use ¾ cup of sugar for each cup of juice cooking 3 to 4 cups at a time. Boil 3 minutes, add sugar, and boil on high heat. Test to see if it makes jelly. Too much sugar will make it syrupy; too little will make it tough. Put up in sterilized jars.

STRAWBERRY PRESERVES

Choose fresh, sweet berries in season. No amount of sugar and cooking will make good preserves out of poor berries.

1 quart strawberries, 3 cups sugar, 1 cup water

Trim tops from the berries, wash and drain thoroughly. Boil together the sugar and water to the soft ball stage, 238°. Add berries, cover, remove from heat and let stand for 10 minutes. Skim any foam from the top. Pour the syrup and berries through a sieve. Boil the syrup to 238° again, and then add the berries again. Let stand for 15 minutes over very low heat. Skim once more. Again remove the berries and cook the syrup to 238°. Add the berries a final time and cook slowly until the syrup is thick. Let stand 24 hours before putting up in jars and sealing.

ORANGE MARMALADE

8 oranges, water and sugar as indicated below

Select shiny, unblemished oranges and wash well. Slice very thin and remove the seeds, and the bitter center membrane. Measure without draining. To each quart of fruit and juice, add 1 ½ quarts water, and let stand overnight. Cook slowly for 2 to 2½ hours, or until the peel is tender. Measure the fruit undrained and add 2/3rds as much sugar. Cook on a fairly high flame until the jelly stage, 220° on a jelly thermometer. Skim off and discard any froth. Put up in sterilized jars.

PEACH MARMALADE
The Carolina Housewife (1847)

"Take very ripe peaches, peel them, take out the stones, and cover them with all the sugar you mean to use for them. A pound of sugar to a pound of fruit is enough to make a very nice marmalade; but if you wish the flavor of the fruit to be very well preserved, take a pound and a half of sugar to the pound. After the peaches have been in the sugar three or four hours, turn them into your preserving-kettle, boil them very rapidly for an hour, if you use a pound, and eight or ten minutes, if you have a pound and a half. Rub it with a spoon through a hair sieve, and fill your jars immediately. Made thus, this marmalade has the transparency of jelly."

147

PEACH JAM

Peaches, about 1 pound of sugar

Blanch peaches in boiling water, and then remove skins and core. Finely slice the peaches and layer with the sugar. Allow to stand 4 hours. Heat slowly until sugar dissolves, stirring constantly. Then heat rapidly, all the while stirring, until the jam is thick. Too much sugar will make it syrupy; too little will make it tough. Put up in sterilized jars.

COUSIN BROOKS NEWTON PREIK'S STEWED FIG PRESERVES

Use an equal amount of sugar and figs. A good figure to start with is 5 pounds each. Use the small pink and lavender "sugar figs" common in Southport, instead of the big green or purple variety. Wash and stem the figs. Pour over with sugar and let stand overnight. Bring to a slow boil stirring constantly, careful not to break the figs. Simmer for about 1 ½ hours, stirring often enough to avoid sticking and scorching. Add thin slices of lemon and cook another 20 minutes. Pour off excess syrup and reserve for serving over pancakes. Put up in sterilized jars and seal.

PRESERVED PEARS
Hood's Practical Cook's Book (1897)

"Pare the fruit and cut it in halves and place it in cold water or it will be discolored. Use one pound of sugar for three pounds of fruit, and one quart of water for three pounds of sugar. When the syrup is boiling take the pears from the water and drop into the syrup. Cook until they can be pierced easily with a silver fork. Fill the [sterilized] jars with fruit and fill to the brim with syrup with syrup, using a small strainer in the tunnel that the syrup may look clear. Bartlett pears are delicious canned and so are the Seckels."

PINEAPPLE MARMALADE
Hood's Practical Cook's Book (1897)

"Pare and grate the pineapples into a pulp, which boil fifteen minutes. Add to each quart of boiled pulp a pint of granulated sugar. Stir and bring to a boil. Fill into glasses or [sterilized] jars. This is a fine preserve, and will keep for years."

QUINCE PRESERVES

The quince thrives in Southport. It produces a beautiful pink flower in the spring, and fairly small fruit later on.

Peel and core enough quince to yield 1 quart fruit. Place 2 cups sugar and 1 cup of water in a saucepan and boil 5 minutes. Add the fruit and boil slowly for 45 minutes or until tender. Put up in about 6 six-ounce glasses.

ENGLISH BRANDIED TUTTI-FRUTTI

Tutti-frutti is of course simply Italian for "all fruits," and applies to numerous foods such as ice cream or candy to which a variety of fruits have been added, such as this recipe for preserves. Tutti-fruiti was a particular delicacy of the Victorians who would add fruits to brandy as they came into season until a large crock had built up. Nowadays, nearly all fruits are available at all times, and the tutti-frutti can be made all at once. For this you will need a large 2-gallon crock with a heavy lid.

Put 1 quart brandy into the crock and add stemmed whole strawberries, raspberries, pitted cherries, pitted and peeled apricots, peaches, pears and pineapple. Cover with 2 cups sugar for each 2 cups of fruit. Store in a cool place. Stir daily for a few days. Cove tightly, or seal in jars, and store for 2 to 3 months before using. Delicious on ice cream, or stir into softened vanilla ice cream and refreeze.

Our neighbor Mary L. Tomlinson, 2005.

8..
Sauces and Gravies for Meats, Seafood & Vegetables

CREAM SAUCE (WHITE SAUCE)

This is the basis of many dishes, from soups to soufflés. It can also be used to top vegetables such as asparagus, broccoli or cauliflower. A wire whisk helps.

2 tablespoons butter
2 tablespoons flour
1 cup hot milk

1/2 teaspoon salt
1/8 teaspoon pepper

Make a roux by melting the butter in top of double boiler and then blending in the flour. You may use a double boiler, or a small, heavy saucepan and cook over very low heat, stirring to avoid scorching. Slowly add the milk, stirring constantly. Bring to boiling point and cook 2 minutes. Season with salt and pepper.

MORNAY SAUCE

A great white sauce made with cheese and egg, the traditional sauce for scallops. This recipe makes about 1 cup.

2/3 cup Gruyère cheese, grated
1 tablespoon butter
1 ½ tablespoons flour
1 cup milk

1 egg
¼ teaspoon nutmeg
½ teaspoon salt
½ teaspoon pepper

Melt the butter in a saucepan over low heat. Sprinkle the flour in and cook 1 to 2 minutes stirring constantly. Slowly add the milk, using a whisk to prevent lumping. Bring to a boil, and cook on very low heat until it has the consistency of heavy cream, stirring frequently. Remove from heat, add the egg, cheese and seasonings, cook slowly about another 3 to 4 minutes.

CHEESE SAUCE

To 1 cup of the Cream Sauce above, add 4 ounces grated cheese, Cheddar, American or one of your choice. Add ½ teaspoon dry mustard and ½ teaspoon paprika. Heat until cheese is melted and blended. Goes great over meats, broccoli or other vegetables.

BÉCHAMEL SAUCE
Adapted from *Favorite Recipes of North Carolina* (1944)

For serving over oysters, stuffed eggs or fish fillets.

¼ cup butter, melted
6 tablespoons flour
2 cups chicken stock, or
   2 bouillon cubes in 2 cups
   water
1 cup thick cream
2 teaspoons lemon juice

1/3 cup Natural American Cheese, grated
¾ teaspoon salt
½ teaspoon paprika
Dash of pepper

Blend butter, flour and seasonings. Add stock and cream, then cheese. Cook until thick. Remove from fire, add lemon juice, mix well.

COCKTAIL SAUCE FOR SEAFOOD

½ cup chili sauce
½ cup ketchup
1 ½ teaspoons Worcestershire
   sauce

2 teaspoons lemon juice
¼ teaspoon salt
Dash of pepper
A few drops of Tabasco sauce

Combine and chill. Goes with almost any cold seafood.

TARTAR SAUCE

This goes great with seafood, especially fried oysters. Make it ahead a few hours so the ingredients can meld. Do not keep it longer than a few days, as the onions may spoil. Mix together:

1 cup mayonnaise
1 tablespoon capers, chopped
1 tablespoon onion, minced

1 teaspoon sweet pickle relish
1/8 teaspoon pepper, coarsely
   ground

HOLLANDAISE

Hollandaise isn't called the Queen of Sauces for nothing. It is the definitive sauce for Eggs Benedict and other specialty dishes. It is superb on vegetables such as asparagus, broccoli, on eggs, or steaks and chops. Nothing is duller than plain, broiled skinless chicken breasts. You might as well dine on cardboard. But cooked with care and topped with Hollandaise, broiled chicken breasts are heavenly.

3 egg yolks	2 tablespoons hot water
2 tablespoons lemon juice	¼ teaspoon salt
or mild vinegar, or half of each	Easy dash of cayenne
½ cup butter or margarine, melted	

Beat eggs in top of small double boiler until smooth but not fluffy. Add the lemon or vinegar juice while whisking, then the remaining ingredients. Stir over low heat until thickened. Yields about 1 cup. May be stored in refrigerator for a week. Important hint: Hollandaise may separate. Don't worry. To warm sauce, just add drops of very hot water and whisk.

BARBECUE SAUCE
Southport's Favorite Recipes (1950)
Contributed by Mrs. O. R. Stubbs

½ cup vinegar	1 teaspoon Worcestershire sauce
½ cup catsup	1 teaspoon mustard
1 teaspoon hot sauce	1 teaspoon salt
1 cup water	

Mix all ingredients together well and pour over fish. This sauce is equally good for pork ribs and chicken.

PUNGENT STEAK SAUCE
Favorite Recipes of North Carolina (1944)

½ cup butter	2 tablespoons catsup
1 tablespoon Worcestershire	1 teaspoon paprika
sauce	2 tablespoons lemon juice
½ teaspoon dry mustard	or vinegar

Combine all ingredients. Add steak drippings. Broil one minute and pour over steak.

153

RAISIN SAUCE FOR HAM OR PORK

This is a classic sauce, usually served with ham.

2 tablespoons butter
2 tablespoons flour
1 ½ cups cider
½ cup raisins
1 teaspoon grated lemon rind

¾ teaspoon prepared mustard,
    English style such as
    Coleman's
1 tablespoon sherry

Combine the flour and butter in a saucepan. Add cider and raisins. Bring to boiling point, and then cook on slow for 10 minutes, stirring. Add the grated lemon rind and the mustard, and slip in a tablespoon of sherry.

TOMATO SAUCE

1 cup tomatoes, stewed and
    strained
1 tablespoon butter, melted
1 teaspoon corn starch

1 teaspoon onion juice
1 tablespoon Worcestershire
    sauce
Salt to taste

Stew until reduced to the consistency of a rich sauce. If too thick, dilute with boiling water. For a spicier sauce, add 6 peppercorns and 2 tablespoons sherry.

CHILI SAUCE FOR HOT DOGS AND HAMBURGERS

1 pound beef, chopped
1 cup tomato ketchup

1 teaspoon prepared mustard
1 tablespoon chili powder

Fry out the beef in a skillet. Mix with the remaining ingredients.

ABOUT KETCHUP

In 1875 the H. J. Heinz Company introduced its bottled tomato ketchup which straightway began to replace the home made sauce. Many 19th Century cookbooks featured recipes for made-from-scratch tomato ketchup. Mary Randolph's *The Virginia House-Wife* of 1824, for example, contains a recipe for "Tomata Catsup" and advises, "Make it in August." Annabella Hill's *Southern Practical Cookery and Receipt Book* of 1867 features two recipes and warns, "It is poor economy to use old corks."

TOMATO KETCHUP
Hood's Practical Cook's Book (1897)

4 quarts of good, vine ripened
   tomatoes
Water to cover
2 grated nutmegs
1 tablespoon pepper

¾ tablespoon cayenne
1 tablespoon mustard
1 tablespoon ground cinnamon
1 pint vinegar
Salt to taste

"Drop the tomatoes in boiling water and boil for 2 minutes. Drain and plunge in cold water. Slip off the skins, and pick over the tomatoes to remove the hard core and any blemishes. Cook the pulp slowly until reduced to one half. Strain through a sieve. Tie the seasonings in a small cloth bag and simmer (do not boil) in the vinegar for an hour or two. Skim off any impurities. Add the strained tomato and cook slowly for 15 minutes. Cool. Add salt to taste. Put up in sterilized bottles and seal. Will keep a long time."

IMITATION WORCESTER SAUCE
Mrs. Hill's Southern Practical Cookery and Receipt Book (1872)

"One gallon of ripe tomatoes washed and cut up. Pour over three quarts of water; let it boil down half. Stir occasionally to prevent the tomatoes from sticking. (A double vessel is valuable in preparing these.) Strain through a sieve; add two tablespoonfuls of ginger, two of black pepper, two of salt, one of cloves, one of red pepper. Boil down to a quart; add a tumbler of vinegar. Strain, bottle, and cork tight."

CARL GREGORY'S BARBECUE SAUCE
FOR BASTING A HOG

1 gallon apple cider vinegar
1 bottle Worcestershire sauce
2 large 16-ounce cans tomato
   sauce

Salt, black pepper and small
   amount of Cayenne pepper
1 teaspoon chopped garlic

Simmer over medium heat for 20 minutes.

BROWN SAUCE

1 tablespoons butter	1 clove
1 tablespoon bacon fat	½ teaspoon salt
¼ cup onion	½ teaspoon pepper
1 shallot chopped fine	Pinch of sugar
2 slices carrot	1 cup brown stock
2 tablespoons flour	½ teaspoon Worcestershire sauce
1 sprig fresh parsley	½ teaspoon ketchup
1 bay leaf	½ teaspoon sherry wine

Sauté the vegetables in the butter and fat slowly until soft. Add the stock, vegetables and bay leaf and clove, and boil for 3 minutes. Strain and discard the vegetables. Add the remaining ingredients and simmer slowly for 15 minutes. Delicious with meats.

DOWN-HOME SAUSAGE GRAVY

8 ounces fresh breakfast sausage	1/2 cup water
2 tablespoons onion, finely	1/8 teaspoon salt
chopped	Tabasco or similar hot pepper
3 tablespoons all-purpose flour	sauce to taste
1 cup cream, or 1 12-ounce can	
evaporated milk	

Cook sausage and onion in skillet over medium-low heat, stirring occasionally, until sausage is no longer pink. Blend the flour with the evaporated milk, then add the water, salt and hot pepper sauce. Mix well. Cook until mixture comes to a boil, and continue cooking for 1 to 2 minutes. Serve over hot biscuits.

RED EYE GRAVY

4 slices country ham, wafer thin	¼ cup water
2 tablespoons butter	¼ cup leftover coffee
1 teaspoon sugar	

Choose country ham so salty it will make your eyes water. Fry ham over medium heat 2 minutes on each side, a little more if you are using a thicker country ham. Overcooking will yield a tough slice of ham. Just as the ham is cooked, add the butter. Remove ham from pan, saving the drippings. Add sugar. As it begins to brown add the water and coffee. Serve over ham or biscuits.

BURNT FLOUR GRAVY

Drippings from fried chicken
  or beef or pork
Flour, a sifting to cover the
  bottom of the skillet
Chicken, beef or ham granules or
  broth

Kitchen Bouquet or similar
  seasoning
Salt & pepper
Water

From the skillet in which you have fried the chicken or meat, drain excess oil, leaving only a thin coating. Toss on a thin coat of flour, shaking pan to even out the coating. Have on hand a 2 cup measuring cup of water. Place skillet over medium heat. Watch carefully as flour begins to brown, then begin to burn. Carefully pour in about a ½ cup of water, stirring quickly with a wire whisk. Gradually add more water, chicken or meat granules and seasonings.

    Note: If you are starting from scratch and have no chicken or meat residue in you pan, and are calorie conscious, simply coat bottom of pan with cooking spray such as Pam and continue the above process. It will still produce a nice, pungent gravy for meats or chicken, rice or potatoes.

TOMATO GRAVY

Tomato gravy is great with meats. Try it on country fried steak or on fried chicken.

2 tablespoons fat
1 pound tomatoes (3/4 cup)
  chopped fine
½ cup milk
½ cup heavy cream

1 cup onion, chopped fine
2 garlic cloves, minced
1 tablespoon flour
1 teaspoon salt
1 teaspoon pepper

Sauté onion and garlic in the fat until glossy and tender. Blend the flour in the cold milk. Add this and the remaining ingredients to the onion and garlic and simmer until the mixture reaches the consistency of gravy.

The pressed glass pitcher once belonged to Mrs. Mary Temple, whose vignette appears on page 374. The ceramic bowl dating from about 1900 was Ma-Ma's. Mary Tomlinson loaned me the antique egg beater.

9..
Eggs & Cheese Dishes

Pa-Pa's Chicken House

When my grandparents married in 1910, they lived near the river. But Pa-Pa wanted "a little place where he could raise chickens." About this time a group of progressive minded citizens founded the Southport Savings & Loan (now Security Savings Bank), which they operated out of a cigar box in the back of Watson's Pharmacy. Pa-Pa went to see Doc Watson and took out the very first loan, $85.00, which he used toward the purchase of two lots and a new house "out in the country" on Atlantic Avenue just north of Leonard Street. He planted a vegetable garden, a scuppernong grapevine, a pecan tree, pear tree, and one of the few apple trees in town, although it never bore enough apples for Ma-Ma to bake a pie. Apple trees have a hard time growing in Southport.

And there was a good-sized chicken house. It was of tin, with big windows, screened with chicken wire naturally, and big tin flaps that during cold days could be lowered down like tents of a carnival concession. So chickens and eggs were very much a part of our diet.

After Pa-Pa died and Ma-Ma gave up raising chickens, I made good use of the abandoned chicken house: I turned it into a playhouse, dressed up the kids in the neighborhood and jump-started my theater career by putting on plays.

HARD BOILED EGGS – COLD WATER START METHOD

Start your eggs at room temperature in cool water. Cover completely with water. Bring to a boil and cook 15 minutes. Drain and plunge the eggs into cold water. This will cause the insides to contract slightly away from the shell, making it easier to peel.

BOILED EGGS – BOILING WATER START

Have the eggs at room temperature. Lower one by one into the boiling water with a slotted spoon. At end of boiling time, drain and plunge into cold water for 20 seconds. Soft boiled – 4 to 5 minutes boiling time. Hard boiled – 15 minutes boiling time.

159

The Egg and I

Those who understand the art of eating a soft-boiled egg are much to be admired. The egg squirms and rolls about in its little china cup, like the chicken itself fleeing the axe. I smash the thing to smithereens, leaving me with a mouthful of gritty eggshells as if I have chewed a 40 watt light bulb. Half of the egg remains in the cup. I am sulky and insolent the rest of the day.

Last year all this changed. On a memorable trip to Austria, the morning's buffet table of my hotel held a chafing dish of beautiful white soft-boiled eggs and a display of shiny white China eggcups. Tiny silver egg spoons lay out artistically. A good night's sleep had left me fit as an Olympic runner, the sun was streaming in the window across the starched, white linens on my table. A cup of good strong coffee with hot milk provided a nice jolt. Once again I rose to the challenge of mastering the soft-boiled egg.

From the corner of my eye, I watched a well-dressed gentleman have his egg. So gracefully and nonchalantly did he tap, tap, tap, the spoon in a perfect circle around the little globe sitting before him! How effortlessly did he remove the top and sink the spoon into the crater! The supple hands and fingers of a hula dancer couldn't have done it better. How I loathed and envied him.

Then, came the epiphany: It was the ritual, I realized! Yes! The ritual made the difference. No rude thoughts of the day must be allowed to intrude. The soft-boiled egg is not to be whacked and gulped down like a Big Mac takeout. The event must unfold with the serenity and holy pace of a Mass.

I took a sip of coffee, breathed three times. Perfectly relaxed, I tapped my spoon evenly around Humpty Dumpty's little belly, removed the dome, and sprinkled it with salt and pepper. My spoon slid easily through the white viscous pudding into the coveted yellow glue, and bore to my waiting lips a perfect lump. Not a shard of shell corrupted my palate, not a dollop of cholesterol escaped my tongue.

Today I look at the world a changed person. There is within me a new peace and confidence and inner glow, as if having been awarded an honorary Ph. D. or initiated into the Royal Order of the Garter. Never again shall I suffer humiliation and defeat by the embryo of a silly, clucking fowl. At last, I have conquered the soft boiled egg.

EGGS BENEDICT

A friend of mine known for wrecking the English language used to call these "Eggs Benefit." Eggs à la Benedict have been in popular cookbooks for more than a century, and nowadays this delicious dish is served in some local restaurants.

Split and toast an English muffin for each serving. Drizzle on a little melted butter. Place onto each half a thin slice of ham, or Canadian bacon or cooked asparagus, or combinations. Add a poached egg to each half, and then top with Hollandaise sauce (page 153). Sprinkle with paprika.

CREAMED EGGS

1 cup Cream Sauce, using the recipe on age 151	Salt and pepper
	Dash of Worcestershire sauce
4 hard-boiled eggs cut into quarters, or sliced	

Serve on toasted bread or biscuits and top with the White Sauce. For variations, add flaked shrimp, salmon, tuna, or diced cooked chicken or ham, or chipped beef.

DEVILED EGGS

No picnic is complete without deviled eggs.

6 eggs, hard boiled	2 tablespoons sweet relish
3 tablespoons sweet and sour mustard	Salt and pepper
	Paprika to decorate
2 tablespoons mayonnaise	

Halve the eggs lengthwise. Scoop out the yolks into a bowl and mix with the other ingredients. Fill the holes and sprinkle with paprika.

POACHED EGGS

Grease a skillet and fill with 1 inch of hot water. Add salt and ½ teaspoon vinegar. Bring to a boil, but not a high boil. Break each egg into a saucer and slip it into the water. Simmer. An egg with firm white and soft yolk takes 2 ½ minutes. Hard poached will take about 4 ½ minutes. Remove eggs with a slotted spatula or spoon.

SHIRRED EGGS

Some refer to this as "baked eggs," but "shirred" is the proper name, dating to old England. Break each egg into individual greased 3-inch baking glasses. Dot with pepper, and sprinkle on salt and pepper. Add 1 tablespoon cream to each if you like. Bake in 350° oven for about 15 to 20 minutes, or until set.

This is my favorite way to fix eggs with grits, and the easiest. I have a small frying pan with a glass top. Lightly grease the bottom, or spray with Pam, then drizzle on butter, and when melted add the egg. Don't lift the lid. When the yolk turns white it will be exactly ready.

SCRAMBLED EGGS

There is nothing easier to cook, nor to ruin, than scrambled eggs. Once on an economy airline flight I was served scrambled eggs that tasted like shredded surgical gloves, poured over with syrup. Thank goodness I had some cheese nabs in reserve.

Beat eggs with 1 teaspoon cream for each egg, add salt and pepper. Heat butter or cooking oil or bacon fat in skillet. Pour in eggs and reduce heat to low. Cook eggs slowly. When eggs begin to firm at bottom, turn gently to cook uniformly. Eggs are ready when they are still glossy and moist, only 2 or 3 minutes. Remember that eggs continue to cook for a short time after removing from the heat, so err on the moist side, unless you like shredded surgical gloves. My sister in law Genie, to my horror, fixed eggs for me by stirring them constantly from the minute she put them over the heat. They were as good as I've ever tasted.

SCRAMBLED EGGS AND FISH ROE

One of my favorite light dinners is scrambled eggs and fish roe. Simply add roughly crumbled cooked fish roe to beaten eggs and scramble. Salt and pepper.

EGGS AND FISH OR SHRIMP

Scrambled eggs and fish are also a great combination. Just add flaked, cooked fish such as salmon or boiled shrimp to the beaten eggs and scramble.

OMELETS

Beat eggs well. Add 1 tablespoon cream for each egg, salt and pepper. Pour into skillet sizzling with a little butter, or a mixture of butter and cooking oil. Cook on low heat until bottom of the omelet is set, lifting it slightly with a spatula to test. To the middle of the pan add about ½ cup of filling, from one of the following or a combination:

> Grated cheese, chopped or flaked ham, crumbled, crisp bacon, cooked asparagus tips, cooked spinach, mixed with a little White Sauce, cooked, chopped broccoli, with a little White Sauce

As soon as the omelet is set, fold over one half onto the other to close. Serve right away.

BAKED FLUFFY OMELET

Separate eggs and beat separately. The yolks should be thick and lemon colored, the whites stiff. Beat into the yolks 1 tablespoon cream per egg. Add salt and pepper. Fold this into the beaten whites. Heat butter in a cast-iron skillet until sizzling, and gently pour in the egg mixture. Bake in preheated 350° oven until golden brown, about 10 to 15 minutes. Remove from oven. Slice the omelet in half. With a wide pancake turner, lift one side and lay onto the other. Remove to warm plate. Top with cheese sauce, creamed ham, chicken or asparagus.

EGG TOAST

An easy and delicious dish for breakfast—or any time you want it—is egg toast. Beat an egg with a little cream or milk in a shallow bowl, dip in slices of bread, coating both sides, and fry in a little cooking oil or butter, or both, until brown. Turn and brown on the other side. Serve with butter, maple syrup, jam or molasses.

MACARONI AND CHEESE

1 8-ounce package of macaroni
2 recipes Cream Sauce, found
   on page 151
Few drops Tabasco sauce

1 cup Cheddar cheese, grated
½ teaspoon dry mustard
¼ teaspoon black pepper

Cook macaroni in boiling water 9 to 10 minutes. Drain and combine with the seasoned cream sauce, the dry mustard, and three-fourths of the grated cheese. Turn into deep baking dish, sprinkle remaining cheese on top and bake about a half hour in 375° oven.

CHEESE TOAST

2 tablespoons butter
3 tablespoons flour
1 cup milk
1 cup grated cheese

Slices of buttered toast
Salt to taste
Dash of cayenne

Melt butter, add flour and blend smoothly, then gradually add milk, stirring constantly, until boiling. Cook five minutes, season, and add the cheese. When melted, pour over toast in a fireproof dish and bake five minutes in hot 450° oven. Serves 4.

WELSH RAREBIT

1 pound American cheese, cut
   into small pieces
3 tablespoons butter
½ cup cream or beer

2 eggs, slightly beaten
½ teaspoon salt
½ teaspoon dry mustard
1 teaspoon Worcestershire sauce

Melt the butter and add the cheese. Cook in a double boiler, stirring constantly, until the cheese has melted. Add the salt and mustard, then the milk gradually, stirring all the while. Then add the slightly beaten eggs and stir until it is thickened. Serve on crisp toast with strips of crispy bacon and tomato slices.

HAM AND MACARONI SCALLOP

1 eight ounce package of
   macaroni
½ cup Cheddar cheese, grated
1 cup minced ham
2 tablespoons butter

1 tablespoon flour
1 cup milk
½ cup buttered bread crumbs
¼ teaspoon pepper

Break macaroni into short lengths and cook in boiling salt water 9 to 10 minutes. Make a sauce by blending butter and flour, add milk and stir to the boiling point. Season with pepper. Arrange in buttered casserole dish alternate layers of macaroni, ham and sauce, sprinkling cheese over each layer of macaroni. Top with buttered crumbs and a sprinkling of grated cheese. Bake 20 to 30 minutes in 375° oven, or until bubbling.

TOMATO AND CHEESE SOUFFLÉ

¼ cup butter
¼ cup flour
¼ cup milk
4 eggs, separated
¾ cup tomato sauce

1 teaspoon salt
Few grains cayenne
¾ cup Cheddar or Gruyerre
   cheese, grated

½ Melt butter over low heat and blend in the flour. Gradually add the egg yolks, milk and tomato sauce. Add the salt, cayenne and grated cheese. Stir until smooth. Add the grated cheese and remove from heat. Beat the egg whites until stiff. Just before baking, fold the mixture into the egg whites. Turn into unbuttered 1 ½ quart straight-sided baking dish. Set in a pan of hot water and bake. For a firm soufflé, bake in pre-heated 325° oven 30 to 45 minutes. For a creamy soufflé, bake 25 minutes at 375°.

PIMENTO CHEESE SPREAD

No picnic is complete without pimento cheese sandwiches, a local favorite.

1 8-ounce package cheddar cheese
1 or 2 4-ounce jars pimento
¼ cup mayonnaise

Dash of Worcestershire sauce
Dash of Tabasco sauce
Salt and pepper to taste

Grate the cheese, chop the pimento, and combine with other ingredients, adding pimento last, and spread on bread or crackers.

Ma-Ma's kitchen scale with some of Southport's favorite vegetables and fruits.

10..
Vegetables & Fruits

The Swamp Garden

Across Leonard Street from our front porch in Southport lies an overgrown tangle of briars and wild things. For over a hundred years gardeners from all over town came here to stake out a patchwork of little plots and grow their vegetables. It was known as the Swamp Garden. Miss Kate Stuart grew vegetables here for her famous inn on the waterfront, and sent green onions for sale at Wilmington by one of the Cape Fear steamers. These gardeners were squatters, for no one knew who owned the land; money was scarce, land aplenty. Old city maps designate the Garden as "Disputed" territory.

This netherland of wet, fertile bog seldom sees frost or freezes—some said it never froze. A little stream runs down the middle and keeps its banks moist and rich. Some call it the Swamp Garden Ditch; some, "Fiddlers' Drain" after the sand fiddlers that live in the creek as it passes through the marsh near the river. Others call it "Bonnet's Creek," after the wicked pirate who during Colonial times when the stream was navigable, would secret his ship up here. We children would play along the banks of this little River Nile to catch tadpoles, salamanders and minnows, and hope to find Stede Bonnet's treasure, which we knew for certain was buried here. Also, I have been assured, it got its name from gardeners who would play tunes on their fiddles when work was done.

There were dozens of little plots in the Garden, some separated by a low, wire fence, some by narrow ditches. Gardeners would lay little bridges of planks across the stream to get from one side to the other. Higher up on the banks overlooking the gardens were giant oaks where they would rest after cultivating their crops. Here were little sheds for storing their shovels, hoes, rakes and supplies. And for hiding their liquor from their wives.

The Garden was abandoned about twenty years ago when the last of old gardeners gave it up. Having coffee on our porch in the morning or an Episcopalian drink in the afternoon, mists often rise from its dark places when none can be seen elsewhere, and fog shrouds it in mystery. Sometimes we see a thin veil of rain falling over it, but only upon the swamp, like a specter in a haunted place that people see and click with a camera, but won't come out in their pictures.

167

TRADITIONAL SOUTHPORT VEGETABLES

Asparagus
Beans
   String beans
   Butter beans, white
   Butter beans,
      speckled
   Great Northerns
   Limas
   Navy beans
   Pole beans
   Pintos (kidney
      Beans)
Beets
Broccoli
Carrots
Corn
Cauliflower
Celery

Collards
Cabbage
Cucumber
Eggplant
Lettuce
Mustard greens
Okra
Onions
Peas
   Butter peas
   Black-eye peas
   Crowder peas
   English peas
   Field peas
   Garden peas
Peppers, sweet or hot
Potato, white
Potato, sweet

Radish
Squash
   Acorn
   Butternut
   Pattypan
   Yellow
   Zucchini
Tomatoes
Turnip greens
Turnip bottoms
Rutabaga turnips
   (Wax turnips)
Purple tops

Processed
   Grits
   Rices

ABOUT ASPARAGUS

Asparagus is a most versatile vegetable. It may be served as a hot side dish topped with butter and lemon sauce or a Hollandaise, prepared in a casserole, or made into soup. It can be chilled and eaten cold, topped with a sprinkle of lemon juice or a drop of mayonnaise, used in salads.

Nowadays asparagus comes fresh, canned or frozen. Choose bright, juicy looking stalks, the pencil thin young sprouts in the spring, or thicker year 'round. Slice off ½ inch from the bottom and place standing up in a glass of cold water in the refrigerator until ready for use. The sprouts will continue to drink the water and stay fresh, like cut flowers. When ready to cook, bend them one at a time until they naturally break, and discard the white bottom part, which will be tough and grainy. Then slice the bottoms for an even look. If the asparagus is thick, trim the thick end section lengthwise with a potato peeler. Thin, fresh early spring asparagus rarely needs trimming. Good, fresh asparagus tips take only a few minutes to cook. As soon as a cake tester goes through, they will have lost their bitterness and should be tender and brittle as butter mints.

White asparagus is green asparagus that has been denied sunlight by banking it over with soil, and harvested when it pokes through the top of the mound. It is more expensive, since its cultivation is more time consuming.

Canned asparagus is almost a different vegetable from the fresh kind. It is limp, but has a richness and sweetness all its own, a bit like spinach. There's no better light lunch or dinner than canned asparagus on toast, topped with a good white sauce. Frozen asparagus is stringy and watery and unsuccessful.

ASPARAGUS CASSEROLE

3 cans cut asparagus
1 can cream of chicken soup
1 can cream of celery soup
Small jar of mushrooms
1 small can water chestnuts,
    cut into small pieces

Grated Cheddar cheese, enough
    to cover casserole generously
Crushed cornflakes

Mix ingredients except cheese and corn flakes. Pour into casserole dish. Cover top with crushed cornflakes, then grated Cheddar cheese. Bake in medium 350° oven about 40 minutes, or until browning and bubbly.

AUNT CONTENT'S ASPARAGUS SUPREME

2 tablespoons butter
2 tablespoons flour
¾ cup milk
1 teaspoon grated onion

1 ½ cups grated Cheddar cheese
3 eggs, separated
1 ½ cups cut green asparagus
Salt and pepper to taste

Make a cream sauce with the butter, flour and milk. Add the onion, cheese and beaten egg yolks, salt and pepper. Add the asparagus. In a separate bowl, beat the egg whites until stiff. Fold into the cream mixture and pour into casserole dish. Bake in a 350° oven for 30 minutes. Serve promptly.

SMOKED-PORK STOCK

For preparing fresh butter beans or string beans, collards or other greens, and many other foods, begin with a cup or more of smoked-pork stock. Stock may be refrigerated for a week or frozen for 6 months.

1 pound of smoked ham hocks,
    ham, or salt pork with streak of
    lean, or a combination of both

1 medium onion, roughly cut
2 quarts water
Salt as needed

Rinse the meat, place in a large stockpot with the onion, and cover with water. Simmer uncovered for a full 2 hours.

169

FRESH BUTTER BEANS

1 quart fresh butter beans   1 cup smoked-pork stock from
¼ pound bacon, salt meat, or ham   recipe above
Salt and pepper to taste   Pinch of sugar

Add enough smoked-pork stock to come to cover the beans. Boil slowly until tender, about 15 minutes. Serve on rice, or as a side dish.

FRESH BUTTER BEANS AND OKRA

Prepare the fresh butter beans with the above recipe. Lay the steamed okra side by side on top of the beans, cover and cook until tender. It's a great combination.

FRESH SNAP BEANS OR OTHER GREEN BEANS
WITH NEW POTATOES

Green beans and little new potatoes can be a meal by themselves. Serve with a bit of cornbread.

Pull the strings from each side of the beans and discard. Wash. Cover beans with about 2 cups smoked-pork stock. Add about a dozen little new potatoes. Boil about 10 minutes. Add beans and cook until both potatoes and beans are tender.

POLE BEANS IN SMOKED-PORK STOCK

Cook pole beans as you would fresh green beans, but they usually take longer before they are tender.

SOUTHERN STYLE GREEN BEANS, USING CANNED BEANS

Green beans right out of the can tastes as if they were seasoned with gun powder. But properly prepared Southern Style they are unbeatable.

Canned green beans   or bacon drippings
Broth, chicken or vegetable   Onions, if desired, sliced
Bacon, 1 or 2 slices or
    Pork fat back,

Drain and wash beans, discarding liquid. In a saucepan, heat broth, chicken or vegetable and pork fat, bacon or drippings for 10 to 15 minutes. Add beans and simmer slowly for 15 minutes.

PREPARING DRY PEAS OR BEANS FOR COOKING

There are two basic ways to prepare dry peas or beans: by soaking in cold water overnight, then slow cooking; or by bringing them to a boil in a large pot, letting sit for an hour, then simmering until tender.

1 pound dry peas or beans	1 medium onion chopped
2 smoked pork knuckles,	Water to cover
or 4 slices of salt pork,	Salt and pepper to taste
or bacon, or a	
combination of meats	

Simmer the meat, onion, salt and pepper in a large boiler on medium-low heat for a long time, an hour or more is not too long. This provides a tasty broth that will be absorbed by the peas or beans. Rinse the peas or beans and add to the pot. Bring to a boil and cook 1 minute. Remove from heat and set aside for an hour. Then resume cooking for about 30 minutes. Be on your guard, for dried peas or beans tend to be crunchy one minute, mushy the next.

HOPPIN' JOHN

Hoppin' John is dried peas or beans with rice. It can be made in many styles. Here is one:

1 pound of dried peas or beans	1 tablespoon butter
½ cup cooked rice	Salt and pepper to taste

Prepare 1 pound of dry peas or beans using the above recipe. Drain and set aside the peas. Boil down the liquid the peas have been cooked in until thick. Return the peas to this broth. Add the cooked rice, butter, and stir.

HERBED & SPICY BLACK EYED PEAS

Years ago I was included in a house party in upstate New York. A blizzard hit and we were snowbound for two days. These were the days when I was paid by the day, so I was hard hit. But our host was a Southerner and a good cook. He cooked up a big pot of herbed and spicy black eyed peas that was memorable, and that snowstorm was the best misfortune I ever had. Use the basic dry pea or bean recipe above. To the broth add the following. They're even better the second day.

1 large onion, cut rough
1 slice raw bacon
2 or more slices salt pork
1 tablespoon sage
1 tablespoon rosemary,
  finely crushed
4 plump garlic cloves crushed

1/8 teaspoon thyme finely
  crushed
1/4 teaspoon Tabasco sauce
2 bay leaves
1 teaspoon ketchup
Garlic salt to taste
A little black pepper

SWEETHEART'S BAKED BEANS

2 16-ounce cans pork & beans
½ can water (8 ounces)
½ cup molasses
1 medium onion, chopped
4 tablespoons ketchup

1 tablespoon vinegar
3 to 4 bacon strips, uncooked
1 tablespoon Worcestershire
  sauce

Mix all ingredients in a baking pan, top with the bacon strips and bake for an hour or more in slow oven, about 325°, or until liquid thickens. I rinse out the bean cans in about ½ cup water and reserve to correct consistency at the end of cooking. My mother says, "I usually bake in large amounts, at least a double recipe, as this can be frozen if left over."

BEETS

Wash and cut off all but 1 inch of the tops. Do not slice or cut, as they will lose much of their distinctly beet flavor, bleed during cooking and look like white turnips. Boil in 6 cups water to which 1 tablespoon white vinegar has been added to preserve color. Boil about 40 minutes covered, or until tender. Cool. Peel and serve whole or sliced.

172

BEET GREENS

Beet greens (tops) make a delicious side dish provided they are fresh. Cook until tender in water with a little vinegar, sugar and salt. Drain. Serve as they are, or add butter.

HARVARD BEETS

2 cups beets, prepared as above, or canned beets, sliced or small whole beets
2 tablespoons butter

3 tablespoons honey
1 teaspoon vinegar
¼ teaspoon nutmeg
½ teaspoon salt

Drain the liquid. In a saucepan combine the butter, honey, vinegar and nutmeg. Simmer uncovered for about 5 minutes. Add the beets and pour the mixture over.

ABOUT BROCCOLI

George H. W. Bush once declared that he was President now, had never liked broccoli, and banished it from the White House. I often agree with him. There's nothing nastier than mushy, watery broccoli made from a package of frozen broccoli left in the freezer too long. But properly prepared from a tender, fresh head, just cooked, broccoli is just fine, so make sure you start off with that. Served topped with a butter and lemon, or a cheese sauce, or with a good Hollandaise, it is delectable. Buy bunches that are fresh looking, with bud clusters compact and showing no yellow color. Keep broccoli cold and humid and use as soon as possible. Cut lengthwise gashes in the stems to assure even cooking. If the head has been around too long and is very dark green and lacks luster, it may be too strong to eat, but will make good soup.

ABOUT CABBAGE

What a gift is the lowly cabbage! It can be used to make coleslaw, salads, stuffed with meats and breading as a main course, or cooked or baked as a side dish and served with butter and sour cream. Cabbage was the first cultivated vegetable of the genus Brassica, ancestor to such diverse relatives as cauliflower and Brussels sprouts. The ancient Egyptians prized it. The Greeks thought that "Cabbage served twice is death." The Romans thought it would protect against a hangover. They were quite wrong. Cabbage arrived in America with the earliest explorers and settlers. And of course, no St. Patrick's Day would be complete without corned beef and cabbage.

173

CABBAGE

To prepare, cut the head in quarters and soak half an hour in salted water, then steam or boil until tender. Cutting the stem crosswise will help assure consistent tenderness. Leftover cooked cabbage may be fried or baked as a secondary dish. It is generally served with vinegar and pepper, but some prefer it buttered.

ABOUT CARROTS

Carrots vary greatly in taste. Freshly pulled small, young carrots have a delicate and sweet taste. Large carrots 2 inches or more in diameter at the base are heartier and richer in taste.

CARROTS

Peel and slice nice fresh, carrots with a high, orange sheen, either thinly crosswise, or in 3-inch strips Julienne style. Drop into boiling water to which a little sugar and salt have been added. Boil for 2 to 3 minutes, then begin testing with a cake-tester or toothpick for doneness. The tester should go in easily; but do not allow the carrots to become mushy. Drain, stir in a little butter or margarine, in a cream sauce, and serve.

TANGY GINGER CARROTS

Peel and drain the carrots. Jullienne, or slice into curls thinly with a potato. Boil until they have lost their crunchiness, but are tender. Drain. In a skillet melt 2 tablespoons butter and 1 teaspoon olive oil. Add 2 tablespoons honey, and 1 tablespoon finely shredded fresh ginger, or ½ teaspoon dried, ground ginger. Sauté carrots in the mixture over low heat to avoid browning the butter for 5 to 10 minutes. Add a little more butter and a pinch of brown sugar. Simmer until hot, and serve.

CARROT SOUFFLÉ

1 ½ pounds carrots, sliced	1 ½ teaspoons baking powder
½ cup butter or margarine	1 ½ cups sugar
3 large eggs	¼ teaspoon ground cinnamon
¼ cup all-purpose flour	

Boil carrots 20 to 25 minutes until very tender. Process carrots and all remaining ingredients in blender or food processor until smooth and fluffy. Bake in 350° oven for 1 hour and 10 minutes or until set. Serves about 6.

CARROT SOUFFLÉ WITH PECANS

To the basic recipe for Carrot Soufflé above, add ½ cup chopped pecans, toasted, and 1 tablespoon grated orange rind before baking.

CARROTS, GERMAN STYLE
Annie May Woodside's Cook Book (1913)

"Clean and cut carrots in one-half inch cubes. Cover with boiling salted water and cook until tender. Make a drawn-butter sauce using carrot water, to which has been added a little sugar and nutmeg. Pour the sauce of which there should be one-half as much as vegetable, over the carrots and cook together five minutes. Serve at once."

CELERY WITH CREAM
The Carolina Housewife (1847)

"Wash a bunch of celery; boil it soft in water; cut the sticks in pieces, two inches long. Make a good sauce, with a pint of milk, flour, and salt; put the celery in, let it have a boil up, and serve."

ABOUT CAULIFLOWER

Of this relative to the cabbage, an old recipe reads, "It is a very taking vegetable, and if cooked just right is delicious. The head should be a creamy white, without spot or blemish. Pick off the outside leaves, and soak in salted water for half an hour. Put into boiling water twenty minutes, or until tender. It may be served with a cream or a Hollandaise sauce, or even plain vinegar and pepper. It is also good cold with a mayonnaise dressing."

Like broccoli, slicing the stem of the cauliflower crosswise in several places will help assure consistent tenderness.

A whole cauliflower on a its own plate or dish, topped with white sauce and sprinkled with paprika, or Hollandaise, and brought to the table makes an impressive dish.

BAKED CAULIFLOWER AND CARROTS IN CHEESE SAUCE
Favorite Recipes of North Carolina (1944)

1 medium head cauliflower	1 cup half & half
1 cup raw carrots, peeled and diced	1 cup Natural American Cheese, grated
¼ cup onions, chopped	Salt
2 tablespoons butter, melted	Paprika

Break cauliflower into flowerettes. Arrange these with carrots in buttered casserole. Cover with onion, seasonings and butter. Pour milk over contents. Sprinkle with cheese. Cover. Bake in moderate 350° oven 1 hour, removing cover the last 15 minutes.

Harry Robinson's Collard Greens

Harry Robinson's general merchandise store was on the east side of Howe Street just north of Moore, a big, rickety, frame building with a false front like out of an old Western movie, decorated with tin signs advertising Orange Crush and Kools cigarettes. It had a counter for selling a few groceries on the right as you entered, and just about everything else you could think of, scattered helter-skelter elsewhere. Galvanized tin pails, speckled blue coffee pots, brooms, rakes, pea-diggers and rocking chairs hung from the ceiling.

At the rear, sitting on a raised platform, was Maude Inman, a woman of enormous proportions, Harry's wife, or girl friend—who knew? She stood guard over the place like a prison warden, usually in a house dress and apron. Small children were terrified to come into the place when she was on duty.

Harry once won a contest, the prize of which was a vacation in the Caribbean. People asked,

"Harry, aren't you getting ready for your trip?"

"Nope," he answered. "No need."

He took with him but one item—an empty suitcase. He'd buy anything he needed along the way and fill his suitcase.

During the early 1950's I was doing some sign painting to make a little extra money. Harry hired me to paint a sign, "701 Service Store," for he was about to sell out and relocate with a store and gas pumps out front on Route 701 just north of Clinton. He had a late-in-life young son of whom he was very proud, and we heard the boy had been hit by a car in front of the new store. Harry, a high-strung man, had picked up his young son and put him in the car, but got so excited he couldn't get the

176

car in the right gear, and raced it swerving and charging in reverse all the way to the hospital.

We were taking Mikael back to N.C. State in Raleigh one day and Daddy wanted to stop by and see how Harry was doing. We found him sitting in a rocker out front of his store having his breakfast—a plate piled high with pancakes and blueberries. He invited us to have breakfast with him, but since it was already past noon, we declined. He told us,

"When I'm eatin' pancakes, I only eat pancakes. When I'm eatin' cabbage, I only eat cabbage. When I'm eatin' collards, I only eat collards!"

Well cooked collards are good enough to eat by themselves. So when you have them next, think of Harry Robinson.

COLLARD GREENS

Collards are great as a side dish, or as a main course with a good piece of steaming hot corn bread fresh out of the oven or skillet; or with corn bread dumplings dropped on top and steamed for a while.

Collards are best in the late fall after a frost has hit them. If you have a head that is nice and rich green and well filled out, but hasn't been visited by a frost, put them in the freezer for an hour. This will break down the fibers just enough.

When serving, have a bottle of hot pepper vinegar handy. Leftover cooked collards freeze well.

1 head of collards
2 cups, or more as need, smoked
　　pork stock from recipe above

Salt and pepper to taste

Cut the stalk and tough lower stems and discard. Wash several times very well. Place leaves on cutting board four or five thick and slice into 2-inch squares. Heat about 4 inches of smoked pork stock in a large stockpot. Add salt and pepper. Add the chopped collards and boil on medium heat about 10 minutes. Turn them every few minutes at first as those on the bottom will collapse first and you want them to cook evenly. When all are collapsed and under the seasoned water, cook on low heat until tender, about another 15 to 20 minutes. Watch them carefully, as some varieties of collards cook very quickly these days.

Cassie and "Joe Poke" Cochran, 1984. Behind them, left to right,
are their children, Gerald, Paul, Joe. Jr., Jimmy, and Jean.

Cassie Cochran's Corn On the Cob

The Cochrans lived in a nice brick house near the city limits. Cassie and
her husband Joe Poke had four strapping boys of my generation, Joe,
Jimmy, Paul and Gerald, and a girl, Jean, who at the time I'm talking
about in the 1950's was a baby. The boys all loved corn, but were always
complaining that they didn't get enough of it. One day Cassie said to her
husband,

"I'm going to fix them. Joe, go out in the field and pull me a
bushel of corn. I'll fill those young'uns up once and for all!"

She made tea, shucked and cooked up a bushel of corn. That's
what they got—tea and corn on the cob. They ate every bit of it. Paul
was the champ—he ate thirteen ears. And none was left over for Joe
Poke.

CORN ON THE COB

Shuck not the corn until you are ready to cook it. To do so ahead of time
will make it starchy. Store in a cool place until ready to shuck. Slice off
top and bottom. Remove shucks and corn silk. Rinse, and drop into a big
pot of boiling water. Boil 1 minute, or until tender. Drain. Butter, salt and

178

serve. Frozen, shucked corn on the cob is never successful. It is mushy and watery, like something drowned and pulled from a pond for crime evidence. Corn in the shucks freezes well. Place in plastic bags, and freeze. When ready to use, thaw, shuck, then steam boil or grill. If grilling, leave in the shucks and grill slowly until steaming hot inside.

CREAMED CORN

Creamed corn put up in plastic freezing containers or washed milk cartons freezes just fine.

1 dozen ears fresh corn	Pinch of sugar, except when
1/3 cup butter	using Silver Queen or other
1/4 cup half & half	very sweet variety
1 cup water	Salt and pepper

Slice off top and bottom. Remove shucks, corn silk and cut off ends. With sharp paring knife, slice each row of kernels from top to bottom. Place the cobs standing up in a very shallow dish or plate one at a time, and with the back of the knife facing downward, drag the blade of the knife down the cob, pressing out the pulp from the kernels. Place the corn pulp in a sauce pan, add butter and a little water, salt and pepper and boil very slowly about 10 to 20 minutes. Add the half & half.

ABOUT EGGPLANT

"Eggplant" is the name we use in North America for the Aubergine, botanically a fruit and not a vegetable. It is a versatile food, goes with many meat dishes, or stands alone as a side dish. Until recently, in our area the eggplant came in one style—plump and purple. Nowadays a dizzying variety of colors and shapes line the shelves of the market. A generation ago most Southerners were used to the basic style of preparation—frying slices in oil, or using it in some pickling recipe. Nowadays there are easily available recipes for Eggplant Lasagna, Moussaka, etc. With the increased sophistication of American cooking, I'm sure that recipes for eggplant alone would fill a fat cookbook. We'll stick to the familiar plump purple variety and the smaller Italian purple variety.

Selecting the eggplant

At her Thanksgiving table a few years ago, my friend Kay Monteleone served the best fried eggplant ever. I asked her to talk me through the recipe.

"Choose fresh, firm, shiny eggplants," She began, "And most important, make certain you choose the male. Not the female. The female has lots of seeds. The male has few."

"How do you tell the difference?" I asked. She put her hand over her face in embarrassment. Kay was up in years, and a conservative, pious woman.

"No one ever told you?"

"No."

"Well... I suppose I will. The male has a pointed tip on the end away from the stalk. The female is indented." (This test seems to be more reliable for the smaller Italian eggplant.)

FRIED EGGPLANT

The eggplant may be peeled or unpeeled, depending your taste. Tender, young eggplant may not need peeling. Cut into ½ inch slices, or slightly thinner if you wish. A salting preparation is necessary to draw out excessive water; otherwise your recipes will be mushy and soggy. Lay on a dry towel and salt. Cover with a towel or paper towel. After 20 minutes, turn and salt the other side, discarding the moist towel. Repeat the process at least three times. When dry, they are ready for cooking.

To fry, simply brown in a skillet with a thin layer of cooking oil, bacon drippings, olive oil, butter, or a combination of these oils. The slices may also be placed on a cookie sheet and browned in the oven. They may be dusted with flour or cornmeal, but this is not necessary.

BAKED EGGPLANT SLICES

1 medium unpeeled eggplant, cut in ½ inches (about 1 pound)	1 tablespoon lemon juice
1 cup mayonnaise	¼ teaspoon salt
¼ cup milk	3 cups finely crushed cheese flavored round crackers

Prepare eggplant slices by sprinkling salt on both sides and place on paper towels. Allow to weep for a half hour. Pat dry. Repeat process. In a bowl combine mayonnaise, milk, lemon juice and salt. Dip eggplant slices into mixture, then coat with cracker or bread crumbs. Place on ungreased baking pan. Bake in 350° oven for 25 to 30 minutes or until slices are crisp and hot. Makes 6 servings.

MUSTARD GREENS

Follow the basic collard recipe on page 177, but use mustard greens.

FRIED OKRA

Frozen okra may be substituted for fresh, but make sure it hasn't been in the freezer too long and frosted over. Avoid old, tough and stringy okra. It won't improve with cooking. Fried okra needs to be served hot.

1 pound fresh okra	Cooking oil in a skillet or Dutch
1 ½ cups corn meal or	oven 1 to 2 inches deep, or fry
cracker meal	in cooker with basket
1 egg	Salt and pepper to taste
½ cup water	

Slice off and discard the greater part of the stem end without cutting into the pod. Okra may be fried whole, or cut into smaller pieces. Wash and roll on paper towels to dry. Beat the egg and water together. Dip the okra into the egg and water mixture, then into the corn or cracker meal. Fry in skillet about 12 minutes until golden brown. Lay on paper towel to absorb excess oil. Salt and pepper.

STEAMED OKRA

Many people take one look at steamed okra and say, "Are you really going to *eat* that?!" They choke at the thought of eating those slimy, gummy little pods wiggling around in a pot of water. Some love them cooked that way—simply stemmed and thrown in a pot of boiling salt water. I'll eat them any way. But overcooking destroys the delicate, unmistakable okra flavor and its interesting texture. Try steaming it for about 10 minutes in a flat-bottomed colander. Flavor with a little butter or margarine, salt and pepper.

SOUTHERN OKRA

Bring okra to a boil, cover and cook gently 8 to 10 minutes, or until tender. Drain and set aside. Fry 4 strips bacon, crumble and add to okra. Sauté ¼ cup chopped onions in bacon fat. Combine okra, bacon and onions, season with salt and pepper and serve.

OKRA AND TOMATOES

This very popular, very easy, very Southern dish goes way back.

2 cups stewed tomatoes
1 tablespoon butter
½ cup onions, chopped
2 cups okra, fresh or frozen
   or canned

1 teaspoon sugar
Salt and pepper to taste

Sauté the onions in the butter slowly until they are glossy. Add the remaining ingredients and simmer slowly. If fresh okra is used, trim the hard stem end and discard the stem. The okra may be left whole, or sliced crossways in 1-inch pieces.

OKRA FRITTERS

Use fresh or frozen okra. Trim stems, but do not cut into pods. Boil 2 cups okra tender but not mushy. Drain well. Dip pods in beaten egg, then roll in cracker crumbs. Fry in hot grease until golden brown.

FRIED OKRA FRITTERS MADE WITH BATTER

Make a batter of self-rising corn-bread mix plus a little flour. Mix with an egg and enough buttermilk to make a thick batter. Stir in uncooked okra, whole pods or cut into 1-inch pieces. Fry in hot oil (not too hot or they will burn before cooking the inside) until golden brown. Salt and pepper and serve immediately.

BAKED ONIONS

Onions, butter, salt and pepper

Choose fresh, firm fairly large onions. Peel. Slice a little off the top and bottom, then slice in half crosswise. Place in a casserole dish, drizzle with butter, then sprinkle with salt and pepper. Cover and bake in 400° oven about 30 minutes. Puncture with a cake tester to see if done.

Note: Baked onions can be cooked in the microwave oven in a matter of minutes. Prepare as indicated below, but cook in a microwave dish with cover. Baked onions are a delicious low carbohydrate substitute for a starch.

CARAMELIZED ONIONS

Caramelized onions are delicious as an accompaniment for steaks and other meats or fowl.

1 large Vidalia or other sweet onion, julienned	2 teaspoons water
1 teaspoon olive oil	Sprinkle of sugar

Simmer slowly over low heat for about 30 minutes, until onions become transparent and amber color.

FRENCH FRIED ONION RINGS
Brunswick Potluck Cookbook
Contributed by Annie Lou Newton

Onions	Accent seasoning
1 pint milk	Salt and pepper
4 egg whites	Oil to deep-fat fry
Flour	

Take large onions and slice in the round. Separate the onion rings and place in enough milk to cover, about 1 pint, and place in refrigerator for 30 minutes. Beat the whites of 4 eggs until frothy. Dip onion rings in egg whites, and then dip in plain flour that has 1/8 teaspoon Accent added, and black pepper and a pinch of salt. Fry in deep fat until a golden brown. Drain on paper toweling.

PUMPKIN PURÉE

2 pounds fresh pumpkin	1 teaspoon salt
3 tablespoons butter	½ teaspoon black pepper
¼ cup heavy cream	Pinch of nutmeg

Peel and chop pumpkin into 2-inch cubes. Boil in salted water for 20 minutes, or until the pumpkin is tender. Drain the pumpkin well. Pass the pumpkin through a food mill or processor and purée finely. Place over low heat and add butter and seasonings.

RUTABAGAS

The rutabaga turnip is a wonderful food. Low in calories, low in carbohydrates, and full of things good for you. They can be served with just butter, salt and pepper, or mashed and flavored with bacon drippings, sautéed onions, bacon crumbs, and Worcestershire sauce. Sour cream is a good additive.

RUTABAGAS MADE EASY

The problem is that the rutabaga is hard to peal raw, and takes an axe to split. So boil it first, let it cool, and then it will be more obedient. The microwave method is to me the easiest and best, and unlike many vegetables, the rutabaga does not suffer from being microwaved. Rinse off the rutabaga. Place in a microwave-proof container and bake about 6 minutes per pound, testing toward the end of the cooking period with a cake tester for doneness. Let it alone until warm to the touch, then peel and process as you like. You may find a wax residue in your cooking container; they are also called Wax turnips. A little hot water will wash it away.

SQUASH—YELLOW SUMMER SQUASH OR PATTYPAN

Choose young, glossy squash that are heavy in relation to their size. The smaller, the tenderer they are likely to be. Young, yellow summer squash need little cooking; in fact, they can be added to salads raw.

STEAMED SQUASH

Squash are good simply washed, top and bottom trimmed, sliced, steamed and served with a little butter, salt and pepper. Some people boil their squash, but this tends to leave them soggy and removed of taste. (The squash, not the people.)

FRIED SQUASH WITH ONIONS AND SCALLIONS

Fry out 2 slices of bacon in a skillet. Sauté sliced squash with chopped onion or scallions. Fry slowly until fully cooked and browned, turning to brown on both sides. Salt and pepper to taste.

SQUASH CASSEROLE

4 cups or more of fresh yellow
  squash, sliced
5 tablespoons butter or margarine
½ cup onion, chopped
4 ounces sharp Cheddar cheese,
  shredded
2 large eggs, beaten

1/4 cup mayonnaise
2 teaspoons sugar
1/2 teaspoon salt
1/8 teaspoon pepper
1 to 2 cups buttery type crackers,
  crushed

Boil or steam squash 5 to 8 minutes until tender but not mushy. Drain well, pressing down with a towel or paper towel to remove liquid. In a skillet, melt ½ of the butter in a skillet, add the chopped onion and sauté about 5 minutes, until glossy but not brown. Remove from heat, stir in the squash, cheese, mayonnaise, sugar and salt. Turn into lightly greased 11x7-inch baking dish. Sprinkle on the crushed crackers. Melt the remaining butter and drizzle over the top. Bake in 350° oven 30 to 35 minutes.

SQUASH FRITTERS

1 cup yellow squash, cooked but
  not mushy, then chopped
½ cup onions, minced, not
  cooked
1 egg well beaten
1 tablespoon canned milk

Salt and pepper to taste
Bisquick or self-rising flour, as
  needed
Vegetable oil and butter, or bacon
  grease, to fry
Red pepper flakes, optional

Strain and pat dry the cooked squash with a towel or paper towel. Mix the squash with the onions and beaten egg, salt and pepper. Sprinkle on and stir in just enough Bisquick or self-rising flour to form a stiff batter. Too much breading will detract from the squash. Heat the oil or grease in a skillet, just enough to sizzle when the batter is added. Drop by spoonfuls into small patties of no more than 2 inches wide, and fry on low heat. Tiny air vents will form, like pancakes. Test with spatula to see if browned on the first side, then turn and brown the second. Serve hot.

TURNIP GREENS WITH BOTTOMS

Follow the basic collard recipe above. As with all greens and things from the earth, wash well. If you like, peel the turnip bottoms, cut into 2-inch cubes, and add to the pot.

VICKIE HARDEE'S BUTTERNUT SQUASH CASSEROLE

Many cooks fix a good butternut squash. My sister-in-law developed this, and wouldn't part with the recipe until she had perfected it to her satisfaction. It's ambrosial. Note: Butternut squash, like the rutabaga turnip, is hard and difficult to cut. An average sized butternut can be tamed by blasting it in the microwave for 5 minutes, then continuing with the recipe.

3 cups of puréed butternut
squash (about 3 squash)
½ cup granulated white sugar
1 cup milk
2 tablespoons all purpose flour
3 eggs
¼ cup butter or margarine

1 teaspoon vanilla
1 teaspoon orange extract
1 cup good quality vanilla
wafers, crushed
¼ cup melted butter
1 cup light brown sugar
¼ teaspoon salt

Cook butternut squash by cutting in half and turning meat side down, then steaming until tender and scooping out the meat. Scoop out the insides and purée in blender or food processor until the consistency of baby food. (Or, you may boil the meats, and then proceed.)

Combine puréed squash, sugar, milk, vanilla, orange extract, salt, flour, eggs and melted butter. Pour into a 4 to 6 cup casserole dish. Bake at 400° for 45 minutes, or until set. In a medium bowl, combine the vanilla wafers, melted butter and brown sugar. Sprinkle over top of cooked casserole and return to oven to brown for 10 minutes. The top should be very, very brown, almost mahogany, and gorgeous.

ABOUT TOMATOES

Some call them "Love Apples." Not Vice President Dan Quayle, who once got into trouble when showing off before a group of school children on TV he went to the blackboard and added an "E" to "tomato." The singular is "tomato," the plural is "tomatoes." Just as the singular is "potato," and the plural is "potatoes."

Grandma Hardee once wrote in her diary, "I still love tomatoes at age 90." She loved tomatoes to the end of her life and lived to 102 ½. And who doesn't love tomatoes! There is nothing like a fresh, plump local vine-ripened tomato, juicy and red as cherry Jell-O, tasting more like a fruit than a vegetable. In fact, it was classified a fruit until 1893 when the Justices ruled it was a vegetable.

Although indelibly linked in our minds with Italy, the tomato actually originated in South America, traveled north to the Aztecs where it picked up its name from their word "tomatl," meaning plump fruit. Then it traveled to north America, and only in the 16th Century did it cross to Spain, Italy and the rest of Europe.

And what a disappointment are so many of the commercially grown tomatoes they stick us with these days—pithy, with tough skins, and tasteless. I think they grow them in caves beside the mushrooms. Hydroponic tomatoes are juicy and photogenic, but too often are bland. If none in the supermarket look any too tempting, try a good brand of canned whole tomatoes.

The tomato is one of the most versatile of vegetables, good for sauces, soups, stews, salads, sandwiches, for flavoring an endless number of dishes, or just eaten as is.

TO KEEP TOMATOES THE WHOLE YEAR
(DRIED TOMATOES)
The Carolina Housewife (1847)

"Take the tomatoes, when perfectly ripe, and scald them in hot water, in order to take off the skin easily. When skinned, boil them well in a little sugar or salt, but no water. Then spread them in cakes about an inch thick, and place the cakes in the sun. They will, in three or four days, be sufficiently dried to pack away in bags, which should hang in a dry place."

SCALLOPED TOMATOES

1 14 ½-ounce canned tomatoes, sliced	½ teaspoon pepper
	2 teaspoons sugar
¼ cup onion, minced	4 slices white bread
Butter to drizzle	7 tablespoons butter, melted
1 teaspoon salt	

Cut off the crusts of the bread and toast it. Lay it in a casserole dish, and drizzle with butter. Sprinkle on the onion, salt, pepper and sugar. Add the tomatoes. Bake in 375° oven for 35 minutes covered, and for 10 additional minutes uncovered.

187

TRADITIONAL SOUTHPORT FRUITS & BERRIES

Locally grown fruits
Apples
Apricots
Cantaloupe
Cherries
Citron
Crab apples
Grapes, Scuppernong
  and Concord
Haw apples
Pears
Persimmon,
  both wild and
  Japanese
Plums, both wild
  and cultivated

Quince
Watermelon

Locally grown nuts
Peanuts (a legume)
Pecans
Chinquapins

The local berries
Blackberries
Blueberries
Huckleberries
Sparkle berries
Strawberries

Imported fruits
Bananas
Cumquats
Grapefruits
Lemons
Limes
Oranges
Pineapple
Tangerines

Carried Away by Carolina Blueberries

The woods in these parts used to abound with many wild berries, blackberries, huckleberries, and sparkleberries, which resemble blueberries but are smaller. You can still find them from time to time if you are lucky. Blueberries are grown commercially hereabouts.

Local Southeast North Carolina blueberries are the aristocrats of blueberries, I swear. There is something about the soil and the salt air and moist climate that gives them a unique aroma and taste. The imported varieties lack the flavor and aroma. Not long ago a push cart on the corner where I live in New York had pints of blueberries for sale. I picked one up, gave it a sniff, and was instantly transported hundreds of miles south to my homeland. "North Carolina berries!" I exclaimed. Sure enough, the label read, "Burgaw, NC." True story.

ABOUT PEARS

"I've never forgiven the pear for not being an apple." Where I read that I forget, but I haven't forgotten the remark, which made me chuckle. I don't know why we treat the pear like a poor relation we are slightly ashamed of. It's difficult to grow apples in Southport, but pears thrive. Chunks of fresh pear add a special touch to fruit cups. Sliced pears preserved in a light sugar syrup have a wonderful, slightly gritty texture and an almost nutty flavor the apple lacks. Poached, they make a delicious dessert that holds its own with any sweet.

POACHED PEARS

Pears	1 teaspoon lemon juice
2 tablespoons butter or margarine	½ teaspoon nutmeg
¼ cup sugar	1/8 teaspoon cinnamon
½ cup water	Dash of salt

Let's start with about four pears. That will give four persons two halves, or eight people a half. Slice in half and scoop out the core. In a skillet boil butter, sugar and water slowly to form a light syrup. Add the lemon juice and spices. Place the pears in the skillet and drizzle on syrup. Poach until tender, about 10 minutes. Drizzle on more syrup. Serve plain with the syrup, or with whipped cream.

"When a man is tired of London, he is tired of life," said Dr. Johnson. We could say the same of fish and grits, meat and potatoes, or rice and gravy.

11..
Potatoes, Grits & Rice

Pounding the Preacher

In the old days, money was very scarce. When a new preacher and his family arrived to take up his ministry, it was the custom for the congregation to give them a "pounding." Each member brought a pound of something—potatoes, flour, etc. A. L. Brown arrived as minister of the Southport Baptist Church in 1937. Two of his daughters remember the day. Myrtle Brown Watson told me,

"They had piled the kitchen table of the parsonage high— foodstuffs, flour, rice, grits and the like. It made us feel good, welcome." Lula Brown McKeithan agreed.

"It made us feel as if we were home." She also recalled that while the Southport church always paid its preacher a salary, there were churches out in the state that from time to time paid off with poundings—"chickens, eggs, vegetables, anything the family needed."

So it made me feel warm to know that only recently the Baptists had given their preacher an honest to goodness old fashioned pounding!

BAKED POTATOES

Baked potatoes will be just fine tossed into the oven and baked. But nobody baked better potatoes than my father, and here's how he did it: Wash and wrap medium sized Idahos in aluminum foil. Bake in hot 450° for two hours. They come out creamy and almost like whipped potatoes, except they are in a nice shell. Before removing from the foil, smash them and roll a bit to break them down. Then split open and top with butter or margarine or other toppings.

TOPPINGS FOR BAKED POTATOES

Any combinations of these are great: shredded Cheddar cheese mixed with sour cream; sour cream with chopped onions and scallions; cottage cheese mixed with butter or margarine; sour cream mixed with cream cheese sprinkled with crisp bacon pieces; sour cream blended with butter or margarine; sour cream with chopped stuffed olives, or chives, or minced garlic; or any of the above seasoned with garlic salt and pepper.

FRENCH FRIES

French fries can be prepared in countless ways, cut thick, cut like matchsticks, peeled or unpeeled, dredged in starch, sprinkled with salt and sugar, you name it. Old Mack's Cafe down on the waterfront used to serve great fries. The following method, though a bit of trouble, is sure to please:

4 large, long Idaho potatoes
Peanut oil
Kosher or coarse sea salt

Peel potatoes. Place in a bowl, cover and refrigerate for 8 hours.

Slicing the potatoes

Using a sharp chef's knife, cut a lengthwise slice about ¼-inch thick off one side of the potato. Lay the potato flat on its side. This makes it easier to cut the potato lengthwise into even slices ¼-inch thick. Working with 2 slices at a time, stack them and cut them lengthwise into relatively even strips ¼-inch wide.

Place in a bowl, cover with water and refrigerate 8 hours more. Drain potato sticks, lay out on dish towels and dry completely before frying.

Use a large Dutch oven or stove-top deep-fryer with frying basket. Heat 2 inches of the peanut oil to 300° using a candy thermometer to make sure you get it precise. Add just enough potatoes to cover the base of the frying basket, and cook until slightly limp, about 1 ½ to 2 minutes. Do not brown. Lift basket and drain fries. Transfer to a baking rack and separate sticks. Repeat with remaining potatoes.

Increase heat to 375°. Again add batches to the oil. Fry until chestnut brown on edges and crisp. Drain and transfer to a bowl lined with paper towels. Immediately season with salt, tossing to coat. Serve. Yield: 4 good servings.

Note: For a slight pork flavor, to every 2 quarts of oil add a 3-inch slice of bacon.

STUFFED POTATO SKINS
Recipes From the Parish of St. Philips in Southport (1907)
Contributed by Miss Florence Price

"Bake several large round Irish potatoes in oven. When done, cut in halves and remove inside, mash and mix with cheese (cut very fine), then season with butter, pepper and salt. Put back in cases and bake till brown."

TWICE BAKED POTATOES

"Twice baked potatoes" is just another name for stuffed potato skins. Follow the above recipe for Stuffed Potato Skins, mixing in any one or more of an endless variety of flavorful toppings suggested in page 191.

LOTTIE HUBBARD'S POTATOES AU GRATIN
Southport's Favorite Recipes (1950)

3 to 4 medium sized white
  potatoes,
  peeled and sliced thin or cubed
1 cup Cream Sauce from page
  151

¾ cup American cheese grated
Salt and pepper to taste
Bread crumbs to cover a
  casserole dish

Boil the potatoes in salt water until tender but not mushy. Line bottom of baking dish with potatoes, cover with the grated cheese, followed with another layer of cubed potatoes and cheese alternately until the potatoes are used up. Cover with white sauce and sprinkle with bread crumbs. Bake in 350° oven about 25 minutes or until well browned.

HASH BROWN POTATOES

¼ pound salt pork
2 cups cold boiled potatoes
¼ cup bell pepper, diced

¼ cup onion, chopped
Salt and pepper to taste

In a skillet fry fat out of salt pork; cut in cubes and remove scraps. There should be 1/3 cup of fat. Cook the diced pepper and onion until glossy. Dice the potatoes and add to the skillet. Cook until the potatoes are brown.

CREAMY POTATO & HAM CASSEROLE

3 cups potatoes cut into ½-inch cubes
2 cups ham cut into ½-inch cubes
1 ½ tablespoons butter
½ cup celery, chopped
½ cup onion, minced
2 tablespoons flour
1 cup chicken broth
4 ounces processed American cheese such as Velveta
½ teaspoon salt
½ teaspoon pepper

In a saucepan melt the butter and blend in the flour. Add the broth and cheese and cook until cheese is melted. Add the remaining ingredients and turn into a casserole dish. Bake 45 minutes in a 325° oven, or until the casserole is lightly browned and bubbly.

SWEETHEART'S MASHED SWEET POTATO IN ORANGE CUPS

This delicious and beautiful dish is great for holidays and festive occasions.

6 oranges cut in half and scooped out. Reserve flesh for ambrosia, juice for drinking, and adding as flavoring
4 to 5 sweet potatoes, boiled, skinned and mashed
1 ½ sticks butter
½ cup brown sugar
2 to 3 eggs, slightly beaten (1 egg for each cup of mashed sweet potatoes)
½ teaspoon nutmeg
½ teaspoon cinnamon
Pinch of ground cloves
1 teaspoon lemon extract
½ cup orange juice, more or less as needed
Miniature marshmallows

Whip the potatoes while still hot with the butter and eggs. Mix remaining ingredients, flavoring with orange juice if mixture is too stiff. Put in orange cups. Bake in 350° oven 20 minutes. Remove from oven, top with marshmallows. When ready to serve, place under broiler until marshmallows are brown. Watch carefully as marshmallows will burn quickly.

SWEETHEART'S SWEET POTATO
SLICES WITH ORANGE SAUCE

This is for a small amount, but can easily be doubled or tripled for a bigger crowd. It is delicious and easy to make.

2 uniformly shaped sweet
   potatoes
¾ cup orange juice

½ cup brown sugar
3 tablespoons butter or margarine

Bake the potatoes in oven for about 30 minutes at 350° or somewhat longer, testing them with toothpick or cake tester until they are cooked but not mushy. They will continue to cook in the oven. Peel and cut into uniform ½-inch slices. Mix the orange juice and sugar in the bottom of a square 9x9-inch pan, add the potato slices, and spoon the syrup over them. Bake for 30 minutes stirring occasionally and spooning the syrup over potatoes until the syrup is thickened.

SWEET POTATO PONE

2 ½ raw, grated sweet potatoes
1 cup molasses
2 cups milk (or 1 cup evaporated
   milk, 1 cup water)
2 eggs
1 tablespoon melted butter,
   margarine, or vegetable
   shortening

1 teaspoon grated orange peel
1 tablespoon brown sugar
1 teaspoon cinnamon

Mix ingredients except for the sugar and cinnamon. Turn into skillet and bake 45 minutes at 350°. Sprinkle the brown sugar and cinnamon on top.

BAKED CHEESE GRITS

1 cup grits
4 cups water
½ cup milk
2 eggs

3 tablespoons butter or margarine
¾ cup grated Cheddar cheese
1 teaspoon salt

Slowly stir one cup grits into boiling salt water. Cook 5 minutes over direct heat stirring frequently. When done add cheese, butter, eggs and milk. Pour into greased casserole dish. Bake in 350° for about 30 to 40 minutes or until firm.

Aunt Lillian "Bitsie" Dozier with her husband, W. G. Faulk, 1930's.

Aunt Bitsie and Her Farm

Lillian "Bitsie" Dozier Faulk (1896-1958), was another of my great aunts, and when I knew her was a widow; William Grady Faulk had died when I was too young to remember him. Except for Mammie and Ted, who, as I have said, were spinsters, just about all of our relatives of Ma-Ma's generation were widows. Fifty years ago men seldom outlived their wives. When Ma-Ma had trouble sleeping, in fact, she would try to put herself back to sleep by counting all the widows in town.

Aunt Bitsie was, (how shall I say it?) a "full figured woman."

"I'll tell my age," she would say, "but don't ask my weight."

She failed to show up at Mammie's one day to take them for a drive, and Ted went into her house and found her on the dining room floor dead of a heart attack. At her funeral the pall bearers huffed and puffed to lift her coffin up the red brick steps of the Baptist Church. I was startled to overhear Deacon "Boobie" Aldridge exclaim,

"My Goodness! Miss Lillian is one *heavy* woman."

She lived in Southport but had a farm near Fairmont in Robeson County where she spent part of the summer. We would visit, and she'd present us with sacks of stone ground grits from corn raised on her place. How wonderful! Freshly ground grits are one of nature's delights. They bear little resemblance to commercial brands we have to make do with,

196

and which taste like cream of wheat. Instead, they burst with the glorious taste of fresh summer corn. Sometimes I try to recreate Aunt Bitsie's grits by adding some fresh corn kernels to the pot, and that helps.

I Take Up Farming

I can't leave Aunt Bitsie without telling about one of our visits to her farm near Fairmont. Fairmont is in a pocket of North Carolina that seems one of the hottest places on earth—Death Valley of the East. Just watch the TV weather news any summer when they show the maps and you'll see. It was *hot.* I was bored. Like all my great-aunts, Aunt Bitsie doted on children and, worried about me, suggested that I go to the garage out back and take the bicycle for a ride. The tires were flat. I strolled over to the tobacco barn where, under the tin awning, the hands were stringing Bright Leaf on long sticks, then lifting it up on racks high into the barn. (Is there any aroma more wonderful than tobacco curing in a hot barn? Clean and pungent, sweet and comforting—Carolina incense. I think not. But of course, as we now know, it kills. Cigarettes are not called "coffin nails" for nothing.)

A teen age kid in coveralls was working the wooden sled they called the "drag," pulled by a mule down the narrow rows of ripe tobacco where the field hands would crop the big gold leaves and pile it on. It looked like an awful lot of fun, and I asked him if I could try.

"Sure," he said, happy to have a break from his servitude.

"How do you get him to go?" I asked.

"It's not a *him,*" he said.

"Then, how do you get *her* to go?"

"It's not a *him or a she.* It's an *it.* A mule's half ass, half horse.

"So how do I get *it* to go?"

"Just say, Gee Haw."

I hopped on the front of the drag, grasped the reins, and told the old mule,

"Gee Haw!"

It obeyed. Away we went down the rows collecting the tobacco. But I didn't know to tell the old half-ass how to stop, and at the end of a row the drag wobbled and nearly overturned. What a disgrace that would have been! Instinctively I pulled on the reins, and the old animal stopped. Then,

"Gee Haw," and away we went. What fun!

When the drag was piled high with the cash crop, I came to the highway and headed back to the barn. The foreman spotted me and looked on with horror.

"Hey you! Who told you you could drive that drag?" he yelled.

"My Aunt Bitsie told me I could," I lied. He shrugged, and for the rest of the afternoon I happily played tobacco farmer.

AUNT BITSIE'S CREAMY GRITS

Avoid instant grits, and use quick grits only as a last resort; both have been processed to death, leaving little corn flavor. Most instructions on packages of regular grits call for a ratio of 4 water to 1 of grits; this calls for 5 to 1.

1 cup grits	1 teaspoon salt
5 cups water	1 tablespoon butter

Cook the ingredients in a saucepan to the boiling pint. Cover, reduce temperature and cook very slowly until done, stirring frequently.

Variations

Very shortly before serving, add a half cup or more of fresh or frozen corn giblets. Wait just long enough for them to get hot, but no longer, as they will release their liquid and dilute your nice creamy grits. Or, after cooking the grits, add grated American, sharp Cheddar or other cheese.

FLUFFY RICE

Please do not use instant rice! The rice has been processed away and it feels like confetti in your mouth. Regular rice is just as easy to fix, and just about as fast. Don't skimp on cheap rices. Even the deluxe rices are inexpensive. Do this:

2 cups deluxe long-grain rice	1 teaspoon butter or margarine
1 teaspoon vegetable oil	4 cups boiling water

Heat the oil and butter in a heavy saucepan with a tight fitting lid. Add the rice and stir just until the grains are coated with the oils and a few become opaque. Add the hot water all at the same time. Bring for a boil. Stir a few times, then cover, turn down to low and stir no more. Cook for exactly 18 minutes. Remove from heat, remove lid and cover with a clean tea towel. Let sit for 15 minutes. (You may also keep rice warm this way, cloth and lid in place, in a very slow oven, for as long as 2 hours.) Fluff with fork and serve. Serves about 6.

OVEN BAKED RICE WITH VEGETABLES

Bake this easy rice dish in a casserole dish with a cover.

1 cup rice
2 cups water
½ stick butter or margarine
2 cups chopped mixed vegetables,
    onion, celery, carrot

2 packets chicken or beef bouillon
1 bay leaf
Pepper to taste

Mix ingredients in the casserole dish, cover, and bake in preheated 350° oven about 45 minutes, or until the rice has absorbed the liquid. Remove and let stand 15 minutes. Fluff with a fork and serve.

My brother Don frying fantail shrimp, 2005. Photo by Vickie Hardee.

12..
Seafood

ABOUT CRUSTACEANS

Shrimp, crabs, crawfish, and lobsters are crustaceans, aquatic invertebrates with jointed limbs and segmented bodies. Shrimp and crabs are the most common in our area. Crustaceans have a rigid outer shell, and can only grow by molting and growing a larger shell. Their new shells are soft, which makes them highly vulnerable during the molting period. Crustaceans are omnivorous and feast on both smaller animal life and plant life.

ABOUT SHRIMP

The first thing you need to know about shrimp is that in Southport it's always *shrimp*, if there is only one or fifty pounds of them. It's like *sheep* in the meadow, and not *sheeps* in the meadow.

The key is *fresh*. A good fresh shrimp has hardly any "shrimpy" smell whatsoever. It should smell only like the fresh sea. A shrimp should smell like a pearl looks, or how you imagine a pearl should smell if it had a scent.

Shrimp of many species are found around the globe, from huge prawns off South America and other places, to bright red medium sized shrimp from Portugal, tiny red Maine shrimp, to pee-wees in the creeks. Fresh medium East Coast shrimp white or brown are the very best. The taste of shrimp is affected by its habitat and weather conditions. Some find the pink Key West shrimp less flavorful, perhaps due to the limestone bottom of the Gulf. Bad floats of seaweed may impart an "iodine" taste. *Avoid* Tiger Shrimp, as they are too tough.

Local Southport shrimp are of the spotted, brown or white varieties. Spotted shrimp show up about May. Brown shrimp run from about July through September when the nets pull in a mix of brown and white. During September through November large white roe shrimp are running.

Shrimp have a delicate meat and take only 1 to 3 minutes to boil or steam, seconds to fry. Some of the recipes in this book have you add shrimp last or late in the process to prevent overcooking.

COMMERCIAL GRADED SIZES OF SHRIMP

Commercially distributed shrimp are graded according to their size. The smaller the numbers, the fewer to the pound and the larger the shrimp. Beware: some markets, even big supermarkets, label as "Large" shrimp that are actually "Medium."

Market name	Count per pound
Super/Extra Colossal	Fewer than 10
Super/Extra Jumbo	16 to 20
Jumbo	21 to 25
Extra Large	26 to 30
Large	31 to 35
Medium Large	36 to 40
Medium	41 to 50
Small	51 to 60
Extra Small to Tiny	61 to 100
Pee-wees	100 and up

A young Jimmy Moore aboard the *Penny*.

Capt. Merritt Moore, left, and John Carr Davis haul in the catch
aboard the *Penny,* off Ft. Pierce, Florida, about 1950.

A few years later, Capt. Jimmy Moore commands the *Penny.*
Photos courtesy of Jimmy Moore.

Lewis J. Hardee, Sr. (1910-1996) in 1940.

A Brief History of the Commercial Shrimping Industry

An account by Lewis J. Hardee, Sr., edited.

The modern shrimping industry was launched at Fernandina, Florida, about 1910. Prior to that time shrimp could be not caught with casting nets in sufficient quantities to make it commercially feasible. It came about because of necessity and the arrival of modern technology. A number of out-of-work menhaden fishermen, including some Scandinavians, Greeks and Italians, had brought with them from the old countries their knowledge of trawling with sailing boats, and began to rig up small craft with automobile engines and trawl for shrimp.

About 1916 my father, John Hardee, and others with business skills, set up operations, and effectively were the pioneers of this new business. At first, shrimp were packed in brine and shipped in barrels by rail to northern cities—not for use as a main course, but sold in bars as snacks on a par with pickled eggs, pigs' feet and sausages.

Gradually much of the East Coast began to discover what heretofore only a few had known, that shrimp are a true delicacy and can be prepared in endless methods and main dishes. By the 1930's shrimp were being packed in ice and shipped by the ton via railroad or truck from ports in the Gulf and along the East Coast far and wide, but mainly to New York. Meat shortages during World War II hastened the popularity of the shrimp as a main course.

The Pink Gold Rush
An account by Lewis J. Hardee, Sr., edited.

In 1949 two men, Everett "Bluff" Peterson and Johnny Salvadore, were in a bar room in downtown St. Augustine. Bluff was one of the best fishermen on the East Coast and Johnny was a shrimp dealer. By chance, they overheard two U.S. naval officers; I think they were lieutenants on submarine duty, talking about how shrimp were interfering with their sonar operation down in Key West. This caught Bluff and Johnny by surprise, because at that time nobody thought there were any shrimp south of Ft. Pierce, Florida, all the way around to Carrabelle, Florida, which is north of Cedar Key on the western panhandle of Florida. They engaged in conversation with these naval officers, and were very impressed with what they heard. There were shrimp off Key West, and perhaps in great numbers.

Johnny and Bluff, and there might have been another person, went down to Key West to see what they could find. At Key West they chartered a party boat and sailed west all the way to Tortugas, using a very small "try net" of approximately twelve feet, which they had brought along. It surprised them that they didn't catch the first shrimp, for they were convinced that the naval officers had been telling the truth.

On the trip back, after dark, Bluff said, "Well, let's make one more try." They made another drag, probably thirty to forty five minutes, and found shrimp. However, it was a shrimp unlike any they had ever seen. They were pink shrimp. Most shrimp caught on the East Coast were brown or white shrimp. It turned out to be a day-burrowing shrimp which came out at night to feed, probably because in the clear Gulf waters it could escape predators.

They agreed to keep their discovery secret until at least after Christmas, because the East Coast was having a fair production until then.

Floyd Dilsaver was working for me at the time as foreman. His brother, Roy, confided in him that I wouldn't have anything to lose by sending my boats to Wilmington for dry dock and overhauling right after Christmas, rather than wait until spring as I usually did. I did so, had them copper-bottom painted, replaced my 100 fathom net-towing cables for ones of 150, and had heavier net-doors installed. In the event that

205

they did find shrimp in commercial quantities, I would be ready to make a run for it.

Early in January 1950, I got word that four boats were about to set out from Ft. Myers for a trial run off Tortugas. I knew the owners of these boats, shrimpers out of St. Augustine, Bluff Peterson, Roy Dilsaver and Frank Hannaberger. Dorothy and I packed suitcases and went to Ft. Myers to see what we could find out. I estimated that the boats would be gone for about a week. On their third morning out we went down to the waterfront; they had not come in. The next morning we did the same, and it was the same story. On our fourth trip to the waterfront, the four boats were in, and the crews were asleep. I inspected the nets and saw that they were not torn up. This was a good sign, for it suggested good, smooth bottoms. Rough bottoms will tear up nets and make shrimping unprofitable.

The men woke up and started making coffee. I asked each captain separately about what they had found. They said they were the most uniform shrimp they had ever seen, running about 26-30 count to the pound. They had shrimped five nights and each one had caught approximately 1,000 pounds headed shrimp a night.

I called Floyd, who was in Southport, and told him it looked like we were going to leave for Ft. Myers as soon as possible. I had seven boats at the time, and another under construction. They went to Ft. Myers, took on ice, fuel and groceries. Having talked with the four boats who made the earlier run, we knew where the shrimp could be found.

The problem with Ft. Myers as a port was that it had no facilities for packing shrimp. I had planned on loading them directly onto a truck, taking them to Southport for washing and icing, and pack them in 100 pound boxes. When my boats got underway for Tortugas, I drove down the Keys to Key West, and located a place where they could come in and pack their catch. I radioed the boats that when they were ready to come in, not to go to Ft. Myers, but to the Gulf dock in Key West. My boats had shrimped about two nights when I contacted them. Afterwards I scouted around and a few blocks from the Gulf dock found a better harbor with a regular fish-packing house, Thompson Enterprises, and made arrangements with them to pack the shrimp.

The next question was, could you market a species of shrimp that nobody had ever heard of? All of our dealings were with white or brown shrimp, which when spoiled turned pink. Now we were faced with marketing a shrimp that when fresh was pink.

The University of Miami conducted tests to determine if they were fit for human consumption. The report was very favorable. There was not much important national news at the time, and the discovery

206

made over-night publicity all over the country. It was a cover story in Life magazine. I don't know exactly who called it the "pink gold rush" but that's what it was. Word got out and in no time boats from all over the East Coast were down there. I was one of the first. In about three weeks there must have been fifty to one hundred. At the peak not long after, there were hundreds of boats working off Key West and Fort Myers Beach.

Among those shrimpers who also migrated to Key West during winters with their families were Dallas Pigott, Merritt Moore, Bill and Charles Wells, Joe Thompson, and V.J. "Puck" O'Neal.

ABOUT FREEZING SHRIMP

Properly frozen and stored in the deep freeze, shrimp keep well a year or more. My father knew how to do it right: After he sold his business and retired, he kept his contacts open, and when the good fall shrimp were running and the price was right he'd buy 20 pounds or more, headed, right off the boat. He'd store up a number of used and washed milk cartons. These he would fill with shrimp, then flash-freeze in the deep freezer. The next day he'd fill the spaces with ice water, and freeze again, then tape the top closed, label and date them. By this method the shrimp are locked in a nearly solid block of ice with no air spaces. When thawed they taste as if they were just hauled from the ocean.

ABOUT BOILING SHRIMP

Add salt to a big pot of water and bring to a rolling boil. Old Bay Seasoning or Crab Boil is a great addition, but not necessary, and may overpower delicate recipes. Do not peel the shrimp before boiling; the hulls help retain the flavor. Add the shrimp, bring to a boil again, and cook 1 to 3 minutes, or until all have turned pink. Do not overcook. Peel completely for creoles or casseroles, leave tail on for shrimp cocktails. Slice down the back and remove the digestive track. Rinse.

THE SHRIMP BOIL

A favorite Southport meal is the Shrimp Boil. Place a big bowl of boiled shrimp, headed or un-headed and still in their shells, in the middle of the table, warm or chilled, and let everybody help themselves. They may be prepared simply as in the recipe for boiled shrimp above, or spicy as in Ressie Whatley's recipe below. Serve with a big bowl of potato salad, green salad, spiced beets, saltines, and seafood sauce.

Headed shrimp are the most convenient, but don't be afraid of buying shrimp whole with the head on. Save the heads for making shrimp stock, a delicious additive to many recipes.

RESSIE WHATLEY'S SPICED SHRIMP
Southport's Favorite Recipes (1950)

1 ½ pounds shrimp, headed and
    washed, shell on
½ cups vinegar
1 teaspoon dry mustard
¼ cup salt

1 teaspoon red pepper sauce
2 teaspoons black pepper
2 teaspoons whole cloves
Water to cover shrimp

Mix all ingredients except shrimp in large saucepan and bring to boil. Add shrimp and cook 3 to 5 minutes, or until all shrimp have turned pink. Set aside and let shrimp cool in the liquid.

LEWIS HARDEE'S FRIED BUTTERFLY SHRIMP

My father made just about the best fried butterfly, or fantail, shrimp you ever tasted, served up only for special guests or special occasions. He'd lay them out in the afternoon and keep them iced until minutes before frying them, then serve them up with a well baked potato, slaw, and sweet, tiny spring peas—Le Seur brand, which he jokingly called Leisure peas.

Fresh shrimp, large – extra large,
    about 8 to 12 per person
1 egg
¾ cup flour

¾ cup fine cornmeal seafood
    breader
Cooking oil such as Wesson
Salt and pepper

Peel shrimp, leaving tail on. Split down back and de-vein, removing dark digestive track. Wash and dry thoroughly. Sprinkle with salt and pepper. Press down the middle so that the two halves form a butterfly. Beat an egg in a bowl. In another bowl, mix the flour and seafood breader. Dip the shrimp first in the egg, then coat with the breader. Arrange and keep on flat pan until ready to fry. May be kept in refrigerator for several hours ahead if desired. Preheat cooking oil in heavy cast-iron pot skillet until very hot, slowly rolling boil, just before beginning to smoke.) Drop in by twos and fry for seconds (about 30 to 45 seconds), or until nicely golden brown. Too much cooking will make them hard and destroy the unique, delicate shrimp taste. Remove and place on paper towels in bowl. Lightly salt and pepper.

My brother Don's method is based on our father's, but achieves a special delicacy of its own by using Zaharain's seafood breader. He warns that Zaharain's delicate seasonings will not keep.

TEMPURA BATTER FRIED SHRIMP OR OTHER SEAFOOD

Tempura is a fairly new but welcome addition to Southport cooking. It's easy, and provides a light, fluffy and delicious crust. It can be used for breading shrimp, fish, carrots, onions, or other foods. This recipe will coat about 1 pound of shrimp.

1 pound of shrimp	½ cup corn starch
1 egg, separated	½ teaspoon dry mustard or ginger
1/3 cup of beer	Flour
1 teaspoon peanut oil	Oil for deep fat frying
1 teaspoon soy sauce	

Beat the egg yolk with the beer, oil and soy sauce. Sift the corn starch and measure ½ cup. To this add the beaten egg yolk mixture and the mustard or ginger. Blend well. Then beat the egg white until stiff and fold into the batter. Dip the shrimp or other food pieces into the batter. Fry a few at a time for about 4 minutes. Drain on paper towels. Serve with a spicy sauce.

JUMBO SHRIMP WITH CRAB STUFFING

8 jumbo shrimp	1 ½ tablespoons herbed bread
¾ cups crab meat	crumbs
2 tablespoons onion, minced	1 ½ teaspoons mayonnaise
2 teaspoons scallions, minced	2 eggs
1 teaspoon green pepper, minced	Salt and pepper
1/8 teaspoon seafood seasoning,	More herbed bread crumbs
such as Old Bay	to bread with

Peel shrimp, leaving tail on. Split down back and de-vein, removing dark digestive track. Wash and dry. Mix the crabmeat in a bowl with the onion, scallions, pepper, seasonings, breadcrumbs, mayonnaise and 1 of the eggs. Chill until firm. Press a tablespoon of the chilled crab stuffing between the butterfly wings, dip into the beaten egg, and then bread on all sides with breadcrumbs. Lay out cookie sheet, place in freezer, and chill until firm but not frozen. Fry in deep fat on medium-low heat 2 to 3 minutes until golden brown.

CAPT. JIMMY MOORE'S SHRIMP BOAT PILEAU

When the shrimpers were away from home port and tied up because of the weather, they'd take turns cooking up a meal in one of their galleys—a fish chowder, chili, whatever was their specialty—and all would share. A favorite was shrimp pileau, but they pronounced it Pearl-oh. It is a favorite Southport dish that goes back as many years as anybody can count. Essentially it is shrimp bogged in cooked rice, tomatoes and sausage. Capt. Jimmy Moore, who for years operated the *Penny,* gave me his recipe:

"Use the rankest Eye-talian sausage you can get hold of. Some bacon. Two cans tomato paste, plus some ketchup. Onions, one or more according to how a person likes onions. Rice. What we use is extra long grain. Wash before cooking to avoid being too gummy. Water. Salt and pepper." Says Jimmy,

"We don't measure nothing. You fry out your sausage and bacon in a Dutch oven. Then add water, onions, rice and tomato paste. And your salt and pepper. That's all the seasonings you need—the sausage takes care of the rest. Then, last, after the pileau has been cooking for twenty minutes, add the shrimp. Cook for an hour."

Incidentally, Jimmy's business card reads, "Official Sage of Oak Island. Known far and wide for his wise advice and counsel."

SWEETHEART'S SHRIMP PILEAU

2 pounds shrimp, headed, peeled
   and de-veined
½ can tomato paste
1 cup canned tomatoes
½ cup chopped onion
½ cup celery

¼ cup chopped peppers
2 tablespoons bacon drippings
   or cooking oil
1 cup raw rice
2 cups water for cooking rice
Salt and pepper to taste

Sauté onion, pepper and celery in the bacon drippings or oil. Add shrimp and cook until they have turned pink. Add tomato paste and tomatoes, rice, water, salt and pepper. Slow cook until rice is tender.

SHRIMP AND GRITS
Thomas Harrelson's Recipe Files

Shrimp and Grits has been a Southport favorite for as long as there have been shrimp and grits, which is a long time. This recipe updates the traditional simpler dish, and is delicious. It makes enough to feed a big crowd, so you may wish to prepare a half recipe.

2 cups yellow grits
8 cups water
1 teaspoon salt
8 ounces extra sharp Cheddar cheese, chunked
1 ½ ounces shredded Parmesan cheese
2 garlic cloves, crushed
1 ¼ tablespoons hot sauce such as Tabasco or Texas Pete
1 ¼ tablespoons butter

Cajun seasoning for shrimp to taste
1 bunch of green onions, chopped
6 pieces of bacon, fried or broiled and crumbled
2 pounds shrimp, peeled and de-veined
Cornstarch as needed
Lemon, salt and pepper to taste
Olive oil and butter, enough to cook the shrimp

Cook yellow grits slowly, stirring frequently to avoid sticking. Salt as directed. Once cooked, add the extra sharp Cheddar cheese in chunks. Add the shredded Parmesan cheese. Add the crushed garlic cloves, hot sauce, and butter. In a separate skillet cook the peeled shrimp in olive oil and butter. Season with Cajun seasoning as they cook. Add lemon and pepper after cooked.

For the gravy

To the shrimp pan juices, add cornstarch and water. Equalize the temperature between the pan juices and the cornstarch water so it doesn't lump up. Add to the pan juices and as it thickens add lemon juice and wine to taste.

To serve

Ladle cheese grits into shallow bowls. Top with shrimp, crumbled bacon bits, and chopped green onions. Pour some of the gravy on top.
Serve immediately. It is good with a side of steamed of asparagus, a mandarin orange salad, and hard rolls.
Any leftovers can be used this way: let grits cool completely, then combine with beaten eggs. Add all leftover shrimp, onions and bacon to the mixture and bake at 350° degrees for 40 minutes. It seems even better the next day.

SHRIMP CASSEROLE

2 pounds of shrimp, peeled and
de-veined
¾ cup rice, cooked
1 can condensed tomato soup,
undiluted
¼ cup green bell pepper, diced
¼ cup minced onion
½ cup almonds, toasted

2 tablespoons butter
3 tablespoons sherry
1 teaspoon salt
1/8 teaspoon mace
1/2 teaspoon black pepper
Dash cayenne pepper
Dash paprika

Cover shrimp with lemon juice and oil and marinate in refrigerator overnight. Stir several times so that shrimp are covered with marinade. Sauté pepper and onions in butter. Drain shrimp lightly and add all ingredients, reserving ½ of the almonds. Pour into lightly greased 1 ½-quart casserole. Cover and bake 20 to 30 minutes in preheated 350° oven. minutes. Remove and sprinkle remaining almonds on top. Serves 6 to 8 generously.

SHRIMP OR CRAB SEAFOOD SOUFFLÉ

This is a delicious, light, main course. Prepare the recipe for Tomato and Cheese Soufflé, page 165. Before baking, fold in 1 cup cooked shrimp or crab meat which has been rolled in just enough mayonnaise to moisten. Serve immediately.

SEAFOOD NEWBURG

This rich, cream dish is one of the most delicious ever concocted. It is most familiarly prepared with lobster meats and served up as Lobster Newberg. However, crab, shrimp or many combinations of seafood may be used.

2 cups seafood
1 cup cream
2 egg yolks, beaten
2 tablespoons butter

1 cup Madeira or sherry wine
1 tablespoon tomato paste
¼ teaspoon salt
Dash cayenne

Melt the butter in the saucepan. Add the wine and cook 3 minutes. Add the beaten egg yolks and then the cream and tomato paste. Beat together and cook on very low heat, stirring, until thickened. Do not overheat or it will curdle. Add the seafood, salt and cayenne, heat and serve.

SWEETHEART'S SHRIMP CREOLE

My mother says, "I usually make a large recipe of Creole sauce. It stores and freezes well for use later. Also, this dish is best made ahead of time and let stand a while, even overnight, for the flavors to meld."

4 pounds shrimp cleaned and de-veined. Save hulls and heads, if you have them, for shrimp broth.
½ cup bacon grease
2 cups onions, chopped
½ cup green onions, minced
2 cloves garlic, minced
1 cup green pepper, or red, green and yellow peppers, minced
1 cup celery with leaves, chopped
1 teaspoon thyme
2 bay leaves, crumbled fine
3 teaspoons salt
1 tablespoon sugar

½ teaspoon pepper
1 6-ounce can tomato paste
1 16-ounce crushed tomatoes. (Use a good brand of crushed tomatoes that is extra thick, with no seeds.)
1 8-ounce can tomato sauce
1 cup stock (See recipe below. Chicken broth may be substituted.)
1 teaspoon Tabasco sauce, or less, according to your taste.
½ cup fresh parsley, chopped
1 tablespoon lemon juice

Prepare the shrimp stock: Place shrimp hulls, and heads if you have them, in a large saucepan. Simmer in 2 quarts water 2 hours. Strain and discard the shrimp hulls and heads. Boil down the broth by half.

In a large Dutch oven, sauté the vegetables, bay leaf, salt and pepper, uncovered on low-medium heat, until onions are transparent—about 30 minutes. Add the tomato paste and sauté 3 minutes. Add the tomatoes, tomato sauce, and stock. Add additional water or stock if necessary. Simmer for 1 hour, stirring occasionally.

Then add the shrimp and cook 6 to 8 minutes, until they are firm and done. Add the Tabasco sauce, parsley and lemon juice. Stir, cover, and remove from heat. Remove from refrigerator an hour before serving. Heat quickly without boiling. Serve over white rice.

[Note: This is a most versatile recipe. I most often quarter this recipe, using only 1 pound of shrimp and adjusting the remaining ingredients accordingly. I usually omit the broth or stock. Also, I personally like to add about ¼ cup chopped ham, and ¼ cup chopped pepperoni, although this latter is a departure from traditional Southport style.]

The Dallas Pigott shrimp trawler fleet in the old yacht basin during the 1950's.
Photo courtesy of Jimmy Moore.

JUMBALAYA

The jumbalaya is a Cajun dish, a reminder of the days in the 1940's when Southport shrimp boats worked out of Louisiana. The following jumbalaya is a delicious one-dish recipe, making life easier all around.

½ cup chopped green onion
½ cup chopped white onion
1 large green pepper, cut into
 strips
1 teaspoon minced garlic
1/3 cup butter
1 pound raw shrimp, headed,
 peeled and cleaned

2 dozen raw oysters,
 or 1 cup cubed ham
1 15-ounce can tomatoes
1 cup chicken broth
½ teaspoon salt
¼ teaspoon cayenne pepper
1 teaspoon sugar
1 cup raw rice

In a large pan, slowly sauté the onion, green pepper, celery and garlic in the butter until tender and glossy but not brown. Add shrimp and oysters and cook 5 minutes. (If ham is used, add this when the rice is added.) Add the tomatoes, chicken broth, salt, cayenne and rice. Stir and cover. Cook 30 to 40 minutes over low heat or until rice is done. If mixture is too dry, add tomato juice. Serve with a green salad.

214

ABOUT FISH

Fish constitute the world's largest supply of "wild" food. They mainly feed on each other. In Shakespeare's *Pericles*, the First Fisherman says, "Master, I marvel how the fishes live in the sea. Why, as men do on land; the great ones eat up the little ones." But how we relish a good fresh fish!

There are enough varieties of fish to suit everyone's taste. There are small fish and prepared alone, or large fish that are often cut into steaks.

Our local waters teem with many varieties of fish:

Fish Common to Southport's Waters

Choice Saltwater Fish for Eating

Croaker. So called because of the croaking sound it makes. A delicious
    small fish.
Drums. They are also called the red bass, the red fish, or the spotted
    tail bass. Small red drum are called puppy drum, and are prized
    eating.
Flounder. This bottom feeding flat fish is a scavenger, with both eyes
    on the grey, upward, side, and none on the white side which
    faces the bottom.
Gray Trout. This also has alternate names such as the sea trout,
    summer trout, and weakfish, among others. It mainly shows up
    in the fall, and is great eating.
Herring. Requires special preparation, as it is small and very bony. It
    is usually fried whole, bones and all, or pickled.
Mullets. Their tiny mouths make them almost impossible to catch with a
    hook; they are mainly caught in nets. The September mullet
    may be heavy with roe, which is to be prized.
Pigfish. A thick fish, it makes a noise like a croaker. Worth eating.
Pompano. An admired fish with delicious, sweet flesh.
Shad. The shad is prized eating, as are their roe which they produce in
    the spring.
Sheephead. See the old Southport recipe for baked sheephead in this
    chapter.
Speckled Trout. Also goes by other names, including the spotted
    weakfish, due to its soft flesh.
Spot. A round black spot on the shoulder gives it its name. It runs in
    schools, and is caught mainly in the fall. It is a small fish.
    When breaded and deep fried and served up with a good pot of
    creamy grits, there is no better eating.
Sturgeon. Good eating, but formidable in appearance. It is bony
    appearance gives it a primeval look.

Whiting. A very popular, delicious fish with a mild, sweet flesh. The bones of
its odd spine fan out into three combs. If larger than a pound, it is
usually filleted, breaded and deep fried, or simply sprinkled with salt
and pepper, buttered and broiled.

Choice Deep Water Fish for Eating

Albacore. A member of the tuna family, this is a prized steak fish.
Atlantic Mackerel. This also goes by the name Boston mackerel or blue
mackerel. It is a large fish, usually filleted or cut into steaks.
Barracuda. This ferocious fish is good eating; it is usually filleted or
cut into steaks.
Bluefish. Its skin is slick and easy to clean. It is an oily fish, but
delicious if prepared just out of the water.
Cabio. Also called the cobia or coal fish, this large species is usually
filleted or cut into steaks.
Dolphin. This beautiful fish with a high, Wagnerian forehead, gives
sportsmen a good tug on the line. The old Southport High
School football team was called the Dolphins, after its tenacity.
King Mackerel. This large fish is abundant in spring and fall; for years
Southport has played host to a King Mackerel Festival, when thousands
are brought in and weighed for a large cash prize. This is a large fish,
usually cut into steaks.
Marlin. You'll see these huge, beautiful blue or white fish, with their
spiked snouts proudly mounted on walls of seafood restaurants. They
are usually steaked.
Sailfish. Like the marlin, the sailfish is another trophy fish for display
in one's den or on a seafood restaurant wall. It is a steak fish.
Spanish Mackerel. The party boats make their living on this large fish,
which is usually filleted or cut into steaks.
Swordfish. The long spike gives it its name. Its steaks are on many
restaurant menus throughout the country. They are the angus steaks of
the sea.

Choice Offshore Bottom Fish for Eating

Blackfish. Abundant from early spring through late winter, the black
fish may be filleted, or cleaned and baked whole.
Grouper. A huge, unusually ugly fish, the grouper is, however,
unusually good eating. It is most often cut into steaks or
chunks.
Hog Snapper. This is usually filleted.
Porgy, or Chicken Snapper. Good eating, usually filleted. Not be confused with
the pogy, or menhaden.
Red Snapper. A very popular fish with a good, sweet taste. It may be filleted or
baked whole; larger specimen are often made into steaks.

Selecting and preparing fish

Fish can be marinated and pickled, baked, broiled, grilled, pan-fried, oven-fried, deep-fried, barbecued, steamed or poached, stuffed, made into chowder and stews.

As with all seafood, the key is *fresh*. The eyes should be clear and shiny. My father would say, "Old fish have sleepy eyes. They have to look you in the eye!"

Fish should have bright pink-to-red gills and have no slime on them. Scales should have a bright sheen. Avoid any with darkening around the edges, or brown or yellowish discoloration. The flesh should be shiny, firm and should spring back when touched. Fish should *smell good*.

Fish cook quickly. When the meat is flaky and with a white color, it's done. And of course, now we know there are huge health benefits to eating fish—especially the fatty parts. So, don't trim the fat from my salmon, please.

THE FISH FRY

Many a church and club in Southport have raised money with a fish fry, and still do. You are likely to be served a piece or two of fried fish, bone in, on a paper plate, along with corn bread and cole slaw. The fish will often be croakers, spots, or other small fish which are usually in good supply and cheaper than other varieties.

Scale, head, gut and wash the fish. Leave bone in for more flavor. Salt and pepper and roll them in corn meal or flour, or a mixture of both. Fry in 2 inches of lard or cooking oil until brown.

The Mullet Are Running

Mullet is such an oily and bony fish I sometimes forget how delicious it can be. They have tiny mouths and are impossible to catch with a hook, so you need a net. They do not freeze well. One fall, years ago, Floyd Dilsaver went fishing over at Oak Island. The mullet were running, he put out his seine net, and hauled in enough to share with friends and neighbors. He brought us a mess fresh out of the ocean. Here is how my mother prepared them. You never had anything so good.

BROILED SEPTEMBER JUMPING MULLET

Cut off the heads, slice them down the middle, and remove the guts and the spine, leaving the scales on as a shell. Sprinkle them with small chips of butter, salt and pepper, broil them in the oven, and eat right out of the shell. Serve with grits and green peas.

OVEN FRIED SPOT
Brunswick Potluck Cookbook
Contributed by Mrs. Pete Lee

6 to 8 fresh spots
¼ cup evaporated milk

2 cups Nabisco type bread crumbs
Salad oil or shortening

Preheat a very hot 450° to 500° oven. Clean the spots, but do not filet. Dip whole salted fish into milk and then roll it in bread crumbs. Place into oiled baking pan with about 2 tablespoons oil or shortening. Put fish into hot oven and bake uncovered for ten minutes. Do not add water. If fish browns more on bottom, turn over carefully with spatula and brown on other side. When done, fish will be brown and crisp on outside, tender and juicy on inside.

MACK'S CAFE FRIED FLOUNDER

Mack's was famous for its fried flounder. You were served a whole flounder, and could order a small, medium, or large fish. It came with a starch—usually grits or a potato dish—a fresh vegetable or two of your choice, perhaps string beans, beets, or slaw, hot rolls, and a dessert—maybe peach cobbler, blueberry dump or apple pie and ice cream.

Scale the flounder, remove the head and clean, but do leave the tail on; it will be crispy and delicious. Score the fish to the bone every inch, dark side up. Dip in milk, then a breading of crushed saltine crackers and a little flour. Fry in deep fat until brown, and the flesh is white and firm, about 3 to 5 minutes, depending on the size of the fish.

BRADY LEWIS'S BAKED MACKEREL
Southport's Favorite Recipes (1950)

1 4 to 5 pound mackerel
1 large onion sliced
3 slices bacon
1 stick butter or margarine,
    or ½ cup bacon drippings

½ lemons
½ cup hot water
1 tablespoon salt
1 teaspoon pepper

Dress fish with head on or off. Gash in 3 places. Place slice of bacon in each gash. Salt and pepper and sprinkle with flour. Slowly fry the onion in butter or margarine or bacon drippings. Then place fish in pan with the onion and bake in a hot oven. As the fish begins to brown, baste often with the hot water. Sprinkle with lemon juice when thoroughly cooked.

SAUTÉED WHOLE FISH

This is a good way to prepare a medium sized whole fish such as trout.

6 whole fish, scaled and cleaned and headed, but not filleted	Heavy cream for dipping Flour for breading
3 tablespoons of butter	Salt and pepper
3 tablespoons of cooking oil or olive oil	Sprinkling of parsley (optional) Lemon wedges

Heat the butter and oil in large skillet. Dip the whole fish in milk, roll in the flour, then cook over medium heat until they are nicely browned. Turn and brown on the other side. Use a large pancake turner to avoid breaking the fish. Add more butter and oil if the flour absorbs too much of the cooking mixture. Remove when cooked through, salt and pepper. Add chopped parsley to the pan, stir and pour over the fish. Serve with lemon wedges.

SAUTÉED FISH FILETS

Cook using the recipe for sautéed whole fish. But take extra care in turning, as fish filets tend to break easily.

FISH CAKES

1 cup cooked fish, flaked	1 teaspoon lemon juice
1 egg, slightly beaten	¼ teaspoon salt
1 cup cold mashed potatoes	Pepper
2 tablespoons flour	¼ cup fat for frying
1 teaspoon minced onion	

Sprinkle the lemon juice over the flaked fish. Combine fish with all ingredients except the flour and form into cakes. Coat the cakes with the flour and sauté in hot fat until brown.

BAKED FISH WITH STUFFING

6 fish filets such as flounder, about 8 to 10 inches long for individual servings, depending on how large you want your servings to be.

½ cup butter or margarine
2 tablespoons bacon drippings
¾ cup celery, chopped
¾ cup onion, chopped
¼ cup green pepper
1 cup bread crumbs
1 teaspoon powdered sage,
   or Old Bay seasoning,
   or poultry seasoning

4 tablespoons fresh or dried
   parsley, chopped fine
Salt and pepper to taste
Lemon juice
Additional butter or margarine
   melted, to drizzle on the fish
6 slices bacon or 3 slices cut
   in half for smaller filets

Sauté the vegetables in the butter and bacon drippings slowly until glossy and tender. Do not overcook because they will cook more during the baking. Add the seasonings and mix. Add the breadcrumbs and mix. In a greased baking dish, form into 6 separate oblong mounds resembling whole fish. Onto each place a fish filet. Brush lemon juice over fish, then brush with the melted butter or margarine. Place a slice of bacon upon each fish. Sprinkle with pepper. Bake in 350° oven about 30 minutes, or until the bacon is brown.

BAKED FISH WITH CRABMEAT STUFFING

To the above recipe, add 1 beaten egg and 1 cup crabmeat.

BAKED SALMON LOAF

1 16-ounce can salmon
2 eggs, beaten
½ cup milk
½ cup bread crumbs, buttered
1 teaspoon lemon juice
½ teaspoon salt

Dash of pepper
½ teaspoon sage
2 teaspoons onion, diced
1 tablespoon chopped parsley
1 tablespoon melted butter

Combine ingredients. Pack into buttered loaf pan. Bake in 350° oven 30 to 40 minutes. Serve with Cream Sauce, Cheese Sauce or Hollandaise.

SWEETHEART'S BAKED WHOLE FLOUNDER
WITH VEGETABLES AND TOMATO SAUCE

This has long been a family favorite. It's a one-dish meal, unless you want to add a bowl of cooked white rice to the menu, and some tiny green peas.

1 flounder, about 2 or 3 pounds for 4 persons, cleaned but not filleted.
5 or 6 small red or new potatoes
3 carrots peeled and cut about the size of the potatoes
5 or 6 small onions about the size of the potatoes
½ green bell pepper, the stem, seeds and white membrane removed
1 can tomato sauce

½ cup dry white wine or vermouth
2 slices raw bacon
4 garlic cloves mashed
½ cup chicken broth
1 teaspoon Old Bay Seasoning or similar, or more to taste
Garlic salt to season
4 thin lemon slices, seeds removed
½ teaspoon pepper

Parboil the vegetables until cooked but not mushy, when a toothpick or cake tester goes through. After a few minutes of cooking, add the tender bell pepper. Drain. Slice the flounder sideways, using a serrated knife the better to cut through the bone, with the center pieces in 1 ½ inch slices. Reassemble the flounder in the center of a greased baking dish. Arrange the parboiled vegetables around the fish. Add the mashed garlic cloves. Splash the fish and vegetables with the wine or vermouth and ½ of the chicken broth, then drizzle with ½ can of the tomato sauce. Place the bacon on top of the fish. Shake on the fish seasoning, a little garlic salt, and the pepper. Cover with tin foil and bake in 350° oven for 30 minutes. Remove foil. Pour in the remaining chicken broth, and then drizzle on the remaining tomato sauce over the fish and vegetables. Place under broiler for about 15 minutes, or until bacon is done and the fish and vegetables are brown. Serve with white rice.

BARBECUED FISH
Southport's Favorite Recipes (1950)
Contributed by Mrs. O. R. Stubbs

Use any large fish, such as rock, bass or flounder. Gash and season on both sides. Pour a little hot butter over the fish and brown on both sides under grill. Baste with barbecue sauce from page 153 and bake in oven at 325° for ½ hour.

BAKED SHEEPHEAD
Recipes From the Parish of St. Philips in Southport (1907)
Contributed by Miss Kate Stuart

"Clean nicely, wipe dry, lay in baking pan with little water, dredge lightly with flour, cut small strips of fat bacon or ham fat and lay on top of fish. When nearly done, cut ripe tomatoes and lay with bacon on top. Stuffing—brown stale bread in oven, pound fine, add melted butter and onion, stuff fish. Serve with sliced lemon."

ABOUT FISH ROE

The eggs of the female fish are known as roe, and what a delicacy are they. Locally, the most commonplace are from shad or mullet which spawn in spring. Pogy (menhaden) roe is usually available at Christmastime. Every spring I look for the apricot colored roe of the shad to show up at my local seafood market, and are they wonderful. Pick over and wash them, puncture with a toothpick or cake tester in a few places to deter buildup of steam and popping, salt and pepper, dust with flour, and sauté in oil. I use a mixture of butter and cooking oil, but lard is also fine. Somehow I always want a pot of creamy grits with my roe, and canned deluxe tiny Spring peas, and pickled beets.

FISH BROTH

Fish broth is easy to make, and great to have on hand for making seafood stews and chowders. It may be used immediately, stored in the refrigerator for 2 or 3 days, or frozen for up to 6 months.

2 to 3 pounds fish bones, heads and trimmings	1 tablespoon lemon juice
4 cups cold water, salted	1 teaspoon salt
1 cup clam juice	½ teaspoon thyme leaves
1 stalk celery with leaves	3 springs or more of parsley
1 small onion, sliced	1 bay leaf

Rinse fish bones with cold water, place in a pot with the other ingredients and boil slowly for 30 minutes, then strain.

ABOUT CRABS

The crabs that abound in our area are Hard Shell Atlantic Blue Claws, and they are considered the aristocrat of crabs. Sometimes they are also referred to as "Blue Crabs." When boiled or steamed they turn bright red. In my opinion, the Chesapeake Bay crabs are just about the best in the world. Their cooler waters seem to impart a clean, fresh quality that stands out. The warmer waters of Florida, the Gulf and South America produce a plumper crab yield nice jumbo clumps, but they lack the oxygenated spring-like taste of those pulled from the Chesapeake. But our local Blues are quite wonderful creatures, with a delicate, sweet taste to the flesh.

The crab season in our locale is year around, except when the crabbers close a couple of weeks out of the year to repair and clean the crab pots. Crabs in our locale are harvested year around. Fall is the best season as they are likely to be plump and full. In cold winter weather they burrow in the mud, but on a warm snap on full moon will come out.

HOW TO BOIL AND CLEAN CRABS

Discard any crabs that are not alive and kicking. In a large kettle, bring 6 quarts and 1 cup of salt to a boil. If desired, add a commercial crab boil such Old Bay Seasoning. If unavailable, add 2 teaspoons allspice, 20 whole cloves; 2 teaspoons thyme, 10 bay leaves crushed, 2 teaspoons celery seeds; 1 teaspoon dry mustard and 1 tablespoon black pepper corns.

Use long handled tongs to transfer the live crabs into the boiling water. Boil for 10 minutes. They will turn red. Drain and allow to cool to room temperature. To clean, insert a firm, blunt knife under the underbelly, or apron, and open. Remove the lungs, little appendages that resemble scratchy, whitish fingers, called the "deadman's fingers as they tend to spoil quickly if not cooked live, or, if dead, kept well iced. Hold the crab under a running faucet and scrape off the eyes and soft entrails. Use nut crackers and picks to remove meat from the body and claws.

ABOUT SOFT SHELL CRABS

Soft shell crabs are only hard shell crabs that have just molted. The time it takes to grow a new shell depends on the warmth of the waters. During warm weather a crab can grow a new "soft" shell in 2 hours, a "paper" shell in 6 to 7 hours. Soft shell crabs are usually sautéed or steamed, and do not require cleaning but may be served whole.

Gathering for a crab boil at Bill Bomberger's place on Walden Creek, summer 1950. L-R: Bill Bomberger, Cousins Jack Dosher and Vera Wescott McKeithan; Ida Potter Watson, Dorothy Dosher Hardee, Miss Annie May Woodside, Minnie Butler, Uncles Paul and Leighton Dosher, Cousin Mary Peacock Bomberger. The little boy is Cousin Tommy McKeithan.

Ma-Ma, Don Hardee & Tommy McKeithan.

Cousin Vera McKeithan.

The Crab Boil at Bill Bomberger's Place
On Walden Creek, Summer 1950

Crab scoops with their long poles, rolls of twine wound around wooden sticks, lead sinkers—basic equipment for catching crabs—still hang out back in our shop, sadly unused.

Let me take you back to the days when our family and friends would pile in Daddy's old black 1938 Chevy pickup and go out to Bill Bomberger's place on Walden Creek at the old Bethel Community for a crab boil. It is a scorching, hot summer day in 1950. My mother sits behind the wheel and drives. Mammie Dozier sits beside her, as she is a large woman and has a little trouble getting around. In the back are my brothers Mikael and Don, Ma-Ma, Cousin Vera and her children Vivian and Tommy, and our friends Ida Potter Watson, Minnie Butler and Annie May Woodside. Daddy will join us later, as will others.

We turn off the highway. The truck rumbles down Old Bethel Church Road, dodging holes filled with water from last night's rainstorm, past the little wooden church, turns off onto an even more primitive dirt road, and comes to a halt in the backyard behind their house. Bill's dogs race to greet us, barking and wagging tails. Bill's old rooster begins screeching his head off; he thinks he's a watch dog. A piglet rushes toward us squealing. This is "Grunt," the pet pig that belongs to Bill's daughter, Barbara; he thinks he's one of the dogs too.

The ladies take the hampers to the house. The Bombergers have a cottage with a screened-in front porch that overlooks Walden Creek. With its crooks and turns through marshes, and banks lined with cedar, cypress, pine and holly, Walden Creek is a beautiful place on earth, pristine and primeval, like the earth before man trespassed.

Bill Bomberger is married to our cousin Mary Peacock. He has a big pot-belly stomach that hangs over the belt of his khaki trousers. He wears a pith helmet and at his side hangs a big hunting knife in a sheath, as if ready for an African safari. He is retired from the Coast Guard and is a tinker. The electric company has not run lines out here yet, so he has a generator in the tin garage out back. It is very noisy, and when it cranks up sounds like a plane taking off.

Mary is pretty and dainty like the rest of the Peacock clan. I rightly should have called this "Cousin Mary's Crab Boil," for Bill gets to sail in his boat and stay cool under its canvas awning or sit on the dock in the breeze, while Mary is stuck in the steaming, sweltering kitchen with pots of boiling water. Bill and Mary always beg for us to come visit more, for so many in the old Bethel Community who have lived here

Bill Bomberger's boat. His cottage can be seen in the distance, right.

since long before the Civil War, have died off or moved away.

My brothers and young cousins and I have not worn shoes since school let out for the summer, but we jump from the truck and head down the blistering hot sandy path to Bill's little ramshackle dock on the creek. We drop lines with sinkers and a chunk of meat tied on. Now we wait.

The left yard of Bill's place drops down to a little marsh branch, on the other side of which live our cousins Liza and William Guthrie. A rickety footbridge leads there. Liza and William have a narrow shack of a house, of three rooms one after the other. It is called a "shotgun house," because you can shoot a shotgun through the front door and out the back without hitting a wall. They also have a tiny screened-in back porch and equally tiny front porch, like Bill's place, overlooking the marsh. Their house smells of sweet potatoes, collards, kerosene lamps, and old day-beds. It is not unpleasant, just very different from modern homes in town. It is a sniff from a century before. Our cousins are sweet, gentle and loving people, and are always glad to see us. They have no radio, no newspapers or magazines, and our visit gives a novelty to their day. But after hugs and reassurances of love and affection, we have little to say to each other. They are very old and frail, and are of a different world.

The canasta cards come out. Ida Potter Watson sits at a card table with Cousin Vera and my two brothers. This is a game three generations can sit down together and play.

Everyone goes to Bill's dock for the crabbing, even if the older folk only sit under the awning on the little wooden bench and watch. The creek is running high now, clear and yellowish as if you were peering

226

through a pane of amber. The crabs are beginning to bite. I sense a jerk on one of the lines, and slowly, very slowly and smoothly, begin to lure to the surface a big, white and blue crab. With the stealth of a spy, my brother Mikael quietly takes the crab scoop by the handle and, also slowly, very slowly and smoothly, slips it into the water underneath the unsuspecting crustacean. Now! With a fast, expert swoop he bags the old fellow and turns it into the crab box. Everyone gets in the act; I have a snapshot of Ida Potter proudly showing off a big, plump rascal she has snapped up in her scoop. Presently we have the crab box nearly filled.

Ida Potter Watson bags a big one.

Minnie Butler, Katie Leiner & Eva Ruark.

Cousin Mary has boiling water rumbling on the kitchen stove in big white enameled boilers with red rims. Here we drop the poor critters, jerking and flailing about in the confusion of their death throes. After a few minutes they grow still and turn bright red. We have no mercy. They are such good eating, and if we wade in the creek on low tide they scare us and we are afraid they will pinch our toes.

Our cousins D.I. and Myrtle Watson, Genevieve and Dan Danford and their son Danny have arrived. Mary sets about making her famous crab stew, and of course Myrtle and some of the other women pitch in to help. They clean the crabs by separating the flesh from the shell and removing the lungs—those scratchy little pencil shaped things

227

you see when you pull off the apron. These are thrown along with the shell into the garbage. They break the crabs in half and add them to the pot. We definitely will not eat the lungs, for these are the Dead Man's fingers and could make you sick, or even kill, as they spoil quickly. Nor will we have ice cream afterwards. After all, everyone knows how Mr. Mel Singletary ate crabs and strawberry ice cream one hot July and blew up and died.

On the screened in back porch, they set out potato salad, fresh vegetables from Bill's field, corn bread, relishes, crackers, iced tea, and pies and cakes for later. All gather. We bow our heads while D.I. says the blessing. Amen, agree the guests. We ladle Mary's crab stew onto our plates, crack open the pinchers, and slurp the flesh out of the breasts. The kitchen, the back porch and the back yard teem with the spectacle of this merry band of diners busy with their feast, like Lords and Ladies in Medieval times.

The pots and pans and dishes have been washed and put away. We gather in the living room. My mother sits at the big, out-of-tune upright piano and accompanies D.I. who serenades us with hymns, never forgetting "Farther Along We'll Know All About It, Farther Along We'll Understand Why." Cousin Joan Burris is up from Florida; we coax her into singing her rendition of "Doin' What Comes Natur'lly." We howl with delight as she makes references to names in our family. Barbara plays the accordion. Her specialty is "Lady of Spain," a real whiz of a piece. How *does* she do it?! She amazes us with her virtuosity. My father, who has been hard at work at his dock, has arrived now, pats his harmonica and plays "Shall We Gather at the River."

We kids grow bored and go out to the front porch to rock in the swing and pick on each other. Cud'n Ella Drew, who has come up from Florida with her family, is roly-poly and always jolly and giggling and full of mischief. When she thinks (mistakenly) that we are out of earshot, she tells a racy joke. I still remember one, but it doesn't belong in a cookbook. And it would ruin her good Christian reputation.

It is growing dark outside now. Bill's power generator, always giving trouble, makes a funny noise, chokes, and the lights go out. Mary goes for the kerosene lamp. But our bellies are full, we've had a good day. Everyone hugs and says good bye, and off we head back home. Since I am young, many years will pass before I appreciate the glories of this day.

One summer some years ago, I was home for a visit. Cousin Vera told me about a patch of blackberries she had spied out near the Bomberger place, and would I take her. She knew how I loved blackberries, and so did she. I've never been one to keep my misery to myself when I could lay it on others, so I'll do so now:

Old Bethel Community was no more, condemned by eminent domain and wiped off the map for the Sunny Point buffer zone and the nuclear plant beginning to rise there. The century-old houses, barns, gardens and fields of my great grandparents and cousins who lived beside the little dirt road, the Bomberger place, all gone. Old Bethel Church, gone. The woods had been leveled like a vast sand lot. It was hard to find a landmark.

"We can n'er recount the hour of splendor in the grass, glory in the flower," wrote Wordsworth. Life moves on. There is no turning back. My high school graduation class found few job opportunities; many of us left for other parts. But one of my brothers, who came along a few years later, got a job at the nuclear plant and never had to leave home to make a good living.

And the turning of the soil to make way for the nuclear plant did wonders for growing things. On that summer day in 1962, Cousin Vera and I gathered a peck of the juiciest, sweetest blackberries I ever had.

Irma and Cash Caroon during his tenure as Mayor of the City of Southport.

The Caroons

Cash and Irma Caroon. I could not invent their names if I were writing a swashbuckling novel. And the two are as interesting as their names. Native North Carolinians, they moved from Oriental to Southport in 1964. Cash remembers that he once said to his wife,

"We've got one dollar left. Do you want to go get ice cream or go to the picture show?"

But they raised a big family of boys and proceeded to develop the major crab processing business in the area, Oak Island Crab Meat Products. Both are energetic and active in civic affairs; Cash served as a City alderman for ten years and as Mayor during 1989-1990.

Today, five million servings of their products are sold annually in the southeastern United States from Maryland to Louisiana to the commercial market—supermarket chains, restaurants, hotels and the military. Their specialties are crab meat, crab meat stuffing, crab cakes, deviled crabs, and shrimp cakes. To handle the volume, a commercial breader is used for the crab cakes. Cash asked the manufacturer for a machine that would bread only one side of his deviled crabs, as the servings are in individual crab shells.

"Can't be done," they told him.

The Caroon crab processing plant in operation.
Photos courtesy of Cash and Irma Caroon.

"I know darn well it can be done," he insisted. So he flew to Sandusky, Ohio, showed the manufacturer how to do it, and with minor alterations to the original, had the breader needed for his business.

All of the crab casserole recipes in this book are to me delicious, but you can't top Irma Caroon's that appear throughout this book. You can start with these:

IRMA CAROON'S CRAB CASSEROLE

1 pound crab meat
1 can cream of mushroom soup
1 beaten egg
1 tablespoon mayonnaise
Juice of ½ lemon
1 tablespoon Worcestershire
   sauce

1 teaspoon parsley
3/4 cup water
1/3 pound grated cheese
1 package Waverly or similar
   crackers, crumbled
1/2 stick margarine, melted
Pimento, chopped, optional

Mix together the mushroom soup, egg, mayonnaise, lemon juice, Worcestershire sauce, parsley and water. Then fold in crab meat. Place in casserole dish, spread on crackers, chopped pimento, and then sprinkled on the butter. Bake at 350° 30 minutes, or until top is brown and bubbly. Note: Ritz or Georgia crackers are also very good on top of most casseroles.

231

IRMA CAROON'S CRAB IMPERIAL

1 pound backfin (lump, white
    crab meat)
1 egg, well beaten
½ cup mayonnaise
2 tablespoons melted butter

2 tablespoons evaporated milk
2 tablespoons pimento or capers
½ cup grated Parmesan cheese
Salt and pepper to taste

Leave crab meat in lumps. Lightly mix with other ingredients except cheese. Place in buttered casserole dish, or in large, cleaned crab backs. Sprinkle cheese on top. Bake at 400° for 20 minutes in casserole dish or 350° for 25 minutes in crab backs.

IRMA CAROON'S CRAB À LA KING

1 pound crab meat, cooked
1 cup diced celery
½ medium bell pepper, diced
2 hard boiled eggs, diced
1 tablespoon Worcestershire
    sauce

1 tablespoon butter, melted
1 pint heavy cream
3 tablespoons sherry wine
Salt and pepper to taste

Simmer celery and bell pepper until tender. Drain. Add cream, crab meat, eggs and other ingredients. Simmer only until heated through. Add wine just before serving. Serve with favorite bread, toasted.

COUSIN MARY BOMBERGER'S CRAB AU GRATIN

1 pound crab meat
1 can cream of condensed
    mushroom soup, undiluted
½ pound Cheddar cheese,
    shredded

1 teaspoon Tabasco sauce
1 tablespoon Worcestershire
    sauce
4 tablespoons sherry

Put undiluted soup in double boiler. Add the cheese, sauces and sherry and stir, and then add the crab meat. Serve on toast.

COUSIN MARY BOMBERGER'S CRAB STEW

2 dozen crabs, cleaned
6 slices salt pork
1 large onion
¼ cup cornmeal

3 cups water
Salt to taste
½ teaspoon black pepper

Make a broth of the water the crabs were cooked in by boiling it until it is reduced by three-fourths. Strain and discard any shells. Fry out the pork in a deep kettle. Add a little of the broth and sauté the onions until they are glossy and soft but not mushy. Break crabs in half, sprinkle with salt and pepper. Place crab halves and claws in kettle with the crab broth and onion. Cook slowly about 1 hour. Thicken with cornmeal. Serve with cornbread or corn muffins, and if you like, with cooked rice.

SWEETHEART'S CRAB CAKES

Store bought crab cakes tend to be crab *flavored* cakes--mostly breading. This recipe is nearly all crab, with good seasonings and just enough binders to hold it together.

1 ½ pounds crabmeat
2 eggs, slightly beaten
¼ cup minced green onion
¼ cup minced white onion
¼ cup fresh or dried parsley
    flakes

2 to 3 tablespoons bread or
    cracker crumbs, enough to bind
1 teaspoon Worcestershire sauce
1 tablespoon mayonnaise
1 teaspoon ketchup
Oil for frying

Shape into cakes carefully, so as to avoid breaking up the crab lumps. Heat oil in skillet until hot, so that the cakes sizzle when they are lowered in on pancake turner. Allow to brown thoroughly on one side before turning, so that the cakes will stay together when turned. Remove and place on good quality cloth-like paper towels such as Viva. Then serve promptly.

233

CRAB AU GRATIN CASSEROLE

1 stalk celery, chopped fine
1 cup onion, chopped fine
¼ pound butter
½ cup all-purpose flour
1 13-ounce can evaporated milk
2 egg yolks

1 teaspoon salt
½ teaspoon ground red pepper
¼ teaspoon black pepper
1 pound crabmeat
½ pound grated Cheddar cheese

Sauté onions and celery in butter until glossy and tender. Blend flour in well. Pour in the milk gradually, stirring. Add egg yolks, salt, red and black peppers, and cook for 5 minutes. Blend well with the crabmeat in a mixing bowl. Transfer to a lightly greased casserole dish. Sprinkle with grated Cheddar cheese. Bake at 350° 20 to 30 minutes, or until bubbly and lightly browned.

COUSIN JOYCE ADAMS'S SEAFOOD HUSH PUPPIES

Cousin Joyce Adams's seafood hush puppies are famous in our family. After a big family seafood cook out, she simply takes leftover seafood and stirs it into a hush puppy mix.

Leftover crab meat or fish, crumbled
1 cup corn meal
½ pint buttermilk
1 egg

1 tablespoon sugar
Old Bay Seasoning, or similar
¾ pint water more or less
1 tablespoon salt
Pinch of soda

Mix leftover fish or crab meat in the hush puppy mix. Shape into balls or drop by spoonfuls into hot oil and cook until they float on top and are brown.

CREAMED CRAB

1 tablespoon butter
1 tablespoon flour
1 cup milk
1 egg beaten
1 pound crab lump meat
½ teaspoon celery seed
1 teaspoon onion juice

Dash of nutmeg
½ teaspoon chopped parsley
½ teaspoon Worcestershire sauce
Bread or cracker crumbs to cover
    a casserole dish
¼ cup butter, melted
Salt and pepper to taste

In a bowl, make a seasoning mixture of the celery seed, onion juice, Worcestershire sauce, salt, pepper, parsley and nutmeg. Fold in the crab meet, taking care not to break the lumps. Let sit for several hours in the cold part of the refrigerator. Melt butter in a saucepan, add flour and stir, then add milk to make a thick sauce. Add the beaten egg. Fold this into the seasoned crab lumps. Turn into greased casserole dish, cover with bread or cracker crumbs, and drizzle on the melted butter. Bake 20 to 30 minutes in 425° oven. Can be spooned onto plates or put in 8 patty or crab shells.

MRS. HAYMAN'S DEVILED CRABS

Mrs. L. D. Hayman was the wife of the preacher at Trinity Methodist Church many years ago. Rev. Hayman, I am told, never tired of fishing and exploring the waters around Southport. The preacher's wife's deviled crabs were praised.

Backfin or claw meat will work in deviled crabs. Save the beautiful lumps for other dishes. If you have picked out your own crab meat, save the crab shells for baking. Or, use oven proof glass crab shells.

1 pound crab meat	1 raw egg
1/3 cup ketchup	1 hard boiled egg, chopped
1 teaspoon Worcestershire sauce	1 teaspoon salt, or to taste
1/3 cup milk	1 ½ cup saltines finely crushed
1 small onion, minced	¼ cup butter or margarine melted
1/2 cup celery, minced	

Sauté onions and celery together until glazed but not mushy. Mix together all ingredients except for the butter and ¾ cup of the crushed saltines, adding the crabmeat last. Spoon into the crab shells. Spoon remaining crushed saltines onto the crab shells and drizzle with butter. Bake at 350° about 25 minutes or until brown on top.

CRAB CROQUETTES
Recipes From the Parish of St. Philips in Southport (1907)
Contributed by Miss Kate Stuart

1 quart of boiled and picked out crabmeat

1 ½ cupfuls bread crumbs

1 level teaspoon dry mustard

1 tablespoonful of Worcestershire sauce

1 scant tablespoonful butter

A little salt

"Mix all together; if too dry add a little water; mould into croquettes, dip in bread crumbs and fry."

SABRE COOKER'S CRAB FRITTERS
Southport's Favorite Recipes (1950)

1 pound fresh crab meat

1 package white crackers such as Uneeda

1 tablespoon butter

2 eggs

½ teaspoon salt

2 tablespoons lard

Crush crackers and add enough water to dissolve. Then put crab meat in and mix well. Add salt, butter and eggs and mix with spoon. Have it of a consistency that you can drop it from the spoon into the hot fat. Keep turning until brown. Serve piping hot.

Cousin Anne Peacock Danz and the Dead Man's Fingers

Our cousin Anne Peacock Danz was a Brunswick County native who lived on the Gunpowder River in Maryland. She once fed her husband Ed crabs for dinner. They had dressed for bed when it occurred to her that she may have failed to remove the dead man's fingers. In a panic she went to the kitchen and rummaged through the trash. To her dismay, she failed to find the dreaded lungs of the crabs. She woke her husband and said,

"Ed," she said, "I hate to tell you, but I forgot to take the dead man's fingers out of our crabs. I'm sorry."

They knew what had to be done. They got dressed and sat up in the living room until the dreaded stomach pains of food poisoning began. Long about dawn, with no sign of illness, Ann said,

"Well, they were nice and fresh, as good a soft shell as you will find."

"Soft shell?!" cried Ed. "Don't you know you can eat the dead man's fingers of a soft shell crab!"

SAUTÉED SOFT SHELL CRABS

Choose soft shell crabs that are still alive. Your seafood dealer can clean the crabs or you can do it yourself. You only need remove the digestive cavity of the crab and remove the eyes. By holding the crab under a cold water faucet you can do this easily with a paring knife and your fingers.

Cooking oil	¾ cup milk
1 tablespoon butter	2 cups all purpose flour
8 crabs	¼ cup cornstarch
2 eggs, beaten	1 tablespoon salt

Dry the crabs, salt and pepper. Mix the eggs and milk in a small bowl. Mix the flour and cornstarch in a second bowl. Dip the cleaned whole crabs, claws and all, in the milk and egg mixture, and then roll in the dry mixture. Sauté in ¼ inch of oil and butter in a skillet at 350°, 3 to 4 minutes on each side, or until brown.

For a variation, make your breading of a seasoned seafood breader, or a mixture of seafood breader with flour.

ABOUT OYSTERS

"He was a bold man who first ate an oyster."

Oysters are sold fresh and in their shells, shucked and in jars or cans. Our local fresh oysters are "Blade Oysters." Sometimes suppliers tack on the name of where they are gathered, such as Topsail Beach Oysters, or Cape Fear Oysters. Local retailers also get in Louisiana or Mississippi Oysters, which are "Rock Oysters," rather than "Blade Oysters." Rock oysters grow in clumps and have thicker shells.

When buying fresh oysters in the shell, make sure they are from inspected waters. Discard any unshucked oysters that are not tightly closed.

There are endless ways to prepare oysters—roasted, steamed, creamed, breaded and fried, or used in soups and chowders. Oysters are great served on the half shell sitting on a bed of crushed ice.

Southporters eat oysters only during months with R's, October, November, through February. At least, they used to. Nowadays we don't know better, I suppose.

Dick Lewis's Oyster Roast

Even now, I can see Dick Lewis, many years after his passing, getting ready for the oyster roast. He is thin and smokes, as everyone did then, and makes a steady living working for the City. Dick is our neighbor across the street, married to Dorcas Ann McKeithan, a cousin of my cousins, whom we call Dork. Just about everyone in Southport is connected in some way, so watch your tongue. It is a cool day in a month with R's. Dick has come back from out in the county in his black 1940's Hudson sedan bearing a gunny sack of oysters, plump, juicy and salty. With a huff and a puff, he lifts the sack into his wheelbarrow and wheels it to the back yard where, under the giant oaks that let in no light, summer or winter, he cleans them. They are creatures from the netherworld of creek bottoms, encrusted with barnacles, and their gray and white and jagged mouths poke through the creek mud, thin and sharp as razors. I can't get through an oyster roast without getting cut. Dork sits in the kitchen drinking coffee, now and then peering out back to see how the oyster roast is going. She doesn't lift a hand to help, nor is she expected to. Her job is to make the cornbread.

Nor does their son, Neil. Dork does everything for him that Dick does not, for she is a one-chick hen. Neil and I, both skinny as twigs, just stand and watch Dick work.

Dick hoses down the oysters and scrubs off the mud, separating the clumps with a hammer. He throws the dead ones filled with cold mud into the trash. After the roast he will use the shells to improve the walk in front of his house. Dig down a few inches and you will find that the streets of Southport, the sidewalks, and the trails through Franklin Square Park, were once paths of crushed shell from oyster roasts like this.

Good handyman that he is, Dick has an electric light rigged up in the back yard. He has everything ready for us. Laid out on a table are heavy rags for grasping the oysters, iron oyster knives, and napkins for the fussy like me. There are only a few of us. Besides Dick and Neil and Dork, only my brother Mikael, Cousin Vera, and her daughter, Vivian, and myself.

Dick has made a grill from a wire mesh set on bricks. He sets a match to the end of a rolled up piece of newspaper, lights the pine wood under the grill, and places on it the first pan of oysters. Dork emerges from the kitchen with a big black cast iron skillet of corn bread. I was wrong about Neil. Dork makes him run into the kitchen and fetch the bottle of vinegar for dipping, and the jug of ice tea. This will be our meal—oysters, corn bread, and ice tea.

We stand around the fire watching the roast, as hungry and impatient as baby birds in a nest waiting for mama bird to come feed them. And here comes Dick with the first pan of hot oysters. Dick has a counter set up against the rear of his kitchen, and here we find a place and eat. We tear off a piece of cornbread and begin gulping down the oysters. Yum. We youngsters like our oysters well cooked and dry. We are squeamish and don't understand how the older folk take them barely warm so they can slurp the juice and gulp down the little critters. My Uncle Paul who is always a tease sometimes opens a big, long, slimy raw oyster, holds it high over his mouth and lets it slide down his throat, then laughs like crazy when we gag.

But no matter. We eat until we can eat no more. No finer feast could be put before a king. This scene will take place across town in many a back yard and kitchen. As it does to this day.

FRIED OYSTERS OR SCALLOPS

1 pint of oysters or scallops	Salt and pepper to taste
1 egg beaten	Oil for frying
1 tablespoon milk	
Dry bread crumbs or cracker crumbs	

Drain oysters or scallops and remove any bits of shell. Dry between towels. Sprinkle with salt and pepper and roll in flour. Mix the egg and milk. Dip the oysters or scallops one by one into the egg and milk mixture, then coat with the dry bread crumbs. Fry in Dutch oven or fryer in deep fat at 375°. Drain on absorbent paper. Serve hot with lemon wedges and tartar sauce.

SCALLOPED OYSTERS

This dish is great as an added attraction to a holiday menu—or anytime.

2 pints oysters
1 1/2 cups seasoned herbed bread
    crumbs
1/2 cup butter
1/8 cup celery, minced
1/2 teaspoon parsley, minced

1/8 teaspoon thyme
1/4 cup cream
1/8 cup Parmesan cheese, grated
A little heavy cream, sherry, or
    Worcestershire sauce may be
    added for a more piquant taste

Drain the oysters. Reserve ½ cup of the oyster liquid. Melt the butter in an oven-proof casserole dish. Add the celery, parsley and time. Sauté gently until the celery is tender. Pour off and reserve the seasoned butter. Fill the pan with alternate layers of oysters, bread crumbs and cream. Pour over the bread crumbs. Sprinkle with the Parmesan cheese. Place in preheated 425° oven for 30 minutes. Serves 4.

COQUILLE ST. JACQUES
(SCALLOPS IN CREAM SAUCE)

Despite its exotic name, this absolutely delicious classic dish is easy to prepare. As an appetizer, count on 3 to 4 sea scallops per person; as a main course, double that number. Prepare a cup of Mornay sauce using the recipe on page 151. This recipe will be sufficient for 4 appetizers. Double the recipe if more is needed. Poach the scallops in water until just barely cooked. Drain. Place the scallops in individual scallop shells lightly greased if you have them, or in small, shallow baking dishes. Pour the sauce over the scallops and broil until golden brown and bubbly, just beginning to blacken at the edges.

ABOUT CLAMS

Clams abound in our local creeks and waters. The local species is the "Quahog Clam." Clams of many species are available fresh in seafood markets, or shucked and put up in jars and cans. Check the Index of this book for other recipes for clams such as clams on the half shell and chowders.

A curious note: We humans aren't the only ones who love clams. Seagulls have learned to snatch them from the river or creek, sail to a great height, and drop them on the hard surface of a highway, where they crack open and can be eaten. Seagulls have only developed this skill recently, within the past half century with the coming of paved roads.

The digestive tracts of clams may contain mud or sand. To remedy this, place them in cold, clear seawater overnight; they will drink of it and cleanse the digestive track. Or, you may run the mud sacks under cold water and wash out. You may have to cut out some of the sacks if they are too large.

Like oysters, fresh clams must be from inspected waters and must be "clammed shut." Discard any that are not closed or that have cracked shells. Open with an oyster knife, or you may find it easier to place them in a pan and bake in a hot oven about 15 minutes until they open. Cover to prevent evaporating the juices. Drain off juices into a tall glass or bottle and let the sand and grit settle to the bottom. Strain and reserve clear juices for your recipes

Clams should be prepared promptly, or put up in containers and frozen for use later. They freeze well. Like oysters, clams toughen easily when cooked; freezing before cooking will in fact help break down the fibers.

Stuffed clams or clams on the half shell are attractive when served in the shell. It is helpful to prepare the shells in advance. Place the shells on a tin sheet and leave outdoors on the ground for a day or two. The ants will do the job of cleaning away the remaining flesh for you. Then scrub, wash, and they are ready for use.

A Clam Dig

My brother Don has a boat and every now and then takes his eldest brother fishing or clamming. He always watches out for him, as this tale will show.

It is a day borrowed from heaven, warm and summery, with just enough cottony clouds here and there to show off the vivid blue skies. The river and the ocean sparkle, clean and clear, like diamonds and emeralds strewn across a mirror. We head to Baldhead Island.

The wind kicks up a bit, the sea runs high and fish aren't biting. Now, I get seasick just walking out on a pier, and the swells begin to make me woozy. "I'm sorry Don," I warn him, "but I'm going to get sick." Not far away is a shoal as big as a city block, a small, sandy island like you see in cartoons with someone shipwrecked on it. We get out, and I lay on my back on the hot sand while my stomach settles. All around is the blue sky, the white sand strewn with layers of seashells glistening and bleaching in the sun. Squawking gulls fly overhead and walk on the beach looking for sea creatures. Pelicans flying overhead suddenly dive head down like a dive-bomber, crash into the water, and scoop up a fish. The first Nor'easter will destroy this little island or deposit it a mile away. But for now, it is our own private paradise, for an hour. It is an allegory for man's existence on this earth.

The fish aren't biting, so my brother heads the boat to one of the little creeks behind Baldhead Island. The tide is very low, and every now and then, he gets into the water out and tows the boat, like Humphrey Bogart and the African Queen. The creek is opaque and warm as bath water. Clams are usually harvested with a forked pea-digger, but on this day we just walk about waist deep, inching forward in the slick mud with our toes until we feel a clam, then reach down and grab it. We make a good haul.

CLAM FRITTERS

1 cup clams diced
1/2 cup onions, minced
2 tablespoons green onions, minced
1/4 cup sweet green bell pepper, minced
2/3 cup cracker crumbs
1 egg

1 teaspoon Old Bay Seasoning or similar seafood seasoning
1 teaspoon soy sauce
Bread crumbs to roll fritters in
Salt and pepper
Cooking oil to cover a skillet to fry

Beat the egg in a mixing bowl. Add the minced vegetables and seasonings and stir. Drain the clams, reserving the juice. Add the cracker crumbs. Add the drained clams and stir, adding a little of the juice if too doughy. Form into fritters shaped like small eggs. Place a layer of bread crumbs in a plate. Lay on the fritters a few at a time. Sprinkle with more bread crumbs and set aside until all are breaded. Fry in medium hot fat. Do not turn until the fritters are browned on the bottom, or they will fall apart, but wait for the egg in them to set, then turn and brown the other side. It helps when turning to guide them onto a small pancake turner with a fork.

An Introduction to Squid

It is surprising how many peoples deny themselves delicious foods because of superstition or some prejudice or other. The strict diet of Hindu Brahmans forbids the eating of onions. Many Jews won't touch pork. The English are not fond of artichokes, probably because the French love them. Lately it's fashionable not to eat beef out of cruelty to animals; but the same people happily dress up in leather jackets.

Having been raised in Southport, I found it a shock when I got out into the world to discover that there are people who actually dislike seafood altogether! I've learned to love just about every thing that comes out of the sea, although that wasn't always so. My first trip to Italy was in the company of one who turned out to be a very disagreeable traveling companion. Arriving late at Pisa, we found but one restaurant open. The kitchen was closed and the owner could only offer us something cold. The seafood salad sounded interesting, and he promptly placed before us a bowl of chopped green peppers and onions in an oil and vinegar dressing, with squid, mussels, tiny octopus and other forbidding creatures wiggling around. "I'm not about to touch that!" barked The Ugly American, and stormed out. He went to bed hungry. I cautiously tasted the strange, exotic dish before me. I've loved seafood salad ever since.

ABOUT SQUID

Choose small, tender squid, as the larger ones can be tough. Your seafood dealer or grocery has probably already cleaned the squid. If not, you must do so. If it is still alive, use caution, as they bite. Grasp the head section just below the eyes. Pull the head free from the trunk. Remove the grayish ink sac. Cut the tentacles free just above the eye section. Save the tentacles but discard the eye section. Remove and discard the innards and small round cartilage at the base of the tentacles, as well as the pointed cuttlebone inside the tail. Remove the reddish membrane that covers much of the squid by par-blanching for a minute or two, then plunging it into cold water to stop the cooking.

You will now have the tentacles and the tubular body. Cut the tube into ¾-inch rings. Use in seafood salads, soups, or fry.

FRIED SQUID

Bread with a mixture of ½ flour and ½ seasoned seafood breading. Fry in deep fat at 365° until golden brown. Salt and pepper. Great as an appetizer or a nice addition to a North Carolina shore dinner.

Cousin Brooks Newton Preik with a platter of Southern fried chicken. 2005.
The family recipe, passed down for generations, is on the following page.

13..
Chicken & Fowl

SOUTHERN FRIED CHICKEN

Is there anything better than homemade Southern fried chicken hot out of the pan, brought straight to the table? Served with rice and burnt flour gravy, or potato salad, and green beans cooked 'till they are nearly mush and almost black? And a pan of hot biscuits still giving off steam, a crock of butter ready for spreading on? And maybe a little honey and chow-chow on the side? I don't think so.

Each Southport cook has a special recipe for fried chicken. It may be marinated overnight in vinegar with a little sugar or in buttermilk for a while before frying, and then dredged in flour, crushed corn flakes or saltines or crackers. Petesy Bill Larsen, who ran a filling station and cafe out at the Sawdust Trail, used to serve up the best you could get outside of Annie Lou Newton's kitchen, and it was a special Sunday treat to go there. It was pan fried. You had to get there right away after church and beat the Methodists or there wouldn't be a table, for he only cooked up so much pan fried chicken, and if there was a crowd and he gave out, he'd throw a batch into the deep fat fryer which wasn't nearly as good–it tasted of fried fish and French fries.

ANNIE LOU NEWTON'S SOUTHERN FRIED CHICKEN
Brooks Newton Preik's Recipe Files

1 tender fryer, cut up	1 to 2 cups cooking oil,
1 cup flour	depending on size of your skillet
Salt and pepper to taste	

Wash and dry the chicken parts. Sprinkle the parts generously with salt and pepper, and seasoning such as Lowries. Bread the chicken parts in a paper bag with flour and more seasoning, shaking to make sure they are covered. Heat cooking oil such as Crisco, 1 to 1 ½-inch deep in a cast iron skillet with cover. Cook on high until browned on one side, covered, about 10 minutes. Lower temperature, turn and cook the other side until done. Total cooking time should be about 20 minutes.

Serve with Annie Lou Newton's potato salad, or rice and burnt flour gravy, and a good Southern green vegetable.

OVEN FRIED CHICKEN

1 2 to 3 pound chicken, cut into
    pieces
1 ¼ cups corn flakes, crushed
1 egg
½ cup cream or evaporated milk

3 tablespoons margarine or
    butter, melted 1 ½ teaspoons
salt
Pepper according to taste
Chicken seasoning (optional)

In shallow dish or pan, mix corn flake crumbs with salt and pepper. Set aside. In a second shallow dish or pan, beat egg until foamy. Stir in cream or milk. Dip chicken pieces in the egg and milk mixture. Coat evenly with crumbs mixture. Place chicken, skin side up, in single layer in well-greased or foil lined shallow baking pan. Do not crowd. Drizzle with melted butter or margarine. Bake in 350° oven about 1 hour until tender. No need to cover pan or turn chicken while baking. Yields 6 servings.

BROILED CHICKEN

Choose a young and tender chicken. Wash and clean, pat thoroughly dry with paper towels. Split down the back, rub with butter and sprinkle with salt and pepper. Place in a pan split side up and under the broiler, but not too close to the coils or flames or it will brown before the insides are cooked sufficiently underneath. Broil about 10 minutes and turn, adding more butter; then brown the other side.

BARBECUED CHICKEN
Favorite Recipes of North Carolina (about 1944)

1 chicken, fryer or broiler
¼ cup or ½ stick butter
½ cup vinegar
3 tablespoons tomato catsup

Chicken broth
Salt to taste
½ pod red pepper
Flour to thicken

Steam whole chicken until done over water to which 1 tablespoon of vinegar has been added. Make a sauce of the butter, vinegar and tomato catsup. Add this sauce to enough chicken broth (slightly thickened with flour) to prevent chicken from sticking. Season with salt and pepper. Pour over chicken and place in oven, basting several times while browning.

EASY CHICKEN CASSEROLE
(PIECES OF EIGHT)

8 pieces of chicken, uncooked,
washed and cut up
1 cup rice, uncooked
1 cup onion, chopped
1 cup celery, chopped

1 can cream of chicken soup
1 soup can water
1 Bell pepper, cut into strips
Paprika
Salt and pepper

In a 9x13-inch baking dish, mix all ingredients except the chicken, pepper strips and paprika. Lay the chicken top, and the pepper strips in between the chicken. Sprinkle with paprika. Cover with foil and bake at 350° for 1 hour. Fluff rice a bit and serve.

MAXINE FULCHER'S CHICKEN CROQUETTES
Southport's Favorite Recipes (1950)

2 cups cooked, chopped chicken
¾ cup thick white sauce
1 egg yolk, well beaten
1 egg, slightly beaten
1/3 cup cracker crumbs

2 tablespoons cold water
½ teaspoon salt
1 teaspoon lemon juice
1 teaspoon paprika
¼ teaspoon celery salt

Combine chicken, white sauce, the egg yolk, lemon juice and seasonings and cook. Cool. Form mixture in cones, cylinders or balls. Roll in the cracker crumbs. Dip in egg which has been diluted with the water. Dip in crumbs. Fry in deep fat at 385° about 2 minutes. Drain on crumpled absorbent paper. Garnish with buttered peas or asparagus tips. Serves 8.

CREAMED CHICKEN

2 cups cooked chicken or turkey
meat, cut into small pieces
1 cup chicken stock
2 cups light cream
3 tablespoons butter
3 tablespoons grated onion

3 tablespoons flour
¾ teaspoon chicken seasoning
Chunks of green or red sweet
peppers, blanched, or
pimentos

Melt butter in saucepan. Add onion and simmer for 5 minutes, until onions are glazed and tender but not brown. Stir in flour. Slowly add chicken stock, cream, and chicken seasoning. Add chicken or turkey. Cook about 5 minutes, or until heated through, stirring occasionally. Serve on biscuits, toast, or rice.

247

Elizabeth Loughlin Harrelson in 1985.

LIB HARRELSON'S CHICKEN AND DUMPLINGS
Tommy Harrelson's Recipe Files

Elizabeth Loughlin Harrelson was the wife of Dan Harrelson, and was like a mother to half the kids in town. Says her son, Tommy,
"This is a dish we had often in our family. Many Southern recipes call for chicken and pastry, with the dough rolled out. In this recipe, the dough is dropped into the broth without being rolled out, resulting in something akin to a biscuit mixed in with the chicken."

1 whole chicken, cut into pieces and skinned	Salt and pepper to taste
	Poultry seasoning to taste
1 onion, chopped	2 hard boiled eggs
2 to 3 ribs of celery, chopped	2 cups self-rising flour
Chicken bouillon to taste	

Place chicken pieces in a pot of water and cook until tender. Cook the giblets and livers separately in water. Remove the chicken pieces and the giblets from the water and let cool. Cut chicken into more than bite sized chunks. Cut giblets into smaller pieces. To the chicken broth add bouillon to taste. Cool some of the chicken broth. Place the flour and

248

poultry seasoning in a bowl and gradually add some of the cooled broth until the proper consistency for biscuits. Put the cut up celery and onions and the cut up chicken and giblets in the remaining broth and bring to a simmer. Add sliced hard-boiled eggs. Add the dumplings one-by-one by using a large serving spoon to scoop out the mixture. They will float to the top when done. Serve in shallow bowls. Salt and pepper to taste.

CHICKEN À LA KING

1 cup white sauce
1 cup cooked chicken pieces

½ cup fresh mushrooms (optional)
1 pimento

Slice mushrooms in half, brown slightly in skillet until they lose their liquid and drain. Use the liquid in making the white sauce for extra flavor. Combine all ingredients, and serve on toast or rice or in party shells.

CHICKEN WITH RICE (ARROZ CON POLLO)

Arroz con pollo is another dish the shrimpers during the 1950's brought back from Key West. It's especially great for parties and gatherings, since it is a one-dish meal and can be fixed ahead.

½ cup olive oil
1 3-pound chicken cut in pieces
1 ½ cups chopped onion
2 cloves minced garlic
1 cup rice uncooked
¾ cup canned tomatoes, chopped
2 cups chicken stock, or ½ can
    consommé with ¼ can water
1 teaspoon saffron

½ teaspoon salt
¼ teaspoon pepper
½ fresh chili pepper sliced,
    or 1/8 teaspoon dried ground
    chili peppers
½ cup tiny green peas, preferably
    fresh
2 canned pimentos, sliced

Heat ¼ cup olive old in large casserole or saucepan. Add chicken and brown well on all sides. Remove chicken and set aside. Sauté onions and garlic in the same casserole for 10 minutes. Remove and set aside. Pour remaining oil into the casserole. Brown the rice in it lightly, stirring constantly. Replace the chicken, onions and garlic. Add tomatoes, stock, saffron, salt, pepper and chili peppers. Mix. Cover and bake in preheated 325° oven 1 ½ hours. Add a little water if rice gets dry. Bake 20 more minutes or until chicken is tender. Place heated peas and pimentos on top of chicken and rice and serve.

FRIED CHICKEN LIVERS

1 pound chicken livers	Salt and pepper to taste
Milk to coat	Cooking oil
Flour to coat	

Choose fresh, firm livers. If the grocer has only soft poor quality livers in stock, wait for another day. Pick over the livers, cutting away and discarding the connecting membranes. Rinse and dry. Puncture each in several places to prevent buildup of pressure and popping. Dip in the milk, then coat with the flour. Fry in hot cooking oil until golden brown. Drain on paper towels, salt and pepper.

CHICKEN LIVERS WITH MUSHROOMS AND WINE

Here is a recipe for chicken stew I adore, and cook up ever six months or so.

1 pound chicken livers	¼ cup chicken stock
¼ cup flour	¼ cup dry sherry wine
½ pound mushrooms, sliced thinly	1 clove garlic, finely minced
6 tablespoons butter or margarine	½ teaspoon crushed sage
2 tablespoons green onions, finely chopped	¼ teaspoon thyme
	Salt and pepper to taste

Pick over the chicken livers, separating them and discarding membranes. Puncture each several times with cake tester or toothpick. This helps lessen the swelling and popping. Dredge in a mixture of flour and water.

In one skillet heat half the butter. Sauté the livers until they start to brown all over.

Meanwhile, in another skillet, heat the remaining butter and add the mushrooms, green onions and garlic. Cook, stirring, until the mushrooms give up their liquid. Continue cooking until the liquid evaporates. Add the mushrooms to the chicken livers. Add remaining ingredients. Cover and cook on low heat until the livers are done, about 15 minutes.

Serve with rice and broiled tomatoes.

ABOUT THE TURKEY

In 1609, this native American bird kept the Jamestown settlers from starvation; wild turkeys were served at the Second Thanksgiving dinner in 1621 (and may have been served at the first, in 1620). Benjamin Franklin preferred it to the eagle as our national symbol, as it is not carnivorous but minds its business and feeds on berries and seeds. The native bird, still prized hunting, is not as plump as its commercially domesticated variety, but both are delicious eating.

The American turkey became an early favorite in the Old Country, even displacing the goose as the favorite Christmas meat in England. The name is thought to derive from a misunderstanding that it originated in the country of Turkey, where it is also popular.

ROAST TURKEY

Nothing is easier than roasting a chicken or turkey. Each cook has his or her favorite method. To use no covering at all tends to dry the bird, and roasting in a tin roasting pan with a lid steams it. I prefer the paper bag method, which allows the bird to brown nicely, and keeps it just moist enough.

Remove and lay aside the bag of giblets for gravy or stuffing, checking both the top and bottom cavities, as different companies hide them in different places. Wash the bird and pat dry with paper towels, trimming and discarding any excess fat. Rub liberally with cooking or olive oil. Sprinkle inside and out with any one or all of these you like: Old Bay Seasoning, garlic salt, rosemary flakes.

Place the turkey in a standard brown paper grocery bag, tucking the end closed or fastening it with steel binder clips. Roasting breast side up will promote a nice brown breast for the table, but tends to yield a dryer white meat. Roasting breast side down will yield a juicier white breast, but some of the skin may stick to the paper and spoil the good look. You decide.

A rule of thumb used to be that you could count on baking your turkey in a 350° oven 20 minutes per pound. But nowadays turkeys are bred to be much leaner and do not require quite that. This chart is preferable, using a preheated 325° oven.

8-10 pounds	17 minutes per pound
10-14 pounds	16 minutes per pound
14-18 pounds	15 minutes per pound
18-20 pounds	14 minutes per pound
20-24 pounds	13 minutes per pound

251

Remove from oven and let stand 15 minutes for juices to return to the flesh. Withdraw from paper bag, or tear away the bag carefully, as steam may pour out. Using wide, pronged roast forks, lift to carving board or plate. Reserve broth for gravy.

Carving the turkey

A carving board with gutters around the edges is best. The wood helps stabilize the turkey better than a slick platter, and the gutters collect the juices. With the neck of the turkey away from you, hold the turkey in place with a long carving fork. With a carving knife, remove one of the breasts by slicing lengthways into the turkey, as near the center bone and as deeply as possible. Separate the white breast from the wing. Then slice the breast crossways. One half of a 15 pound turkey is more than enough for a dozen persons to start on. You may wish to delay slicing up the remaining half to keep it moist.

TURKEY GRAVY

4 cups turkey broth. If roasted turkey doesn't yield enough, add canned turkey or chicken broth.	1 cup flour
	3 tablespoons Kitchen Bouquet or similar seasoning
1 ½ cups cold water	2 teaspoons salt
	Pepper to taste

Fill a glass jar or vessel with the cold water. Add the flour on top and shake until dissolved. Add to broth and other ingredients and simmer in sauce pan, stirring occasionally to avoid scorching. If you wish to add giblets, boil the liver, heart and kidney until cooked through. Slice off the hard membranes of the kidney, and then cut all three into giblets.

CREAMED TURKEY

Follow recipe for Creamed Chicken on page 247, but substitute turkey meat.

FRIED MARSH HEN OR QUAIL

4 marsh hen or quail
½ cup buttermilk
½ cup flour
Salt, pepper & cayenne pepper

2 slices bacon
Bacon, or bacon drippings,
or duck fat, usually
commercially available

Wash, dry and quarter the marsh hen or quail. Each bird will yield 2 small breasts and 2 small legs. Fry out 2 slices bacon in a skillet. Save the crisp bacon for snacking, but leave the lard in the pan. Add enough cooking to bring the fat level up to ¾-inch. Dip the pieces into buttermilk. Salt, pepper and dredge in flour, shaking off excess. Heat the oil. Fry until golden brown. Drain on paper towels before serving. Goes great with mashed potatoes, or rice and burnt gravy, and any good Southern green vegetable. Feeds 4 skimpily, so add more if you are big eaters.

QUAIL IN WINE AND CREAM

4 quail, cleaned and trussed
Oil, enough for sautéing the
onions and spices
½ cup onion, chopped
1 ½ cups cream
2 whole cloves
1 bay leaf

1 teaspoon peppercorns
1 tablespoon garlic, chopped fine
1 1/2 cups dry white wine
1/2 teaspoon salt
1/8 teaspoon pepper
Dash of cayenne
1 teaspoon chives, chopped fine

Sauté the onions, cloves, peppercorns, garlic and bay leaf in the oil for about 4 minutes. Add quail and brown on all sides. Add the remaining ingredients except for the cream and simmer 30 minutes. Remove the quail and set aside. Strain the sauce; discard the cloves and other spices. Add the cream and heat, but do not boil. Pour over quail. Serve each person 1 quail. Serves four.

Lewis J. Hardee, Sr., hunting, 1956.

Marsh Hens and Fried Quail

In the early winter when the weather turned cold and overcast, when the shrimp weren't running and the boats were tied up, and there was a good high tide running to flush them out, Daddy would go marsh henning. He'd get out his black, high rubber boots, shotgun and red cartridges, load up the skiff in the back of his '38 Chevy pickup, and head to the creeks and marshes where the marsh hen lay. The tide would be high and lapping at the tops of the marshes, now bronze and dying for the winter.

Late in the afternoon he'd return with his bounty, a string of these marvelous little game birds. He'd dress them, my mother would fry them up, and we'd have a feast. You get four small pieces out of a bird, two brown breasts and two thighs. Nothing tastes better. I can only give you an idea of how the marsh hen tastes, akin to wild duck or quail, gamy without being strong, but unique. And with every mess of them you'd crunch down on a buckshot or two.

More than once my father told me how, as a young man growing up on the East Coast of north Florida, he went with his father and a party of shrimpers laid up by the weather, to return with more than 400 birds, which they dressed, iced, shared with neighbors, and ate for breakfast, dinner and supper. I don't know when I had a marsh hen last. My brother Don or his friend Dickie Aldridge occasionally went hunting and brought us a mess. But, alas, I suppose those days are over. Quail is available in our modern supermarkets, so the recipe for fried quail above on page 253 is about as close as I can get to capturing the lost delight of marsh hen.

PREPARING GAME BIRDS

Pluck and dress as you would a freshly killed chicken or turkey. The wax method is helpful. Scald and rough-pick the birds, dip in melted paraffin wax. Allow to harden, then peel off the wax, which should take most of the pinfeathers and down. You may also singe any remaining feathers with a chef's blowtorch or a long-handled match.

Daddy's Hunting Dog

My brother Mikael wanted a dog. This was summer 1954, before Hazel changed everything. Phil King over at the beach had a litter of springer spaniels for sale and my father was glad to get one, since he could double as a pet and a hunting dog. He was a beautiful dog with glossy brown hair and white spots. But he was the runt of the litter and soon earned his name, "Trouble." At the first sign of thunder he'd find a way to get inside the house and plop, dripping wet with rain, onto the middle of the bed in the back bedroom. There he'd lie shivering with his head on his paws looking up at you with the most pathetic look you ever saw on a dog's face, and you couldn't budge him until the storm rolled past. Once, dear Ma-Ma tried to stop him from getting past her at the front door and he came close to knocking her down getting inside the house. I can hear Ma-Ma now,

"Con-sarn it, Trouble! You're ruining Dorothy's carpet!"

When Trouble was old enough, Daddy decided it was time to take him duck hunting, and giving a whistle, loaded his hunting gear into the pickup and headed for the marshes, Trouble sitting proudly in the seat beside him, panting with his long pink tongue hanging out. But hardly an hour went by before the truck drove up out front. Daddy was wet and covered with mud from head to foot, spitting mad. At the first blast of his shotgun, Trouble had jumped a foot high, leapt from the skiff and charged terrified into the marshes.

"Never saw a gun-shy spaniel in my life!" Daddy grumbled. Our brave retriever, it turned out, was a lap dog.

ROAST WILD DUCK

From time to time, our father would bring home a wild duck he had bagged, and what a delicacy! He'd pluck and clean it, and my mother would roast it. The wild duck bares little resemblance to the domesticated Long Island duck you get in supermarkets. Its meat is dark purple and richly gamy, and oh, so good. Wild duck is much less fatty than the domesticated breed, and requires fat in cooking to preserve moisture and tenderness.

Whole wild duck, cleaned
1 medium onion, peeled
1 apple, peeled, cored and cut
 into pieces
1 stalk celery, cut into 1-inch
 pieces
Butter or lard

Clean, wipe and dry the duck. Rub the insides with lard or butter to help keep the juices in. Sprinkle generously with flour. Place a whole peeled onion, apple and celery inside the duck and place in roaster. Scatter any extra vegetables beside the duck. Lay 2 strips of bacon over duck, and fasten with tooth picks. Place uncovered ducks in preheated 500° oven. Immediately reduce heat to 350° and bake about 20 minutes, depending on size.

ROAST DOMESTIC DUCK

4 to 5-pound duck	1 cup orange juice
3 cups apples, pared and cut	1 teaspoon fresh garlic, chopped
1 cup raisins (optional)	Salt and pepper

Clean and singe duck. Rub liberally with the garlic. Fill the cavity with the apples and raisins. Roast uncovered in 325° oven, about 20 to 30 minutes a pound, basting often with the orange juice. Allow to stand 15 minutes. Allow grease to rise in pan, siphon off, and use residue for making the orange gravy.

ORANGE GRAVY FOR DUCK

3 tablespoons orange peel	Salt
1 cup orange juice	Dash of cayenne
1 cup drippings from pan	2 tablespoons currant jelly
½ teaspoon prepared mustard	1/3 cup dry white wine

Boil the ingredients on medium heat until the consistency of gravy.

Lewis J. Hardee, Jr., with a holiday ham. 2005.

14..
Meats

Beef Goes Through the Ceiling

We had gone shopping in Wilmington and Cousin Vera wanted to stop by the A.& P. before we headed home to pick up some 8 O'Clock coffee and a few things she couldn't get in Southport. My mother was happy to oblige, and we enjoyed prowling through the store. This was in the late 1940's.

"I want you to see this!" cried Vera. "I can't believe it." She led us to the meat cooler, and there was T-bone steak, marked $1.00 a pound.

"A *dollar* a pound!" she exclaimed.

"We won't be able to eat!" said my grandmother, shaking her head. "I never thought I'd see the day when steak hit a dollar a pound."

Oliver's Grill

The closing notice posted in the window of Oliver's Grill in 1985 broke many hearts. For years Ed Oliver and his wife Toni, in their little sandwich shop on Howe Street, had turned out the best hamburgers known to man. When you entered, your senses quickened and you drooled with the smell of hamburgers frying, onions, beer—whatever made up the heart of Southport cooking in those years.

The little hole-in-the wall had only four hard wooden booths, a half dozen wood stools without backs at the counter, and a dark, wooden floor. Cases of beer and food supplies were piled here and there. The menu was limited, mainly hamburgers, hot dogs, sandwiches, milk shakes, soft drinks and beer. Toni tells me that when they first opened in 1949, the hamburgers sold for 15 cents, hot dogs for a nickel, and a sandwich was 10 cents. They did not take reservations or telephone orders. Toni, always on the run, would write down your order in a jiffy with hardly time to catch her breath, and rush behind the counter to help Ed with the cooking. Customers packed the place. Routinely, Ed lowered the blinds to the door hours before they actually closed for business in the afternoon, so they could eventually get home. The Olivers refused to gouge people, kept the prices low, but built a beautiful brick home on the river.

259

Ed and Toni Oliver
shortly before they retired
and closed their famous grill in 1985.

Sign in Oliver's Grill window
announcing the closing.

OLIVER'S CLASSIC HAMBURGERS

Their famous hamburgers made their fortune, and Toni shared with me the secrets of how they were made: The meat was Swift's, a combination of chuck and sirloin, regularly delivered on Thursdays. The patties were not made days ahead of time, but only a few at a time as needed. The meat was rolled into small balls of about ¼ pound each, and then flattened.

The patties were placed on the grill, and after a few minutes pressed with a pancake turner to squeeze out the excess fat, and turned once. After turning, they'd place standard Merita buns on top for warming. The condiments were Sauer's mustard, Hunt's Ketchup, Heinz hamburger pickle chips, and chopped onion. Toni says, "The onions were sweet in the summer time, and in the winter we did the best we could." In later years, they would offer lettuce and tomato topping and a few other variations, but the above was the Classic Oliver's Hamburger.

POT ROAST

Salt and pepper the roast on all sides, then coat with flour. Heat a Dutch oven with about 1/8-inch of lard until meat will sizzle when added. Roll the roast around in the hot grease to sear on all sides and seal the juices in. Cover, and slow cook in 300° oven for about an hour and 15 minutes to two hours, or until tender. For the last 30 to 45 minutes, add carrots, potatoes, a small turnip, and white onions around the roast. After the meat and vegetables are done, remove from the Dutch oven and use the drippings for gravy.

The electric crock-pot slow-cooker method is excellent for pot roast. Begin the meat and vegetables with a little broth in the morning, and they will be ready for the evening meal.

GRAVY, USING THE POT ROAST DRIPPINGS

Shake cold beef broth and flour in a jar. Add the broth first, then the flour, to avoid the flour sticking to the bottom. Use the proportions 4 oz broth to 1 tablespoon flour. Add this to the drippings in the Dutch oven and cook until thickened. Add 1 tablespoon Kitchen Bouquet or similar gravy helper. Adjust salt and pepper.

CHICKEN-FRIED STEAK

Round steak, cut into slices   Lard or vegetable oil
  ½ to ¾ inch thick   Salt and pepper
Flour

Pound the steaks with a meat pulverizer on both sides. Sprinkle with salt and pepper, then dredge in flour on both sides. Fry in a skillet in about ½ inch of hot grease. Bacon grease or lard is the best; vegetable oil will do.

SWISS STEAK

2 pound bottom round steak   1 cup mixed carrots, peppers and
½ teaspoon chopped garlic   celery, chopped fine
Flour to season   Salt and pepper to taste
¼ cup bacon or ham drippings   1 cup hot beef stock
½ cup onions, chopped fine   ½ cup tomato sauce

Slice into serving size portions and beat both sides of the slices with a macerating mallet to tenderize. Rub generously with the garlic. Flour. Heat the bacon or ham drippings in a heavy, iron casserole dish. Sear and brown the slices on both sides. Sprinkle on the vegetables, add salt and pepper, and pour on the hot stock and tomato sauce. Cover and bake in preheated 300° oven 1 ½ to 2 hours.

BRAISED SHORT RIBS OF BEEF

2 pounds beef short ribs   1 teaspoon paprika
1 tablespoon garlic, chopped   Salt and pepper to taste
½ cup onion, chopped   Oil, to sear the beef

Heat enough oil to cover the bottom of a Dutch oven nearly to the smoking stage. Sear the beef on both all sides. Add enough water to cover bottom of Dutch oven. Add remaining ingredients and cook in 300° oven 2 ½ hours.

CREAMED DRIED BEEF

Prepare 1 cup Cream Sauce using recipe on page 151. When smooth and thick, add dried beef shredded. Serve on toast.

TO CORN BEEF
Key to the Pantry (1898)

"To every gallon of water add 1 ½ pounds of salt, ½ pound of sugar and 1 ounce of saltpeter; boil and skim. When cold put in the beef. Put the beef in water one day to draw out the blood."

FLORIE JOHNSON'S CORNED BEEF AND CABBAGE
Southport's Favorite Recipes (1950)

1 medium cabbage, medium sliced	1 ½ cups toasted bread crumbs
Salt water to cover cabbage	Butter to dot the top of the casserole
Butter to dot the casserole.	Pepper
1 can corned beef	

For the white sauce

1 cup water	1 tablespoon cornstarch
½ cup evaporated milk	Salt and pepper

Boil the cabbage in salted water for about 6 minutes. Drain, saving water. In a saucepan blend cold water and evaporated milk with the corn starch. Cut the corned beef into small pieces and add to the white sauce. In a baking dish place a layer of bread crumbs, then alternate layers of the cooked cabbage, creamed corn beef and bread crumbs. Sprinkle bread crumbs and pepper on top, and dot with butter.

CORNED BEEF HASH
Annie May Woodside's Cook Book (1913)

"Chop lean, cold boiled corned beef, add an equal quantity of boiled potatoes which also been chopped, not mashed, and either two minced small onions or a few drops of onion juice. Season to taste with salt and pepper and turn into an iron skillet in which a heaping tablespoon of mixed butter and lard has been melted. Add just enough water to the hash to make it moist, cover the skillet and put to cook over a slow heat—a stove lid over a gas flame turned low gives the requisite temperature— and cook until a thick brown crust is formed."

MEAT LOAF

A good meat loaf with a crispy, dark brown crust is one of my favorite foods. Here's my recipe.

2 pounds ground beef	¼ teaspoon thyme leaves
1 pound ground pork	1 teaspoon salt
1 large onion, finely chopped	1 teaspoon black pepper
½ cup dry bread crumbs	1 bay leaf finely crumbled
2 eggs	2 bacon slices

Mix all ingredients except the bacon. Grease the bottom of a loaf pan or dish. Form the meat into a long loaf and place in the pan. Lay the bacon strips over the meat. Roast at 325° for about 1 ½ hours. Remove the loaf when done, and use the drippings as the basis for a nice brown gravy. Meat loaf is just as good served hot or cold the next day, or on sandwiches.

STOVE TOP MEAT LOAF WITH TOMATO SAUCE

My easy stovetop method makes a crunchy crust top and bottom, and produces its own tasty, tomato sauce. Prepare 1 recipe of meat loaf, above.

Fry out the bacon in a 10-inch medium weight skillet. When crisp, remove and crumble the bacon. Add a little more cooking oil to the skillet. Mix all other ingredients, including the crumbled bacon, form into a round loaf, and place on a plate. Heat the oil in the skillet to the sizzling point. Slide the loaf into the hot grease. Reduce heat, cover and cook on low heat about 20 minutes, until the egg has set the meat mixture and the bottom is browned and crisp. Drain off and reserve the liquid. Lift the loaf onto a plate, and turn over. Add a little cooking oil to the skillet and increase the heat again to the sizzling point. Slide the loaf back into the pan. Pour off the fat from the reserved liquid from the first cooking and discard; mix with half of one 6-ounce can of tomato sauce. Pour half of this mixture over the meat loaf and cover. Reduce heat, and cook another 10 minutes. Drizzle the remaining tomato sauce around the sides of the skillet and stir in the juices to make a gravy. Serve with rice, and green peas or beans.

BEEF STEW

2 pounds beef, cubed
1 ½ cups beef stock or bouillon
2 slices salt pork
2 slices bacon
2 tablespoons flour
¼ teaspoon dried thyme leaves
Fistful of fresh parsley chopped
Child's fistful of celery leaves
1 medium onion, quartered

1 bay leaf
1 ½ cups carrots peeled
    and sliced
1 ½ cups potatoes peeled and
    sliced
1 tablespoon catsup
½ teaspoon Worcestershire sauce
Salt and pepper to taste

Season the beef cubes with salt and pepper, and dredge in flour. Fry out the meat in a heavy Dutch oven. Sear the meat, turning frequently and adding more fat if necessary. Add the stock or bouillon to cover the beef and the seasonings. Bring to a boil, reduce heat and simmer for about 1 ½ hours, until the meat is tender. Add carrots and potatoes, and more stock if needed and cook 30 minutes longer. To thicken, add small balls of butter and flour and stir.

BEEF STEW WITH VEGETABLES

Follow recipe for Beef Stew. About 30 minutes before the meat is done, add the peeled and sliced potatoes and carrots, and also small white onions, stalks of celery, or white turnips.

SAUTÉED CALF'S LIVER

1 ½ pounds sliced calf's liver
3 tablespoons butter
1 slice bacon, or more

3 tablespoons cooking oil
Flour to coat
Salt and pepper

Remove the tough membranes from the liver. Fry out the bacon; remove and set aside when crispy. Pour off the excess bacon drippings and save for other recipes later, but leave some drippings in the pan. To this add the cooking oil and butter and heat. Salt and pepper the liver slices, then dredge in flour and sauté quickly, about 1 minute per side. They should be crispy and brown, but slightly pinkish inside. Add an additional sprinkling of salt and pepper. Serve with string beans and either rice with burnt flour gravy or mashed potatoes. The oil residue from sautéing the liver is just right for making burnt flour gravy.

265

VEAL LOAF
Recipes From the Parish of St. Philips in Southport (1907)
Contributed by Mrs. Charles Hewett

3 pounds raw veal	Butter size of egg
3 eggs	1 teaspoon pepper
3 tablespoonfuls of cream	1 tablespoonful salt
4 pounds of crackers	1 tablespoonful sage

"Beat the eggs and cream together, chop the veal very fine, adding the well pounded crackers and seasoning. Now mix the eggs and form into a loaf. Bake two and one-half hours, basting oven with butter and hot water."

ROAST SUCKLING PIG

Scald the pig by immersing in very hot water (but not boiling water) for 1 minute. Remove from water and with a very dull knife scrape any hairs that may remain. Cut a slit from the bottom of the throat to the hind legs and remove the entrails, being careful not to break the brains. Wash thoroughly in cold water and chill. Fill with any desired poultry stuffing and truss the opening. Roast in moderate 350° oven 3 to 4 hours. When serving, place an apple in the mouth of the pig and serve with candied sweet potatoes and applesauce.

Hood's Practical Cook's Book of 1897 gives this additional advice, "Roast pig is not a common family dish, but on the farm it might well become so, especially where the family is large enough. A well-cooked roast pig is quite as delicious as Charles Lamb described it to be. The pig should not be over five weeks old, nor under three, and it should be thoroughly cleaned. It should be stuffed either with potato or bread stuffing, highly seasoned with sage, salt, pepper and onions, if onions are liked. Mash the potatoes, or, if stale bread is used, moisten it, add melted butter and a beaten egg. Skewer the legs, forward and backward, and rub the pig all over with butter, salt, pepper and flour. The baking pan should have a little water, and the oven should be slow at first, but hot enough to brown at the close. Baste often, and bake from two and a half to three hours. Apple sauce goes with roast pig."

Charles Lamb's Dissertation Upon Roast Pig

In his classic memoir of growing up in Southport, *The Old Man and the Boy,* Southport author Robert Ruark cites Charles Lamb's "A Dissertation Upon Roast Pig" as one of the pieces of writing that made an impression on him. It is a wonderful piece of whimsey, as delightful and vivid today as when written in 1822. Here is a synopsis:

Ho-ti, a Chinese swineherd, leaves his eldest son in charge of things while he goes hunting in the woods. Bo-Bo is a "great lubberly boy" fond of playing with fire. He accidentally sets the house afire, roasting a pig trapped inside. He smells something so novel and enticing he sticks his hand into the pig and "he tasted—crackling!"

Ho-ti returns. "You graceless whelp," he cries, "what have you got there devouring? Is it not enough that you have burnt me down [my house] with your dog's tricks, and be hanged to you, but you must be eating fire, and I know not what—what have you got there, I say?

"O father, the pig, the pig!" exclaims the son. "Do come and taste how nice the burnt pig eats." Ho-ti is repelled by such a barbarous thought, but nevertheless tastes the pig. Lamb writes,

"Nothing but fires from this time forward." And Lamb also recommends as an accompaniment to pork,

"Pine-apple is great."

BAKED HAM

Place ready-to-cook Smithfield ham in a pan, fat side up. Cover bottom of pan with a little water. Bake 325° for approximately 18 minutes per pound, until temperature with a meat thermometer has reached 148°. Allow to sit before carving so the juices can return to the meat.

BAKED HAM SLICES AND APPLES

2 large, thin slices raw ham	½ cup brown sugar
1 teaspoon dry mustard	1 tablespoon butter
2 teaspoons vinegar	2 apples

Mix together the mustard and vinegar. Spread the mixture thinly on the ham. Slice apples very thin and spread two layers on the ham. Sprinkle well with the brown sugar. Roll the ham the long way. Hold together with metal skewers or tie with string. Place in baking pan and dot with butter. Bake in moderate oven 25 to 30 minutes. Baste several times while cooking.

267

BROILED OR SAUTÉED HAM SLICES

Slice ham in ¼-inch slices. Cut the edges in a few places to help prevent curling. Smear butter over each slice and broil about 15 minutes. Or, sauté on both sides in butter and a little oil until lightly brown.

BAKED HAM, HONEY GLAZED

I never understood why it's a "roast beef" but a "baked ham." Both are roasted.

1 14-pound ham preferably smoked	3 bay leaves
	3 fresh thyme sprigs
6 to 8 small onions peeled	1 clove
4 celery stalks chopped into 2-inch lengths	1 cup cold water
4 carrots chopped into 2-inch lengths	

The honey glaze

1/3 cup light brown sugar	1 ½ teaspoons ground pumpkin pie spice
1/3 cup honey	
1 ½ teaspoons mustard	About ½ cup cloves

Soak the ham overnight in cold water, changing the water twice. [This is unnecessary with many prepared hams. Read the instructions on the label.] When ready to bake, rinse under cold water and dry well. Score the ham criss-cross to form diamond shapes. Stick a clove into the middle of each diamond. Place the ham fat side up on a rack in a roasting pan with ½ inch water. Mix the honey glaze, and paint the ham. Bake uncovered in preheated 320° oven for 20 minutes per pound, basting a few times with more honey glaze, until lightly caramelized. Let sit for 20 minutes for the juices to settle. Remove ham and vegetables from the oven, putting aside the vegetables for serving later. Reserve the liquid for a ham gravy.

SAUCE FROM A HONEY GLAZED HAM

Your pan will have collected a cup or more of juices from the cooked, honey glazed ham. It will be dark, and rich with the honey glaze and ham juices. Pour this into a saucepan and set in the freezer for about an hour, or long enough for the fat to rise to the top and become firm. Lift this off and save for seasoning other dishes. The remaining sauce will probably need no additional work except for heating up. It will be great on rice.

HAM AND PINEAPPLE

1 slice of ham 1-inch thick, center cut, cured	2 tablespoons butter
	1 can sliced pineapple
2 cups milk	

Soak the ham in the milk for 4 hours. Remove from milk and place in hot pan with the butter. Cook slowly in a skillet until brown, turn and brown on the other side. Transfer ham to another pan and place in warm oven where it will remain warm but not cook. Put slices in pan with the ham juice and brown on both sides. Then place ham on platter with slices of browned pineapple surrounding it. Mix the pineapple juice with the ham gravy and pour over the ham.

BOILED HAM

1 fresh, uncooked ham	½ cup brown sugar
1 bay leaf	1 teaspoon pepper
1 onion	1 teaspoon salt
Sprigs of parsley	1 teaspoon powdered tarragon
1 quart of sweet pickle vinegar, or one pint of cider vinegar	1/3 cup butter, melted
	Water to cover
1 cup of cracker crumbs	

Thoroughly brush and clean the ham in lukewarm water in which a teaspoon of borax has been dissolved. Soak overnight in cold water. In the morning, shave off every particle of the hardened surface. Place it in a large kettle and cover with cold water. Heat slowly, removing the scum as it begins to boil. Add the bay leaf, onion, parsley and vinegar. Simmer, allowing 20 minutes to the pound. When done, allow to remain in the liquor until cold. Peel off the skin, trimming any ragged edges. With a cloth, sop up the melted fat from the top. Mix the cracker crumbs, sugar, salt, pepper, tarragon with the butter. Spread over the fat surface, bake in the oven until brown and crisp.

269

FRIED COUNRY CURED HAM AND RED EYE GRAVY
The Proverbial Church Cookbook (1991)
Contributed by Marie Swan Royal

4 slices country cured ham,   1 teaspoon sugar
   cut ¼ thick, uncooked   ½ cup water
2 tablespoons butter

"Place ham slices in unheated skillet. Turn heat to medium. Cook 2 to 4 minutes on each side. (Do not overcook as it causes ham to be tough.) Put butter in skillet just as you turn ham. Remove from pan. Pour drippings in gravy bowl. Do not loosen ham particles from pan. Add sugar to pan. When sugar begins to brown, add water and stir rapidly loosening particles as you stir. Heat to boiling. Mix into drippings and serve immediately. Gravy is delicious served over ham or grits."

HOW TO CORN A FRESH HAM
According to Dickie Marlowe

For years, fresh corned ham was a special treat at Christmas at our house. It must be brined for several weeks, but you will have an unforgettably wonderful dish. The meat will be tender and very light gray. Have your butcher prepare a fresh whole ham of about 16 pounds, or a half ham of about 8 pounds, by puncturing it with a brining fork. Or, you can prepare it yourself by puncturing it all over with an ice pick.

There are two basic methods for corning a ham, by immersing it in brine for about a week, or by packing it in salt for a month. The latter is described by my childhood friend Dickie Marlowe, grandson of Mrs. Ina Norment of whom I have written earlier. Dickie learned the method years ago from Mr. Toler, butcher for Dan Harrelson's Grocery for many years. Dickie says,

"Rinse the ham. While it is still wet, pat on a layer of salt. Place it in a bag and store it in the refrigerator for 4 weeks. Every week check the ham to see if it needs more salt. When it is ready, rinse the ham completely. Then simmer it in clear, unsalted water for about 4 hours or more, until tender. Then brown in the oven if you wish."

Serve with mashed potatoes and a green vegetable, and have Tomat Butter and Hot Pepper Jelly handy.

TO CURE HAMS
Key to the Pantry (1898)

"Cut out your hams. Salt them the next day, never salt them the same day it is cut out. Rub salt on the skin side and hock first, then the raw side rubbed well. Mix equal parts of saltpeter and red pepper, take a spoonful of the mixture and rube on raw side, especially around the bone. Pack it down in salt the day after it is cut. If there is any danger of the hogs freezing, pile them on each other to prevent. Let it stay six weeks or longer, and hang up to smoke well before the first of March. Smoke a little every day for two weeks, until the meat shows smoke. Take down and rub with hickory ashes before fly time. After you rub with ashes, knock it on the table to keep too much from sticking. The ashes keep worms away. Hang up again. Treat shoulders the same way. For middlings, do not put any saltpeter and pepper on, but ash like hams."

ROAST LOIN OF PORK

Loin is the best of the three cuts of pork that are good for roasting, the others being a fresh ham (leg) and the shoulder.

4 pound loin roast
Salt and pepper

Roast uncovered in a 350° oven until the thermometer registers about 175°. Remove and let stand 10 minutes before carving so that the juices can settle. Serve with boiled new potatoes, small green peas, and Sarah Rebecca Drew's Tomat-Butter.

PICKLED PIGS FEET
Hood's Practical Cook's Book (1897)

"Pigs feet are a toothsome delicacy." They are cleaned and boiled as for souse [see page 273], and pickled without removing the bones. They are served cold, or may be fried or broiled. They should be boiled for a half hour, or until thoroughly cooked. Serve them plain, fried until brown in butter, or broiled.

BOB MIDYETTE'S COUNTRY RIBS
The Proverbial Church Cookbook (1991)

Bob is a superb cook. For years, he ran The Pharmacy Restaurant on Moore Street, the first restaurant in town to feature gourmet cooking.

2 ½ pounds country ribs
1 cup dark brown sugar, packed
¾ cup vinegar
½ cup water

4 bay leaves
1 teaspoon crushed red pepper
1 tablespoon rubbed sage
½ teaspoon salt

"Salt ribs several hours before cooking. Mix sugar, vinegar, water and spices in a pan; simmer and add ribs. Cook in covered sauce pan on medium to low on stove top for 2 to 2 ½ hours or until meat falls away from bones. Serve with sauce. Delicious with cole slaw, cornbread and baked sweet potatoes!"

SCRAPPLE, SOUTHPORT STYLE
(LIVER PUDDING)

1 slice of calf's liver, single
    serving size
1 pork chop
1 ½ cups beef broth
1 cup white corn meal

2 tablespoons finely grated onion
1 slice bacon, finely chopped
1 tablespoon sage
1 teaspoon salt
1 teaspoon pepper

Remove the membrane from the liver. Boil the liver and pork chop until very tender. Discard the liquid and the pork chop bone. The above measurements assume you will wind up with 1 measured pound of cooked meat. (I cook it for ½ hour in a pressure cooker.) Put meat through a grinder or blender, adding beef broth so it will blend well. Pour this and remaining ingredients into a sauce pan, mix well, and cook until the corn meal is done and smooth. Pour into a small 4x6-inch loaf pan and bake on the middle shelf in a 370° oven 30 minutes. Slice and pan-fry in grease. Serve with grits and eggs over easy. This freezes well. Cut into serving size slices, wrap individually and freeze in plastic freezer bags.

SOUSE

Ma-Ma used to make souse, which I foolishly avoided. The recipe is scary, but the taste is enticing, if different. This is based on *Hood's Practical Cook's Book*:

Use the leftover pieces of the pig after the ham, ribs, etc. have been used—the pig's head, the thick fat jowls, ears, feet, and fore part of the leg. Thoroughly cleanse and scrape the skin. Place in salt brine overnight. Discard the brine. Scrape the skin again and once again place in brine overnight. Then place in a kettle, cover with cold water, bring to a boil and simmer until the bones will come out easily. Shuck the meat and discard the bones, gristle, and excess fat. Chop the skin into small pieces. Pack these down hard along with the meat in a stone jar. Cover with vinegar and store away. It will settle down into a compact mass. "It can be cut out and served cold in slices, or warmed up in a spider, or browned, as desired."

HOG'S HEAD CHEESE
Mrs. Hill's Southern Practical Cookery and Receipt Book (1872)

"Split the head apart—the upper portion only is used; scrape it well. The brains must first be removed; cut off the nostrils and throw them away; cut off the ears; clean and scrape them well; they are to be boiled with the head, the tongue and feet. When entirely done, take them from the broth; remove all bones; grind or chop the meat, tongue and ears together. Pick the meat from the feet carefully; season with salt, pepper, mace, allspice, and a few cloves to taste; place a cloth in the bottom of a pan, large enough to cover the cheese; pack the meat in; cover it well with the cloth; lay a tin plate on top, and a weight upon that. When cold, remove the cheese to a plate; garnish with lemon and green sprigs of parsley. Eat for supper or luncheon, with French mustard or pickles. If this is to be kept long, put it in spiced vinegar. The vinegar should not be strong, and should be changed occasionally."

CHITTERLINGS
Mrs. Hill's Southern Practical Cookery and Receipt Book (1872)

"Take the intestines and maws selected for chitterlings (and take only those which are in good condition); cut them open with a sharp knife. Hog chitterlings are best—indeed the only kind in general use. Turn and wash them in several waters; scrape them; lay them to soak in weak salt and water two days, changing the water and washing them well; when changed, in fresh cold water. Boil them until tender; pack them in a jar. Pour over weak vinegar to cover them; renew the vinegar as may be necessary. Cut them in pieces if large; roll in corn meal or bread crumbs, and fry until hot in boiling lard, or dip them in thin batter and fry until the batter is a golden color; very little cooking is required. This is a popular dish, very rich; but should be attended by a very neat, careful person, and not suffered to lie a moment that can be avoided after being taken from the animal until they are cleaned and in soak. The water should be changed often and the vessel in which they are put to soak washed clean each time of changing. Seasoned like oysters, they make a good mock oyster."

ABOUT PORK CHOPS

In the old days, Southport cooks mostly threw their pork chops in the pan and fried them, or grilled them, and they turned out fine. The problem is that today's hog farms breed pork that is much leaner, and pork, especially chops, tend to be tough and dry. I think they put the pigs on low carb diet or tofu. So it's hard to come up with a classic Southport chop. But here are some recipes that bring back the old Southport taste and are juicy and tender. Don't worry about having them a little pink; trichinosis has been eradicated in the U.S.

PAN SAUTÉED PORK CHOPS

Wash the chops and pat dry with paper towels. Combine olive oil and butter in a skillet on medium-low heat, just hot enough that the chops lightly sizzle when placed into the pan. Cook about 2 minutes on the first side to sear, then turn and cook 3 to 4 minutes on the other until it is light brown. Cook until just past the raw stage, still pink and juicy. As the thickness of the chops varies, a precise cooking time is difficult to predict, so as they are nearing done, slice into the thick part of the chop with a sharp knife to check. The first side you have cooked may not have browned; that is all right. Serve it gray side down, browned side up.

BREADED PORK CHOPS

This works equally well for center cut or a second cut of chop. Select as many chops as you wish for your meal. Dip in milk, then coat with bread crumbs. Brown on both sides in a little butter and olive oil. Salt, pepper, and serve.

BAKED PORK CHOPS WITH ONIONS

Pork chops, preferably with
bone in, 1-inch thick,
about 1 per person.
1 good sized onion, cut crossways
in round slices

Butter
Olive oil
Dale sauce, or a mixture of soy
and Worcestershire sauce

Sauté onion slices slowly in skillet with butter and olive oil until translucent and tender, but do not brown. Set aside. Preheat oven to 350°. Sear chops in hot skillet. Add more butter and olive oil and bake uncovered in oven until tender. Top with onions and serve.

LIZZY ROBINSON'S BAKED PORK CHOPS
AND SPANISH RICE
Southport's Favorite Recipes (1950)

4 pork chops
1 cup raw rice
1 green pepper, stem and
membranes removed,
and chopped
2 stalks celery

1 cup tomatoes, cooked
1 medium onion, chopped
Salt and pepper to taste
Cooking oil or bacon
drippings to cover the bottom
of a skillet

Boil rice until tender and drain. Brown chops on either side and remove from pan. Then brown the onion, celery and pepper. Add the tomatoes. Then blend all together in baking dish with chops placed on the top. Bake 15 minutes in 450° oven.

LEMON BAKED PORK CHOPS

6 pork chops ½-inch thick   6 slices lemon
½ cup ketchup   Salt and pepper to taste
½ cup water   Flour to coat
2 tablespoons brown sugar   Cooking oil

Brown chops on both sides in the oil. Place in baking dish. Mix together the ketchup, water and sugar. Pour over chops. Lay slice of lemon on each chop. Bake in preheated 350° for 45 minutes.

STUFFED PORK CHOPS

Select as many 1-inch thick rib pork chops as needed. Make an incision in the side of each to form a little pocket. Fill with the following bread filling."

2 cups bread crumbs   ¼ cup melted butter
1 tablespoon chopped onion   Sage to taste
1 cup chopped apples   Salt and pepper to taste

Place the stuffed chops in a lightly greased baking dish. Bake in slow 325° oven about 40 minutes until brown.

BARBECUED SPARE RIBS

I have not come across a commercial bottled barbecue sauce that beats the sauce in this simple recipe. I have a rule of thumb: if barbecue sauce doesn't taste good licking it before cooking, it won't be any better when cooked.

2 pounds of best quality spare ribs, baby back if available
Burgundy wine, for the first marinade, which is optional.

The sauce for the second marinade and the cooking

½ cup tomato ketchup   2 teaspoons Worcestershire sauce
½ cup honey   1/8 teaspoon cayenne

Slice the ribs into individual pieces or leave the slab intact, as you prefer. I prefer to have individual ribs, as you get more gooky coating to the bite. Marinate in Burgundy wine several hours or overnight. Drain and pat dry. Mix in a bowl the tomato ketchup, honey, Worcestershire Sauce and cayenne. Marinade ribs until ready to cook. Paste with more barbecue sauce. Barbecue on low heat on grill until charred, or in slow 325° oven for 2 hours, turning when half through and painting again with the sauce.

Serve with scalloped potatoes, cole slaw and fresh Carolina-grown sliced tomatoes.

ABOUT EASTERN NORTH CAROLINA PIT BARBECUE

Barbecue comes in many ways. Texas barbecue is typically beef slathered with sauce. In the North, what they call a barbecue is often just a cookout with steaks and hamburgers.

Eastern Carolina pit barbecue is unique to the Coastal Plain of North Carolina from Virginia to South Carolina. It is pit-roasted, shredded and chopped pig, smoked for a long time and basted with vinegar. During the years I was driving I-95 two or three times a year between New York and Southport, my first stop on crossing from the Virginia line into North Carolina was for a Carolina style pit barbecue sandwich, with coleslaw, a little ketchup and hot sauce. A little cafe at Newton's Crossroads had just about the best, lean chopped pork, with chunks of gristle and sometimes little chips of bone that I didn't mind a bit. I knew I was back in the Good Ole North State.

Edgar Finch's Pit Barbecue

You come by your love of Carolina barbecue early. In the late 1940's and early 1950's Mr. Edgar Finch would do a barbecue for the Baptist Church benefit that was just about the best you could get. Ladies of the church put up signs in Watson's and Leggett's Drugstore windows and sold tickets. Edgar's barbecues were so anticipated that word of mouth was usually enough.

Edgar had a good voice and sang in the church choir. He owned a farm not far from town—"the old Finch place," where he raised tobacco and crops and pigs. He'd donate the pig and the oak firewood and do all the work with the help of Mr. Afton Smith and other volunteers. Out in the park behind the church they'd dig a pit about 6x4 feet and about 1 to 2 feet deep, line it with oak logs for the firewood, and overlay an iron grill. They'd slaughter the pig, gut it, cut it in half and lay it out on the grill, "still in his shell," as Afton told me.

On a cold night in winter when the picture show let out, we kids would walk home together and if Edgar had his barbecue going, stop and watch. You could smell the oak fire and pungent smell of the pig sizzling long before you reached the pit. They had a light strung up and kerosene lamps to work by, and tables set out. Edgar and Afton and the others tended the fire all night long and into the next day, taking turns basting and turning the pig. All during the night people would drop by and bring coffee and food and lend a hand. About noon next day, they would start pulling (shredding) and chopping the pork and fixing the paper plates—barbecue, coleslaw or rolls. Once, to everyone's amazement and delight, they took in $200, about $3,000 in today's money.

A PIT BARBECUE

Here's what you will need for your barbecue:

1 Baptist Church
2 shovels
4 volunteers with strong backs to dig a big pit and tend the barbecue,
    or a few more, if anyone is prone to get sleepy about 2 a.m.
2 kerosene lamps
    Or, lights strung out back to see by
1 pig
1 volunteer with a strong stomach for slaughtering the pig
1 butchering knife
1 50-gallon drum for searing the pig
Branches of fresh pine needles for the searing
Metal seals with sharp edges from Mason or Ball jars, or knives, for
    scraping the hide
Hickory chips for smoke
Oak logs or slabs
Vinegar based barbecue sauce for seasoning

Cooks will argue over the exact ways to have a pit barbecue, but our neighbor, Carl Gregory, gave me a detailed description of a classic pit barbecue that is as good as it gets:

For a 100-pound hog, you will first dig a pit about 4-feet wide x 6 feet long, 1 foot deep. Line the pit with cinderblocks up to a total height of 16-inches. Over this, place 4 to 5 black 6 to 7 foot iron pipes or rods (not galvanized, which might kill you), for holding the pig above the fire. The cooking will take about 14 hours, 12 on the flesh side, 2 additional on the skin side.

First, kill the pig by shooting it in the head or slitting its throat. Heat a 50-gallon drum over a fire at a 45-degree angle to a simmering

278

temperature of 175-200°. To this hot water add a couple of fresh branches of green pine needles. The rosins from the pine will form a thin glue-like coating to facilitate the removal of the hairs from the skin.

Immerse the pig and simmer for about 1 minute, no more. Do not immerse longer, nor should you allow the water to boil, as this will prematurely begin to cook the flesh. With sharp-edged sealing Mason or Ball sealing caps from canning jars, or knives, scrape off the hairs from the skin and discard.

In the meantime, get the fire going. Over kindling in the pit, place hickory chips which have been soaked 24 hours so they will provide lots of smoke. Upon these place oak logs. Ignite the kindling and let burn a while.

Tie the pig upside down and slit the throat if you have not already done so to let some of the blood run out. Remove the head, slit down the belly and gut. Place the head in a large pot along with the liver and the "lights" (the lungs). This will be used to make souse, hashlet, or other dishes. Wash out the cavity thoroughly.

Open up the hog and flatten out, legs extended, and place between lengths of wire fence fashioned to form a sort of flat cage. This will help in managing the hog when placed over the fire. Test the temperature of the fire. It should be hot enough so that the hand will be uncomfortable when thrusting it just under the pipes that will hold the pig over the fire. Place the hog, in its "cage" flesh down, over the smoking fire. Do not turn. Baste the pig every 30 minutes with a mixture of half water, half red apple cider vinegar, salt and pepper. After 12 hours puncture the skin well with ice picks or thin knife blades, and add hot coals to increase the heat. Now, thrust 2 long iron rods as handles within the "cage" on either side of the carcass and turn it over, skin side down. Cook for an additional 2 hours so the grease will run out into the fire. The pig should now be thoroughly cooked.

Remove the pig from the "cage" and place on a long table covered with oilcloth. (Some cooks use a table fashioned with a lip around the edge to form a shallow trough; this keeps the meat from falling from the table.) Chop the meat with a cleaver. Skin and set aside the skin for cracklings or fried pork skins. Chop and cut the ham, shoulder and other choice parts into small pieces. Keep some meat on the ribs and set aside or refrigerate to enjoy as spare ribs later.

North Carolina pit barbecue is traditionally served with Tabasco or Texas Pete hot sauce, and a mild vinaigrette sauce made of vinegar, water, salt, a pinch of sugar and ground black pepper. For those who like it a bit spicier, add flakes of red pepper. Serve with barbecue sauce.

CRACKLINGS

Cracklings are the residue from rendering pork. The rendered grease becomes lard when cool. Cracklings are a delicious addition to cornbread and stuffing.

3 to 4 pounds of firm fat from pork loins, or from a pit-barbecued pig. Lard 1-inch deep in a skillet

Cut the fat into half inch cubes and cook on low heat in a large pot, stirring often to assure even browning. The fat will turn brown when it begins to get very hot. When all of the fat is browned, place in a colander to drain. The residue is the cracklings. Absorb excess grease on paper towels.

ABOUT VENISON

The woods around Southport are home to thousands of deer. Their eyes will shine like cats' eyes in your headlights at night as they graze beside the highway. You will see hunters with their trucks parked beside the highways with their dogs and guns waiting for the drive.

Fresh killed venison is apt to be tough. It will be tenderer and of better flavor if allowed to hang at least 2 weeks in a refrigerator or cold locker. Then it may be used immediately, or frozen for use later.

BRAISED VENISON

As venison tends to be tough, this slow cook method helps to tenderize the meat.

2 pounds venison	½ cup chopped celery
2 slices salt pork	¼ cup carrot, peeled and diced
1/8 cup fat	1 tart apple, cored and chopped
1/4 cup hot water	1 teaspoon lemon juice
Flour, to cover the venison	
½ tablespoon vinegar	

Grease the venison with the salt pork. Pat on the salt, pepper and flour. In a Dutch oven, brown the meat on all sides in the hot fat. Add the hot water and vinegar. Cover and cook until tender, about 2 ½ hours. Check every now and then, adding a little more water if necessary to keep it from drying out. Add the celery, carrot and apple a half hour before completing the cooking. Serve with hot pepper jelly, or Tomat-Butter.

BROILED LOIN OF VENISON

Brush ½ inch slices with melted butter or olive oil, salt and pepper. Broil or sauté 5 minutes on each side. Serve with butter creamed with salt, pepper, finely chopped parsley, adding drops of butter drop by drop during the creaming.

ROAST VENISON

Place the leg, loin or saddle in a roasting pan. Cover with the marinade below. Cover and refrigerate for 12 to 24 hours, turning and basting from time to time. Drain. Place bacon slices over the meat and roast at 350° for 20 minutes per pound for rare, 22 for medium rare. Increase the heat to 450° for the last 15 minutes to brown the surface.

The marinade

1 cup cider, heated	½ teaspoon salt
2 tablespoons oil	¼ cup each of celery
1 slice onion	¼ cup of sliced carrot
2 bay leaves	Sprig of thyme or rosemary

VENISON PEPPER STEAK
Contributed by Vickie White Hardee

2 pounds venison	1 teaspoon oregano
1 cup onion, roughly cut	1 tablespoon parsley
2 cups green bell pepper, stem and membrane removed, roughly cut	½ teaspoon thyme
	A sifting of flour
	1 cup cold water
Lard to fry	Salt and pepper to taste

Slice venison cross-grain into small strips of about 1x3 inches. Fry in the lard until crisp. Drain on paper towels. Pour out most of the oil, leaving enough to sauté the onions and peppers. Place the venison pieces in a Dutch oven, sift in the flour. Stir, and add the cup of cold water. Lay the peppers and onions on top, cover, and bake in slow oven ½ to 1 hour.

ROASTED OPOSSUM
Key to the Pantry (1898)

"Clean thoroughly and scrape it. Put it into a stovepan with sufficient cold water, a pod of red pepper and salt. Baste frequently to make it crisp. Cook well done. Serve cold."

FRIED SQUIRREL
Key to the Pantry (1898)

"Cut up the squirrels, salt and pepper them; dredge with flour and fry as you do chicken."

STUFFED BELL PEPPERS

4 bell peppers	1 tablespoon dried basil
1 pound hamburger meat	2 tablespoons minced garlic
2 tablespoons minced salt pork	½ cup fresh parsley, washed,
1 cup rice, cooked	dried and chopped finely
½ onions	Salt and pepper
½ cup green scallions	1 15-ounce can tomato sauce
½ cup carrot, finely shredded	Parmesan cheese, freshly grated
1 tablespoon dried oregano	Seasoned bread crumbs
1 envelope beef granules	

Choose plump, squat bell peppers, rather than tall ones, with "even feet" so they will remain upright in the pan. Cut off tops, remove seeds and membranes. Drop in boiling water, making sure they are totally submerged, and parboil them about 2 to 3 minutes, until you can puncture them with a cake tester. Do not overcook. Drain and set aside. Fry out the salt pork in a skillet, then remove to a mixing bowl. Crumble and fry out the hamburger meat, then drain and add to the bowl. Sauté the carrots, onion and scallion about 3 to 4 minutes. Mix together all ingredients except the tomato sauce. Fill the bell peppers with the mixture. Cover the pepper skins lightly with olive oil, or olive oil spray. Spoon on enough tomato sauce to cover the tops. Sprinkle with bread crumbs and the Parmesan cheese. Place the stuffed peppers in an uncovered baking dish and bake in 350° oven about 45 minutes. Pour the remaining tomato sauce into the hot baking dish. Wait a few minutes and serve with a contrasting vegetable such as steamed yellow squash.

SWEETHEART'S SOUTHPORT STYLE
MEAT SAUCE FOR SPAGHETTI

1 pound ground beef	1 6-ounce can tomato paste
½ pound ground lean pork	4 tablespoons olive oil
1 medium onion, chopped	4 tablespoons butter
1 carrot, grated	2 bay leaves
1 stalk celery	2 whole cloves
1 cup beef bouillon	1 teaspoon thyme
1 14-ounce can tomatoes	Salt and pepper

In a Dutch oven, heat the oil and butter and sauté the garlic and onion slowly until glazed and tender. Remove and put aside. Brown the beef and pork, stirring to break up the big lumps. Add the garlic and onion and remaining ingredients except for the tomato paste. Cover and simmer for 2 hours, occasionally stirring. If sauce is too thin, allow to cook for a while uncovered. Add the tomato paste, and adjust flavors with salt and pepper.

SOUTHPORT STYLE MEAT BALLS FOR SPAGHETTI

1 pound ground beef	1 teaspoon salt
½ pound ground lean pork	¼ cup fresh parsley, chopped
2 eggs	1 teaspoon dried basil, or
½ cup herbed bread crumbs	1 tablespoon fresh basil
2 cloves garlic, minced	Butter and olive oil for browning
1 teaspoon ground black pepper	

Mix the ingredients. Form into small balls. Heat the olive oil and butter in a skillet and brown the meatballs, turning to brown evenly on all sides. They need not cook thoroughly, but can complete their cooking in the spaghetti sauce.

Desserts may be fancier, but they don't get any better than
good old apple pie.

15..
Pies, Cobblers, Etc.

ABOUT PIE CRUST

Ready made frozen or refrigerated pastry is so readily available these days, that it's easy to forget how superior a well turned out homemade piecrust can be. Good pastry should be flaky, tender and delicate. Here are a few hints: All ingredients should be cold, including flour and dry ingredients, mixing bowls, surfaces and utensils. And the mixing should be done quickly. Use cold vegetable shortening such as Crisco, or butter or lard. Cut into flour with two knives or a double-bladed pastry cutter. Mix quickly until the fat, now covered with the flour, is the size of small peas. This mixture may be reserved in the refrigerator until ready to use.

When ready, sprinkle cold water evenly onto the flour-fat mixture, about 2 to 4 tablespoons to 1 cup flour. Some trial and error may be necessary to master this technique. Too little water, and the crust will break; too much and it will be hard and brittle. Toss with a fork. If making two crusts, divide into 2 balls. Coat the board and rolling pin lightly with flour and roll out the pastry. Roll from the center of the dough to the edges to form a circle slightly larger than the pie pan. Place the crust into the pie pan and press down slightly along the edges into the pan. Trim the overlapping crust away with a knife.

BASIC PIE CRUST

1 ¼ cups all purpose flour
1 teaspoon sugar
1 teaspoon salt
¼ cup vegetable shortening

1 tablespoon butter or margarine
4 tablespoons (approximately)
   ice water

In a medium bowl, combine the flour, sugar and salt. With a fork, cut in the shortening and the butter or margarine in the flour and sugar mixture until it is uniformly crumbed. Add the ice water a tablespoon at a time, mixing with a fork, until the dough can be pressed into a ball. Flatten slightly, wrap in plastic wrap and chill for 20 minutes. Roll out the dough on a floured surface into a 12-inch circle and fit into a 10-inch pie plate or deep 9-inch pie dish.

SOUTHERN PASTRY

2 cups flour, sifted   1 cup shortening
½ teaspoon salt   6 tablespoons ice water

Sift flour and salt, then cut in shortening. Shape into 2 balls. Chill thoroughly. Roll out into 2 9-inch pie crusts, or 1 9-inch crust with a top crust.

EGG PIE CRUST

3 cups all purpose flour   1 egg slightly beaten
1 teaspoon salt   3 tablespoons water
1 cup vegetable shortening such   1 teaspoon vinegar
   as Crisco

Cut shortening into the flour and salt until the size of peas. Add beaten egg, water and vinegar. Divide into three equal parts. Flatten each on floured pastry board with rolling pin. Makes enough for one double piecrust and one single.

MERINGUE TOPPING

This classic meringue topping may be used for pies of many sorts, tortes, cobblers, or puddings.

3 to 5 egg whites, depending on   1 teaspoon sugar per egg white
   how high a meringue you   ¼ teaspoon cream of tartar
   wish, room temperature   ½ teaspoon vanilla

Beat egg whites and cream of tartar until frothy. Gradually add the sugar and beat until stiff and glossy. Blend in the vanilla. Spoon onto top of pie, torte, cobbler or pudding with spatula. Bake in 350° oven 10 to 15 minutes or until the meringue is nicely browned.

    About "weeping:" Weeping (little tears of honey-like syrup that form on the meringue) occurs if the sugar has not been well blended into the egg whites, or when the meringue is baked in too hot an oven.

APPLE PIE

The flavor of the pie rests on the quality of the apples. Avoid mealy, flat tasting apples, but choose firm, juicy tart apples such as winesap.

4 or 5 apples	2 teaspoons cinnamon
Butter	¼ teaspoon salt
1 cup white sugar	Pastry dough for the crust
2 cups brown sugar	

Line the bottom of a pie tin with a pastry shell. Peel, core and slice apples into thin slices. Place a layer of apples on the pastry shell, dot with butter and strew with a portion of the sugars, cinnamon and salt. Add another layer of apples and repeat the process. Lay the top crust on, seal the edges, and prick in several places with a fork, in decorative patterns of snowflakes or such if you like. You should have enough layers to make a mound with the final layer, as the apples will cook down a bit. Place on a cookie sheet to catch any drippings. Bake in 400° oven for 20 minutes, reduce temperature to 350° and bake another 25 minute, or until crust is browned and the apples cooked through.

PORK APPLE PIE
Recipes From the Parish of St. Philips in Southport (1907)
Contributed by Lillie Morse

"Make nice paste, line bottom and sides of a large pot. At the bottom lay a large slice of fresh pork with most of the fat trimmed off. Season with salt and pepper, and add pieces of the paste. Next put a thick layer of sliced apples sprinkled with sugar, continue till the vessel has been filled. Moisten with sweet cider. Bake in a slow oven."

OLD FASHION BLUEBERRY PIE

This recipe will also work for blackberry or other berry pies.

4 cups fresh berries	2 tablespoons butter
2 tablespoons flour	1/8 teaspoon salt
1 cup sugar	1 pie shell, unbaked
1 tablespoon lemon juice	

Pick over the berries, discarding stems and leaves. Wash and drain well. In a bowl mix the flour, sugar and salt. Line a 9-inch pan with the rolled pastry, or use the frozen shell. Fill with berries. Sprinkle over them the lemon juice and dot with butter. Use enough berries to form a mound, as the berries will cook down a bit. Place on a cookie sheet to catch any drippings. Lay on the top crust and puncture with fork to vent, fanning out in straight lines from center to form snowflake pattern. Or, for lattice top crust, cut pie dough into ½-inch wide strips and arranged lattice fashion. Bake in a 400° oven for about 45 minutes.

CREAMY BAKED CHEESECAKE

2 8-ounce packages cream cheese, softened	3 eggs
	¼ cup lemon juice
1 14-ounce can sweetened condensed milk	1 8-ounce container sour cream

For the crust

1/3 cup butter or margarine, melted	1 ¼ cups Graham cracker crumbs
	¼ cup sugar

For the crust, combine butter or margarine, crumbs and sugar and press firmly into 8-inch torte pan. For the filling, in large mixing bowl beat the cheese until fluffy. Gradually beat in the sweetened condensed milk until smooth Add the eggs and lemon juice and mix well. Pour into the piecrust. Bake 50 to 55 minutes in preheated 300° oven. Cool completely, then spread the sour cream on top. Chill thoroughly. Serve plain cut into wedges, or top with strawberry or other glazing before serving.

CHOCOLATE PIE
Contributed by Ann Warren

Guaranteed delicious!

¾ cup sugar
2 cups milk
4 tablespoons flour
3 to 4 tablespoons cocoa

Pat of butter or margarine
3 egg yolks, separated
¼ teaspoon vanilla flavoring
1 pie shell, baked

Mix sugar, flour and cocoa. Add milk and cook in heavy saucepan until it begins to thicken. Beat egg yolks in small mixing bowl. Add to yolks several spoonfuls of custard mixture and mix well. Add this to the custard and continue to cook to desired thickness. Remove from heat and add pat of butter or margarine. Stir until well blended. Pour into baked piecrust. Use egg whites for a meringue, using the recipe in this chapter. Spoon on meringue and bake at 350° 12 to 15 minutes, or until meringue is nicely brown.

COCONUT CREAM PIE

1 9-inch pie crust, baked
1/3 cup all-purpose flour
½ cup sugar
2 cups milk
3 egg yolks, beaten

2 tablespoons butter
1 ½ teaspoons vanilla
1 ½ cups moist shredded coconut
1 piecrust, baked

Use a double boiler. Combine the sugar, flour and salt. Add the milk and boil about 20 minutes or until mixture becomes like a very thick pudding. Beat frequently with a wire whisk to avoid lumps. Add the beaten egg yolks and stir well until smooth and thickened. Remove from fire and add the butter, coconut and vanilla, and mix. Pour into the baked pie shell. Top with meringue using one of the recipes for meringue in this chapter. Sprinkle on some shredded coconut. Bake about 15 minutes in 350° oven, or until lightly browned, depending on the thickness of the meringue.

MA-MA'S LEMON MERINGUE PIE

Whenever I came home from college or the Army for visits, Ma-Ma never failed to bake me a lemon pie, which I craved. I still do. Her filling may also be used for small lemon tarts.

½ cup cold water
6 ½ tablespoons cornstarch
1 ½ cups hot water
1 ¼ cups sugar
3 large egg yolks, beaten

Juice of 2 juicy lemons, about ½ cup
2 tablespoons butter
Pinch of salt
1 9-inch pie crust, unbaked

Dissolve cornstarch in the cold water in a heavy saucepan or double boiler. Add the hot water, sugar, salt, and cook over low heat until it comes to a boil thickened, coats the spoon and is about the consistency of sweetened condensed milk. Add butter. Pour small amount of hot mixture into beaten egg yolk, and then mix all. Cook, stirring, until it has the consistency of a thick pudding. Add the lemon juice. Pour into 9-inch pre-baked pie crust. Top with a high meringue. Bake on bottom rack of a 350° oven 15 or more minutes or until the meringue is nicely browned.

ABOUT CHESS PIE

Chess pies are predominantly Southern, and one of the most delectable of desserts. The basic chess pie is of eggs, butter and sugar, with varying flavorings and textures such as chocolate, tangerine, lemon-buttermilk or pumpkin. The familiar pecan pie is a vanilla chess with pecan nuts added. The origin of the word "chess" is debated. It may take its name from Chester, England; for the fact that it holds up well in a pie "chest;" or for the time a woman apologized for her dessert: "It's ches' pie."

LEMON CHESS PIE

1 cup sugar
1 stick butter, melted and cooled
3 eggs, beaten
1 cup light corn syrup
¼ cup cornmeal

1/3 cup lemon juice
1 tablespoon cornstarch
¼ teaspoon salt
1 unbaked piecrust
Cornmeal to sprinkle on top

Mix ingredients well and turn into the piecrust. Sprinkle generously with cornmeal. Bake in preheated 350° about 55 minutes, or until firm. If piecrust begins to over-cook, place a sheet of tinfoil over and cook until done.

ABOUT KEY LIMES

The Key limes are small, about the size of golf balls, and delicate yellow when ripened. They have a distinctive taste apart from the larger, sharper, green variety. The name is something of a misnomer, since they originated in Malaysia and were not brought to the Keys and cultivated until about 1913; but even after a hurricane destroyed the groves, the name stuck. They are the most popular lime in parts of the world, but seldom found out of the South in the United States. Key limes nowadays they come mostly from the Florida mainland, Mexico, Honduras and Egypt.

KEY LIME PIE

This is my favorite, because it's as close to the Key Lime pie of memory as I can make. It's "as easy as pie" and absolutely delicious. Some prefer their Key Lime pie baked in a Graham cracker crust. I like it both ways.

1 8-inch pastry shell, regular, not deep	4 teaspoons sugar for the meringue
1 can sweetened condensed milk	½ teaspoon cream of tartar for the meringue
½ cup fresh Key Lime juice	
4 eggs separated	

In a mixing bowl beat the egg yolks, then add the sweetened condensed milk and limejuice. Mix well, and pour into pie shell. Top with Meringue Topping using recipe on page 286. Or, cover rim of piecrust with a strip of aluminum foil to prevent browning. Pre-bake in 350° oven about 15 minutes until brown. Cool to lukewarm. Add the pie filling and bake in 350° oven about 10 minutes until pie is set. Remove foil from crust. Add whipped cream to each slice before serving.

A Dismal Memory of Key Lime Pie

During the Key West years one Saturday, Daddy took our family and some friends to lunch in a restaurant near the pier where his boats moored. To my juvenile brain, it was the last word in tropical modernity and glamour—pink brick columns with floor-to-ceiling windows slanted outward. Hibiscus and bougainvillea blossoms frolicked, palm trees waved in the Gulf breeze—a far cry from Quack's Sea Shack in Southport.

I forget what I ordered for the entrée—the most expensive thing on the menu Daddy would allow, I'm sure. And for dessert, I ordered a favorite, Key Lime pie. The waitress placed before me one of the most delectable concoctions imaginable—a cloud of whipped cream over a huge wedge of translucent, light-yellow filling languishing upon a flaky, brown crust. Alas! At that same moment the waitress placed the bill before Daddy. Being a wise and prudent man, he immediately double-checked it.

"Forty cents!?" he exclaimed. *"That pie is forty cents?!"*

"I guess so," I replied, knowing full-well that Lee's Chinese Restaurant charged only ten cents, the La Concha Hotel Dining Room, only fifteen.

"I'm not about to pay for that!" said my father, and snatching the plate from under my nose, handed it back to the waitress.

"Daddy, please!" I begged.

Oh, the cruelty to which parents subject their children! No lime pie! No six-inch high, forty-cents-a-slice Key Lime pie with a cloud of whipped cream! Daddy was right, of course. Shrimp, our livelihood, at that time wasn't bringing forty-cents a pound wholesale.

PEACH PIE

8 to 9 ripe fresh peaches	Pinch of salt
1 cup brown sugar	Butter to dot
About 1 teaspoon cinnamon	Pastry for 2 crusts,
A few drops of Bourbon	a top and a bottom

Line a 9-inch pie tin with pie crust. Peel and slice the peaches into eights and place on the pie crust. Mix the sugar and cinnamon, and pour the mixture over the peaches. Dot with butter and sprinkle with the Bourbon. Lay on the top crust, seal and puncture with a fork several times. Place a cookie sheet underneath to catch any drippings. Bake at 450° for 10 minutes, then at 375° for 30 to 40 minutes, until crust is brown.

292

MERINGUE SHELL

A meringue shell is easy to make. It makes a delicious and festive dish when filled with chocolate pudding, or vanilla pudding, juicy strawberries, raspberries, peaches or other fruit, or combinations thereof, then topped with whipped cream and brought to the table, or when baked as small, individual servings.

3 to 5 egg whites	½ teaspoon vanilla
1 cup sugar	¼ teaspoon cream of tartar

Let the egg whites stand in a small mixer bowl at room temperature for 1 hour. Cover a baking sheet with plain brown paper or foil, and draw a 9-inch circle. Add the vanilla and cream of tartar to the egg whites and beat with electric mixer on medium speed until soft peaks form. Add the sugar 2 tablespoons at a time, beating on high speed until the stiff peak stage. With a spatula, spoon the meringue into the circular shape on the brown paper, building up the sides to form a pool. Bake in 300° oven 50 minutes. Turn off the oven and let the meringue dry in the oven for 1 hour. Do not open door.

ORANGE MERINGUE PIE
Cousin Mary Mulling's Recipe Files

1 cup sugar	2 tablespoons butter
4 tablespoons cornstarch	3 eggs, separated
¼ teaspoon cream of tartar	1 teaspoon lemon juice
1 1/3 cups orange juice	1 8-inch pie shell, baked
Grated rind of one orange	

In saucepan, mix sugar, cornstarch, cream of tartar, then add orange juice. Cook over medium heat until thick, stirring constantly. Allow to boil 1 minute, still stirring. In a separate bowl beat the egg yolks, then beat in ½ of the hot mixture. Add this to the saucepan with the rest of the mixture. Add the butter, orange rind and lemon juice. Boil 1 minute, stirring constantly. Turn into the baked 8-inch pie shell. Beat the egg whites until stiff, add a tablespoon of sugar and ¼ teaspoon cream of tartar, and continue to beat until the stiff-peak stage. Top pie with the meringue and bake in 325° oven 8 to 10 minutes or until the meringue is light brown.

SWEETHEART'S PECAN PIE

1 ½ cups pecan halves, slightly
   toasted
1 stick butter or margarine,
   melted and cooled
1 cup sugar
½ cup light corn syrup

½ cup dark corn syrup
3 eggs, beaten
1 teaspoon vanilla
¼ teaspoon salt
1 piecrust, unbaked,
   or 14 mini-pie crusts

Mix all ingredients and pour into unbaked pie crust. Place on cookie sheet and bake in preheated 350° oven 35 to 40 minutes. Or, pour into 14 mini-pie crusts and bake about 30 minutes, until crust is brown and pies are set.

PUMPKIN PIE

This is one recipe I'd recommend using canned pumpkin rather than boiled fresh pumpkin. I've never had pumpkin pie with fresh pumpkin turn out as good as with a good brand of canned pumpkin.

1 15-ounce can pure pumpkin
1 12-ounce can evaporated milk,
   undiluted
2 large eggs
¾ cup granulated sugar
½ teaspoon ground cinnamon
½ teaspoon ground ginger

1/2 teaspoon ground nutmeg
1/8 teaspoon ground cloves
Pinch of salt
1 9-inch deep-dish pie shell,
   baked
Whipped cream to top

Prepare a baked pie shell, the edges of which have been covered with foil strips to avoid burning after the filling has been added and the pie returned to the oven. Let cool. In a bowl, mix sugar, salt and spices with the pumpkin. Beat separately the 2 eggs in another bowl, and add to mixture. Gradually stir in evaporated milk and mix well. Pour into the baked pie shell. Bake in preheated 425° oven 40 to 50 minutes or until knife inserted near center comes out clean. Cool on wire rack for 2 hours. Serve immediately or refrigerate. Top with whipped cream before serving. Makes 8 servings.

EVELYN THOMPSON'S COCOA PECAN PIE
Jean Thompson Poole's Recipe Files

1 cup sugar
1/3 cup unsweetened cocoa
3 eggs, slightly beaten
1 cup light or dark corn syrup
1 tablespoon margarine,
    melted

1 teaspoon vanilla
1 cup pecan halves
1 unbaked 9-inch pastry shell

In medium bowl, stir together the sugar and cocoa. Stir in eggs, syrup, margarine and vanilla until well blended. Stir in pecans. Pour into pie shell. Bake in 350° oven for 50 to 60 minutes. Center should be softer than outer edges. Cool. Garnish with whipped cream or Cool Whip if desired.

ERLINE PERRYMAN'S SWEET POTATO PIE
Erline Perryman's Recipe Files

Sweet potato pie was never one of my favorites. It always seemed heavy and packed, as if someone accidentally sat on it. But dear Erline Perryman recently brought us one that changed my mind. It's absolutely heavenly. I can see why Erline is on the committee at her church that takes meals to the sick and shut-in.

2 ¼ cups cooked sweet potatoes
    mashed
¾ cup granulated sugar
½ cup firmly packed brown sugar
½ cup packaged French vanilla
    instant pie pudding
¾ cup evaporated canned milk

2 large eggs at room temperature
4 tablespoons butter
1 teaspoon ground cinnamon
1 teaspoon vanilla
¼ teaspoon nutmeg
1 pie shell, unbaked

In a large bowl combine ingredients by hand, or with an electric beater at medium speed. Spread evenly into unbaked pie shell. A 9-inch Pyrex dish works well. Bake at 450° for 10 minutes. Reduce temperature to 350° and bake 40 minutes longer, or until done. Cool on a wire rack. Garnish with whipped cream.

COUSIN MARY BOMBERGER'S SHOO-FLY PIE

¾ cup molasses
2 ¼ cups flour
6 tablespoons shortening
¾ cup brown sugar
¾ cup boiling water

¾ teaspoon soda
¾ teaspoon cinnamon
Pinch of salt
One 9-inch pie shell, uncooked

Combine molasses, soda and water and pour into pie shell. Reserve liquid to mix with some of the flour mixture. Rub together flour, salt, shortening, sugar and cinnamon. Sprinkle on top of the molasses/soda/water mixture. Bake in moderate 350° oven about 35 minutes, until filling is a rich brown.

ABOUT COBBLERS

The cobbler is a deep-dish berry or fruit pie often with a rich biscuit dough instead of pastry. For most of the recipes in this section, various fruits or berries may substituted with equal results.

APPLE COBBLER

3 large apples
1 cup sugar
½ teaspoon nutmeg
½ teaspoon cinnamon

½ cup butter
1 recipe buttermilk biscuit
   dough (Bisquick may be used)

Peel, core and slice apples very thin. Roll out 3 thin layers of biscuit dough the diameter of the deep dish or casserole to be used. Lightly butter the vessel. Place on the bottom a layer of the biscuit dough, then a layer of the sliced apples, sprinkle on part of the sugar, cinnamon and nutmeg and dot with butter. Add another layer of biscuit dough and repeat the process, ending with a top layer of the biscuit dough. Bake on bottom rack of oven in a 370° oven 35 to 45 minutes, or until the apples are done and the cobbler is brown and bubbly. Serve with hard sauce or whipped cream.

BLUEBERRY COBBLER

1 stick butter or margarine	2 cups blueberries
1 cup milk	¼ teaspoons mace
1 sup sugar	Dash of nutmeg
1 cup flour	Dash of cinnamon

Put butter in a 9-inch square baking dish and place in 350° oven until butter melts. Mix flour, sugar, and then milk in mixing bowl to make a thin batter. Pour over the butter to cover bottom of dish. Place berries over top and sprinkle with spices. Bake about 30 minutes in 350° oven.

BLACKBERRY COBBLER

3 cups fresh blackberries	1 tablespoon cornstarch
¾ cup plus 2 tablespoons water	Dots of butter or margarine
¼ to ½ cup sugar	1 teaspoon cinnamon

For the dough

1 cup sifted cake flour	2 tablespoons vegetable
1 tablespoon sugar	shortening
1 ½ teaspoons baking powder	1/3 cup milk
¼ teaspoon salt	

Heat berries in a saucepan with ¾-cup water and sugar. In a small bowl whisk together cornstarch and remaining 2 tablespoons water until cornstarch is dissolved and add to berry mixture. Bring mixture to a boil and boil 1 minute. Pour mixture into a 2-quart baking dish. Dot with butter or margarine and sprinkle with cinnamon. To make dough: In a large bowl, sift together flour, sugar, baking powder and salt, and with a pastry blender or two knives blend in shortening until mixture resembles coarse meal. Add milk, stirring until combined well. On a lightly floured surface, with floured hands pat dough out until ½ inch thick. Top berries in dish with dough and prick top to vent, or drop by teaspoons over berries. Bake in preheated 400° oven 20 minutes. Serve warm with ice cream or whipped cream.

APPLE DUMPLING
The Southern Cook Book (1939)

2 cups flour
4 teaspoons baking powder
1 teaspoon salt
4 tablespoons shortening

1 cup milk
6 apples, cored and pared
Sugar
Cinnamon

Sift flour, baking powder and salt. Cut in shortening. Add milk and mix to smooth dough. Turn onto floured board and divide into six portions. Roll each large enough to cover one apple. Place apple on each piece of dough. Fill with cinnamon and sugar. Wet edges of dough and fold over apple. Place on greased baking pan and bake in moderate 350° oven until apples are tender, about a half hour.

AUNT CONTENT'S CHERRY COBBLER

1 10-ounce can sour red cherries
1 ¾ cups sugar
1 cup sifted flour
    plus 3 tablespoons more
1 cup sugar

½ teaspoon salt
1 teaspoon baking powder
2 tablespoons butter
½ cup milk

Mix ¾ cup of the sugar and 1 tablespoon flour, add to the cherries and bring to a boil. Pour into a baking dish. Mix 1 cup plus 2 tablespoons flour, 1 cup sugar, the salt, baking powder and cut in the butter. Add milk and stir. Pour cherry mix into a baking dish. Drop this mixture on top of the cherry mixture and bake 30 minutes in 350° oven.

PEACH COBBLER, OR OTHER FRUIT COBBLER

Follow the recipe on page 296 for apple cobbler, but substitute another fruit.

APPLE CRISP
Southport's Treasure of Personal Recipes (1952)
Contributed by Mrs. Doris Hickman Stephens

Doris was one of the superb cooks at the Southport High School lunch room during the 1950's.

6 apples, peeled, cored and
    quartered
1 cup sugar
¾ cup flour

1 teaspoon cinnamon
¼ teaspoon nutmeg
1 stick butter

Combine sugar, flour, cinnamon and nutmeg. Cut in the butter. Make a crumbly mixture. Place the apples in a baking dish or pan. Cove with the mixture. Bake 35 minutes in a 375° oven.

PEACH CRISP

4 cups fresh peaches, cored,
    peeled and sliced
1/3 cup brown sugar
¼ cup oatmeal
¼ cup flour

½ teaspoon nutmeg
¼ teaspoon cinnamon
2 tablespoons butter or
    margarine, softened

Coat 8-inch baking dish lightly with oil or cooking spray. Line dish with peaches. In a separate bowl, mix the remaining ingredients. Sprinkle over the peaches and bake in 375° oven for 30 minutes, or until peaches are bubbly and golden brown. Serve warm or cold, with ice cream or whipped cream.

Cousin Vivian McKeithan Jones, 2004, with some of the Christmas baking—
nut bread and fruit cake.

16..
Cakes & Cookies,
Frostings & Fillings

Josie Newton and her husband, H. B. "Mitty" Smith,
at Atlantic City, 1920's.

Josie Smith's Sad Cake

In the old days when a cake went into the oven, children and men were banished from the kitchen or made to tiptoe around as if they were walking on eggs. The least bump could cause the cake to "fall," resulting in a "sad cake." Chocolate cakes are particularly prone to fall. Some men, like old Doc Watson, craved the rich, compressed, doughy cake, and begged their wives, "Please bake me a sad cake."

Josie Newton Smith lived in a handsome white house on Lord Street. She subscribed to *Time* magazine and from her bay window could see the world and knew everything that was going on in town. She was a precise, high-strung woman, and like all of the Newton clan, was bright as they come, and full of words and wit.

But she hated the kitchen. Once she attempted a pound cake and complained to a neighbor that it failed.

"Do you mean, it fell?" asked the neighbor.

"Did it fall?!!" she exclaimed. "So hard I had to go under the house to get it out of the oven!"

TROUBLESHOOTING

A fallen cake could be the result of too much sugar liquid or shortening, or too little flour. Or, the temperature was too low or allowed to fluctuate during cooking.

A heavy, dense cake could be caused by too much liquid or shortening, too many eggs, or over-mixing. The temperature may have been too high. Also, the baking powder or baking soda may be old. Check the expiration date on the container.

A crumbling cake may mean too much sugar, leavening or shortening, or under-mixing.

A soggy bottom could mean too much liquid, eggs were insufficiently beaten, it wasn't mixed or baked enough.

ONE-TWO-THREE-FOUR CAKE
Swans Down Cake Flour Method

The One-Two-Three-Four Cake has been used in Southport for over a hundred years, and since 1894, Swans Down cake flour has been famous throughout the South and in Southport.

1 cup butter or margarine, softened	3 teaspoons baking powder
	½ teaspoon salt
2 cups sugar	1 cup milk
3 cups cake flour, sifted	1 teaspoon vanilla
4 eggs	½ teaspoon almond extract
1 cup milk	

Butter and flour three 9-inch cake pans. In a mixing bowl cream butter and gradually add sugar, creaming until light and fluffy. Add eggs one at a time, beating well after each addition. In another bowl, sift flour with baking powder and salt. Add flour mixture alternately with milk and flavorings to creamed mixture, beating after each addition until smooth. Pour batter into cake pans. Bake in preheated 300° oven 30 to 35 minutes. Cool 10 minutes, remove from pans and let cool completely on racks.

CLASSIC WHITE CAKE

3 cups flour, sifted
1/3 cup soft shortening
1 3/4 cups sugar
1 1/3 cups skimmed milk

4 egg whites, stiffly beaten
3 ½ teaspoons baking powder
2 teaspoons vanilla
¾ teaspoon salt

Cream together the shortening and sugar until fluffy. Sift together the flour, baking soda and salt. Mix the vanilla into the milk. Alternately stir the flour mixture and the milk into the fluffy sugar and shortening. Fold in the egg whites. Pour into 2 9-inch layer pans, or a 9x11x3-inch rectangular pan. Bake the layers in preheated moderate 350° oven for 30 to 35 minutes; the long pan, 35 to 45 minutes. Cool on wire racks.

TURTLE EGG CAKE
Brunswick Potluck Cookbook (1960's)
Contributed by Mrs. Delphia Oberjohann

Turtles are an endangered species and protected by law. Regular hen eggs must be substituted for turtle eggs. You might like to see the article, "When Turtles Cry," on pages 344-345.

3 cups self-rising flour
½ pound butter
2 hen eggs
2 cups sugar
10 turtle egg yolks (about
    6 yolks of large hen eggs
    provides an equivalency)

Pinch of soda
Pinch of salt
1 teaspoon lemon extract
Milk

Cream sugar and butter. Beat turtle egg yolks and unseparated hen eggs, salt and soda until fluffy. Add to sugar and butter. Add lemon extract. Add flour and enough milk to make the batter smooth and creamy. Have oven preheated to 400°. Put cake in oven. Bake 10 minutes, then turn oven to 350° and bake 45 minutes until done.

303

Dwight McEwen, about 1960, in a rare photo of him without a coat and vest.

Dwight McEwen, Esq.

Dwight McEwen was a gentleman of the old school. He wore a light brown mustache stained with tobacco, and walked and sat erect as a general. Mr. Mac, as we called him, always dressed in a suit with a vest. A watch chain dangled on his fob. He was a close friend of our family, and no Christmas went by that Ma-Ma didn't wrap up a red tin of Prince Albert for his pipe. He was a lawyer and a court reporter, and his office and little apartment were above the old Post Office where Mammie Dozier was his secretary. He'd sit on her porch and visit in the late afternoon or on Sunday mornings and smoke his pipe, and was given to grand remarks such as, "The King James Version of the Bible is the grandest work of poetry and philosophy in the English literature!" Long after Mammie could no longer work he kept her on his payroll, though he had no legal obligation to do so.

He was one of the first persons in Southport to own a motorcycle, which he rode up and down the River Road between Southport and Wilmington where he worked as a Court Reporter. Mr. Mac was divorced and lived alone, and I suppose by necessity became a good cook. Here's his sour cream pound cake.

304

MR. MAC'S SOUR CREAM POUND CAKE

½ pound butter (2 sticks), softened
3 cups sugar
6 eggs
3 cups sifted flour

½ pint (8-ounce) sour cream
¼ teaspoon soda
1 teaspoon vanilla and 2 teaspoons almond extract, or 1 vanilla and 1 lemon extract

Cream together the butter and sugar. Blend in the eggs one by one with a sprinkle of the flour as each egg is added. Add remaining flour and the baking soda. Blend in but do not whip the sour cream. Turn into ungreased circular tube pan and bake in preheated 325° oven for 1 ½ hours. Let sit for 15 minutes, invert the pan to release the cake, then place upright on a cake dish.

SUPERMOIST CHOCOLATE CAKE

2 cups all-purpose flour
1 cup sugar
3 tablespoons baking cocoa
2 teaspoons baking soda

1 cup water
1 cup mayonnaise
1 teaspoon vanilla extract

In large mixing bowl, combine flour, sugar, cocoa and baking soda. Add water, mayonnaise and vanilla. Beat at medium speed until thoroughly combined. Pour into greased 9-inch square, or 11x7x2-inch baking pan. Bake in preheated 350° oven for 30 to 35 minutes or until cake tests done when a cake tester or toothpick comes out clean. Cool completely.

APPLESAUCE CAKE

1 cup butter
2 cups sugar
4 cups flour
2 cups applesauce
2 eggs
1 cup nuts
1 cup raisins

1 teaspoon baking soda
1 teaspoon vanilla
1 teaspoon cinnamon
½ teaspoon allspice
½ teaspoon cloves
½ teaspoon nutmeg

Cream butter and sugar, then add the eggs. Add soda to applesauce, and then add this to the mixture. Add remaining ingredients and mix. Turn into 2 8-inch loaf pans ¾ full. Bake in preheated 300° oven 1 hour or longer.

CARRIE DREW FULCHER'S ITALIAN CREAM CAKE
Julie Ann Harrelson's Recipe Files

Tommy says, "Carrie Drew, like her sister, Annie Lou Newton, was a fine cook. One of her specialties is this cake that she offered at times to church bake sales and for auction at fund raising events. This cake was always one of the most popular, bringing in well over $100 on several occasions."

2 sticks of butter	1 cup buttermilk
6 eggs, yolks and whites	1 teaspoon vanilla
separated	1 small can angel flake coconut
2 cups self-rising flour	2 cups finely chopped pecans
1 teaspoon baking soda	2 cups sugar

Preheat oven to 350°. Grease and flour 3 cake pans. Measure out and place al ingredients in small containers so mixing can proceed smoothly. Beat the 6 egg whites until very stiff and set aside. In another bowl, cream butter and sugar and beat with mixer until smooth. Add egg yolks, and beat well. Combine flour and soda and add to batter alternately with buttermilk. Stir in vanilla, coconut, and 2 cups of finely chopped pecans. Fold in stiff egg whites. Do not beat. Pour batter into 3 cake pans and bake in preheated oven 25 minutes at 350° degrees.

For the frosting

2 8-ounce package cream cheese	1 can angel flake coconut
1 stick of butter, softened	Pecan halves
2 boxes of 10x powdered sugar	Maraschino cherries
2 teaspoons of vanilla	

Simply mix all ingredients and ice cake when layers have cooled. Top with coconut, pecan halves, and maraschino cherries for decoration.

MA-MA'S OLD TIME SPONGE CAKE

Ma-Ma wrote, "The weight of the eggs in sugar, and half their weight in flour; this enables you to make a cake of any size you desire. You will look far to find a better sponge cake."

5 large eggs, separated
1 cup granulated sugar
1 cup pastry flour sifted

Grated rind and juice of 1 lemon
Pinch of salt
Confectioner's sugar, about ½ cup

Line a 11x16 inch shallow pan with wax paper or cooking parchment. Beat yolks until thick and very creamy. Add sugar and beat till light colored. Beat in the lemon rind, juice and salt. In a separate bowl, beat whites till stiff and nearly dry. Sift in the flour lightly over the beaten egg whites and fold 'till just barely covered. Do not stir, but fold, careful not to break down the air bubbles. After the flour has been folded into the egg whites, fold in the egg and sugar mixture. Spread the batter onto the lined pan. Bake in preheated 350° oven 40 to 50 minutes. Do not over-bake. When done, turn onto a fine towel that has been generously sprinkled with confectioner's sugar. Peel off the paper. If the sponge cake is to be used for a jelly roll, immediately roll and set according to the instructions below for jelly roll.

HERMITS
Key to the Pantry (1898)

8 egg yolks
2 cups sugar
½ cup butter
½ teaspoon soda
3 tablespoons sour cream
2 cups seeded raisins or
    currants

1 teaspoon powdered cinnamon
½ teaspoon powdered cloves
Flour sufficient to make a
    soft dough

Roll out a half inch thick. Cut into squares. Place an inch apart on greased tins, and bake in quick oven [450°].

MA-MA'S JELLY ROLL

1 recipe of Ma-Ma's Old Time Sponge Cake from page 307
1 cup of whipped jelly or jam, grape, strawberry, raspberry, apple, or whatever you prefer

When the Old Time Sponge Cake has been baked and turned onto the sugar-covered towel, roll up into the towel and allow to cool and set, about 30 minutes or a little longer. Unroll, spread on the jelly or jam and roll back up again and cover with waxed paper. When ready to serve, remove from paper and slice crossways in 1-inch thick circles.

ANGEL FOOD CAKE

Many Southport cooks ice their angel food cake with vanilla or chocolate frosting, but that seems like gilding the lily to me. Angel food cake is great just as it is, or topped with peaches or strawberries and syrup.

1 cup sifted cake flour	1/4 teaspoon salt
1 ½ cups sugar	1 1/3 teaspoons cream of tartar
1 1/3 cups of egg whites, about 12 medium sized eggs	1 1/2 teaspoons vanilla or almond extract

Sift the flour and measure into a big mixing bowl. Then sift it four times with ¼ cup of the sugar and the salt. Sift in the rest of the sugar. Beat the egg whites in a large bowl until foamy and white but not stiff. Add the cream of tartar and beat until stiff enough to form stiff peaks. Sprinkle 2 tablespoons of sugar over the beaten egg whites and beat until just blended. Beat in the remaining sugar a little at a time. Add vanilla or almond. Fold in the flour with a rubber spatula, sprinkling about ¼ cup over the egg whites at a time. Pour the batter into an ungreased 9 or 10-inch circular tube pan and bake in preheated 325° oven 40 to 60 minutes until the top is nicely brown. Remove from oven and turn pan upside and let hang until cool. Remove from pan and set on a cake dish.

DEVIL'S FOOD CAKE

Is it too irreverent to follow angel food with devil's food?

2 cups flour
1 ½ cups sugar or firmly packed
   brown sugar
¾ cups cocoa
2 eggs
1 cup milk

1 ¼ cups butter or margarine
1 teaspoon baking soda
½ teaspoon salt
1 teaspoon red cake coloring
2 teaspoons vanilla

Cream together the butter or margarine with the sugar. Add the 2 eggs, beating well after each addition. Add remaining ingredients. Bake in greased and floured 9x19-inch pan or two 9-inch square pans in preheated 350° oven about 35 minutes.

MA-MA'S HOT MILK CAKE

This cake is so delicious, with a rich and moist crust, it doesn't need icing. It holds up well when kept in refrigerator and served cold.

¼ pound butter
1 cup milk
2 cups flour
2 cups sugar

3 eggs
1 teaspoon vanilla
1 teaspoon baking powder
Pinch of salt

Put milk and butter in sauce pan and bring to boil. Set aside to cool. Beat eggs, add sugar and beat until creamy. Add flour and milk alternately, then salt and vanilla. Just before putting in pan, add the baking powder and mix well. Bake in greased square 9-inch pan in preheated 350° oven for 40 to 45 minutes, or when a cake-tester comes out clean; or in two 4½x9-inch loaf pan about 50 minutes; or in 5 4x6-inch loaf pans for about 40 minutes.

EASY PINEAPPLE-COCONUT CAKE
Myrtle Watson's Recipe Files

Some of the most delicious cakes are also the simplest. Myrtle Watson's pineapple–coconut cake falls into this category.

Bake a recipe of One-Two-Three-Four Cake on page 302, or a package of yellow cake mix. Let cool. Puncture top with a fork all over. Spoon on a can of crushed pineapple, not drained. If the cake is to be eaten soon, layer on a nice thickness of heavy whipped cream. If not, layer on Cool Whip. To either the whipped cream or Cool Whip, sprinkle on a generous layer of fresh frozen coconut flakes. Delicious.

BANANA LAYER CAKE

A more delicious cake you can't find. But since it calls for fresh bananas that turn dark quickly, it should be used promptly.

1 recipe for One-Two-Three-Four
Cake, page 302, or packaged
yellow layer mix

1 recipe Classic Seven-Minute
Frosting, page 334
2 bananas

Bake the cakes in 3 9-inch layers. Cool. Spread bottom two layers with one-half recipe of the Classic Seven-Minute Frosting. Lay on sliced bananas. Place top layer on and ice with remainder of the frosting on top and sides.

ALMOND MACAROONS

1/2 pound almond paste
1 cup sugar
3 egg whites, unbeaten
1/3 cup confectioner's sugar

2 tablespoons pastry or cake flour
1/8 teaspoon salt
1/2 cup or more thinly shaved
almonds

Mix the almond paste thoroughly with your hands. Add bit by bit the sugar and unbeaten egg whites. Blend thoroughly and sift in the confectioner's sugar, flour and salt. Cover cookie sheets with brown paper, not waxed. Place teaspoonfuls of the batter on the paper and flatten into tiny mounds, or shape with a pastry bag and tube. Sprinkle and press on the almonds. Cover and let stand for 2 hours. Bake 30 minutes at 300°.

Leila Jane Sellers. Photo courtesy of Susie Carson.

HUCKLEBERRY OR BLUEBERRY CAKE
Susie Carson's Recipe Files

Susie Sellers Carson has contributed a generous number of old Southport recipes for this book. Huckleberries used to be more common than blueberries, as they could be gathered nearby in the woods. This recipe was used by Susie's mother, Leila Jane Sellers (1892-1972), who would send it to her husband, Ledrew, serving in France during World War I. "Postage wasn't so expensive in those days," remarked Susie.

½ cup butter
¾ cup milk or buttermilk
1 cup berries, dredged in flour

1 cup sugar
2 cups self-rising flour
3 eggs, beaten

Cream butter and sugar. Add eggs and milk. Lastly, add berries which have been dampened and covered with dry flour. This is necessary to keep the berries from sinking to the bottom of the pan. Pour into 9x9-inch baking dish or pan. Bake 35 to 45 minutes in preheated 350° oven or until lightly browned.

311

CHIFFON CAKE

This cake appeared about 1950 and for a while was the rage of the town. It was a radical method, using cooking oil instead of firm shortening, eliminating the need for cutting the shortening into the flour or creaming the sugar and shortening together. It is delicious and may be served plain, or frosted.

2 cups flour	2 teaspoons vanilla
1 1/2 cups sugar	3 teaspoons baking powder
1/3 cup Wesson oil	1 teaspoon salt
7 eggs separated	½ teaspoon cream of tartar
3/4 cup cold water	

Sift together the flour, sugar, salt and baking powder. Add the Wesson oil, egg yolks, cold water and vanilla. Beat until smooth. In separate bowl beat the egg whites until very stiff. Add the cream of tartar and beat slowly until mixed. Fold whites into flour mixture. Pour into ungreased circular angel food pan. Bake at once in preheated 325° oven for 55 minutes, then an additional 10 minutes at 350°.

ORANGE CHIFFON CAKE

Follow the recipe for chiffon cake above, but substitute ¾ cup orange juice for the cold water, and 2 teaspoons orange extract for the vanilla.

COCONUT LAYER CAKE

1 recipe for One-Two-Three-Four Cake, or a packaged yellow cake mix.

Coconut frosting

2 cups grated coconut	1 cup water
Juice and rind of one large orange	2 egg whites
2 cups sugar	½ teaspoon cream of tartar

Mix coconut with juice and rind of orange and let stand while making frosting. Dissolve sugar in water and boil syrup until it forms a soft ball when dropped in water or spins a thread about 3 inches long when dropped from a spoon. Whip egg whites until frothy. Add syrup in a thin stream, whipping constantly. When frosting is fluffy and forms peaks, mix in cream of tartar. Divide coconut mixture among three layers. Spread frosting on two layers, top with third layer and frost top and sides of cake.

LEMON JELLY/COCONUT LAYER CAKE

1 recipe One-Two-Three-Four Cake, page 302,
    or a packaged yellow cake mix
1 recipe for White Butter Icing, page 334
1 recipe for Classic Seven-Minute Frosting, page 334
1 can coconut, grated
1 recipe Great Grandma Davis's Lemon Jelly Filling, page 336

Bake in 3 9-inch layers. While layers are slightly warm, spread each layer with a thin coating of the White Butter Icing. This will keep the crumbs from coming through the Seven-Minute Frosting. Spread the bottom layer with Great Grandma Davis's lemon jelly filling and sprinkle on grated coconut liberally. Repeat for the second layer. Spread the Seven-Minute Frosting on the top layer and sides, and pat on grated coconut.

LADY BALTIMORE CAKE

1 recipe for Classic White Cake, page 303, or use a packaged cake mix. Bake this in 3 layers. Use a double recipe of Seven-Minute Frosting, page 334. To one half of the frosting add:

1 cup chopped raisins	1 cup chopped figs
1 ½ cups chopped nut meats	½ teaspoon lemon extract

Mix thoroughly and spread on the bottom two layers of the cake. Spread remaining icing over top layer and sides. Sprinkle top with additional chopped figs, raisins and nuts.

LORD BALTIMORE CAKE

Follow the recipe for Lady Baltimore Cake, except to one half of the Seven-Minute Icing add:

½ cup dry macaroon crumbs	½ cup candied cherries, quartered
¼ cup chopped pecan meats	¼ teaspoon orange extract
¼ cup chopped almonds, chopped	2 teaspoons lemon juice

SCRIPTURE CAKE
Recipes from the Parish of St. Philips in Southport (1907)

No Southern cook book could hold up its head without a recipe for Scripture Cake, or Our Lord's Scripture Cake, as it was also called. It takes it name from the mention of its ingredients in Bibical passages— flour from 1st Kings 4:22, sugar from Jeremiah 6:20, butter from Judges 5:25, figs from Nahum 3:12, milk from Judges 4:19, almonds from Numbers 17:18, salt from Leviticus 2:13, eggs from Jeremiah 17:11, leavening from Amos 4:5, and spices from Genesis 37:25.

4 ½ cups flour	2 cups figs
2 cups sugar	2 cups raisins
2 tablespoons baking powder	2 cups almonds
½ teaspoon salt	½ teaspoon nutmeg
1 cup butter, softened	½ teaspoon cinnamon
½ cup milk	½ teaspoon allspice
2 tablespoons honey	¼ teaspoon ground clove
2 eggs	

Sift together the sugar, flour and baking powder. Cut in the butter with a fork or pastry cutter. Beat together the milk, eggs and honey, and blend with the first mixture. Add the fruits, nuts and spices and blend well. Pour into an ungreased 10-inch tube pan and bake in 325° oven for about 1 hour. Let stand for 10 to 15 minutes, then invert, let hang until cool, remove from pan and set upright on a cake dish.

NORTH CAROLINA TIPSY CAKE
Key to the Pantry (1898)

"Prepare all the ingredients in time to build your tipsy cake several hours before using, and let stand in very cold place. Make enough sponge cake to bake in two layers, nearly an inch thick when done. Make a rich custard of 1 pint milk and 3 eggs. Sweeten to taste. Let it be very thick, and flavor with vanilla. One large glass of sweet wine (scuppernong or misch preferred), 1 pint cream, 1 pound blanched almonds. Sweeten your cream slightly, and flavor delicately with a little of the wine; then whip until stiff enough to stand alone. To build: Put a layer of cake in the bottom of a deep glass bowl. Pour wine over slowly until the cake is about soaked through. Stick almonds (endwise) thickly in the cake; then a layer of custard, then whipped cream, and so on until bowl is full. Ornament the cream on the top of bowl with crystallized cherries or violets. Serve in ice-cream plates or saucers."

314

SALLY RAMSEUR'S GINGERBREAD
Southport's Favorite Recipes (1950)

½ cup sugar
½ cup butter
1 cup molasses
2 ½ cups flour
1 egg

1 teaspoon cinnamon
1 teaspoon ginger
2 teaspoons baking powder
1 cup hot water
½ teaspoon salt

Cream shortening and sugar. Add beaten egg and molasses, then flour and flavorings which have been sifted together. Add hot water, mix and bake. Bake in 350° oven 30 to 35 minutes. Serve with Great Grandma Davis's lemon sauce.

ANNIE MAY WOODSIDE'S NUT BREAD
Southport's Favorite Recipes (1950)

3 cups sifted flour
1 cup chopped nuts
1 egg, beaten
1 cup milk

4 tablespoon shortening, melted
½ cup sugar
1 teaspoon salt

Sift flour. Measure 3 cups. Add baking powder, salt and sugar. Mix well then sift into mixing bowl. Stir in nuts. Beat egg until foamy, then stir in milk. Add this to flour mixture, stirring only until mixed. Stir in shortening. Pour into greased loaf pan and bake in moderate 350° oven about 1 hour or until crust is brown on top and the bread shrinks slightly from sides.

SPICE CAKE

2 cups flour, sifted
½ cup shortening
2 cups brown sugar
3 eggs, separated
1 cup thick sour cream

1 teaspoon baking soda
2 teaspoons cinnamon
1 teaspoon cloves
½ teaspoon nutmeg
¼ teaspoon salt

Sift flour, salt, soda and spices together three times. Cream shortening with sugar until fluffy. Add the beaten egg yolks and beat thoroughly. Add sifted dry ingredients and cream alternately in small amounts beating well after each addition. Beat egg whites until stiff but not dry and fold into batter. Pour into greased 9x9-inch square pan and bake in preheated moderate 350° oven 40 to 50 minutes.

BLUEBERRY CRUNCH

3 cups blueberries	1 15-ounce can (2 ½ cups)
1 cup sugar	crushed pineapple, undrained
1 box yellow cake mix	1 teaspoon nutmeg
½ cup melted butter	1 teaspoon cinnamon
1 cup chopped pecans	½ teaspoon salt

Mix the crushed pineapple with the nutmeg, cinnamon and salt, and pour over bottom of lightly greased baking 9x13-inch baking dish. Layer blueberries over this. Sprinkle with lemon juice and ¾ cup of the sugar. On top of the fruit sprinkle dry cake mix and drizzle with the butter. Top with the nuts and sprinkle with the remaining fourth of a cup sugar. Bake in 350° oven 25 minutes. Remove cake, take a knife and cut through to the bottom so juice will rise to top. Bake another 15 minutes, or until the cake is done.

MACK'S CAFE BLUEBERRY DUMP CAKE
Betty McGlamery Cochran's Recipe Files

1 pint fresh blueberries	1 ½ stick butter or margarine,
1 small can crushed pineapple,	melted
not drained	½ cup nuts, chopped
1 recipe packaged yellow	
cake mix	

Wash and pick over berries. Place berries and pineapple in baking dish. Spread on cake batter. Place nuts on batter. Drizzle melted butter or margarine on top. Sprinkle on chopped nuts. Bake in 9x13-inch metal baking pan 1 hour in 350° oven, or at 325° if using a glass baking dish.

TEA LOAF

1 package pound cake mix	1/3 cup raisins
1 cup blueberries	3/4 cup nuts chopped
½ teaspoon cinnamon	1 teaspoon nutmeg
2 cups confectioner's sugar	1 teaspoon lemon juice

Prepare the cake batter, and gently fold in the berries, nuts, raisins and spices. Pour into 3 small or one large loaf pan. Bake according to package directions, allowing 10 minutes less time. Turn out on rack and cool. Mix confectioner's sugar with lemon juice and spoon over loaf.

SWEETHEART'S PINEAPPLE UPSIDE DOWN CAKE

1 recipe One-Two-Three-Four ½ cup butter
Cake, page 302, or cake mix ½ cup pecan nuts, chopped
1 15-ounce can crushed pineapple Maraschino cherries
1 8-ounce can pineapple slices
1 cup brown sugar

Prepare the cake mix and set aside. In a heavy 10-inch cast-iron skillet melt the butter, and then add the brown sugar and the crushed pineapple. Cook slowly until it has boiled down into thick syrup, about 20 minutes. Remove the syrup and pineapple mixture from skillet and set aside. Arrange pineapple slices in the bottom of the skillet; a 10-inch skillet will accommodate one in the center surrounded by six slices. Place a cherry in the middle of each pineapple ring. Pour the syrup mixture onto this, and then pour on the cake batter on top. Bake in preheated 350° oven until the top is brown and crusty, about 35 minutes. Let stand 10 minutes, and then turn out on a serving dish, pineapple side up. Serve with whipped cream or ice cream.

LEMON BARS
Swans Down Cake Flour Method

1 1/8 cups cake flour 1 cup granulated sugar
1/2 cup butter, room temperature 1 teaspoon baking powder
1/2 cup confectioner's sugar ¼ teaspoon salt
2 eggs 3 teaspoons lemon juice

Combine flour, butter and ¼ cup confectioner's sugar. Press into an 8-inch square pan making a rim to hold filling. Bake for 20 minutes. Combine remaining ingredients, beating until fluffy. Pour and spread evenly over hot crust. Bake 25 minutes or until firm in the middle. Cool. Cut into squares and sprinkle with remaining confectioner's sugar.

LEMON CRACKERS
Key to the Pantry (1898)

"Two eggs, 2 ½ cups sugar, 1 cup lard and butter mixed, 3 light tablespoons of carbonate of ammonia pulverized and mixed with 1 pint of sweet milk. Season with essence of lemon. Flour to make a stiff dough. Work well. Roll thin as for pie-crust, stick with a fork, bake in a quick oven. Nice with chocolate or tea."

317

BROWNIES

This recipe should convince anyone of the superiority of made-from-scratch cooking. These brownies are absolutely delicious. Do not overcook.

1 cup sifted all-purpose flour
2 squares unsweetened chocolate
1 cup sugar
¼ cup butter or margarine
2 eggs well beaten

½ teaspoon salt
½ teaspoon double acting
   baking powder
1 cup chopped walnuts or pecans
1 teaspoon vanilla

Melt the chocolate and butter or margarine in the top of a double boiler. Remove from heat and add remaining ingredients, mixing thoroughly. Pour into an 8-inch square pan. Bake for 350° for about 30 minutes. Cool and cut into squares.

BLONDE BROWNIES
Contributed by Margaret Connaughton

1 1/3 cups sifted all-purpose flour
1 teaspoon baking powder
½ teaspoon salt
½ cup butter
1 cup light brown sugar,
   firmly packed

1 egg
1 teaspoon vanilla
½ cup chopped English walnuts

Sift flour with baking powder and salt. In large bowl, beat at medium speed butter, sugar, egg and vanilla until smooth. Stir in flour mixture and nuts until well blended. Spread evenly in lightly greased 9x9x1½-inch pan. Bake in preheated 350° oven 25 to 30 minute, or until surface springs back when gently touched with fingertips. Cool a bit. Cut with sharp knife into bars while still warm. Makes 34 small brownies.

FROSTED CARROT CAKE

2 ½ cups all purpose flour   3 cups finely grated carrots
2 cups sugar   1 cup pecans, chopped
½ cups salad oil   1 teaspoon baking soda
1/3 cup milk   2 teaspoons baking powder
4 eggs

Mix ingredients except for carrots and chopped pecans, starting on low and increasing speed to high, for about 5 minutes. Add the carrots and chopped pecans and beat on slow until mixed. Turn into greased torte pan and bake in preheated 325° oven about 1 hour, or until toothpick or cake tester inserted in center comes out clean. Cool completely on wire rack.

The frosting

1 8-ounce package cream   ¾ cup powdered sugar
  cheese, softened   ¼ cup chopped pecans or
2 tablespoons butter or margarine   mixed nuts
½ teaspoon vanilla

In a small bowl, with mixer at medium speed, beat the cream cheese, butter or margarine and vanilla until smooth. Gradually beat in the powdered sugar until fluffy. Stir in the nuts. Spread on the cake.

Mary Mintz's Piano Recital

You felt very grand if someone offered you petits fours. Mary Mintz, wife of Judge Rudolph Mintz, was a highly gifted musician and a classy lady. She taught music in their home on Bay Street. The piano was in a spacious room with a bay window. My mother was a pupil of hers at the time, and at her annual recital, played Liebestraum. I played something out of John M. Thompson, I forget what, only happy that I didn't forget my place and have to start over. At the little reception that followed, Mary served punch and tea-sandwiches and little petits fours, glazed over in pink and white icing. I thought this was about the most delicious confection I had ever tasted—and still do.

PETITS FOURS

Use the Classic White Cake recipe in this chapter, baking it in a square or rectangular pan. Cut into squares of about 1 ½ inches. For variety if you wish, cut out some with a round cookie cutter. There will be some waste, but they will make a beautiful presentation.

Place the little cakes on a rack with a cookie sheet to catch the candy drippings. Make a batch of the petits fours frosting, below. The icing will be white and smooth. Spoon the icing over half the cakes. Stir in a drop of pink or green coloring to the other half and ice the remaining cakes. After they have cooled, remove the iced cakes to a platter. Decorate with colored decorator's icing, available in tubes at the grocery store if you wish, but this is not necessary.

PETITS FOURS FROSTING

2 cups sugar   Confectioner's sugar
1/8 teaspoon cream of tartar   (1 cup or more)
1 cup hot water

In a sauce pan boil the sugar, cream of tartar and water to the thin syrup stage, 226°. Cool to lukewarm, about 100°. Add confectioner's sugar a bit at a time until the mixture is just thick enough to coat a spoon. Ladle icing over one of the cakes as a test. Adjust the thickness if necessary.

CREAM PUFFS MADE WITH BUTTER

½ cup boiling water   ½ cup all-purpose flour, sifted
¼ cup butter   2 eggs, well beaten, separately

Preheat the oven at 425°. Combine the boiling water and butter in a saucepan and heat until the butter melts. Add the flour all at once, stir hard until the dough forms a ball in the center of the pan. Remove from heat and let stand 5 minutes. Add 1 of the beaten eggs. Beat. Add the other beaten egg. If the dough is not stiff, let stand 10 minutes. Drop by spoonfuls onto a cookie sheet leaving room for expansion. Bake about 20 minutes for small puffs, more for larger ones. Reduce the temperature to 375° and continue baking 10 to 20 minutes or until the puffs are firm and crusty. Test doneness with one of the puffs. If it flattens out, bake the remainder more. Prick puffs with a sharp knife to let steam escape. When cool, fill with Rich Custard from the recipe on page 352, or whipped cream or any cream filling.

CREAM PUFFS MADE WITH OIL

¼ cup cooking oil   2 eggs
½ cup boiling water   Dash of salt
½ cup flour, sifted

Combine water and oil in a saucepan and bring to a boil. Add flour and salt all at once and stir vigorously until smooth and the mixture comes away from sides of the pan. Remove from heat and beat in the eggs one at a time, beating until smooth. Drop by spoonfuls 2 inches apart onto greased baking sheet, making 6 puffs. Bake in hot 450° oven for 10 minutes, then reduce heat to 400° and bake 25 minutes longer. Cool. Slice off top of each puff and fill with Rich Custard Filling from the recipe on page 352 or vanilla custard or whipped cream. Sprinkle with confectioner's sugar.

RESSIE WHATLEY'S FRUIT CAKE
Ressie Whatley's Recipe Files

As you can see, this will make enough to give a cake to everyone you know.

1 pound butter
1 pound sugar
1 pound all purpose flour
1 teaspoon baking powder
1 dozen eggs, beaten
4 pounds white raisins
¼ pound citron
1 pound mixed fruits
1 package each red and
  green cherries
¼ pound green pineapple

¼ pound red pineapple
½ pound dried orange peel
½ pound dried lemon peel
1 pound English nuts
1 pound Brazil nuts
1 pound pecans
1 pound almonds
2 packages figs
Juice of 1 orange
Dates

Cream the butter and sugar. Sift together the flour and baking powder, and add this to the first mixture. Mix in the eggs, orange juice. Then add the remaining ingredients. Pour into deep loaf pans and bake on slow 225° oven for 4 to 5 hours. Decorate the top with pecan haves and pieces of red and green cherries. [You may wish to sprinkle with brandy every week until the cake is used. This keeps it moist and improves the flavor.]

ENGLISH FRUIT CAKE

5 ½ cups cake flour, sifted
2 ½ teaspoons baking powder
¼ teaspoon mace
1 cup shortening
1 ¾ cups brown sugar
3 eggs, beaten
1 teaspoon lemon extract
3 ¼ cups raisins

¼ cup candied orange peel
¼ cup candied lemon peel
¼ cup citron
¼ cup candied pineapple
¼ cup candied cherries
1 cup chopped nuts
1 cup orange juice

Sift the flour, baking powder and mace 3 times. Cream shortening and sugar until fluffy. Add lemon extract. Slice the candied fruits and add to the mixture. Add dry ingredients and orange juice alternately. Pour into 10-inch tube pan and bake 2 to 2 ½ hours in 300° oven.

VANILLA WAFERS

½ cup vegetable shortening
1 ½ teaspoons vanilla
1 cup sugar
2 eggs, unbeaten
2 tablespoons milk

2 ¾ cups all purpose flour
2 teaspoons baking powder
1 teaspoon salt
1 egg, well beaten

Blend shortening and vanilla. Gradually add sugar, creaming until light and fluffy. Add eggs one at a time, beating well after each addition. Add milk and blend well. Sift the dry ingredients together into the first mixture and blend thoroughly. Chill in refrigerator until firm. Roll dough on lightly floured pastry cloth or board to 1/8 inch thickness. Cut with 2-inch cookie cutter, and place on greased baking sheets. Brush cookies with egg. Bake in 400° oven for 7 to 12 minutes until lightly brown.

LADY FINGERS

1/3 cup cake flour
1/3 cup confectioner's sugar
1 whole egg

2 egg yolks
2 egg whites
Confectioner's sugar to dust

Sift the cake flour 3 times. Sift in the confectioner's sugar. In a separate bowl, beat the egg and egg yolks and vanilla until thick and lemon colored. In another bowl, whip the egg whites until stiff but not dry. Fold the sugar carefully into the egg whites. Beat the mixture until it thickens again. Fold in the egg yolk mixture. Pour into greased ladyfinger tins. Bake 15 minutes in 375° preheated oven. When cool, dust with confectioner's sugar.

BUTTER COOKIES

½ cup butter, room temperature
½ cup sugar
1 egg
1 cup all-purpose flour, sifted

¼ teaspoon salt
1 teaspoon vanilla
¼ teaspoon nutmeg

Cream the butter and sugar well. Add the egg, vanilla, nutmeg and salt and mix. Add the flour and mix. Shape the dough into small balls and flatten with the hand, or roll and cut with cookie cutter. Bake in moderate 375° oven until the edges are light brown, about 12 minutes.

Susie Sellers Carson at a recent dessert tasting.

Susie Sellers Carson

Susie Sellers Carson was born out the road a few miles at Supply, but has lived and worked for most of her life in Southport, and is as much a part of our town as our live oaks and the old town pump in Franklin Square Park. Her education did not stop with graduation from Southport High School as Valedictorian of the class of 1937, but continues to this day. In recent years she has shared her vast knowledge of Southport and local history through writings and teaching; she is our town's unofficial historian.

Among her books are *By Faith We Serve,* a history of the Southport Baptist Church, *Joshua's Dream,* a history of Southport that has gone into multiple printings, and most recently *Joshua's Legacy,* which treats many of the colorful personalities that have been part of our history. She considers her running column in the *Wilmington Star-News,* "A Bit of History," her "crowning glory," since it reaches such a wide audience. For years she has edited *The Whittler's Bench,* the newsletter of the Southport Historical Society, of which she is a long time member. She teaches a popular course in local history for the Brunswick County Continuing Education Department.

Her career was as legal secretary to the noted lawyers S. Bunn Frink and E. J. Prevatte. Her daughter, Kathryn Carson Kalmanson is a professional librarian at Salisbury State University in Maryland. Susie lives on Atlantic Avenue with two cats, Curious Jane, and Dudley Doowright ("who won't do right") says Susie.

And, to the point of this book, she has contributed a wealth of recipes and historical information.

324

ENGLISH TEA CAKES
Susie Carson's Recipe Files

This recipe belonged to Susie Carson's great aunt, Lina Stallings. Having been passed down from Lina Stallings grandmother, it probably dates from the Revolution. Susie says, "I have baked these cookies for many people and they are always liked."

2 cups all purpose flour
½ cup butter, softened
1 cup granulated sugar
1 egg
2 tablespoons cream
2 cups plain flour

1 teaspoon baking soda
¼ teaspoon salt
1 teaspoon vanilla extract
Raisins
A bit more granulated sugar

Combine butter, sugar, egg, cream, and vanilla. Beat until light and fluffy. Combine flour, salt and baking soda and stir into the creamed mixture, mixing well. Chill 2 hours. Roll out small portions of dough at the time on a lightly floured board. Dough may be rolled thick or thin. Cut with a 3-inch cookie cutter. Sprinkle each cookie with granulated sugar and press one or two raisins into the center of each cookie. Place on a greased baking sheet and bake in a 375° oven about 8 minutes or until lightly browned. Cool and store in tightly covered containers. Yield: about 4 dozen cookies.

SUSIE CARSON'S CHOCOLATE PECAN DROPS
Susie Carson's Recipe Files

½ cup shortening
4 tablespoons cocoa
1 cup light brown sugar,
    firmly packed
2 eggs
1 teaspoon vanilla

1 ½ teaspoons flour, sifted
3 teaspoons baking soda
¼ teaspoon salt
½ cup milk
1 cup pecans, chopped

Cream shortening and cocoa together. Add sugar gradually, creaming until light and fluffy. Add eggs, one at a time, beating after each addition. Sift dry ingredients together 3 times and add to creamed mixture alternately with the milk. Fold in the pecans. Drop from teaspoon onto greased cookie sheet and bake in 400° oven 10 to 12 minutes. Frost with chocolate or sour cream frosting. Makes 3 dozen.

CHEWY OATMEAL COOKIES WITH NUTS, RAISINS AND DATES

½ cup shortening, softened
1 ¼ cups sugar
2 eggs
½ cup molasses
1 ¾ cups flour, sifted
1 teaspoon soda

1 teaspoon salt
1 teaspoon cinnamon
2 cups rolled oats
½ cup nuts, cut up
½ cup raisins
½ cup dates, pitted and chopped

Blend the shortening with the sugar, and then beat in the eggs and molasses. In a separate bowl, sift together the flour, soda, salt and cinnamon. Blend the two mixtures together. Blend in the oats, nuts, raisins and dates. Drop teaspoonfuls on lightly greased baking sheet, leaving about 2 inches in between to allow for expansion. Bake in 400° oven about 10 minutes, or until lightly browned. Makes about 40 cookies. Guaranteed delicious!

OATMEAL COOKIE SANDWICHES WITH CREAM FILLING

Follow directions for chewy oatmeal cookies above, but omit the nuts, raisins and dates. Roll dough into small balls about 1 ½ inch in diameter, then press into small circles about ¼ inch thick. Place on lightly greased cookie sheet and bake in 400° oven about 10 to 12 minutes, or until lightly browned. Do not overcook. Let cook. Spread half of the cookies with filling below, and top with the remaining cookies, sandwich style.

The filling

2 cups confectioner's sugar
1/8 cup each of butter and
   vegetable shortening, room
   temperature, blended

1 teaspoon vanilla
Dash of salt
Milk as needed

Mix the butter and vegetable shortening together with the vanilla and salt. Mix in the confectioner's sugar. Blend in 1 teaspoon milk, and continue to add milk ½ teaspoon at a time, blending after each addition, until the consistency of smooth paste.

ABOUT GRAHAM FLOUR

Some recipes in the old cookbooks used in Southport call for Graham flour, a form of whole wheat flour developed in the 1830's by Sylvester Graham, a forerunner of the health food movement. Graham flour must be used quickly or refrigerated, as it quickly turns rancid.

GRAHAM CRACKERS

This recipe closely replicates the use of Graham flour with all-purpose, whole-wheat and rye flours, all readily obtainable today.

½ cup all-purpose flour
1 ¼ cups whole-wheat flour
½ cup light rye flour
½ cup sugar
1 teaspoon baking powder
½ teaspoon baking soda
¼ teaspoon ground cinnamon

½ teaspoon salt
½ cup cold butter, cut into
 pea-sized bites
2 tablespoons honey
2 tablespoons molasses
¼ cup cold water
1 teaspoon vanilla extract

With an electric mixer, mix the flours, sugar, baking powder, baking soda, salt, and cinnamon. Add the cold butter and mix until the mixture resembles coarse meal. Add the honey, molasses, water, and vanilla. Mix until the dough comes together in a ball. Between 2 sheets of waxed paper, roll the dough ½-inch thick. Chill for 1 hour. Bake in the middle of the oven and preheat to 350°. Lightly flour the dough and roll 1/8 inch thick. With a sharp knife or pizza cutter, cut into 2-inch squares. Arrange the crackers on nonstick pan, or line a pan with parchment. With a fork, prick several holes in each cracker. Bake for 15 minutes, until lightly browned at the edges. Makes 48 crackers.

GRAHAM GEMS
Recipes From the Parish of St. Philips in Southport (1907)

1 pint Graham flour
2 teaspoonfuls baking powder
1 tablespoonful sugar

1 tablespoonful lard
Milk or water as needed

"Mix baking powder and flour, rub the lard through it, stir with milk or water till it is thin enough to drop from a spoon. The pans should be hot and thoroughly greased. They should stand on the stove while being filled, and also a moment later, until the gems begin to rise, then they must be put on the upper grate of the oven. Then will bake in fifteen minutes if the oven is hot [450°]."

LEILA JANE SELLERS' SOFT MOLASSES COOKIES
Susie Carson's Recipe Files

Says Susie, "I call these Leila Jane's Molasses Cookies because these are the kind she made for us as far back as I can remember."

½ cup butter, melted
3 cups flour, more or less
1 cup molasses
2 tablespoons milk

½ teaspoon salt
1 teaspoon baking soda
1 tablespoon ground ginger

Combine molasses and butter and mix well. Add milk. Sift 1 cup flour with the salt, soda and ginger. Blend and add to the molasses mixture. Then add enough of the remaining flour to make a dough stiff enough to be rolled. Chill. Roll to ½ inch thickness. Cut and bake on a greased cookie sheet in a moderate oven about 8 to 10 minutes. Makes about 60 cookies.

PECAN SNOWBALLS
Brooks Newton Preik

1 stick butter, softened
1 cup flour
3 tablespoons powdered sugar
1 ½ teaspoons vanilla, or almond
    or rum flavoring

½ cup pecans, finely chopped
Confectioner's sugar to coat

Combine first four ingredients in a food processor and pulse until thoroughly mixed. Add nuts and pulse just until blended. Remove dough and roll into small balls about the diameter of a quarter. Bake on an ungreased baking sheet for about 13 minutes at 350. Do not overbake. Bottom should be a light golden brown. Overcooking makes cookies dry and tasteless. When cool, put in a plastic bag with powdered sugar and shake until well coated.

GINGER SNAPS

1 cup shortening
1 cup sugar
1/3 cup hot coffee
1/3 cup molasses
5 cups cake flour

1 teaspoon salt
1 teaspoon soda
2 teaspoons ground ginger
1 teaspoon cloves
1 teaspoon cinnamon

Cream shortening and sugar. Add hot coffee to the molasses, and add to the creamed mixture. Sift dry ingredients together. Add gradually to liquid mixture. Chill thoroughly. Roll out on a pastry cloth 1/8 inch thick. Cut out with round cookie cutter. Bake in moderate oven 330° 17 minutes. Makes about 14 dozen 2-inch cookies.

GINGERBREAD MEN

½ cup molasses
¼ cup sugar
3 tablespoons butter
1 tablespoon milk
2 cups flour

½ teaspoon each of
baking soda, salt, nutmeg,
cinnamon, powdered cloves,
ginger

Bring the molasses to the boiling point. Add the sugar, butter and milk. Sift together the flour, baking soda and spices, and add to the mixture, and beat well. Cover the dough and chill. Dust a board lightly with flour or confectioner's sugar. Roll out about a cup at a time, keeping the rest of the dough cool. Roll as thin as possible and cut with a small gingerbread-man cookie cutter. Cut with cookie cutter and place on ungreased cookie sheet. Bake in moderate oven 330° about 15 minutes.

COUSIN MARY BOMBERGER'S TOLL HOUSE COOKIES

½ cup butter
6 tablespoons white sugar
6 tablespoons brown sugar
1 egg, lightly beaten
1 1/8 cups flour

½ teaspoon soda
A few drops of hot water
Dash of salt
½ teaspoon vanilla
1 cup chocolate chips

Blend the butter and sugars. Add and blend the beaten egg, soda, a few drops of hot water, the salt and vanilla. Add the chocolate chips and stir. Drop ½ teaspoonfuls onto a greased baking sheet. Bake in 375° oven until brown.

Clara Belle "Daughter" Cooper Daniel,"early 1950's.

A Memory of Caramel Cake

Daughter Daniel's mother had died. Clara Belle Cooper Daniel was the real name of our neighbor and dear friend, but everyone called her Daughter. I didn't know her real name until I was fully grown. Her husband Ed ran the City electric plant out on Howe Street. My father called me and said,

"Ed has to work, and Daughter doesn't drive and has no way to get to the funeral. Would you consider driving her down there? You can take the station wagon."

I was home on vacation from Chapel Hill, and glad to do so. This was the mid-1950's.

Daughter came from a big family. Her sister Alease also lived in Southport but was embarrassed to have Daughter ride with her. Alease wanted us to call her "Ale*ése*" and got angry if we pronounced it "*Ale-eeze.*" And Daughter, you see, was a country dumpling of a woman, and childlike. Alease, after all, worked as a sales lady at the Wonder Shop in Wilmington, and had her reputation to uphold. So "it wasn't convenient" for Alease to have her sister ride with her to Andrews for the funeral.

On a hot summer day we set out in Daddy's two-tone brown and tan 1953 Chevy station wagon for Andrews, which is on the other side of Georgetown in South Carolina.

330

"Daughter," I asked. "Are any of your people connected to the Coopers that the Cooper River was named after?"

"Yes. That was..." she answered, and proceeded to give me a detailed genealogy. Daughter could remember the smallest details and facts even if they didn't add up to much.

The old Cooper home was right out of Tennessee Williams—a big two-story house with fat, square columns and a wide front porch on both floors overlooking a railroad track. It had been white at one time. Pontiacs and Buicks and Fords with license tags from all over were parked willy-nilly on the sand front yard. The family stood about hugging each other and catching up.

Daughter mounted the very high, collapsing and treacherous steps to her home. Old Mrs. Cooper was laid out in a darkened room with the shutters drawn, a brass funeral parlor candlelabra casting a discreet light. Their colored cook gave Daughter a big moist hug and exclaimed,

"The Lord got himself a *good* woman this day!"

In the kitchen off the rear of the house was more food than I had ever seen at a wake. On the stove someone had brought a wash pan big enough to take a bath in, heaped with white rice. I glanced on the screened-in back porch, and there, among the desserts, was a six-inch high layer cake with caramel frosting—the kind that's like candy and is hard to make. I drooled. But just then four young grandchildren with no necks spied the cake and patted their hands with glee.

"Oh, goodie!" cried one. "Caramel cake!"

"Keep away from that cake," barked the cook. "That's for after!"

The long cortege of cars to the church and the funeral is a blur in my mind. All I could think of was how to beat it back to that cake before those evil children got a hold of it. And I did. After the funeral, I by-passed the line to the fried chicken, made a bee-line to the back porch and cut big, selfish slices of that caramel cake for me and Daughter. Oh, was it good! How sad it ran out before Alease got any.

CARAMEL FROSTING – EASY FUDGE METHOD

½ cup brown sugar firmly
  packed
1 ½ cups white granulated sugar

1 ½ cup milk
2 tablespoons butter

Combine sugars and milk and bring to a boil, stirring constantly. Then boil without stirring until a small amount forms a soft boil in cold water, or until mixture reaches the soft-boil 232° temperature on a candy thermometer. Add butter. Cool and beat until right consistency to spread.

The Angel Maker—Marion St. George

I've already told you that Marion St. George was one of the good cooks who worked in the school lunch room. Her picture appears on page eighty-one with the lunch room staff. But I haven't told you about the first time I saw her, nor about her caramel frosting.

The grand opening of the lunchroom was a day of some excitement, as prior to this we had to bring our own lunches from home. The students filed into the lunch room one class at a time, beginning with the first grade. When our grade got to the serving counter, we looked in horror at one of the women dishing out the food—Marion St. George. Her bottom lip was purple and rolled down like a shotgun cartridge, the chin mutilated and nearly missing. And she had a habit of cupping a hand around her chin unconsciously trying to hide it.

"Gag!" we muttered. "A freak show." Kids are not nice, you know.

When I arrived home after school, our neighbor Myrtle Trunnel was sitting at the kitchen table with my mother having a cup of coffee.

"How could they expect us to eat! Looking at this!" I exclaimed with youthful intolerance. The wise, compassionate souls who raised me patiently explained that Marion, or Mammy as we came to call her, as a child had accidentally tripped in the yard and fell into the coals of a fire under an iron caldron of boiling soap, and had been maimed.

"Better the scars on the outside than the inside," said Myrtle.

We soon came to know Mammy St. George as one of the most lovable and affectionate of women. Her soul radiated beauty, blinding you to her mutilation. Someone called her "an angel maker," for, when you were with her you felt like an angel. Sometimes if she saw us drooling over the big pan of cobbler on the lunch counter, with a twinkle in her eye she'd slip you an extra spoonful. Beauty within is what counts.

Not long before she died, I visited her in her house on Lord Street where she lived with her sister. She gladly gave me her recipe for caramel frosting. It's one of the most difficult recipes to fix, and many a cook has given up after two or three tries, but when it turns out well, it's worth it—simply memorable, the best caramel cake you'll ever eat. It's a very, very old recipe. And to sink your teeth into a layer cake frosted with it—creamy, and slightly fudge-like, golden tan and absolutely delicious—is to transport you back into an old Southport kitchen a hundred years ago.

MARION ST. GEORGE'S CARAMEL FROSTING

You will need a medium size saucepan and a 10-inch cast iron skillet. You will boil milk and sugar in the saucepan, and caramelize the sugar in the skillet.

1 large can evaporated milk
4 cups sugar
¼ stick of butter, or a little less

1 teaspoon vanilla
Pinch of salt

Pour the evaporated milk and 3 cups of the sugar in the saucepan on medium heat. In the skillet pour the sugar and begin to cook on very low heat. Stir both constantly. Here is the catch: The milk and sugar mixture must come to a full, rolling boil exactly when the sugar in the skillet is caramelized. Spoon or drizzle the caramel syrup into the boiling milk and sugar mixture while stirring. If the caramel crystallizes, your frosting is a flop. Start over. If the milk and sugar are not rolling boil, your caramel syrup will simply harden and you have flopped. But if the two mixtures combine, you are home free. Add the butter and cook until the mixture has reached the soft ball stage, like fudge. Beat until creamy. Add the vanilla and salt. Spread on cooled cake layers. If the frosting becomes too stiff, add a little canned milk.

If crystals begin to form before sugar caramelizes, brush them with pastry brush dampened but not dripping wet. Add drop of two of water and stir a bit.

PENUCHE ICING

½ cup butter
1 cup brown sugar, packed
¼ cup milk

1 ¾ cups confectioner's sugar, sifted, maybe a little more

Melt the butter in a saucepan, add the sugar, and boil over low heat for 2 minutes. Add the milk and return to a boil, stirring constantly. Cool to lukewarm. Add the confectioner's sugar a bit at a time. Cool to lukewarm temperature and stir until the icing is thick enough to spread.

MOCHA ICING

¼ cup butter
3 teaspoons cocoa

1/3 cup confectioner's sugar
1 tablespoon strong, clear coffee

Cream the butter, add cocoa and sugar, and moisten with coffee to the consistency desired for icing.

WHITE BUTTER ICING

3 cups confectioner's sugar,
  sifted
1/3 cup shortening, softened

3 tablespoons heavy cream
1 ½ teaspoon vanilla

Blend together the sugar and shortening. Stir remaining ingredients until smooth.

MARSHMALLOW FILLING
Annie May Woodside's Cook Book (1913)

5 teaspoons of powdered gum
  Arabic
1 cup cold water
1 cup pulverized (confectioner's)
  sugar

1 egg white
½ teaspoon vanilla extract

"Dissolve the gum Arabic in the water. Add the sugar and cook over a gentle heat until thick enough to form a soft ball between the fingers when a little is dipped into ice water. When this stage is reached, pour the boiling mixture over the beaten white of the egg. Add the flavoring, and spread between the layers of cake, using a knife dipped into hot water to spread it smoothly."

CLASSIC SEVEN-MINUTE FROSTING
Dorothy Hardee's Recipe Files

2 egg whites
1 1/2 cups sugar
1/3 cup water

1 ½ teaspoons corn syrup
¼ teaspoon salt
1 teaspoon vanilla

Combine egg whites, sugar and water in double boiler. Cook over boiling water 7 minutes, beating constantly with rotary beater until peaks form. Remove from heat and add vanilla. Beat until cool and thick enough to spread. Covers the top and sides of 2 9-inch layers, or 2 dozen cupcakes.

BANANA CAKE
Mrs. Bryant Potter
Southport's Favorite Recipes (1950)

½ cup butter
1 ½ cups sugar
2 eggs
1 cup bananas, mashed
1 teaspoon vanilla or lemon extract

2 cups flour
½ teaspoon baking soda
¼ teaspoon salt
½ cup milk
Poppy seeds (optional)

Cream butter. Add sugar. Add lightly beaten eggs. Add bananas and beat well. Add sifted dry ingredients alternately with milk. Bake in tube pan for 45 minutes at 350°. Optional: Add 2 tablespoons poppy seed to the batter. Sprinkle and press on more poppy seed when removed from oven.

Mrs. Plaxco's Lemon Cake

Mrs. Plaxco was a small, genteel woman always with a pink, delicate, powdered face. Her husband, Frank, was the manager of the Brunswick Navigation Company's pogie plant, and they lived in the handsome white brick house on Moore Street still standing on the same block just east of the new Episcopal Church. One summer day Mrs. Plaxco invited my parents and me over to their cottage on Long Beach for cake and lemonade. After some chit-chat she went into her kitchen and brought out the most beautiful lemon layer cake you ever saw, a glossy and glorious vision in pale yellow. She cut into it and served each of us a modest size slice. Out of this world! Cool yellow frosting, with lemon jelly filling between moist, vanilla flavored cake. Mine was devoured in seconds. What shall I say of the portion—sufficient? All I really needed? Modest? *Genteel? Stingy!?* When she went into the kitchen for something, I whispered to my mother, "I want another slice."

"*Don't you dare!*" she snapped.

For the rest of our visit I looked longingly at that cake, thinking, surely she will offer us another slice. She did not!

That crushing deprivation, I am convinced, led to my life-long lust for lemon-jelly cake. Not to impugn the memory of dear Mrs. Plaxco, I'm sure that had she the slightest inkling of my lust for her ambrosial confection, she would gladly have given me the whole cake. Luckily, I have Great Grandma Davis's equally divine recipe for lemon filling, which follows on page 336. Moral of story: *Always offer second helpings!*

Great Grandma Mary Allen Jones Davis, about 1925,
with two of her Hardee grandchildren.

GREAT GRANDMA DAVIS'S LEMON JELLY FILLING

This is a very, very old recipe, since Great Grandma Mary Allen Jones
Davis was born in 1857 and learned cooking from her mother. They were
from near Beaufort, North Carolina. It's great for lemon jelly filling on a
cake, or as a dessert sauce.

1 stick butter softened   3 tablespoons water
1 cup sugar   ¼ cup lemon juice and some
2 large eggs, slightly beaten   grated rind

Mix in saucepan and cook on low heat until thick as cream, constantly
stirring. This will keep for weeks in the refrigerator, as long as nobody
discovers it and eats it all up. For the dessert sauce, do not cook as long.

336

Grandma Ella Content Davis Hardee,
on her 90th Birthday in 1972.

GRANDMA HARDEE'S FLUFFY NO-COOK COCOA FROSTING

Should you wish to live to age 102 and six months as did Grandma Ella Davis Hardee, add this to your diet.

½ cup vegetable shortening   2 tablespoons milk
   such as Crisco   2 tablespoons cocoa
½ cup butter or margarine   1 teaspoon vanilla
4 cups confectioner's sugar, sifted   Pinch of salt

Cream butter and shortening. Add vanilla. Gradually add sugar, cocoa and salt. Scrape sides and bottom of bowl often. Icing will appear dry. Add milk and beat at high speed until light and fully. If too dry, add a little more milk.

337

CHOCOLATE FROSTING
WITH MARSHMALLOWS AND NUTS

2 cups granulated sugar
½ cup cocoa
½ stick butter or margarine
½ cup milk
1 tablespoon Karo syrup

1 teaspoon vanilla
Pinch of salt
1 cup marshmallows miniatures
¾ cup pecans

Combine ingredients except for marshmallows and nuts. Let stand for a while. Then bring to a boil, stir and boil 1 minute. Ice a 2-layer cake. While still warm, top with marshmallows and pecans.

CHOCOLATE FUDGE ICING

2 cups sugar
2 tablespoons light corn syrup
3 squares (ounces) unsweetened
    chocolate

½ cup milk
1 teaspoon vanilla
2 tablespoons butter

Cook sugar, syrup, chocolate and milk slowly to the 232° or very soft ball stage when dropped into cold water. Remove from heat, add vanilla and butter. Cool without stirring until lukewarm. Beat until creamy and thick and spreads easily. Covers tops of two 8-inch cake layers and top.

Cousin Betty Hardee Zander displaying an English trifle made with lady fingers, in our Grandma Ella Content Davis Hardee's compote dish. 2005.

17..
Puddings, Ice Creams, Dessert Sauces, Etc.

LEILA JANE SELLERS' BANANA PUDDING
MADE-FROM-SCRATCH, THE OLD SOUTHERN WAY
Susie Carson's Recipe Files

Susie Sellers Carson provided her mother's very old, authentic Southern recipe for banana pudding. Susie adds, "I do not use a double boiler. I mix the milk with flour, sugar and salt and heat it all slowly to a gentle boil, stirring constantly."

3/4 cup sugar
2 eggs, separated
1/3 cup flour
2 cups milk, scalded

1 ½ teaspoons lemon juice or
    vanilla extract
3 medium bananas
Vanilla wafers

Mix sugar, salt and flour. Gradually add this to the scalded milk. Cook 15 minutes in a double boiler, stirring constantly until thickened, then occasionally. Beat egg yolks a little and stir some of the hot custard into them, then stir into the mixture in the double boiler. Stir and cook 2 minutes. Add lemon juice. Cool.

Line a 7-inch casserole with vanilla wafers. Then add alternate layers of bananas, custard and wafers, ending with custard. Top with a meringue.

The meringue topping

Beat the 3 egg whites until stiff, and add 2 tablespoons of sugar. Spread on top of the pudding. Bake in a slow 325° oven for 15 to 20 minutes.

DORCAS ANN LEWIS'S EASY BANANA PUDDING

I can't imagine a Southport cook who doesn't know how to cook up a banana pudding. Some top theirs with whipped cream. I like Dork's because she adds an extra touch of vanilla flavoring, and tops it with a big meringue.

1 package vanilla pudding mix   ½ box vanilla wafers, or more
2 bananas, sliced thin   1 teaspoon vanilla flavoring

Prepare the pudding mix as directed. Add the extra vanilla and stir. Line a baking dish with a layer of the vanilla wafers. Spread a layer of the pudding over this. Place a layer of the banana slices on this. Repeat the process until the ingredients are used up. Top with a meringue made of at least 4 egg whites and a little sugar and pinch of cream of tartar. Bake in 350° oven about 15 minutes, or until the meringue is nice and brown.

MA-MA'S BREAD PUDDING

This is genuine old-time bread pudding. Ma-Ma would add leftover cooked fruit such as apples or pears to the pudding mixture before baking. Serve with her Butter Sauce, page 367.

4 cups cubed bread   1 cup raisins
1 cup milk   1 teaspoon cinnamon
2 eggs   1 teaspoon vanilla
½ cup sugar

Beat eggs and milk together with the sugar, spice and vanilla. Stir in bread cubes until well moistened. Add raisins. Bake in greased casserole dish at 350° for 40 minutes, or until set.

HASTY PUDDING
Mrs. Hill's Southern Practical Cookery and Receipt Book (1872)

"Wet up three tablespoonfuls of fine corn meal with cold water; stir it to three tumblerfuls of boiling water. Add salt to taste; stir frequently until the meal is thoroughly cooked, and the mush sufficiently thick. Eat cold or warm with sweet milk or syrup. Cut cold mush in slices, and fry.
    Add to this quantity of mush two well-beaten eggs, a quarter of a pound of butter, sugar, and spice to taste. Bake in an earthen dish."
    [About 1 hour in a 350° oven should do.]

CHOCOLATE PUDDING

1 egg	1 ¾ cups all purpose flour
1 cup sugar	¼ teaspoon salt
2 tablespoons soft butter	¼ teaspoon cream of tartar
1 cup milk	¼ teaspoon baking soda
2 squares unsweetened chocolate, melted	

Beat well the egg, sugar, butter and chocolate. Beat in the milk. Sift together the flour, salt, cream of tartar and baking soda; blend in the milk. Combine all ingredients and cook over low heat until thickened.

FIGGY PUDDING

Figgy pudding dates back to Cornwall, England, where it was traditionally eaten on Palm Sunday, possibly in memory of the Christ's cursing of the barren fig tree on that day. It is prepared in many ways.

1 cup boiling water	1 egg, well beaten
1 cup dried figs, chopped	½ cup sugar
½ cup chopped apples,	½ cup molasses
¼ cup carrot, chopped	½ cup nuts, chopped
½ cup breadcrumbs	1 tablespoon lemon juice
½ cup flour	1 teaspoon salt
2 tablespoons butter	1 teaspoon soda

Pour the boiling water over the fruits. Beat in the egg. Stir in the sugar and molasses. Blend this in the fruit mixture. Sift together the flour, breadcrumbs, salt and soda, and add to the mixture. Pour into greased 1-quart mold. Tie up in cheese cloth or steam bags, place in steamer over boiling water and steam for about 2 hours. Serve hot with Foamy Sauce, or any dessert sauce.

When Turtles Cry

We were over at Long Beach at our friends, the Harold St. Georges. It was June and school was out for the summer. The St. George cottage, like most on Long Beach in those days, wasn't much to brag about. "Miz" Alice was frugal and hadn't taken down the blackout shades (cream on the outside, black on the inside), left over from the War when shore lights might draw Nazi submarines. Alice was neat as a pin, but the linoleum floor was always crunchy underfoot because sand would manage to get in from the beach without fail, either on the feet of bathers or by nature's own mischief. A mosquito or two would find its way through the rusty screen on the front porch to buzz around and bite. The sofas and mattresses were always damp and smelled as if a baby had wet.

Dinner was over and we boys were anxious to quit this rustic outpost of civilization and get back to our comfortable homes on the mainland. Suddenly, someone knocked on the front door and told us there was a turtle down the beach laying eggs.

My friend Neil and I went to the car and found the flashlight. Alice hunted up hers, and our expedition descended to the strand—Alice, my mother, Ma-Ma, my brother Mikael, Neil and myself. A full moon lit up the balmy evening, making long, silvery, moon-rivers on the infinite expanse of the ocean.

Full moon in June is when the great loggerheads come ashore to lay their eggs. They are easy to find. Walk along the strand until you spot turtle tracks, and sure enough, you will find mama-turtle up next to the sand dunes making a nest.

The turtle was not far from the house, and a small crowd had gathered. Someone out pleasure driving on the strand had pulled up and had his headlights trained on the turtle. The great sea monster, as big as a card table, had dug a hole with its fins, then laboriously turned around and began to drop the eggs, plop, plop, into the hole. Turtle eggs are the size of ping-pong balls, white and pliable like thin celluloid, and there will be several dozen. Mrs. Loggerhead was born at this place; after hatching, her baby turtles will scamper across the beach to the surf as fast as they can to avoid predators. Years later they will return to this same spot to lay their eggs. Scientists can not tell us how they know to return to the site of their birth, but they do.

Turtles cry when they lay eggs, and we flash lights in their eyes to witness the tears running down her face. I fantasize it's because Mrs. Loggerhead knows what a hostile and treacherous world she has brought her young into, and weeps for their future; the reality is that the tears come when turtles are out of the brine of their natural element. I myself feel a little pang of guilt at violating the privacy of her birthing, away from the sea creatures and fellow turtles of her briney habitat. Alone on the beach under the stars, this is the most private and intimate moment of her life.

She covers the nest with sand, well knowing that the strange creatures who inhabit dry land have discovered her secret nesting place, and may spoil it even before she has made her way back into the ocean. But this June ritual to the beach began a million years before her, so she does what her ancestors have done for that million years and begins to lumber back to the surf. Neil and Mikael and I take turns riding on the turtle's back, balancing with our arms to stay upright, like beach boys on a surfboard. There is something thrilling and marvelous about riding a turtle's back on a moon-swept night as she heads back to her home in the sea. You share the triumph of this mother who has just propagated her species. For a brief moment under the cold, brilliant stars, with the moon lighting up the world like daylight, with the vast ocean stretching before you, and the giant, ancient sea monster under your feet, you feel totally insignificant, a speck in the cosmos, in the most wonderful way; and you thrill with a sharp, keen hurting awareness of being alive and part of nature.

The grownups discuss whether or not we should rob the nest of its eggs. Even then, I now realize, there were notions about conservation; in the end, we leave half of the eggs in the nest. Poaching parties such as ours nearly wiped out the loggerhead on the East Coast; they are now a protected species.

Murl and Margaret Swan Hood.
Photo courtesy of Ron Hood.

TURTLE EGG DUFF

The duff, that steamed pudding of flour, milk, eggs and seasonings, recalls the ancient English roots of Southport's cooking. The famous turtle egg duff is quintessential Southport fare, as it derives from old England and makes use of turtle eggs which until recent years were plentiful—and legal. (Nowadays the duff is made up with regular hen's eggs.) Recipes for steamed puddings in old English cookbooks such as *The Cook's Oracle* of 1817 differ little from the Southport egg duff. When sweetened, laced with currants or raisins, it was passed out to sailors, who styled it, "plum-duff."

Margaret Hood lived for years on Baldhead Island, where her father, Southport legend Capt. Charlie Swan, was lighthouse keeper. The recipe they used for turtle duff was printed in Ethel Herring's 1967 biography, *Capt'n Charlie.*

2 dozen turtle egg yolks.
½ cup granulated sugar
¾ cup self-rising flour
½ teaspoon salt

1 tablespoon shortening, melted
1 teaspoon vanilla extract
½ box seedless raisins

346

Whip eggs with a small amount of water until fluffy. (Only the yolk of the turtle egg is used; the white will not cook properly. 1 dozen large hen eggs provides an equivalency.) Add sugar and blend well. Sift flour with salt and soda and add to mixture. Blend well. Add shortening and vanilla. Dredge raisins in flour, then add to the mixture. Add a small amount of water to the mixture, just enough to mix well. Pour into well greased duff mold. [Note: Duff molds are also called plum pudding or steam pudding molds, tube pans with a lid, so that after cooking for 45 minutes, the pan may be inverted to complete the cooking. An angel-food cake pan will work. Fill the pan ¾ full with the batter and cover as tightly as possible with aluminum foil. Place the tube pan inside a second pan of water large enough to hold the tube pan with the water level 3/4ths to the top. Boil for about an hour. Test for doneness; a knife should come out clean when done. Turn onto a plate, slice, and serve with a dessert sauce.]

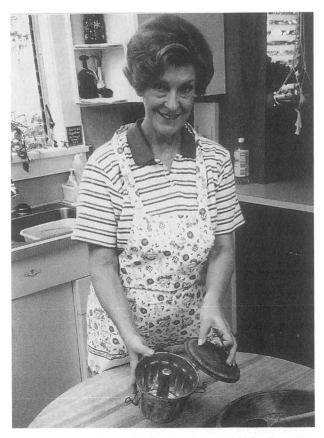

Our friend Dean Rhodes displays Margaret Swan Hood's duff pan, inherited by her son, Ron Hood, who loaned it for this photograph.

347

LEMON PUDDING CAKE
Favorite Recipes of North Carolina (about 1944)

The top will be like cake, the under portion a delicious lemon jelly.

3 tablespoons flour	1 cup milk
3 tablespoons butter	Juice of 1 lemon
1 cup sugar	Rind of 1 lemon, grated
2 egg yolks, beaten	2 egg whites

Combine flour, butter and ¾ cup sugar. Add egg yolks, milk, lemon juice and rind. Beat well. Add remaining sugar to stiffly beaten egg whites, fold into first mixture. Pour into buttered baking dish, place in pan of hot water. Bake in moderate 350° oven 1 hour. Chill. Top with whipped cream.

PERSIMMON PUDDING

1 pound ripe persimmons	½ teaspoon cinnamon
½ cup sugar	½ teaspoon nutmeg
½ cup milk	½ teaspoon allspice
2 tablespoons flour	

Skin the persimmons and steam until they are very soft, remove the seed, then purée. Mix with the remaining ingredients and cook to the consistency of pudding. Serve with ice cream or whipped cream.

SUSIE CARSON'S CREAMY RICE PUDDING
Southport's Favorite Recipes (1950)

½ cup uncooked rice	1 teaspoon vanilla
3 cups boiling water	¼ teaspoon nutmeg
½ cup raisins	1 ½ teaspoons salt
2 eggs slightly beaten	
1 1/3 cups sweetened condensed milk	

Wash rice and put in top of double boiler. Add water and salt. Cover and cook rapidly over boiling water until rice is tender, about 40 minutes. Add the milk and raisins. Slowly add beaten eggs, stirring constantly and rapidly. Continue cooking for 15 minutes. Remove from heat. Add vanilla and nutmeg.

ENGLISH PLUM PUDDING
Susie Carson's Recipe Files

This recipe is in the ancient Yorkshire tradition. An old Yorkshire saying goes, "In as many homes as you eat plum pudding in the twelve days following Christmas, so many happy months will you have during the year."

2 cups plain flour	1 ½ cups mixed, diced
1/3 cup sugar	glazed fruits
1/4 cup shortening, melted	1 teaspoon salt
2 eggs, beaten	1 teaspoon soda
1/3 cup molasses	2 teaspoons ginger
1/3 cup milk	½ teaspoon nutmeg
1 cup raisins	1 teaspoon cinnamon
1 ½ cups chopped nuts	

Sift together the flour, sugar, salt, soda and spices into a mixing bowl. Make a well in the mixture and add shortening, eggs, molasses and milk. Mix thoroughly. Stir in fruit and nuts and mix thoroughly. Grease and lightly flour a pudding mold or smaller molds. Fill 1/3 full of batter. Cover with a tight fitting lid or aluminum foil. Place in a kettle with a rack on the bottom. Add enough boiling water to come half way up sides of mold. Cover kettle and bring to a boil. Simmer at boiling temperature, for a 1 ½ quart mold 3 hours. Adjust time for smaller molds. Check the water level from time to time. After completing the cooking, let stand a few minutes. Turn upside down onto a serving plate and serve with a dessert sauce.

CAROLINA PLUM PUDDING
The Carolina Housewife (1847)

"Six pounds of raisins, four pounds of currants, four and a half dozen eggs, two pounds of citron, half an ounce of mace, one pint of brandy, six pounds of suet, four loaves of bakers' bread, two pounds of brown sugar, one table-spoonful of salt. The above ingredients will make twelve small puddings. Boil them in cloths two hours. When done, hang up in the same cloths, without opening until you use them. Then boil one hour longer. The pudding will keep perfectly well all winter."

ABOUT MOUSSE

The mousse is a light, spongy food, often made fluffy with beaten egg whites and chilled or frozen. It takes it name from the French word meaning "froth."

CHOCOLATE MOUSSE

1 ounce (square) unsweetened
   chocolate
1 ¼ cups evaporated milk
¼ cup water

7 tablespoons sugar
2 eggs, separated
1/8 teaspoon salt
1 teaspoon vanilla

Melt chocolate over hot water. Scald ¼ cup milk and sugar over boiling water. Pour over egg yolks, stirring well. Add salt. Return to double boiler and cook 5 minutes, stirring constantly. Add gradually to melted chocolate, beating until thoroughly blended. Cool. Chill remaining milk until very, very cold and whip until very stiff. Fold chocolate mixture into milk, add vanilla. Spoon into individual parfait glasses and freeze until firm. Top with whipped cream. Decorate with a few shavings of chocolate and serve.

FRESH STRAWBERRY MOUSSE

2 envelopes unflavored gelatin
1 cup milk
1/8 teaspoon salt
2 pints strawberries, sliced

1 cup sour cream
3 egg whites
¼ cup sugar

In a saucepan, sprinkle gelatin over milk. Place over low heat and stir constantly until gelatin dissolves, about 5 minutes. Remove from heat. Add salt and strawberries. Stir about 5 minutes. Add sour cream, stir until blended. In a bowl, beat eggs until stiff but not dry. Gradually add sugar and beat until very stiff. Fold into strawberry mixture. Turn into 1 large mold or individual molds or parfait glasses. Chill. Top with whipped cream and a fresh, whole strawberry. Makes about 6 servings.

ABOUT CUSTARDS

The custard is a cooked or baked dish mainly of eggs and milk. It may be sweetened as a dessert dish, or flavored with cheese, fish or other ingredients as an entrée. Included in this section are dessert custards only. Soft Custard, also called "Boiled Custard," is thinner and often used as a sauce for fruits or other desserts.

CLASSIC BAKED EGG CUSTARD

A classic, delicious in its simplicity.

3 eggs
½ cup sugar
3 cups scalded milk

1 teaspoon vanilla
¼ teaspoon salt
Nutmeg to sprinkle on top

In a mixing bowl beat eggs enough to blend evenly. Add the sugar and salt and mix. Slowly add the scalded milk, beating with a fork. Add the vanilla. Pour into buttered custard cups. Set cups in a pan of hot water about an inch deep. Bake at 350° for about 45 minutes. Test by inserting a knife into the custard near the edge. If it comes out clean, it will firm when it cools. Makes 6 small custards. Note: for extra-special flavor, add ¼ teaspoon freshly ground vanilla beans before baking.

COCONUT CUSTARD

Add ½ cup finely flaked coconut to the Classic Baked Egg Custard recipe above before pouring into the baking cups.

CARAMEL CUSTARD (SPANISH FLAN)

¾ cup sugar
1 teaspoon butter
2 tablespoon water
4 eggs, well beaten
1 large can evaporated milk

1 1/3 cups scalded milk
1 cup sugar
1 teaspoon vanilla
A bit of grated lemon peel

Boil water and sugar together until sugar turns golden brown. Add the butter. Quickly remove from heat and pour equal amounts into 8 custard cups. Beat together the remaining ingredients. Pour into the 8 custard cups. Place cups in a pan of hot water and bake at 350° oven for 35 minutes. Turn out flat on dessert plates to serve. May be served warm or chilled.

CHOCOLATE CUSTARD

Add 1 ½ ounces melted unsweetened chocolate to the Classic Baked Egg Custard recipe on the preceding page before pouring into cups and baking.

ORANGE CUSTARD
Mrs. Hill's Southern Practical Cookery and Receipt Book (1872)

"The yolks of eight eggs; before breaking them, balance their weight with sugar; balance the weight of three with butter. Cream the butter, sugar, and yolks together. Grate the outside peel of two oranges; add this with their juice. Line the plate with puff paste as in the preceding directions; pour in the custard, and bake."

RICH CUSTARD

¾ cup sugar
2 tablespoons cornstarch
1 cup milk
1 cup heavy cream
4 egg yolks, well beaten

2 tablespoons butter
1 cup heavy cream, whipped
1 ½ teaspoons vanilla
1/8 teaspoon salt

In a double boiler, combine the sugar, cornstarch and salt. Stir in the milk and cream. Cover and boil over the hot water for 8 minutes without stirring. Uncover and cook 10 more minutes, stirring occasionally. Add the egg yolks, butter, and cook 2 more minutes. Cool a bit. Add the vanilla, and then fold in the whipped cream. Chill.

TAPIOCA CUSTARD

Tapioca always sounds like a Caribbean dance, but actually, it is a Brazilian seed from the cassava plant, with a long history of use in English milk puddings. Pearl tapioca makes the best custard.

3 tablespoons quick-cooking
  tapioca
½ cup sugar

¼ teaspoon salt
2 eggs, beaten
½ teaspoon grated lemon rind

Combine tapioca, sugar, salt, eggs and milk in a double boiler and cook 7 minutes. Stir and cook 5 minutes longer. Remove from heat and fold in the vanilla and grated lemon rind. Will thicken as it cools. You may also add dates, diced banana, chopped pineapple, apples or other fruits.

ABOUT CHARLOTTES

Charlotte, North Carolina, is not the only namesake for Queen Charlotte of England (1744-1818). So is the "Charlotte," the delicious and famous two-hundred year old dessert. The Charlotte is akin to English Trifle, of sponge cake or lady fingers with whipped cream or a gelatin type pudding. It is of two kinds, baked or unbaked, and of many flavors such as chocolate, caramel, lemon, vanilla or of berries or fruits. A wine or liqueur may be added.

The Charlotte is the invention of a French chef working for the English monarchy. Food historians think "russe" was added at a banquet honoring Tsar Alexander I of Russia. The Charlotte showed up in the South about the first quarter of the 19th Century.

CHOCOLATE CHARLOTTE RUSSE

This version of the recipe is chocolate flavored and unbaked.

1 ounce (square) chocolate	1 ¾ cups whipping cream
2 tablespoons cold water	½ teaspoon vanilla
2 teaspoons unflavored gelatin	Pinch of salt
¼ cup boiling water	Ladyfingers
6 tablespoons sugar	

Dissolve the gelatin in warm water. Melt chocolate over low heat. Add boiling water and cook slowly until thickened, stirring constantly. Add the sugar, salt and ¾ cup of the cream. Cook 3 minutes longer. Remove heat and add the gelatin. Stir until dissolved. Cool. Chill. Add the vanilla. Whip the remaining cream and fold into the chocolate mixture. Line a mold with lady fingers or sponge cake, and pour on the pudding. Chill until firm and serve.

APPLE CHARLOTTE
The Carolina Housewife (1847)

"Cover the bottom of a baking-dish with a layer of grated bread; strew over it bits of butter about the size of a hickory-nut; then put a layer of sliced apple, then one of brown sugar and a little powdered spice and grated lemon-peel, then another layer of butter, and so on until the dish is full, taking care that the bread and butter are the last layer. Bake for several hours, in a very slow oven. The apples must be pared and sliced very thin. Peaches, or any other fruit, may be made in the same way."

VANILLA CHARLOTTE RUSSE
The Carolina Housewife (1847)

"One pint of milk made into a custard with the yolks of six eggs, and six ounces of white sugar, flavored with vanilla bean, one ounce of isinglass [gelatin] dissolved in milk, and mixed with custard, one pint of cream, whipped to a froth, and mixed gradually with the custard; stirring the whole constantly with a large spoon. The mould to be lined with light sponge cake, cut in strips, and placed on the bottom around the slices; then filled with the mixture, and the top covered in the same manner, with the cake. The mould to be surrounded for some hours with ice, until the Charlotte is completely frozen; then turned out as you would ice cream."

SYLLABUB
Recipes From the Parish of St. Philips in Southport (1907)
Contributed by Lillian Dosher

Brooks Preik has pointed out to me that Charles Dickens called every dessert a syllabub. In the South it has traditionally referred to some sort of nog-like drink made with cream and flavorings. Some version or other of this old dessert shows up in just about every antique Southern cookbook. This recipe was submitted to the St. Phillip's cookbook by my great-aunt Bitsie, whom I write about in "Aunt Bitsie and her Farm," pages 196-197.

1 quart of cream   1 goblet sherry wine

"Sweeten to taste. Whip till thick."

APPLE BROWN BETTY

2 tablespoons melted butter   ½ cup orange or pineapple juice
2 cups bread crumbs, toasted   1/3 cup sugar
4 apples, cored, peeled and sliced
Grating from rind of 1 lemon
    or orange

Butter the bread crumbs and place into a baking dish, alternating layers with the apples, making the last layer of crumbs, and sprinkling each layer with the fruit juice, water and sugar. Bake 1 hour in 350° oven, covered for the first half of the cooking. Serve with hard sauce or cream.

354

ENGLISH TRIFLE

The name is thought to derive from the Old French term "trufle," meaning something of little importance. The French have long looked condescendingly at English cooking. I much admire French cooking, but snobbery in cooking shows a mind closed to the earth's delights. Trifle is one of the great desserts. It is made in many variations. Basically it is left-over cake, preferably sponge cake, layered with pudding, fruits, and topped with whipped cream.

Place a round of sponge layer cake or lady fingers in a deep terrine. Spread on a layer of Rich Custard, using the recipe on page 352. Sprinkle with rum or sherry and scatter on a layer of mixed fruit—small chunks of pineapple, peach, sliced seedless grapes, and a few maraschino cherries chopped. Canned fruit will do, but fresh is best. Build up layers of this and top off with heavy whipped cream. Chill several hours until firm.

SOUTHERN CORN PUDDING

3 cups corn, cut and uncooked
3 eggs, lightly beaten
3 tablespoons melted fat
3 tablespoons sugar

1 1/8 cups milk, scalded
Salt and pepper to taste
1/2 cup walnuts, chopped

Combine all ingredients except walnuts in a greased baking dish. Sprinkle on the chopped walnuts. Bake at 350° for 30 to 40 minutes or until firm. Serves 6 to 8.

Ida Potter Watson and her friend Minnie Butler, 1940's, in a
characteristically jolly mood. Photo courtesy of Elizabeth Watson Griffin.

Loaves and Fishes: Ida Potter Watson

On summer afternoons when berries were in season, she'd invite us over
for her specialty, blackberry or blueberry dumplings with hard sauce. Ida
Potter Watson was special, sweetness itself, a dessert dumpling of a
woman. There is so much to tell about Ida Potter, as our family called
her, or "Pottie" as her friends in the FF Club and her grandchildren called
her; but here I must be content with just a few words.

Her husband, George Y. Watson, died in 1920 of influenza, not
having reached his fortieth birthday, leaving her with five children to
raise. Her father-in-law, "Papa Doc" Watson, watched out for the family,
and they lived in his big, imposing two story, white columned house that
stood on Howe Street cattycornered from the Baptist Church, although
they were Methodists.*

---

* "Papa Doc" had moved to Southport from South Carolina "wearing one brown shoe
and one black shoe," but founded Watson's Pharmacy, for years a Southport institution,
and was a founder of Southport Building and Loan Association (now Security Savings
Bank).

It never occurred to her not to be generous even when, like most families in town, there wasn't a lot to be generous with. To her guests at a meeting of the FF Club or her church group she'd say,

"Have some more cookies. There are lots more left in the kitchen," which made the ladies helping serve very nervous, for they knew that sometimes none were left.

When she died in 1962, the family presented me with a silver teaspoon with the U.S. Capitol embossed in the bowl, the Library of Congress, Mount Vernon and other shrines on the stem. She had brought it back as a souvenir of a bus trip to Washington in 1948 with her friends Minnie Butler and Miss Annie May Woodside for Truman's inauguration. They laughed and giggled all the way. When no food was available in the stops en route, they shared their picnic lunches with the bus driver and their fellow travelers, and like the story of The Loaves and Fishes, no one went hungry.

The Watson home, southwest corner of Howe and Nash Streets, now removed.

IDA POTTER'S STEAMED BERRY DUMPLINGS

1 cup flour
1 teaspoon baking powder
¼ cup sugar

½ cup milk, more or less,
    enough to make a stiff dough
1 cup berries

Blackberries, blueberries, or huckleberries may be used. Mix flour, sugar and baking powder. Blend in milk, then add berries. Form into small balls. Place in double boiler and cook on medium heat for 30 minutes. Serve with hard sauce.

Note: Cousin Brooks Newton Preik tells me that her mother made the sauce with a can of evaporated milk, lots of sugar, and lots of nutmeg. "We loved it." she says.

BAKED APPLE DUMPLINGS

6 apples
2 cups flour, sifted
2 cups sugar
2 cups water
¼ cup butter
1/3 cup milk

¾ cup shortening
2 teaspoons baking powder
¼ teaspoon cinnamon
1 teaspoon nutmeg
1 teaspoon salt

Make the sauce by combining the sugar, water, cinnamon and nutmeg. Cook 5 minutes. Add the butter. Pare and core the apples. Sift together the flour, salt and baking powder. Cut in the shortening. Add milk all at once. Stir until flour is moistened. Roll ¼-inch thick and cut into 5 inch squares. Place one apple on each square, sprinkle with sugar and spices and dot with butter. Fold corners and pinch edges shut. Place 1 inch apart on a greased pan. Pour over sauce. Bake 35 minutes in a 375° oven.

AMBROSIA

6 Valencia or naval oranges
2 cups grated coconut (optional)
2 cups banana slices

¾ cup confectioner's sugar
    or less
½ cup orange juice

Peel the oranges, cutting away all the white pith. Cut the juicy flesh from the membranes. Discard the membranes and any seeds. This should give you about 5 cups. Add other ingredients. Chill and serve. Will yield 12 servings.

BAKED APPLES

6 apples
¾ cup sugar, white or brown
1 teaspoon cinnamon

1 teaspoon nutmeg
6 tablespoons of butter
Water

Wash and core the apples with an apple corer. In a bowl mix the sugar, cinnamon and nutmeg. Place the apples in a baking dish and fill the cavities with the sugar and spices mixture. Place a tablespoon of butter on top of each. Fill the baking dish with ½ inch water. Bake in 350° oven for one half hour, or until the apples are tender, basting frequently with the syrup.

BANANA FRITTERS

2 bananas
Lemon juice
1 tablespoon sugar
2 tablespoons butter

1 cup flour
¼ cup milk
¼ teaspoon soda
Lard for frying

Peel and slice the bananas cut into halves lengthwise and then cut each piece crosswise. Sprinkle with lemon juice and let stand an hour. Combine the sugar, butter, flour, milk and soda. Dip the pieces of banana into the batter. Fry in hot lard. Serve with a sauce.

Sauce for the topping

1 cup sugar
¼ cup hot water

1 teaspoon vanilla

Boil the sugar and water. Add vanilla and serve.

PEACHES AND CREAM
Mrs. Hill's Southern Practical Cookery and Receipt Book (1872)

"Peel soft juicy peaches, quarter them, put a layer of peaches, one of sugar, sprinkling it on very thick until the desired quantity is prepared. Spread thickly over the last layer of peaches powered loaf sugar [confectioner's] sugar. Set the dish upon ice or in a very cool place an hour before using; do not bruise them. Some persons like them best mashed fine, sweetened, and a little grated nutmeg added; in either way serve in small deep plates; eat with rich cream."

ABOUT ICE CREAM

It came as a surprise to me to learn that ice and ice cream helped define American cooking long before the days of commercial refrigeration. And the large numbers of recipes for ice cream and ices in very old cookbooks—*Key to the Pantry* of 1898 contains thirty-two—were puzzling, since home refrigeration was not available until many years later. Recipes routinely read, "Place in freezer and freeze hard." Then, of course, I realized they were referring to the ice cream churns in which rock salt is used to melt commercially obtained ice, lowering the temperature to well below freezing.

I have earlier described the iced mint julep served to the English diarist Frederick Marryat during his tour of America during 1837-1838. Of ice and ice cream, he wrote,

"There is one great luxury in America, which is the quantity of clear pure ice which is to be obtained wherever you are, even in the hottest seasons, and ice-creams are universal and cheap."[*] In 1855, my Davis ancestors migrated from Beaufort, North Carolina, to the St. Marys River that divides northeast Florida from Georgia, where they had saw mills, and where in 1884 Grandma Ella Davis Hardee was born. Sailing ships that called for the timber and naval products brought with them from the north blocks of ice that were kept for long periods in a shed well-insulated with sawdust. Grandma never pronounced it *ice*-cream as we do with such familiarity, but Ice-*cream*. Somehow, her wonderful, antique pronunciation made you think of rich cream, iced. So, eat lots of ice cream. But call it Ice-*cream*.

---

[*] Frederick Marryat, *A Diary in America,* p. 216.

The Southport Ice Plant

The Southport ice plant was two blocks east of Howe on Leonard Street, and the old WB&S short line railroad ran just past it. Ice was long imported to Southport via sailing ships and, after artificial refrigeration, from Wilmington via steamboat. In 1913 a group of civic minded Southport men decided Southport needed its own ice plant and chartered the Southport Ice Manufacturing Company. The WB&S hauled in the ammonia and supplies needed for the operation.

My grandmother Dosher's property was just across the fence near the ice plant. The WB&S had ended passenger service by the time I came along, but when an occasional steam engine went by, I'd run with glee to the back fence to watch as it chugged and hissed and rattled down the tracks past the ice plant, then disappear through the woods to make its way down to the depot near the river.

During the 1940's Mr. Mike Sanders took over the ice plant operation. When the machinery was making ice, Ma-Ma's house shook like an earthquake was hitting, and dishes rattled in the cabinets. I asked her if it didn't wake her up at night. "Only when it stops," she answered.

During hot summer days, we kids would go to the plant and buy a nickel's worth of ice for drinks, sometimes to make our own sherbets. Mr. Sanders, or Mr. Roy Swain who worked for him, would go into the freezer, and from behind a black rubber flap covering a little door, would emerge our little pyramid of ice, too small to sell on their regular route, but just enough for our summer treat. They'd tie it with a piece of jute and off we'd go with our prize, sucking on splinters of cold ice all the way home.

Beside the plant was a narrow cement trough for the discharge of warm water from the operation, slimy-green with algae. We'd sit in our bathing suits under the plant waiting for the release of the water, then slide on its crest down to the drain, where it emptied underground into the Swamp Garden Ditch. My mother's generation had done the same.

On August 27, 1940, there was a big commotion downtown on East Moore Street. The depot was ablaze. Like half the town, we went down to watch it. This was all very scary but exciting to a young child; but don't we enjoy being scared? Suddenly there was a terrific explosion. The firemen moved us away from the blaze toward Atlantic Avenue. We later learned that an ammonia tank intended for the ice plant had exploded. A piece of metal tore through the house of Mr. Willie Walker making a hole big enough "to drive a horse and cart through." The blast killed Mr. Willie Walker who was watching the fire from about seventy-five feet away.

ICE CREAM

Recipes for homemade ice cream are accommodatingly inexact, as they can be adjusted to suit your tastes, using the equipment you might have on hand, with relative ease and success. Most ice cream recipes use one of three basic mixes, to which different flavorings or fruits are added:

> Custard style mix, to which whipped cream is added.
> Canned sweetened condensed milk is used as the basis, to
> which whipped cream is added.
> Egg custard method. This is similar to the plain custard mix,
> but eggs are used.

Most recipes for home-made ice cream call for one of three basic methods of freezing:

1. Refrigerator freezer method, using refrigerator trays. These recipes usually date from the days when freezer compartments in home refrigerators were quite small, and the compartment for making ice cubes in trays was usually the only place cold enough for freezing ice cream. The advantage is that the freezer trays are shallow and freeze quickly; the drawback is that standard freezer trays don't hold much, and 2 or 3 trays may be required for one batch of ice cream. To use this method, allow the mix to freeze until ice crystals form. Scrape the partially frozen mixture from the sides of the trays. Beat. Add whipped cream if the recipe calls for it, return to freezer and let freeze again until hard.

2. Refrigerator freezer method, using stainless steel mixing bowls. This method is similar to the refrigerator-tray method, but allows for a full recipe to be managed in a single mixing bowl, rather than in 2 or more ice cream trays. Freeze the ice cream mixture until extremely cold and partially frozen around the edges. Beat. Add whipped cream if the recipe calls for it, add additional fruits if desired, return to freezer and let freeze again until hard.

3. Churned method, using a hand cranked churn or an electric churn. For these, follow manufacturer's instructions.

362

ICE CREAM BASE – CUSTARD METHOD

1 cup half & half

1/2 cup sugar

1/8 teaspoon salt

1 tablespoon all purpose flour

½ teaspoon vanilla

1 cup whipping cream

Pre-set the freezer to the coldest setting. Scald the milk. Gradually add the mixture of sugar, salt and flour and vanilla. Stir over low heat to the boiling point, and boil for 1 minute. Cool. Pour into freezing tray and freeze for ½ hour. Whip the cup of whipping cream until barely stiff. Turn the partially frozen tray into a chilled bowl and beat with cold rotary beater until smooth but not melted. Fold in the whipping cream. Return to freezer. Freeze until firm, stirring now and then.

ICE CREAM BASE- SWEETENED CONDENSED MILK METHOD

1/3 cup sweetened condensed milk

½ cup water

½ teaspoon vanilla

1 cup heavy cream

Blend sweetened condensed milk and vanilla thoroughly. Pour into freezing tray or stainless steel mixing bowl and place in freezer until crystals form around sides. Whip the cream until barely stiff, then fold into the milk mixture. Return to freezer and freeze until half-frozen. Beat again. Scrape sides of trays or mixing bowl. Return to freezer and freeze until solid.

VANILLA ICE CREAM

Use either of the ice cream bases above. Add an additional teaspoon of vanilla extract before turning in the whipped cream.

CHOCOLATE ICE CREAM

Use either of the ice cream bases above. To the mixture, add 2 ounces melted chocolate squares.

BANANA ICE CREAM

Use either of the ice cream bases above. After the first freezing, and before turning in the whipped cream, add 1 ½ cups well mashed bananas mixed with 1 tablespoon lemon juice and 2 tablespoons sugar.

FRESH STRAWBERRY OR PEACH ICE CREAM

Use either of the ice cream bases above. Add 1 cup mashed strawberries or peaches which have been mixed with ½ cup sugar. After the first freezing, before turning in the whipped cream, add another ½ cup or more of fresh chopped strawberries or peaches.

PINEAPPLE ICE CREAM

3 cups milk	1 ½ cups crushed pineapple,
½ cup sugar	both pulp and juice
1 egg, beaten	1 teaspoon vanilla

Beat the ingredients together well. Partially freeze in stainless steel mixing bowl. Beat, return to freezer, and freeze until hardened.

LEMON CUSTARD ICE CREAM

1 cup sugar	½ cup lemon juice
1 cup boiling water	2 tablespoons grated lemon rind
2 eggs, beaten	Dash of salt
3 cups milk	

Mix together the flour, sugar and salt in top of a double boiler. Add the boiling water and heat until it boils, stirring constantly. Pour slowly over the beaten eggs. Return to the boiler and cook 3 minutes, stirring all the while. Remove from fire and cool. Add the milk, lemon juice and rind. Pour into stainless steel mixing bowl and partially freeze. Beat, return to freezer, and freeze until hardened.

BUTTER PECAN ICE CREAM

1 ½ cups milk	Butter, to brown the pecan meats
½ cup sugar	2 eggs, separated
½ teaspoon salt	1 cup heavy cream
1 cup pecan meats,	1 teaspoon vanilla
roughly chopped	

Mix the sugar, salt and milk. Brown the pecans in butter. Beat the egg whites until stiff, but not dry as for a meringue. Whip cream until thick and holds a peak, but do not over-beat. Add the vanilla and fold in the egg whites, milk and pecans. Pour into stainless steel mixing bowl and place in freezer until half-frozen, stirring every 30 minutes, until nearly frozen, then freeze until firm.

The Big Snow of 1989

Just off the coast from Southport runs the Gulf Stream, whose warm waters keep our town bathed in warm, moist and salty air. Seldom do we see snow, even though it may blanket the land only a few miles inland, and when it does fall, seldom sticks more than a few hours. 1989 was a major exception. Just before Christmas of that year it began to fall. Before it had stopped two days later, more than eighteen inches had fallen, breaking a double record—it was the largest amount of snow ever recorded in Southport, and the only snowfall on record at Christmas. The town was unrecognizable, wrapped in white and silver tinsel. The miniature snow village under our Christmas tree had become alive just outside our doors! The snow-covered black limbs of our giant live oaks formed a canopy of silver and white overhead; our birdbaths were huge, white mushrooms. Once familiar houses were snow castles, streets were lanes of glitter. Until the streets became impassable, we rode around town snapping pictures from the car. Besides ourselves, Rev. P.D. Midgett, documenting the miraculous event from his van with his video camera, seemed to be the only soul about. Children, who you would have thought couldn't be contained indoors, stayed put, transfixed by the wizard responsible for this winter fantasy. Other than P.D., the only moving creatures we saw were two long-tailed dogs who frolicked across fences, leap-frogged across each other on the snow covered streets, dove under houses, then burst forth again on their jubilant jaunt through this once-in-a-lifetime fairy land.

SNOW CREAM

On those very rare occasions when I was growing up that we had snow, Ma-Ma would send us into the yard with a bowl to collect nature's surprise, and she'd make us a dish of snow cream. Here's how she did it: She'd separate 2 eggs, beat the yolks in ½ can of sweetened condensed milk, beat the whites until stiff, then fold in the egg and sweet milk, and add a little vanilla. Add this to the bowl of snow and serve immediately. Crushed pineapple or peaches may also be added before turning into the bowl of snow.

ABOUT SHERBETS

The sherbet, also spelled sherbert, is an ice usually made with milk and egg white or gelatin.

GRAPE SHERBET
Key to the Pantry (1898)
Contributed by Miss Kate Stuart

This recipe from Mrs. Grover Cleveland "at the White House" was included in the copy of the above cookbook used at the Stuart House. Kate Stuart has written in the border, "Try it."

"One quart of grape juice (sweetened to taste), 2 cups of orange juice, with 1 cup of sugar. Turn into a freezer. When half frozen, add the beaten white of 1 egg and 1 tablespoon of sugar. Take out dasher, and set away to harden."

LEMON SHERBET

¼ cup lemon juice	¼ cup boiling water
¾ cup sugar	½ cup whipping cream
1 teaspoon plain gelatin	1 egg yolk, lightly beaten
2 tablespoons cold water	1 egg white, beaten until stiff

Mix the lemon juice and sugar. Dissolve the gelatin in the hot water, and then add the cold water. Add this to the fruit mixture and stir. Freeze this for 1 hour. Then whip the cream, and then add the egg yolk and egg white. Place the partially frozen sherbet in a cold bowl and beat with rotary beater until creamy. Fold in the whipped cream mixture. Return to tray and freeze for about 3 hours.

STRAWBERRY OR RASPBERRY SHERBET

Follow the basic lemon sherbet recipe above, but reduce the amount of lemon juice and add crushed strawberries or raspberries.

ORANGE SHERBET
Recipes From the Parish of St. Philips in Southport (1907)
Contributed by Norma Brinkman

1 pint orange juice
1 pound sugar

2 tablespoonfuls gelatin
1 quart water

"Cover gelatin with cold water. Soak for one-half hour. Boil sugar and water together for five minutes, add gelatine, then set aside to cool. When cold, add orange juice, strain, freeze and add meringue."

PINEAPPLE SHERBET
Annie May Woodside's Cook Book (1913)

½ pint canned pineapple
Juice of 2 lemons
2 cups sugar

3 cups milk
1 cup cream

"The pine apple must be fine-chopped, and then mix all in order given. Freeze, let stand two hours. This will serve eight people liberally."

SNOW CONES

The snow cones sold today at carnival and beach concessions were in Southport long referred to as "sherbets." Like snow cones, Southport sherbets were simply shaved ice in a paper cup poured over with fruit flavored syrup, not ices made with gelatin and milk. During the years when ice plants provided the town with blocks of ice, small, steel hand-shavers were easily available at many general merchandise stores. Mr. Willie McKenzie did a big business with Southport sherbets, which he made with a big, hand cranked commercial ice shaver.

MA-MA'S DESSERT BUTTER SAUCE

A delicious, versatile sauce, great with many desserts.

¼ cup butter
½ cup granulated sugar

1/3 cup light cream or
undiluted evaporated milk

Combine ingredients in a saucepan. Cook over low heat for 5 minutes.

CHOCOLATE SAUCE

Delightful over fruits such as poached pear, or ice cream.

1/3 cup semisweet chocolate
¼ cup cocoa

¾ cup granulated sugar
1 ¼ cups water

In a saucepan cook the water, chocolate and sugar until melted. In a bowl mix the cocoa with 3 tablespoons of water to form a smooth paste. Pour this mixture over the chocolate and bring to a boil, constantly whisking. Simmer uncovered for 5 to 10 minutes. Do not allow to boil. Serve hot or cold.

CHOCOLATE CREAM SAUCE

1 ounce chocolate
2 tablespoons hot water
1/3 cup sugar
1/2 cup hot milk

½ cup heavy cream, whipped
2 eggs
¼ teaspoon cinnamon
½ teaspoon vanilla

Melt chocolate, add sugar and hot water, and cook until smooth and glossy. Add milk. Beat eggs and combine with mixture. When cold, add cinnamon, vanilla and whipped cream.

HARD SAUCE

I never understood why Hard Sauce was called Hard Sauce. It's not as runny as syrup, but is definitely not hard, and is definitely not hard to eat.

1 stick butter or margarine
1 cup sugar (powdered, white,
    or light brown)
1/3 cup milk or canned
    evaporated milk

1 teaspoon vanilla
¼ teaspoon nutmeg

Melt sugar and butter, add warm milk, and stir. Serve over berries, berry dumplings, fruitcake, plum pudding, or just about anything not too sweet.

BROWN SUGAR SAUCE WITH NUTS

3 tablespoons butter or margarine   1 cup chopped walnuts or pecans
1 cup firmly packed brown sugar   1 teaspoon vanilla
½ cup half & half milk

Melt butter, stir in brown sugar and cook 5 to 8 minutes. Remove heat.
Stir in half & half, nuts and vanilla.

WINE OR BRANDY SAUCE FOR PUDDING
Our Favorite Recipes (1974)

½ cup butter   ½ cup powdered sugar
¼ cup brandy or sherry wine   2 egg yolks
2 pounds granulated sugar

Beat all ingredients except brandy or wine. Add this one drop at a time
Beat until ready to serve.

PUDDING SAUCE
The Carolina Housewife (1847)

"Six heaping table-spoonfuls of loaf sugar, half a pound of butter,
worked to a cream; then add one egg, one wineglass of white wine, one
nutmeg.—When it is all well mixed, set on the fire until it comes to a
boil: it is then fit for use."

GREAT GRANDMA DAVIS'S LEMON SAUCE

This is great for pouring over slices of cakes, dessert dumplings,
blackberries, strawberries, or just about any dessert that could benefit
from a little touch of lemon sweetness. Follow the recipe for Great
Grandma Davis's Lemon Filling on page 336, but do not cook as long as
for filling.

My cousin Erica Jones, cousin Vivian McKeithan Jones' granddaughter. 2005.

18..
Candies

ABOUT CANDIES

Candy making is an art in itself. Each of the recipes in this book is from a reliable source, but expect to be challenged by some. I have had good luck with many of them, but also some failures using the same recipe on a later date. The temperatures and humidity of the day you are making candy, as well as the temperature of the candy syrup, play a big role in candy making, and it is important to follow recipes carefully and measure ingredients carefully.

In years gone by, cooks used the cold water method exclusively to test candy temperatures whereby you drizzle a little of the syrup in a cup of cold water, and the shape that results tells you which stage you have reached—the "soft ball," "firm ball," "soft crack," or "hard crack." This has always seemed messy and arbitrary to me, as I never could tell exactly the difference between a firm ball and a hard ball, for instance.

Using a candy thermometer is a definite help, but is no guarantee of success. Test your thermometer. If it hits 212° as the water begins to boil, it is accurate. Make sure the prong sits deep enough in your syrup or mixture to register properly.

Temperatures

Soft Ball. 232 to 240° Fahrenheit. Syrup will make a soft ball when picked up but will not hold its shape. This is the temperature for fudge, penuche and fondant.

Firm Ball. 250 to 268°. Syrup makes a ball that will hold its shape. For divinity and taffy.

Soft Crack. 270 to 290°. Syrup falls hard but not in brittle threads. For butterscotch and toffee.

Hard Crack. 300 to 310°. Syrup forms brittle threads that break. For brittles, lollypops and caramel or candy apples.

A rule of thumb is that for every 500 feet above sea level you live, add 2° to the temperature required. For most candies, you should use a good sized, heavy pot, and wooden spoons. A marble slap is good to have for cooling some candies, but a large platter will do. A pastry brush is handy for wiping away any crystals that may form on the sides of the pot.

The Halloween Carnival

Halloween without candy apples would be like Thanksgiving without a turkey. I spy a candy apple and am immediately drawn back to the Halloween Carnivals the Southport High School P.T.A. used to put on, for never was there a Carnival without a card table full of bright red, shiny candy apples for sale.

The Halloween Carnival was a major fund raiser for the school, and an eagerly awaited event. It was held in the old gymnasium that used to be attached to the rear of the Masonic Lodge, a curious old wooden building with the red brick chimney of the Lodge at one end, and a balcony that ran around all sides overlooking the basketball court. At the rear end was a pair of steps that led to the east and west balconies.

A large and excited crowd would be standing in the chilly air outside of the gym waiting for the doors to open. And what wonders did we behold! Overhead were draped crepe paper streamers in orange and black, and against the walls the concessions were lined up. The Barnum & Bailey Circus held no greater spectacles. Each of the twelve grades sponsored some sort of concession. The Fish Pond was great fun. You'd pay a nickel or dime, they'd give you a bamboo fishing pole with a little basket on the end of the string, then toss it over a bed sheet draped across a wire, and reel in your prize—a piece of candy or little toy. There was a Fortune Teller booth and a Kiss Me booth. There was a Hit the Prize stand where you'd toss a ball and hope to knock some prize off its stand. There was a Popcorn Stand, a Hot Dog Stand, and a Drink Stand. The Senior Class always laid claim to the House of Horrors—the stairs and part of the balconies rigged up and covered over with cardboard and outfitted with wicked and horrible things. Throughout the evening you'd hear the screams of us poor devils who'd pay our dime for the privilege of climbing the steps to the east balcony to be scared out of our wits. There in the near darkness would be ghosts and skeletons and headless bodies and wild, cackling crazy sounds. ("I just escaped from Dix Hill Insane Asylum *and I am coming to murder you!!!"*) They'd scream at you, *"Now you are going to feel what it's like to touch a human heart!"* and slap a cold beef liver (in a plastic bag) onto your palms. At the exit, they'd hurl you down a cardboard slide rigged up on the west staircase.

But the candy apples are what got me started on this little reminiscence, and here's the recipe:

CANDY APPLES

6 to 8 medium-sized apples
2 cups sugar
½ cup butter
1 teaspoon vinegar

½ cup cream
½ cup water
Pinch cream of tartar

Dissolve sugar and water in a saucepan. Add the cream of tartar, butter, vinegar and cream. Cook, stirring constantly to 290° or the soft-crack stage. Remove from heat. Put a skewer or popsicle stick in each apple. Dip each apple into the boiled syrup and place on a buttered surface to harden.

ANNA McKENZIE'S BROWN DOGS
Susie Carson's Recipe Files

2 pounds light brown sugar
3 pounds raw peanuts
¼ teaspoon baking soda

¼ cup butter
Water
1 teaspoon vanilla flavoring

Roast the peanuts until light brown. In heavy pot, mix sugar with enough water to dissolve. Cook over medium heat, stirring occasionally, scraping sides of pot. When white streets begin to form on sides of pot, add the baking soda and stir well. Mixture will foam up. Add the vanilla flavoring and the butter. Add the peanuts and mix well, then turn heat low. Spoon into well greased muffin pans. If mixture starts to harden in pot, add a little water, stir well, cook down and fill muffin tins as quickly as possible. Makes about 3 dozen.

OLD BRUNSWICK TOWN CARAMEL BARS

2 cups brown sugar
1 stick butter
½ cup chopped nuts

2 eggs
1 ½ cups flour
1 teaspoon vanilla

Cream sugar and butter, then add well beaten eggs, flour, vanilla and nuts. Cook at 325° about 35 to 40 minutes. Cool and cut into squares.

CARAMELS

1 16-ounce package light
   brown sugar
1 14-ounce can sweetened
   condensed milk

1 cup light corn syrup
1 cup butter

Line an 8-inch square baking pan with foil, including the edges. Coat with cooking spray or cooking oil. Melt 1 cup butter in 3 quart sauce pan over low heat. Stir in the sugar and the corn syrup until smooth. Bring to a boil, cook until candy thermometer reaches 235°. Stir by hand 1 minute until mixture is smooth. Pour into the pan and let stand 3 hours, or until cool. Cut caramels into 1-inch pieces with a buttered knife. Wrap each with plastic wrap.

Mrs. Mary Temple's Store

Mrs. Mary Temple ran a store on Howe Street. It was a tiny little doll house of a building sheathed in fake red-brick asphalt siding, sitting squat on the ground with the boughs of a big cedar tree hanging overhead. The front yard was white sand, which daily she swept clean. Mrs. Temple was our principal supplier of candy. Her face was powder white as confectioner's sugar from the candy she sold, and never saw daylight. She'd shove aside a cardboard Dutch door she'd rigged up to keep people out of her living area, waddle in behind her candy counter, and patiently wait while we made our selections.

Besides the candies, which she kept in big glass jars stacked one on top of the other, there were a few loaves of Merita bread for sale and not much else. The cold drink box hadn't held a block of ice since old Mr. Temple died years before and was empty and dusty. The shelves were empty of goods, and held cardboard boxes of Lord Knows What. There was a glass cabinet with spools of J. & P. Coats thread in funny purples and colors that didn't sell, so old they would break.

It took forever to decide what to buy with your nickel or dime. Almost everything was a penny apiece. There were grape colored bubble gums, yellow, chewy Mary Janes, Crayola-colored jaw-breakers, pink marshmallows covered with cocoanut, orange colored peanut butter candies in the shape of peanuts, tough Double Bubble gum, and *chocolate dice.* That was just about our favorite. Some woman out in the county made them in her kitchen and peddled them to the stores. They were a chewy dark brown candy filled with peanuts which, when sliced into one inch cubes, looked like dice.

MARY TEMPLE'S CHOCOLATE DICE

I'm quite proud of this recipe, replicated from memory. How often did I long to have a taste of Mary Temple's chocolate dice just once more. Well, while working on this book, I spied an old recipe and said to myself, that just might be it! The first batch was a failure, crunch and sugary. But I felt I was on to the secret and kept at it. And lo! Mrs. Temple's dice, or as close as I can come to it. I gave a batch to Neil Lewis, who said, "Where on earth did you get the recipe!!?" Here it is.

2 cups sugar
¾ cup light corn syrup
½ cup butter

2 cups heavy cream
8 ounces unsweetened chocolate
2 cups roasted peanuts, shelled

Boil the sugar, syrup, butter, and 1 cup of the cream over medium heat, stirring constantly. Cook to firm ball stage, 254°, beat in the remaining cup of cream, and boil again to 254°. Stir in the chocolate until mixed, then peanuts. Spread into a buttered 7-inch square pan. When cool, cut into 1-inch cubes with a sharp knife.

CHOCOLATE TURTLES

½ pound of soft caramels, using
   recipe for caramels, page 374
2 tablespoons heavy cream

1 ½ cups pecan halves
4 squares semisweet chocolate

Melt the caramels with the cream over hot water. Let cool 10 minutes. Arrange pecan halves in groups of three on lightly greased baking sheet, one for the head, two for the legs. Spoon melted caramel over the nuts and let stand for 30 minutes. Melt the chocolate squares over hot water, remove from heat and stir until smooth. Spread over the caramel turtles, but not over the nut pieces. Makes about 24 turtles.

CHOCOLATE CHERRY CORDIALS

6 ounces Semi-Sweet Chocolate
   chips
5 ¾ ounce package
   Chocolate Chips

2 tablespoons shortening
1 tablespoon milk

Melt chocolate pieces and shortening in double boiler slowly. Stir to blend well. Remove from heat and cool to 78.°

While cooling, prepare the centers:

4 dozen maraschino cherries,
   drained
¼ cup butter
1 tablespoon milk

2 to 2 ¼ cups confectioner's sugar
1/8 teaspoonful almond extract
1/2 teaspoon vanilla extract

Cream butter with sugar and milk well. Blend in vanilla and almond extract. Add additional sugar if mixture is too sticky. Mold a small amount around a cherry, being careful to cover each cherry. Place on waxed payer covered tray. Cover and chill.

The dipping:

Heat the cooled chocolate to 78° over warm water. Keep the temperature steady while dipping. Drop centers into the chocolate. Roll to coat completely and remove with fork. Draw fork across rim of pan to remove excess chocolate. Drop from fork upside down onto waxed paper, swirling a thread of chocolate from fork across top for a decorative touch. Chill. Store in a cool place a couple of days to set.

CHOCOLATE-COATED PEANUTS

1 6-ounce package semi-sweet chocolate
2 ½ cups roasted shelled, skinless peanuts, lightly salted

Melt chocolate in top of double boiler over hot but not boiling water. Add peanuts and stir. Turn out on waxed paper, separating with a fork. Store in air-tight containers.

CLASSIC CHOCOLATE FUDGE

3 cups sugar
1 cup milk
3 squares unsweetened chocolate
3 tablespoons light corn syrup

3 tablespoons butter or margarine
1 1/2 teaspoons vanilla
1/8 teaspoon salt
1/2 cup chopped walnuts or pecans

Cook chocolate and milk in 3 quart heavy sauce pan until milk is scalded and chocolate is melted, stirring constantly. Add sugar, corn syrup and salt. Cook over medium heat, stirring until sugar dissolves. Wipe off any crystals that may form on side of saucepan. Cook without further stirring to soft ball stage, 236 to 238°. Remove from heat, add butter but do not stir. Cool until lukewarm 110°. Add vanilla. Beat until candy starts to thicken. Stir in nuts and pour into a lightly buttered 8-inch square pan. Cut into 36 pieces.

CHOCOLATE FUDGE
SWEETENED CONDENSED MILK METHOD

18 ounces semi-sweet chocolate
1 14-ounce can sweetened
  condensed milk

½ to 1 cup chopped nuts, optional
2 teaspoons vanilla extract

Melt the chocolate, sweetened condensed milk and salt in a heavy saucepan until melted. Stir in vanilla, and nuts if wanted. Spread into a 9-inch square pan lined with foil. Chill 2 hours until firm. Turn onto cutting board, remove foil and cut into squares. Store in refrigerator.

GRANDMA HARDEE'S COCOA FUDGE

¾ cup cocoa
3 cups white granulated sugar
1 small can evaporated milk

2 tablespoons light Karo syrup
2 teaspoons vanilla
1/8 teaspoon salt

Combine cocoa with sugar and salt. Add milk. Bring to a boil, stirring frequently until a small amount dropped in a cup of water forms a small boil 236 to 238°. Remove from heat, add syrup and beat until mixture thickens. Pour into buttered pan and cut into squares. For a variation, add nuts or coconut to mixture before putting into buttered pan.

VICKIE HARDEE'S CHRISTMAS FUDGE

2 cups of sugar
2/3 cup skim Pet can milk
½ stick of blue bonnet margarine
12 regular sized marshmallows
cut into fourths (do not use the
miniature marshmallows)

1 cup semisweet chocolate chips
1 tablespoon of vanilla
1 cup of chopped pecans

Vickie says, "This fudge never fails for me and is delicious! I usually make it only at Christmas and then some years I have had to make as many as ten batches. You will need a 3-quart pot and an 8x8-inch pan. Spray with Pam or grease with butter.

"Place the first four ingredients in a 3-quart pot. I use a copper bottom pot. Bring to medium boil constantly stirring the sugar, milk, butter, and marshmallows. Start timing when boiling begins and stir continually for ten minutes. It's important that you time it exactly, not one minute longer or one minute shorter. Take the mixture off heat when the 10 minutes are over. Quickly add the semisweet chips stirring while they melt. Then add one tablespoon of vanilla while stirring. Finally add one cup of nuts and stir. Pour the mixture into an 8x8-inch greased pan while it is still hot and flowing. Set aside and let cool till the next day. Cut and place in tin lined with wax paper."

CHOCOLATE-COATED RAISINS

Follow the recipe for Chocolate Coated Peanuts on page 376, but substitute raisins for the peanuts.

HOREHOUND CANDY

8 cups boiling water
1 ½ quarts loosely packed
horehound leaves and stems.
4 cups sugar

1 ¼ cups dark cane syrup
1 tablespoon butter
1 teaspoon cream of tartar

Simmer the horehound covered for 20 minutes. Drain and retain only the dark and bitter brew. Add remaining ingredients to the brew and boil to the hard crack stage, 300°. Skim off any scum. Pour into a buttered 15x10x1-inch pan. Cut into pieces before it sets.

COUSIN BROOKS NEWTON PREIK'S CARAMEL FUDGE

Candy does not get better than this timeless Brunswick County caramel fudge that cousin Brooks Newton makes, based on the recipe of her mother, Annie Lou Knox Newton. It is essentially that of Mammy St. George's caramel frosting, requiring great skill and perhaps some practice, as the temperatures of the two pots, one to caramelize the sugar, the other to boil the milk and other ingredients, must be carefully synchronized and mixed at exactly the right moment. As Brooks says, "This is one of the most difficult recipes to turn out right." But her instructions come as close as you can find to help achieve success, and the intrepid will be rewarded with a special delight.

1 can Carnation evaporated milk	¾ stick of butter
4 cups sugar	1 ½ teaspoons vanilla
1/8 teaspoon salt	1 cup chopped pecans

"Put 3 cups of the sugar, salt and evaporated milk in a large, heavy pot, about a 6-quart pot. Bring to a boil stirring constantly. At the same time, put the remaining 1 cup of sugar in a small iron skillet and stir over high heat until sugar melts and turns a light golden brown. *Do not overcook* or fudge will be dark and bitter. Pour the melted sugar immediately and slowly into the other pot, stirring constantly with a long wooden spoon. The mixture will bubble up rapidly and care must be taken to keep the pot from boiling over. It is difficult to do the preceding alone, since both pots need stirring constantly and at the same time, but it *can* be done. Continue cooking on medium heat and add butter and vanilla. Candy must then be beaten until it begins to harden a little around the sides of the pot. The amount of time for this varies. I use an electric mixer but my mother preferred to beat by hand. It takes some practice to know when is just the right moment to pour into a greased pan or dish to finish hardening. Right before the candy is poured, a cup of chopped pecans can be added, but move very quickly or the candy will get too hard to pour. It is best to cut it into squares before it is completely hardened."

379

DIVINITY

Do not attempt divinity on a warm, muggy day. As my mother says, "Divinity knows the weather."

2 ½ cups sugar
½ cup light corn syrup
½ cup water
2 egg whites

¼ teaspoon salt
1 teaspoon vanilla
Pecan halves

Use an electric mixer and beat the egg whites with the salt to stiff peak stage, but not dry. In a heavy quart saucepan, combine sugar, syrup and water and cook without stirring until the sugar dissolves. Cover; cook without stirring 1 minute until sugar on side of pan melts. Uncover. Cook on high heat without stirring until temperature reaches 235°. In a thin stream, slowly pour half of the hot syrup over the egg whites while beating with the electric beater. Cook the remaining syrup to the 260° hard-ball stage, then slowly drizzle and beat into the mixture. Continue to beat until it is just stiff enough to hold its shape when dropped from a spoon, about 5 minutes. Mix in the vanilla. If you wish, divide the batch of candy into thirds, stirring a few drops of red food coloring into one, and green into another, for a festive look. Drop by spoonfuls onto waxed paper. Press a pecan half into the center of each. Allow to dry out uncovered for 30 minutes to several hours, until bottoms of the candies are no longer sticky, and they are easily removed from the waxed paper. It should be firm but delicate and frothy. Store in a sealed container.

SEA FOAM

Sea Foam is Divinity's half sister, but equally divine.

1 ¾ cups light brown sugar
¾ cup white sugar
½ cup hot water
¼ cup light corn syrup

¼ teaspoon salt
2 egg whites
1 teaspoon vanilla
½ cup broken walnuts (optional)

Combine sugars, water, corn syrup and salt in heavy sauce pan. Cook stirring constantly, until sugar dissolves and mixture reaches a boil. If sugar crystals form on sides of pan, wipe them off with a pastry brush dampened but not dripping wet. Continue cooking without stirring at a very low boil to hard boil stage 260°. Remove from heat. At once, beat egg whites until stiff. Pour hot syrup slowly in thin stream over egg whites beating constantly with electric mixer on high. Add vanilla. Continue beating until candy loses gloss and forms peaks. This will take about 10 minutes. Stir in walnuts or pecans. Drop rounded teaspoons on waxed paper, swirling to make attractive peaks. Makes about 30 to 36 pieces.

ENGLISH TOFFEE
Favorite Recipes of North Carolina (about 1944)

2 cups almonds	5 tablespoons water
1 cup sugar	$\frac{1}{4}$ teaspoon salt
1 cup butter	Sweet chocolate

Blanch almonds and toast a golden brown in oven. Put half through food chopper and cut remainder into large pieces. Combine sugar, butter and water, and boil to 300° (brittle when dropped into cold water, stirring constantly). Remove from fire, add broken nut meats and pour into buttered pan. Grate sweet chocolate over top and sprinkle generously with chopped meat nuts. Cool 10 minutes. Turn upside down on waxed paper and sprinkle with grated chocolate and nut meats. Cut into 1-inch squares.

MAPLE SUGAR CANDY
Annie May Woodside's Recipe Files

2 cups maple sugar	1 cup nuts
$\frac{1}{2}$ pint cream	

Boil sugar and cream together until it strings, then beat thoroughly and add nuts. Lay on buttered pan and cut into blocks.

SUGARED PECANS
Contributed by Cousin Jean T. Lindquist

1 egg white, cold	1 teaspoon salt
1 tablespoon water	1 teaspoon cinnamon
1 cup sugar	1 pound pecan halves

In a large bowl, beat the egg white and water to a froth. Drop all pecans in at once and stir until all are coated and the white is gone. In another bowl, mix sugar, salt and cinnamon. Then drop all pecans into this sugar mix and stir well. Spread on a rimmed, non-greased cookie sheet. Bake in 300° oven 30 to 35 minutes, stirring after 15 minutes. Cool. Store in air-tight containers.

PENUCHE-COCONUT DROPS

This is a replication of the penuche-coconut drops we used to buy at Mrs. Mary Temple's store. Penuche is a delicious fudge of Mexican origin.

3 cups brown sugar
¼ teaspoon salt
1 cup heavy cream
2 tablespoons butter

1 teaspoon vanilla
1 cup chopped nuts
Shredded coconut lightly toasted

Toast the coconut in the oven. Dissolve the sugar, salt and cream in a large pan, constantly stirring until you have reached the boiling temperature. Cover and cook 3 minutes, until the crystals on the sides of the pan are washed down by the steam. Uncover and cook on low heat without stirring to the soft-ball stage, 234°. Remove from heat and add the butter. Cool to 110°. Beat until smooth and creamy. Add the vanilla, nuts and shredded coconut. Drop by spoonfuls onto waxed paper.

SNICKERDOODLES

3 ¼ cups all purpose flour, sifted
1 ½ cups sugar
3 eggs, well beaten
1 cup (2 sticks) butter
1 cup hickory nuts or walnuts,
    chopped coarsely

½ cup currants
½ cup raisins, chopped
½ teaspoon salt
1 teaspoon baking soda

Sift together flour, salt, baking soda and cinnamon. Set aside. Work butter until creamy, and then add sugar, a little at a time, beating until smooth. Beat in eggs thoroughly. Stir in the flour combination, nuts, currants and raisins. Drop from a teaspoon onto a greased cookie sheet, about 1 inch apart. Bake in a preheated 350° oven for 12 to 14 minutes. Cookies keep well in an airtight container. Makes about 10 dozen.

COCONUT MACAROONS

3 egg whites
½ cup sugar
2 cups coconut, shredded

½ teaspoon salt
1 teaspoon vanilla

Beat the egg whites with the sugar and salt until stiff. Fold in the coconut and vanilla. Drop by teaspoonfuls onto greased pan. Bake at 325° for 30 minutes. [The recipe for Almond Macaroon on page 310 may be used, substituting coconut for the almonds.]

382

minutes. [The recipe for Almond Macaroon on page 310 may be used, substituting coconut for the almonds.]

SOUTHPORT HIGH SCHOOL LUNCH ROOM
ONE MINUTE CANDY
May White Moore's Recipe Files

This is the way the staff at the old Southport High School lunch room used to make candy.

2 cups sugar	2 cups oat meal, old fashioned
½ cup cocoa	½ cup peanut butter
½ cup milk	1 teaspoon vanilla
1 stick margarine	Nuts, or coconut

Mix ingredients. Bring to a boil, and boil one minute, stirring constantly. Remove from heat. Drop onto aluminum foil or wax paper

ABOUT POTATO CANDIES

Candy made with a potato base, either Irish Potato or Sweet Potato seem unlikely. But they have a long history in Southport and for good reason; they are easy to make, and have an unexpectedly light, even effervescent quality.

CHOCOLATE POTATO CANDY

3/4 cup well boiled, mashed Irish potato	About 4 ½ cupfuls confectioner's sugar
1/3 cup cocoa	1 teaspoon vanilla

In a large bowl, mix the mashed potato, salt and vanilla. Begin beating in the sugar and coca until the mixture becomes dough-like and can be rolled into individual candy-size balls. Chill. Then coat with Chocolate Cherry Cordial coating.

MRS. WILLIE FULLWOOD'S IRISH POTATO AND
PEANUT BUTTER CANDY WHEELS
Aline Harrell's Recipe Files

Mrs. Fullwood was the wife of the grocery store owner, Willie Fullwood, whose vignette and photograph are on pages 16-17. She gave this unlikely candy recipe to the mother of Aline Harrell. Aline in turn passed it on to me. She entered it in the 1969 New Hanover County Fair and took the blue ribbon!

½ level cup Irish potato, mashed   1 small jar creamy peanut butter
About 5 cups (2 boxes)
    confectioner's sugar

Mash the potato. Gradually add small amounts of powdered sugar until you can roll it into a dough ball. At first the mixture will be thin enough to beat with a spoon; gradually it will become harder to mix, and you will have to knead it like dough. When the consistency of piecrust, roll out onto waxed paper to the thickness of piecrust. Spread a thick layer of creamy peanut butter over the rolled-out dough. Now, roll up like a jellyroll, about ¾ inch thick. Leave overnight, and then slice into wheels. Cover individual pieces in plastic wrap.

FAT MARR'S IRISH POTATO CANDY
Susie Carson's Recipe Files

This version of potato candy makes a good compliment to Mrs. Fullwood's Candy Wheels. During the Great Depression, "Fat" Marr was the cook at Camp Sapona, a C.C.C. unit (Civilian Conservation Corps) located on the north side of Leonard Street a few blocks east of Howe. Susie Sellers Carson gave me his recipe for chocolate covered potato candy.

½ cup unseasoned, well mashed   1 cup flaked coconut
    white potato   1 teaspoon vanilla extract
3 cups confectioner's sugar   2 squares semi-sweet chocolate

While potato is hot, beat in sugar and coconut, then vanilla. Press into a lightly greased 8-inch square pan. Melt chocolate and pour over top. Chill and cut into squares. Keeps indefinitely in airtight containers in refrigerator.

SWEET POTATO CANDY

1 medium sweet potato, unpeeled
2 pounds confectioner's sugar
1 cup flaked coconut
1 ½ cups nuts, finely cut

¾ cup light raisins, finely cut
1 teaspoon vanilla or rum extract
¼ teaspoon salt

Boil, bake or steam the potato until tender. Peel and mash through food mill or use blender to remove any fibers. Mix in a 2-quart bowl with salt and 1 pound of the sugar. Mixture will liquefy, and then thicken. Add the coconut, nuts and raisins alternately with the remaining pound of sugar. Add vanilla. Mix well. Turn mixture onto a marble slab or other service and knead well. Line two 12-inch lengths of aluminum foil with waxed paper; dust lightly with additional confectioner's sugar or coconut. Divide candy in half. With lightly buttered palms, pick up candy and form a ball, then into a short roll in the hands. Place on waxed paper and continue to roll, working from center to both ends, holding paper firm with one hand while the other continues rolling until candy is about 1 inch in diameter. Roll up firmly in waxed paper and foil and chill several hours. Repeat the rolling process with the other half of the candy. Cut into slices. Makes about 48 pieces, or 3 pounds.

ABOUT PULLED CANDIES

Taffies and other pulled candies such as butter mints are made by pouring hot candy syrup onto a marble slab or platter, letting it cool, then working like dough or otherwise pulling them. Great care must be taken when picking up the hot syrup, for it is dangerous. The edges will cool first. When cool enough to touch, pick up edges and fold back into the hot middle. When still hot but cooled enough to handle, pick up with greased hands, pulling it into a rope loop, then folding the loop together, and again stretch into a rope. Repeat this until it is nearly cool and hardly has any give. Then work in the flavoring and or coloring. Pull again, then lay out on a marble slab or counter top. Some cooks when working alone, throw the candy rope over a hook to stretch. We always use two people, pulling the candy in a hand-over-fist motion. When done, divide into 3 or 4 batches and stretch each batch into rope about ½ to ¾ inch thick. Lay out on marble slab or platter, snip into individual pieces, or cut with a sharp knife.

Should the candy get sugary, place in a saucepan with 2 tablespoons corn syrup and ¾ cup water. Cook over low heat until the taffy dissolves, then cook according to the recipe.

PULLED CANDY

What fun we had on a cold day having a pull candy party. You need at least two people for the pulling.

2 cups sugar   ¼ cup water
¼ cup vinegar   Drop of vanilla

Cook sugar, vinegar and water without stirring until syrup spins a thread when a little is dropped into a measuring cup of cool water. Pour onto greased slab of marble or heavy platter. Follow directions for pulling candy above.

PULLED BUTTER MINTS

2 cups sugar   Pinch of cream of tartar
1 cup water   4 drops of peppermint extract
¼ cup (½ stick) butter or
   margarine

Combine sugar, water, butter and cream of tartar in 2 quart heavy saucepan. Stir over medium heat until sugar is dissolved. Then cook without stirring over high heat to the hard ball stage 260°. Wipe off any crystals that may form on sides of pan. Pour onto buttered marble slab or large platter. Follow directions for pulling candy above. When nearly cool, work in the peppermint.

MOLASSES TAFFY

1 cup molasses   1/8 cup salt
2 teaspoon vinegar   2 tablespoons butter
1 cup white sugar

Cook over high heat the molasses, vinegar, sugar and salt to the boiling point. Cover, and without stirring cook syrup on fairly high heat to just below the firm-ball stage, 250-268°. Cut the butter into small pieces and drop in the hot syrup. Boil to just below the soft-crack stage, 270-280°. Spread out the syrup over a slab and sprinkle with 4 drops of oil of peppermint. Do not scrape pan. Pull according to the directions for pulling candy above.

MOLASSES TAFFY SWEETENED CONDENSED MILK METHOD

1 can sweetened condensed milk   1/8 teaspoon salt
1/2 cup molasses   Butter

Combine sweetened condensed milk, molasses and salt in heavy saucepan. Cook over medium heat, stirring constantly, to 250° or the semi-firm ball stage. Pour into a buttered 8-inch square pan and let stand until cool enough to handle. Butter your hands and pull taffy away from the edges, then pull until shiny and light colored. Twist into a rope about ¾ inch thick. Lay out on a marble slab or waxed paper and cut into 1-inch lengths with kitchen scissors.

MOLASSES-PEPPERMINT TAFFY

Work in 4 drops oil of peppermint to either taffy recipe while pulling.

SALT WATER TAFFY

2 cups sugar   1 ½ teaspoons salt
1 ½ cups water   2 teaspoons glycerin
1 cup light corn syrup   2 tablespoons butter

Dissolve over low heat the sugar, water, corn syrup, salt and glycerin. Cover and cook 3 minutes, or until the sides of the pan are free of crystals. Uncover and cook without stirring to the late-hard-ball stage, 268°. Remove from heat and add the butter. Do not scrape pan. Spread out the syrup on a slab in two or three puddles if you wish. Pull according to the taffy pull instructions, adding drops of different coloring and flavoring to the separate batches.

BUTTER MINTS

1 16-ounce package   2 tablespoons butter
   confectioner's sugar   1/4 teaspoon mint extract
4 ounces cream cheese   1/8 teaspoon vanilla extract

Melt the cream cheese and butter in a large sauce pan on low heat. Stir constantly until smooth. Gradually stir in the sugar. Add the mint and vanilla, stirring well until blended. Divide into two portions. Roll each into a 12-inch rope. Cut into ½-inch pieces. Let stand, uncovered, about 4 hours.

CREAM MINTS
Annie May Woodside's Cook Book (1913)

1 pint sugar
½ pint water

1/8 pound butter
Oil of peppermint, a few drops

"Put on fire and boil slowly till it will form soft ball when dipped into cold water (not ice water). Pour out on a damp or greased platter. When cool enough to press fingers into it, make a small hole in it and add 6 to 8 drops of peppermint extract, or 3 or 4 drops of oil of peppermint. Use a silver or wooden spoon in working it. When cool enough, work as dough and put away between purified paper. After a day or two it will be ready for use."

MARZIPAN

Marzipan is a mainly decorative confection made by pressing the dough into small molds to create delightful objects of infinite variety—pears and oranges and fruits, little toys, or other decorations.

1 8-ounce cup almond paste
1 egg white
¼ teaspoon clear vanilla or rum
    butter flavoring

3 to 4 cups confectioner's sugar

Break up paste into bowl. Add egg white and flavoring and mix. Add confectioner's sugar, one cup at a time until mixture looks and feels like stiff dough. Knead until smooth. Separate into several batches, adding drops of food color appropriate for mold—orange for tiny "orange slices," green for "lime slices", etc. Roll in confectioner's sugar and press into molds. May be stored in refrigerator, or in air-tight containers. May be frozen.

POPPYCOCK

Cracker Jacks are a commercial brand of poppycock. The prize that comes with this recipe is its delectable taste!

8 cups popped popcorn
1 1/3 cups sugar
1 cup butter
2 cups almonds and pecans

1 teaspoon vanilla
½ cup light Karo syrup

Combine sugar, butter, vanilla and syrup in a saucepan. Cook over medium heat until caramel brown in color (about 15 minutes after it comes to a boil). While hot, pour over popcorn and nuts. Mix gently. Spread in clusters on a greased cookie sheet.

FONDANT

2 cups sugar
1 ¼ cups water
2 tablespoons light corn syrup

½ teaspoon vanilla or other
flavoring

In a heavy saucepan heat the sugar and water on low heat, stirring, until the sugar melts. Cover and boil 3 minutes. Remove cover and boil *without stirring* to the soft ball stage, 238° on a candy thermometer. This may take 20 minutes or longer. Wipe off any crystals that form on the sides of the pan with a wet pastry brush. Allow to stand until lukewarm. It will be a clear, thick syrup. Pour onto a marble slab or large platter. Scrape the syrup from the outsides to the center repeatedly with a spatula or frosting spreader. The syrup will begin to turn white. When white and firm, add ½ teaspoon vanilla, or other flavoring, and knead until smooth. Cover with a cold damp cloth and allow to stand one half hour. Cut or shape into pieces. Roll the pieces in nuts or candy sprinkles. You may let stand 3 or 4 days before using. Makes about a pound.

PECAN LOGS

Prepare 1 recipe of fondant, above. Roll the candy into a long rope, or 2 ropes, about 1 inch thick. Spread 8 ounces of chopped pecan nuts onto a sheet of waxed paper. Lay the fondant ropes on the chopped pecan meats, and roll up in the paper, pressing the meats in the candy hard enough to stick. Allow to stand several hours. Cut into individual pieces 2 to 3 inches long, and wrap these in waxed papers.

STUFFED DRIED FIGS

Steam 1 pound of dried figs for 15 minutes, or until softened. Cool. Stuff with fondant candy using the recipe above on page 389 .

NOUGAT

The ancestry of nougat can be traced back to medieval times. Here's another recipe that needs a dry day. For years my mother made up at batch of nougat at holiday time. Some was used to stuff dates, and some was mixed with nuts or fruits as candy.

1 cup plus 6 tablespoons sugar	1 cup blanched almonds
1 tablespoon water	½ cup blanched pistachio nuts
1 1/3 cups light corn syrup	½ cup candied cherries, chopped
¼ cup egg whites	
2 tablespoons butter cut into small chunks	

In a heavy 2-quart saucepan cook 6 tablespoons of the sugar, the tablespoon of water and 1/3 cup of the corn syrup. Cover and cook 3 minutes so the steam can wash down any crystals that may have formed. Uncover and boil to the soft-ball stage, 234°. Remove from heat and let stand while you beat the egg whites in a mixture to the stiff peak stage. Add the syrup gradually to the whites and boil about 5 minutes until thickened, beating constantly.

In a second pot, place 1 cup of the corn syrup and 1 cup sugar. Cover and cook over low heat without stirring for 3 minutes. Uncover and boil on high without stirring to just under the hard-crack stage, about 285°. Remove from heat and let stand for a few minutes. Combine the two mixtures. Add the butter, almonds, pistachio nuts and candied cherries. Pour into a buttered 8x8-inch pan dusted with confectioner's sugar. Let stand in a cool place for 12 hours.

RESSIE WHATLEY'S GLAZED PEANUTS
Ressie Whatley's Recipe Files

1 pound light brown sugar	Pinch of salt
3 cups raw peanuts, shelled	Enough water to moisten

Place ingredients in cast iron skillet and cook slowly for 1 hour. Put in greased muffin tins and cool.

CARAMELIZED PEANUTS

2 ½ cups roasted peanuts with red skins
1 cup sugar
½ cup water

Heat water and sugar in a heavy pot until sugar is dissolved. Add peanuts with skins still on. Stir constantly until sugar syrup has evaporated. Dump into large baking pan. Spread around in pan and do not crowd. Bake in 300° oven for 30 minutes, turning with a wooden spatula every 10 minutes.

CHINESE CARAMELIZED WALNUTS

These are great as snacks, or used as a little something special with ham or turkey.

2 cups plump unbroken walnuts   1 teaspoon coarse salt
2 teaspoons corn oil   2 tablespoons sugar

Place the nuts in a bowl and cover with boiling water. Let stand 30 minutes. Drain and pat dry. Preheat oven to 300°. Spread the nuts in a flat pan. Bake on the middle shelf of the oven for 30 minutes. Reduce the heat to 250°. Turn the pan around and let bake an additional 10 minutes. Bake until nuts are almost dry but with a touch of moistness at the center. Heat the corn oil in a skillet over moderate heat, add the nuts and stir until coated. Sprinkle with salt, then with the sugar, a bit at a time, stirring to coat. Cook until sugar melts and caramelizes around the nuts, about 2 or 3 minutes. Yields 2 cups.

EASY PRALINES
Dorothy Hardee's Recipe Files

1 pound package light brown   1 tablespoon vanilla or maple
  sugar   extract
1 6-ounce can evaporated milk   1 cup chopped nuts
1 tablespoon butter   Pinch of salt

Combine sugar, milk, butter and salt. Bring to a boil. Stir gently on low heat to soft ball stage 238°. Remove from heat. Allow to cool. Add vanilla and beat with electric mixer until creamy. Stir in nuts. Drop by spoonfuls onto waxed paper.

PRALINES

2 cups packed light brown sugar
1 cup granulated white sugar
1 cup light cream
¼ cup light corn syrup

1/8 teaspoon salt
1 teaspoon vanilla
2 cups pecan meats

If the pecan meats are unbroken halves, chop most roughly, reserving enough to place a half on top of each piece of candy. Cook the sugars, milk, corn syrup and salt to boiling in a heavy 3-quart Dutch oven, stirring constantly. Reduce heat to medium and cook, without stirring to 234° or the soft ball stage. Cool without stirring about 1 hour. Add the vanilla and pecan halves. Beat about 1 minute until the mixture just coats the pecans but is still glossy. Drop by spoonfuls onto waxed paper. Let stand uncovered for about 2 hours. Top each with an unbroken pecan half.

TUTTI FRUTTI CANDY

As has been pointed out earlier, "tutti frutti" is simply Italian for "all fruits," and may apply to ice cream, cakes, or other recipes, including this one for candy: To the nougat recipe on page 390, mix in 1 cup of chopped candied fruits, oranges, cherries, and dates.

PEANUT BRITTLE

1 ½ cups shelled raw or
   parched peanuts
½ teaspoon salt
1 cup sugar

½ cup corn syrup
½ cup water
1 ½ tablespoons butter
½ teaspoon lemon extract

Spread the peanuts in a pan. Sprinkle with the salt. In a saucepan cook the sugar, corn syrup and water to the hard crack stage, 300°. Add the nuts, butter and lemon extract. Pour into a shallow buttered pan. When cool enough to handle, press down with your fingers to make as thin as possible. Break into interesting but irregular pieces. Yield: about a pound.

ROCK CANDY

I won't mention the name of the store where we used to go to get rock candy, except to say that it wasn't Mrs. Mary Temple's, Dan Harrelson's, Galloway's, or Mr. Willie McKenzie's. But I grumbled to Cousin Vera one day that I didn't think I got my full quarter pound.

"Well, Dummy, don't you know?!" she barked. *"He made his fortune weighing his thumb!"*

2 ½ cups sugar
1 cup water

Use a disposable 8-inch aluminum pan. Boil without stirring to the hardball stage, 247° to 252°. Pour syrup over the strings into pan. Cover with a foil and exercise patience, as it will take a week to crystallize. Lift out the candy. Rinse quickly in cold water, and then place on racks in a very low oven to dry. Break into tiny pieces, place in a bowl and serve with coffee or tea. Makes attractive decorations, especially at Christmas.

*And that's a nice way to end this book—
thinking about Christmas!*

Index to the Recipes

400

401

403

Index to the Reminiscences
and Articles
Listed according to their appearance in the book

Index to the Photographs

About the Author

Prof. Emeritus Lewis Hardee recently retired from Wagner College, Staten Island, as Head of Theater, following a career in music theatre, writing, composing and conducting. He has said,

"My career was in New York, but my heart is in Southport, where it has always been, and will remain."

A native of Southport, he was graduated from Southport High School class of 1954, then attended U.N.C. Chapel Hill where he earned a B.A. in Radio TV Motion Pictures, a M.A. in Music in Musicology, and did post graduate studies in composition at Columbia University. During 1960-1962 he served with the U.S. Army as a Specialist with the Counter Intelligence Corps.

He is composer and/or author of musicals, including *Revolution!*, the outdoor musical drama produced in Southport in 1976 as part of the Bicentennial Celebration. Two, *The Little Prince* and *The Prince and the Pauper*, have toured the United States. His historical writings include *Three Southern Families, a History of Connecting Hardee, Jones and Davis Families of Coastal North Carolina*, published 1995 by the Southport Historical Society; and *The Lambs Theatre Club*, 2005, by McFarland & Company.

A long-time member of The Lambs, the oldest theatrical club in the United States, he currently serves as its Historian, and is Vice President of The Lambs Foundation, Inc. He is a subject of record in Marquis *Who's Who in America*.